RUNNING

Running

A Global History

Thor Gotaas

REAKTION BOOKS

Published by
Reaktion Books Ltd
33 Great Sutton Street
London EC1V 0DX, UK
www.reaktionbooks.co.uk

First published in English 2009

This book was first published in 2008 by Gyldendal Norsk Forlag, Oslo, under
the title *Løping: En verdenshistorie* by Thor Gotaas
Copyright © Gyldendal Norsk Forlag 2008

This translation has been published with the support of NORLA

English-language translation by Peter Graves © Reaktion Books Ltd

Printed and bound in Great Britain
by Cromwell Press Group, Trowbridge, Wiltshire

British Library Cataloguing in Publication Data
Gotaas, Thor.
Running: a global history.
1. Running – History.
2. Running – Social aspects.
I. Title
796.4'2'09-dc22

ISBN : 978 1 86189 526 4

Contents

Foreword

It is of course impossible to write a complete version of the world history of running. In the oldest sources there is relatively little to choose from and the sources are often anecdotal. An author has to take the sources that exist, weave them together and try to create the broadest picture possible.

For the period after 1800 there is an abundance of interesting source material and then it becomes a matter of choosing and excluding.

Even though a book of this kind will be coloured by the time and place of its author – Norway, Europe, shortly after the year 2000 – I have tried to cover the whole world. I have also tried to pick out the long and significant threads that emerge in a subject as large as this. Nevertheless, the book bears the impress of being written by a European who sees the world from Scandinavia. That is inevitable, just as it is inevitable that the book also bears the impress of its author's preferences and sympathies in the choice of events and cast of characters

As the title suggests, *Running: A Global History*, this book does not pretend to be anything other than *one* version of the history of running in the world – namely, the author's version.

1
Messengers and Forerunners

It's said that some messengers on long assignments would
crop off their hair and have the message written on their
scalps. The hair would grow and the recipient would have
to give the messenger a haircut to read the message.
—Unknown source

There was a young girl in Mainz in Germany in the eighteenth century
who took the life of her own child: she was filled with shame and despair
after becoming pregnant outside marriage. Her crime was discovered. She
was arrested, charged and sentenced to public execution.

It came to the appointed day. On the way to the place of execution the
citizens looked at her and her escort and many felt it was wrong that such
a sweet young thing should be in the hands of the executioner. A noblewoman,
trembling with sympathy, thought the girl ought not die and hastened to
call upon Prince Johann Friedrich Karl von Onstein, who wrote a letter of
reprieve and summoned his runner to take the news to the Supreme Court
as fast as possible.

The judges carried out the prince's wishes and the ropes round the wrists
of the pale and terrified girl were untied. She fainted and collapsed into the
arms of the priest – finally free after this awful nightmare.

The runner was the hero of the day; the citizens carried him home in
triumph and the prince rewarded him generously. But, terrified by the
thought of arriving too late, the runner had ruined himself physically and
the terror had taken root in his heart: he died soon afterwards, to the great
sorrow of the prince and the people.[1]

From Hut to Hut

The office of runner occupied thousands of specially trained men in many
cultures for many hundreds of years. Rumour had it that you could hammer
nails into a runner's feet, so hard were they. Not absolutely true, perhaps,
but their feet were undoubtedly hard, whether the messengers were operating in Europe, Africa, America, India or China. Of all these, it is the Inca
runners who are best known.

When the Spaniards arrived in South America and conquered the Inca
Empire in 1532, that empire stretched from the present border between
Ecuador and Colombia to the Rio Maule in Chile and had an estimated
population of ten million. The success of the Incas as empire builders and

rulers was put down among much else to good communications and a
well-developed network of roads. The roads were as straight as possible in
order to save the traveller time and consequently they often ascended steep
slopes by means of long staircases. The roads were carved in rock or supported
by walls and along the greatest of them were milestones to show the distances
– one mile was equivalent to six thousand paces. There were suspension
bridges made of lianas across the rivers, and other primitive bridges that it
was a risky business just to cross.

Professional runners, *chasquis* (the word means 'to exchange', 'to give
and take'), ensured an efficient system of messengers. They were selected
from among the best and most reliable people, trained from a young age
and sworn to a duty of silence. They were proud of their profession and
obedience to the law was a matter of course in a realm where the theft of
maize from an Inca's land led to a death sentence. The runners lived in small
huts along the roads – four or six men in each, depending on how important
the particular lines of communication were. Two of the men always sat ready
in the doorway, watching the road. As soon as they saw a messenger coming,
one of them went to meet him. He would run alongside the messenger,
listening to the simple oral message three or four times, or he would take
over the piece of knotted string that contained the messages. The knotted
string was the Inca system of letters and they possessed neither an alphabet
nor the wheel. Smaller pieces of string of different colours were tied on to
a length of string, either running parallel or sticking out from a set point:
knots referred to numbers, colours to meanings. The runner himself did not
need to be able to read all the knot-codes – he was often transporting secret
messages and there were experts to interpret them.

After taking over a message a runner would proceed as fast as possible
to the next hut a few miles farther on and the process would be repeated,
while the first runner sat down and waited for the next errand to arrive.
Since every stage was relatively short, they kept up a high speed. They carried all kinds of news of varying importance, from district governors to the
supreme leader – the Inca himself: local news, instructions from above,
information about crops and animal husbandry. Over the bridges and
along the roads that reached from the coast to the high mountain region at
over 13,000 feet (4,000 m), there were messengers constantly on the move,
covering nearly 200 miles (320 km) in 24 hours in stages. The messengers
chewed coca leaves to renew their energy and the messages were passed on
without interruption until they reached the recipient.

Like their equivalents in many other countries, the messengers were
immediately recognizable: they wore tall feathers on their heads and they
announced their arrival by blast on a conch trumpet they carried on a cord
round their waist. They were armed with a club and a sling in case they met
enemies. At any one time there were thousands of runners on duty, working in fifteen-day shifts and receiving food and lodging from the state. They
were so important that they earned the same amount as the mayors.

A *chasqui* playing a
pututo (conch shell).

These messengers transported everything imaginable to the Inca in Cuzco, including exclusive food such as snails and sea-fish. Even though it was located far inland, by the afternoon the court could receive fish taken from the sea that morning. There was also another kind of messenger, *hatun-chasquis*, who transported larger and heavier errands and whose shift lasted only half a day.

Particularly important messages from the ruler were accompanied by a red thread or by a staff with markings. At each hut there was a beacon ready to be lighted to warn of serious trouble such as invasion or rebellion. The runners on duty would light the fires and the message would rapidly be passed to the capital, where the ruler and his council resided. Thus, even before he knew the cause of the alarm (that information arrived by messenger), the Inca leader could order the army to march in the direction the alarm had come from.[a]

Cuzco was the centre point for the runners in the Inca Empire; it was regarded as the centre of the world and was the main residence of the Inca himself, the Son of the Sun. The city lies some 11,500 feet (3,500 m) above sea-level and had over 200,000 inhabitants at the height of the Inca Empire. When the empire was at its greatest, the most distant parts lay 1,000 miles (1,610 km) from Cuzco but messages would cover that distance in five days.

Messengers left the city every day and others arrived at the palace. When the runners met out along the roads, those going to Cuzco always gave way to those coming from there, in such respect was the city held.

The sources tell us that the Incas viewed the natural environment with humility and devotion. That was also true of the messengers. To the Incas even the smallest thing possessed a soul, everything was alive and worthy of respect, and man should try to win the favour of all beings. The runners racing across high plains and mountains did not see nature as a wasteland but rather as filled with a rich flora of spirits and objects, rocks and animals, all belonging to the world man lived in and was subject to. Every step the runner took was watched over and guarded by millions of beings. Rather than fearing isolation along unpopulated stretches or in the darkness of night, the Inca runner was fearful that the host of spirits around him would desert him if he did not behave and think properly. They lived in a world filled with threat and could never be sure what malice might be perpetrated by enemies and natural forces. Runners knew that the messages they carried and their speed of delivery were significant for the whole of society and its survival in war and peace, crop failure and natural catastrophe. Before crossing a river the runner would drink a little of its water and ask the river to be gentle as he crossed. The sight of a bat, the sound of a bird, a strange dream – all these things lodged in the messenger's mind and had a symbolic import. 'Alas! It was bound to happen', he would say when fate struck. To the Incas, everything was subject to the disposition of the spirits.[3]

Apart from the messengers there were other groups who had to prove their competence in running. To become a member of the Inca upper class it was necessary to have a four-year education in which a running race was the most important test. At schools in Cuzco this important elite group was instructed in the language of the rulers, in religion and in the knot codes by the best scholars. During their last year they studied history and took supplementary courses in surveying, geography and astronomy. They were not going to be messengers but they still had to run.

On the day of the examination, *huaracu*, in the Inca twelfth month (November), the candidates gathered in the great square in Cuzco to pray to the Sun, the Moon and Thunder. Before the examination all the young men had their hair cut short and were dressed in white, with black feathers on their heads. Together with their families the whole group went to the neighbouring hill, Huanacauri, in order to live on a strict diet of water and raw maize and to perform rituals and dances. A few days later they were given red and white blouses and slept in tents along with their families. There remained a five-mile race to Huanacauri, one of the holiest places for far around, where, according to legend, one of the brothers of the first Inca had been turned to stone on the summit. Before this metamorphosis, however, he had been given wings and resembled the bird the Inca ranked above all others – the falcon, since it could fly and stoop so fast. The word *huaman* meant both falcon and speed, and the many words that began with *hua* show the importance of the falcon in Inca folklore. This race was run under the sign of the falcon.

Speed was vital in the Inca Empire to retain power and uphold order and that was true both of message-runners and military troops on the march. Falcons, runners and soldiers were closely linked in a country whose only means of transport was by foot. One of the groups conquered by the Inca was the Cara, who had neither message staffs nor knotted string and thus fell easy prey to the Inca.

Before the day of the race the organizers placed animal figures carved in stone-salt on the summit, which was the finishing line: the figures depicted the falcon, the eagle, the wild duck, the humming bird, the snake and the fox. There was much jostling once the competition started since every one of them was prepared to give his all to win honour and the goodwill of the gods. When the runners arrived they grabbed the figures – the first taking the most noble birds, the last getting the worthless reptile. Thus each man carried the proof of his own strength or weakness and the spectators knew who to praise and who to mock. To fail to finish was shameful.

That night the competitors slept at the foot of the hill and in the morning they ascended a peak on which two stone falcons had been erected. Then a rough fight took place between two teams of the young men, followed by them testing their skill with the bow and the slingshot. Next came tests of will in which they were beaten but must not show pain and they had to remain at their posts for ten nights without sleep. The candidates also had to stand motionless without blinking while an officer swung a club over their heads and threatened their eyes with his sword.

Those who passed the examination were received by the highest Inca and given specially sewn short trousers, a diadem of feathers and metal breastplates. Their ears were pierced with gold needles so that they could wear heavy ear ornaments – a visible sign of belonging to the elite, the 'long-ears'. There were further ceremonies before they were accepted into the elite: dances and ritual bathing, the presentation of weapons and a feast. Finally they had to clear a patch of ground.[4]

Even though the Incas also included running as one of a number of sporting activities, both at large annual athletics meetings and also at smaller events, this is much less frequently mentioned than the messenger relay system, which became the distinguishing mark of the empire and impressed everyone. The messengers functioned as the nervous system of the empire and it was through them that the Inca took control and held it. The Spaniards saw the usefulness of the messengers and retained them: a Spanish mounted messenger took twelve or thirteen days from Lima to Cuzco whereas runners covered the distance in three days.

Messengers and Trick Runners

Since the fifteenth century there have been running messengers in Central
Europe, either working full-time as messengers or carrying out particular
tasks for nobles and landowners. There is a saying that tells us something
important about the serf's relationship to his master: 'You shall serve him
six days a week and on the seventh you shall carry messages.'[5]

In 1573 in Breslau in Poland there were forty messengers under the
jurisdiction of a senior messenger. They had good wages, fixed shifts and privileges such as being excused military service. Central Europe consisted of
small states, which often meant that the distances covered were short because
those states situated closest together tended to communicate most; in spite
of that, however, messengers might well cover 60 miles in a day. They were
remunerated according to the length of the mission and earned nothing
when resting. Message runners were a distinct professional group in Germany
by the beginning of the seventeenth century and that is reflected in a
number of family names: Läufer ('runner'), Löper and Bott ('messenger').
The job often passed from father to son.

There were ordinances concerning routes to be taken and who was to
be informed and called upon. The journeys could be tortuous, with many
people to inform. The saying 'A runner and a liar' suggests that messengers might have been prone to exaggeration and lies when they arrived in
a strange place dripping with sweat and ready to return home as soon as
possible.[6]

For a man who travelled a great deal and picked up news as he went,
it was tempting to lie when surrounded by inquisitive citizens. There was
something exotic about the arrival of a messenger – registering at the city
gate before a final sprint to his appointed goal, and then the whole ritual of
shouting out news or handing over documents in a society in which many
were illiterate. Indeed, not all messengers could read. It's said that some
messengers on long assignments would crop off their hair and have the
message written on their scalps. The hair would grow and the recipient
would have to give the messenger a haircut to read the message. Regulations
prescribed that the messenger should pass on news in exchange for gratu-
ities and to fail to do so could be punished by exclusion from the profession.
Any breach of duty was punished severely.

By comparison with those who were more static in terms of residence,
the messengers were both well-travelled and knowledgeable. They belonged
to a profession that crossed national boundaries and had a great deal of
contact with people of a higher social class, even though the runners themselves came a humble background. They enjoyed considerable esteem and
the career was a springboard to increased social status.

To hinder or injure messengers was forbidden and they had diplomatic
immunity even in wartime, when they traversed battlefields carrying information about negotiations. The actual messages were well-protected against

wind and rain inside a capsule in the staff or message stick. Some of them kept wine in a flask in the end of their staff and took swigs of it along the way, and they ate hard-boiled eggs and other provisions. They were dressed in a special uniform in the colours of their city and bore a cudgel, spear or short sword to protect themselves against dogs, robbers and other miscreants. Their identity was confirmed by a badge and a pass bearing the coat of arms of their city.[7]

In Germany the age of message runners in public service came to an end around 1700. Better roads and better communication by horse made them superfluous as the German postal system developed, even though only four men were needed to deliver all the post in Berlin in 1712. Gradually postmen took over the missions of the message runners, at the same time as the quantity of mail increased with the delivery of newspapers, journals and private post.

The unemployed German messengers found new employers after 1700: kings and noblemen employed forerunners to announce their arrival at important celebrations and meetings. Since horse-drawn carriages rarely moved faster than five or six miles an hour a nimble man could easily stay in front of them.

Originally forerunners had a different function. The roads were so bad during the fourteenth century that servants ran in front of the carriage to find the best possible track. Later it became their job to ensure a pleasant journey and to light the way with torches in front of the carriage in the dark. They preferred to run in line abreast and it made a characteristic sight along the highways: a great man, such as the Sultan of Turkey on his travels, could be heard and seen at a long distance because of the sounds of jangling bells, creaking carriage wheels, singing and the loud chattering of the runners.

In the sixteenth century the sultan kept a household of a hundred runners from Persia, who were called *peirles* – footmen. Out in the countryside they ran backwards alongside the carriage, tumbling and doing tricks to entertain the sultan. They were running jesters, who kept the sultan's company happy on their travels. He had favourites among the runners – those who caught silver balls in their mouths and chewed on them as horses chew on their bits. In one hand they carried a sugar-sweet piece of dried fruit to keep their mouths moist – a good thing to have in a hot country like Turkey.[8]

A newspaper advertisement in Breslau on 24 January 1798 shows the qualities aristocrats were looking for in men of this kind:

Runner sought. We seek a young runner of good physique and appearance, clean shaven, well-trimmed and well-behaved, who can run fast and keep going for long distances. Anyone fitting the above description should apply to the castle in Kratzkau before the 28th of this month, where he will have excellent prospects.[9]

If a number of candidates of equal quality were to apply, there would be a selection process.

In England the Duke of Queensberry stood on his balcony in Piccadilly and made applicants keep running until they sweated. The runner who sweated least and looked least exhausted got the job. 'I have use for you, young man', the duke said to those who passed the test – it also helped to be well-dressed and to look elegant. An easy running style and a showy costume were the ideal. It is claimed that messengers were attractive to women and illustrations depict them as well-proportioned and determined. They were fit and active in comparison with the flabby noblemen and were easily recognizable because of their thin faces and slim bodies.

On one particularly warm day the applicants were running backwards and forwards in uniform for the duke while he was lying back indolently on the balcony. He liked one of the men in particular and, happy to see such a fine fellow, made him carry on for a long time. Finally the duke called: 'That's enough for me', at which the runner pointed at his smart, borrowed uniform and shouted back, 'This is enough for me', and ran away too fast for anyone to catch him.[10]

In England messengers were called 'running footmen' and were employed by the nobility from the seventeenth century on to carry messages and to compete for money – just as some men kept racehorses. A footman should be young and dashing, have well-shaped legs and be unmarried. As he got older he might become his master's servant and hand over the more energetic tasks to younger colleagues.

Running footmen had to obey orders promptly and run important errands irrespective of the time of day or season of the year as, for instance, when the Earl of Home in Scotland sent his lackey with an important message to Edinburgh one night, a good thirty miles away. The following morning the earl came down to breakfast and saw the runner asleep on a bench, snoring. Had he forgotten his errand and slept the night away? The earl was on the point of castigating him when he realized the man had been to Edinburgh during the night and had returned.

Whatever little whim the employers of men like these might have, whether they wanted something fetched or delivered, medicine collected from the doctor or small surprise gifts taken to a lady they admired, off hurried the runner. An occasion of this kind arose for the Duke of Lauderdale when his servants were laying the table for a great dinner. They were short of a number of items of silver cutlery to make the table setting perfect so the duke ordered the long arm of the estate to run to his other residence some fifteen miles away and fetch cutlery. The lad ran as if possessed and got back just before the guests were going in for dinner.

Runners had a strong sense of status and professional pride, as is shown by an episode in Milan in Italy in 1751. The runners in the service of the nobility there noticed that the police were wearing bandoliers and shoes with multicoloured ribbons, claimed that they had sole right to such attire and demanded that the police cease wearing them. When the police refused, the runners attacked one of them and forced him to remove his shoes on the public street. The police were threatened with death if they continued to wear this clothing: 'The two sides were on the point of attacking each other when the governor intervened and ordered the police to wear only blue bandoliers in the future, and the ribbons decorating their shoes should be the same colour as the shoes themselves. Both sides were satisfied with this and parted without coming to blows.'[11]

The messengers considered it a matter of honour to deliver messages fast and they drove their bodies mercilessly. Young men frequently only lasted three or four years in the profession and many of them died worryingly early. But one or two of them held out for twenty or even forty years. One such man was Joachim Heinrich Ehrke, who served at the court of the Grand Duke of Mecklenburg in Germany for 43 years from the 1790s. When he grew old he trained younger successors and was in charge of eleven men, including three of his sons.

Ehrke took his job as trainer seriously. He insisted on dietary rules, demonstrated breathing exercises and instructed his pupils in geography. He recommended breathing through the nose and pressing one's sides to relieve a stitch – to counteract which his pupils drank a herbal infusion. There was a widespread story, possibly true or perhaps a myth, that one of them had an operation to remove his spleen – that being where the pain is felt – to prevent stitches. This may be wishful thinking, but they did train in heavy shoes and run through sand and newly ploughed fields, lifting their knees extra high as they went. Their training sessions really did push them to the limit.

Ehrke knew that the training of runners for employment by the nobility was a profession in a number of European countries. The *Medicinal Handbook for Runners* from Breslau in 1782 contained advice on how to run faster, increase stamina and avoid stomach problems. The medicinal prescriptions in the book can hardly be called doping but belief in the drugs is in itself revealing since competition was intense and the profession was renowned for such feats as covering daunting distances or winning races against horses.[12] In hilly country, narrow streets or lanes a man could even beat a carriage with a six-horse team, but on good straight roads in flat country the horse was superior.[13]

The nobility set much store by having fast horses and resilient runners, both being important in practical and in status terms. The Viennese grandees around 1800 preferred Italian runners, whereas the French preferred the Basques. Men from Wallachia (Romania) were also sought after. It was an honour to get a place at court, to leave one's poor surroundings behind and move to official housing near the castle of the king, prince or emperor. Court runners brought glory to their families and homes and gained entry to a storybook world. The imperial court in Vienna employed fourteen runners at the beginning of the eighteenth century.

By the end of the eighteenth century hundreds of runners had lost their jobs and the profession almost disappeared as a result of social changes. The French Revolution of 1789 led to a demand for more democracy and less aristocratic luxury but the number of runners also declined drastically in England and Germany. The nobility lived rather more soberly than before and the employment of runners no longer had the same status.

There was a French saying – 'To run like a Basque' – about the mountain people from the Basque region. When Basque runners lost their jobs with the nobility, they started holding two-man races (*korrikalaris*) – major betting events in which the participants were dressed in a traditional loose shirt, sandals, long trousers and with a sash around their waists.

The Basques favoured long distances, nothing less than six or seven miles and preferably fourteen, fifteen or more. Unlike the English footmen the Basques did not run fixed routes: it was up to them to find the fastest route to their destination and a good topographical sense and resourcefulness in hilly country counted for a great deal. Only the start and the finish were defined. Once challenge races became popular in the Basque region whole villages and towns began to support local men and to make competition fairer fixed routes were defined; this in turn inspired solo runs against the clock.[14]

The firmly rooted traditions in Vienna and Austria meant that the nobility there held on to private runners for some decades into the nineteenth century, and the runners there belonged to a guild, with journeymen and fixed entrance tests. In Vienna the annual test for accreditation as a journeyman was held in the spring and the qualification time was 11 miles in 1 hour 12 minutes. From 1822 on the run was held in the Prater Park on 1 May.[15]

That year many of the citizens of Vienna rose early to watch the 'Running Festival in the Prater'. The first people arrived at the starting line at 5 a.m. since the competition was to begin at 6 a.m. There were trainers and seconds, spectators who had bought tickets and occupied a stand similar to a tent, all kinds of people both on foot and mounted, all dressed up for the occasion and eager for the results. There were soon over 3,000 people present and listening to the military band, which was playing Turkish music.

The ten or twelve runners got ready, dressed in light shoes of soft green leather, tight close-fitting clothing and headgear in the colours of their employers. In normal circumstances they wore their own red, green or blue uniforms but for the spring race all of them turned out in white and only the headgear revealed who their masters were. They carried whips in their hands – usually to deal with angry or aggressive dogs but in this case to sweep aside spectators who pressed too close in the narrow city streets.

They were an exclusive group – one from each master – and they had staked a lot on being victorious. Their masters had overseen their training and had been instructing the trainers for months before the competition. Victory was of great significance and would be the talk of the town for a long time even outside aristocratic circles.

The starter shouted 'Quiet in the line!' and called each man forward by the name of his master. The identity of the runner was of little interest, more attention being paid to his employer, whether victorious or defeated. When the starting shot went they set off to wild cheering, with riders and creaking carriages in tow, including a carriage with a doctor and first-aiders, while the music in the park whipped up the excitement further. Then it was out onto the streets, puffing and blowing, where the crowds cheered and clapped, patted the runners on their backs and looked out for their favourites. A runner would sometimes break down, need medical help and lie there on the street surrounded by the crowd while a doctor tried to revive him. The runners gave their all in the name of their masters and knew that a top placing would lead to honour, a pecuniary bonus and a place in the runners' hall of fame.

When the first man home arrived at the finish the shouts of bravo and the master's name echoed and his employer would hurry forward to congratulate his runner and bask in the glow of victory. Moments like this outweighed all the expense and effort involved in keeping a stable of runners.

At the finish the participants were wrapped in blankets and well looked after. To the sound of a fanfare of trumpets the first three were called up to receive their prizes – a flag of honour adorned with an eagle going to the winner. Then they all marched off under a banner and the three winners were treated to breakfast at a café while the money changed hands. Betting played some part in it but the Austrians were not the enthusiastic gamblers the English were.

The distance in the Prater is not given exactly but times were recorded and Franz Wandrusch won in 40 minutes in 1845. But neither spectators nor runners were bothered about times and it was only the first three places that mattered. There was an element of the carnival about it all, as the modern idea of sport with records kept and records broken did not yet exist in Vienna.

The 1847 spring race in the Prater was the last. After the 1848 revolution in Austria the competition was not repeated and the nobility ceased to keep runners. Some of them became manservants and continued in the service of their masters, others became independent runners, as noble men's runners had already done in many countries. The best Viennese runners were famous far beyond Austria and used their place of origin for publicity purposes.

Trick running was an old idea that belonged within the circus tradition. In many countries, particularly in England, running had been a marketplace entertainment for centuries. German and Austrian trick runners toured Europe, reaching as far as Russia, where a performance before the Tsar in St Petersburg was the high point of their fame. It was a prestigious and profitable event, but also an excellent testimonial and something to show off about afterwards. The runners accompanied acrobats and artistes who moved from town to town along the 'jugglers' routes' – the routes artistes followed around Europe between the courts of great men and princes and the major towns. Other groups, too, who had not been noblemen's runners or forerunners, joined in to make up a motley crowd of itinerant entertainers: they often came from southern Europe and were small, often family troupes of acrobats who walked the tightrope and performed balancing or strongman acts.

Thus the runners were not merely competing for attention with each other by running fast and well or far and entertainingly, they were also competing with experienced entertainers. To meet this sharp competition the runners became more versatile and, like the entertainers, they became brash self-publicists.

The mere sight of unusually dressed strangers in a sleepy small town would arouse curiosity and set the rumour mills going. A parade through the streets whipped up interest, particularly if the runner belonged to an ensemble whose shouts in foreign languages were accompanied by musical instruments. They would take up their stance on the square and their leader would blast on his trumpet to all four points of the compass before announcing the time and place of the performance. If the parade failed to whet the appetites of the public sufficiently the troupe would hire the town drum to announce the performance or produce flyers and read them aloud in doorways all round the town. The more affluent groups in the business stuck up posters but that cost rather more than newspaper advertisements. And since far from all the inhabitants would be literate or take newspapers, proclamations and word-of-mouth were more effective.

Runners lived by impressing the public and by offering something new and more spectacular on each visit. In order to perform they needed the permission of the local authority and in some towns they – like other travelling entertainers – had to pay 10 per cent of their takings to the fund for the relief of the poor and up to a third of their takings to local people in need.[16]

Performing runners lacked both the security and the social setting of runners to the nobility. They were in the same situation as contemporary artists and authors who now had to rely on a free market after having previously been supported by aristocratic patronage. On the other hand runners – whether they were men or women – were now free to perform independently as long as they had the written permission of a ruler or other dignitary.[17]

Runners had been part of the street scene for many years and by the middle of the nineteenth century people were demanding something extra, something with more to it than just speed, if they were to pay for a performance. Many of the runners dressed in enormous hats and colourful clothes and changed them during the performance, without, however, simply becoming clowns. Wilhelm Goebel from Prussia, who ran four *versts* in 12 minutes (a *verst* is 3,500 feet or 1,066 m), emphasized comedy when he ran with weights, in armour or carrying grandmothers on his back. He did balancing tricks, had a number of acrobats with him, and arranged races in which the challenger was given a lead of a hundred and fifty paces to increase the excitement. Runners ran forwards and backwards, up hill and down dale, in narrow streets and great squares.

The German runner Peter Bajus, born in 1795, was among the fastest of all. After the market for runners to the nobility declined in Germany and the neighbouring countries he moved to London and won fame for being particularly successful at running for wagers. When he returned to his homeland in 1824, the Grand Duke of Hessen-Darmstadt employed him. Bajus was unusual for his age in that he was a trick runner first and only thereafter a runner to the nobility:

> He is slim, with a rather thin face, strongly built in the legs and with strong sinews; his head is less than one-eighth of his height, hollow chest, well-turned legs, slightly protruding ears, strong hands and feet. He is never ill; he is neither a great eater nor a great drinker; phlegmatic by nature; he goes pale in the face when making the most enormous efforts, but never gets very hot; he has never – not even when running into the wind – felt pressure in his chest or had a stitch.[18]

It took Bajus eighteen minutes to run three and a half miles, a distance that would take normal walkers an hour. Big and strong as a bear, Bajus could carry 220 lbs (99 kg) for half an hour without stopping and 330 lbs (150 kg) for a quarter of an hour. He was a rare combination of being both big and light on his feet, equally good over all distances, a folk hero who inspired songs and stories. People called him 'deerfoot' and writers calculated that, given his pace, he could run round the world in 150 days.

As an excellent representative of the disappearing breed of forerunners Peter Bajus remained active until 1844, when he decided once again to prove himself at running for wagers. Although the 49-year-old could cover eighteen miles in two hours, he took a tumble in a competition with young men and came limping home. Even though he was exceptionally good for his age, he could no longer beat the best young men.

Apart from in Great Britain, trick running was at its most popular in Europe between 1840 and 1850. With the development of modern sport from the middle of the nineteenth century onwards trick running drew less attention, particularly as a different sort of person was taking up running and the contexts in which running was done – gymnastic associations, for instance – were also changing.

Runners continued to carry out important missions up to the middle of the nineteenth century: they were mankind's original form of communication, of alerting their fellows. But as horsemen, carriages, trains, telegraph and telephones took over their functions, runners became a superfluous and old-fashioned curiosity. Runners had run long and short distances, alone or in groups, for entertainment or for money, and when these motives no longer existed people found other reasons to run.

Seen from the perspective of global history, modern organized running is a recent activity, but the prehistory of running consists of much more than lap times and records, even if they are part of the picture. We shall follow the development of running from the earliest times and see why people across the whole world, in different countries and different periods, have run. The global history of running is not as obvious as one might at first think. It is full of amazing surprises and curious stories, even if the actual business of running has always been quite straightforward.

When, then, did human beings start running?

2

A Primordial Human Trait

The sons of the kings had to run every day and they received no
food until it was done – so they went out in the morning.
—Unknown Egyptian Source

The biologist Dennis Bramble and the anthropologist Daniel Lieberman
have argued that two million years ago man developed from his ape-like
forefathers because he had to run long distances hunting animals on the
African savannah. The climate had changed and large areas of forest had
turned into savannah with the result that new living conditions arose.
This gave the species *Australopithecus*, which was able to run, an important
advantage and, as time passed, it also favoured an anatomy that made
long-distance running possible. If that was the case, then running skills were
important for human evolution: the anatomy and body changed when our
forefathers were forced down on to the ground and, anatomically speaking,
running made them human.[1]

Bramble and Lieberman disagreed with the established theories that
saw running merely as an extension of walking on two legs. *Australopithecus* began to do *that* four and a half million years ago, at the same time as
he was swinging from tree to tree. Even if *Homo* walked on the ground, it took
at least three million years for *Homo sapiens* to arrive. During this period
our forefathers bore little resemblance to human beings and consequently
the ability to walk could not have been the most decisive point of change
in human evolution. Compared to man, *Australopithecus* had short legs,
long arms and a muscular, ape-like body. Bramble and Lieberman state: 'If
natural selection had not favoured running, we should have continued to
look more like apes.'[2]

The two men studied 26 characteristics of the human body. They also
studied the fossils of *Homo erectus*, 'upright man', who is assumed to have
lived between 40,000 and 1.8 million years ago, and the fossils of *Homo
habilis*, 'handy man', sometimes referred to as 'original man', whose skeletal
remains are over 2.5 million years old. The tendons in the legs and feet,
elastic joints and efficient toes turned the species into runners. Man took
long paces and his body absorbed the impact when the feet hit the ground:
he had good balance and the skeleton and muscles reinforced the body and
made it better adapted to running without overheating, not least because
of millions of sweat glands.

Although man is slow on his feet in comparison to many species, the ability to sweat and tolerate heat enabled him to tire out faster animals when hunting. Given training, man can achieve extreme endurance and this makes it possible for him to hunt much faster animals such as antelope on hot days: the bushmen of Africa still chase antelope until the animal overheats and becomes an easy prey.

Running is a primordial human characteristic and is put to many different uses.

A Royal Long-Distance Run

King Shulgi ruled over the southern cities of Sumeria from 2094 to 2047 BC. He was all-powerful: priest and king, general and taxman. The king ensured that the inhabitants delivered corn and other goods to the temple offices, the temple also being the bank and the office that paid out wages.

In 2088 BC feasts of thanksgiving were to be held in the holy cities of Nippur and Ur. King Shulgi promised to attend both feasts between one sunset and the following sunset and to do so he had to run from Nippur to Ur and back, a total distance of 200 miles (320 km).[3] He was dressed in sacred apparel that no one else was permitted to wear, with a cap and shirt of expensive materials and a false beard. Like most Sumerians he was short and had a large, arched nose and dark eyes.

After many hours he approached Ur, one of the most sacred cities in Mesopotamia and the residence of the moon god Nanna. He passed irrigated fields and fruit gardens, the water coming from the River Euphrates that flowed immediately outside the city walls. In the distance rose the Ziggurat, the stepped pyramid that was the home of the moon god and the goal of the king's run. King Shulgi entered the city gate through the thick walls of baked clay and ran on through narrow streets, past small houses, towards the northern part of the city where all the sacred shrines were located. He ran to the tower of Nanna's temple, surrounded by great walls and gardens, then he climbed the many steps up into the temple which was filled with pots, bowls and jugs with food and drink for the god.

King Shulgi made solemn offerings of food and other things before the statue of Nanna in order to pay homage to and placate the god. The king was merely the god's deputy and it was Nanna who held all the power and was the special protector of Ur.

Then King Shulgi began his run to Nippur. He passed the oldest temple in Ur, where his eldest daughter lived as the high priestess, and so left the small city.

The Sumerians inhabited fairly flat country with good roads; there were no mountains and valleys, no rivers to cross and he was running during the cool season. King Shulgi knew the value of keeping a steady, comfortable pace and not stopping for too long. He drank water and ate dates, grapes, bread and honey at the huts that lay every couple of hours' walking time along the road. His servants accompanied him with food and jugs of water and with torches to light his way at night. The king was not alone in the darkness and he was well looked after. It was a strange little procession under the starry sky, with the king in front alternating between running and walking and his servants behind, ready to help at the slightest hint.

King Shulgi passed large parks and temples outside Nippur, entered the city gate before his deadline and went directly to a feast for the sun god Utu and the fertility goddess Inanna. On behalf of his people he made a sacrifice before a statue. The king had done his duty and performed a great physical feat in accordance with unwritten rules, thus ensuring his posthumous fame. The king embellished it with the help of scribes and the bearers of oral tradition.

Some of the oldest written documents in the world are preserved from these cities in southern Mesopotamia, 'the land between the rivers' Tigris and Euphrates in what is now Iraq.[4] The people of this region began to practise agriculture about 8000 BC and they used advanced methods of irrigation to improve their crops. This led to a great concentration of people and some of the first cities in the world grew up in Mesopotamia before 3500 BC. Message runners had a central part to play in what is the oldest bureaucracy known to mankind. They delivered official documents around the kingdom and they were held in high esteem, receiving olive oil, beer and land as payment.[5]

Young men began their careers by carrying letters between the capital city and governors in the provinces. Later they led slave-trains and organized the transport of food and building materials. The messenger Ir-Nanna did his job so well that he became head of the royal chancellery and of all the messengers, and later administrative officer and governor. The certainty that being a messenger could lead on to advancement within the hierarchy of the state attracted ambitious types and the continual journeys back and forth across the country provided them with an excellent background for moving on to more important roles.

Archaeologists have not found the remains of any sporting arenas in Sumeria but boxing and wrestling are referred to in poetry and in administrative texts. Ball games were played and jugglers and acrobats gave performances in a society in which many inhabitants had leisure time and valued good physical health. Running was often linked to cultic festivals and religion and sport were closely connected, such as when the king's fastest messengers brought sheep and goats to be sacrificed to the gods before feasts and banquets.

The Runs of the Pharaohs

An organized kingdom grew up in the Nile valley in Egypt between 3100 and 3000 BC and there is archaeological evidence of archery, wrestling, boxing and horse-racing: the Egyptians also ran, swam, rowed, fenced and played ball games. The messengers here were running infantrymen, men who escorted powerful people travelling in horse-drawn carriages, and soldiers selected as fast runners.

The kings are best known for a running ritual that took place at the thanksgiving festival Heb Sed, 'the festival of the fox brush' – the name referred to the tail on the back of the pharaohs' clothes in early Egyptian times.

Heb Sed originated with the foundation of the pharaonic state and was celebrated for almost 3,000 years. At first it was a military festival with parades and flag-bearers and it included a run in which high-born prisoners of war ran round markers symbolizing the borders of the state before being executed. In later times only the king ran.

Rameses II (1303–1213 BC) sat on the throne of the pharaohs in Egypt for 66 years from 1278 BC.[6] Before his coronation he had to run at a crowded festival held at one of the pyramids to prove himself worthy of the throne. He was all alone out on the 150-yard track but received the help of supernatural powers. He drank fortifying tonics and ate sacred food.

Thirty years later he had to run the same distance again to demonstrate his continued vitality and ability to rule, and from then on he had to repeat the run every third or fourth year at a thanksgiving festival held below the towering pyramids, where even his subjects were present to see him undergo the test. Everything in society, even daily life itself, was dependent on Rameses since he was the centre of the world and the guarantor of harmony. He and he alone had direct contact with the gods and could share their mighty powers. As the representative of the gods he maintained their work of creation and a weak and enfeebled ruler could endanger the whole cosmos. Rameses successfully performed these runs, which also symbolically marked out the territory of the kingdom, until he was over 90 years old.[7]

Archaeologists have found few traces of competitive running in Egypt but there are references to people as being 'the swiftest of the swift' and comments such as 'I surpassed all in the city in speed, both its Nubians and its Egyptians'.[8]

A recently discovered stone monument by the old road from Memphis to the oasis at Fayum, dated between 6 December 685 and 5 January 684 BC, has provided a little more information about Egyptian running. King Taharqa was ruling at that time and, on his orders, a stone was carved and erected 'in the western desert, west of the palace' with an inscription concerning 'running training for the army of Taharqa, son of the Sun'.[9]

The king had selected soldiers to train in the desert to carry out lightning attacks. On a tour of their training camp he saw to his great joy that they were in excellent shape and he organized a race from Memphis through the desert to Fayum. The monarch accompanied the race in a carriage but left it at intervals to run some of the sections with the men – an unheard-of practice for such a powerful individual. It was of great importance to the men that the king could quite literally move at their level. They rested for two hours in Fayum in the middle of the night before they all started back to Memphis, where they arrived at dawn. The first to arrive received extra pay and all those who finished were given a prize. According to the memorial stone they took four hours for the 30 miles from Memphis to Fayum and a little longer on the way back, as the men were tired and the temperature had risen.

Running in Mesopotamia and Egypt was often a religious ritual, sometimes connected to the military life, and a means of communicating with the gods. It was also the predecessor of another flourishing Mediterranean sporting culture, that of the Greeks, which has been a good deal more influential in the development of modern sport.

3

In Honour of the Gods

Runners have over-developed legs.

—Socrates (469–399 BC)

Ageus was the name of a boy born in the Greek city state of Argos around 350 BC. We do not have any details about his formative years but will rely instead on the rich sources from that period about running.[1] Like other free-born Greek boys of the time Ageus would certainly have come into the care of a gymnastics teacher, *gymnastes*. The boys were only six or seven years old when they started wrestling, doing gymnastic exercises and running under proper guidance. They made their debut in torch-lit runs and local religious festivals, ran relays or one against one within the context of the same *gymnasium* (*gymnos* = 'naked'). Ageus ran naked and barefoot, embrocated with olive oil, at a sports ground that was roofed in case of bad weather. There was running water close by and bathing facilities after training, friends and older teachers – everything a boy needed to become a good man and a good warrior. Close relationships with adult men were common in Ancient Greece although the boys would later marry and form their own families. Parents required their sons to keep company with men in order to learn about life.

There were competent trainers in Argos. The city is among the oldest in Hellas, highly developed and protected by walls to keep enemies at bay. It was renowned for its skilled sculptors and architects. The inventor of the discus came from here and astronomers climb up a tower to observe the stars. This is the city state in which Ageus grew up.

The trainers drilled technique and explained the importance of running in sand, both because it is hard and because it is good for the legs.[2] They attached weights to their feet or wore armour – these were well-known tricks in ancient times. The youngsters raced back and forth in the stadium but rarely went out in the country since the competitions they were targeting were held on tracks of about 200 metres in length: the one at Olympia was 192 metres.[3]

But Ageus was not the sprinter type; he was lightly built and had stamina. His stamina increased year by year and long distance was the ideal discipline for him.

Ageus' first races were in his native city but later the group from his gymnasium go beyond the city walls, keen to sharpen their skills against

Pottery amphora decorated in the Fikellura style with a running man, *c.* 530–500 BC.

others of the same age-group, since in Hellas the youngest running class – even at Olympia – was the under-thirteens. The philosopher Aristotle and others warned against the ruthless exploitation of young bodies since the best child runners seldom reached the top as adults.

Ageus' performance curve went upwards and in 327 BC he decided to take part in the Olympic Games. It did not happen before he had been tempered in competition at different levels. Ageus was also a full-time messenger for his home city, always ready to carry out tasks and errands, whether about war, banquets, weddings, entertainments or sacrifices. He was a man everyone in the city knew, someone they saw moving around with important communications, someone who was present when important things were happening.

In the late autumn of 327 BC Ageus began his preparations for the following year's Olympic Games in August. Ten months was the usual training period for professional athletes aiming for success at Olympia. He had to train full time, following his trainer's advice about diet, rest, sunbathing, sleep and technique. He had to avoid eating too much or drinking too much wine, and had to watch his weight, though that looked after itself, given long training sessions and his job as city messenger. The trainers recommended celibacy and serious athletes refrained from sex before important competitions in order to build up their strength.

Hectic months of improving his form passed. Ageus trained, feeling ever stronger and ready for the great contest, for soon the Olympiad – the period between Olympic Games – would be over. Smaller competitions formed part of his build-up, along with tests against friends and runs in the country around Argos.

Ageus communicated with the gods before his departure, as the Greeks did to seek success and good fortune, and he made promises that had to be fulfilled if the victory were to be his. He was not competing alone: gods and spirits from the past were all round and would watch over everything that happened – men are merely small pieces in the great game, even in the sporting arena. He lived in a society in which everything was in the hands of the gods: human activities, events, buildings, natural formations, trees and rivers. All the things he saw and heard in nature were signs that he attempted to interpret in order to know whether the gods were joyful or wrathful. He also directed his prayers to earlier good athletes from Argos, whether alive or dead, seeking their help.

It was with a solemn, heavy but proud sense of duty that Ageus and his companions – his father and brothers – set out from Argos for Elis. Ageus was to represent his home city in the greatest and most illustrious of all Greek sporting festivals, in Olympia on the west coast of the Peloponnese, about eighteen miles from the sea, where the Greeks have been competing since at least 776 BC, but probably for much longer. While growing up Ageus had heard stories about famous runners, *heros*, heroes who were like demi-gods, and his dream was to achieve what they achieved. He was willing to suffer torment to achieve their status and to know that those who came after him would mention his name in solemn tones and pray to statues of him. An heroic performance would also bring glory to his family and his city, and would demonstrate a connection with the divine powers. Now it was Ageus' turn to meet the best of the best.

They arrived in Elis, which was packed with tense and ambitious sportsmen waiting for the first full moon after the solstice, the start of the Olympic Games. Ageus registered with the judges in Elis, which was where the athletes lived, ate and trained, isolated from the world outside for the last month before the games. The same thing happened at the other great Greek games – collective training and then selection by the judges so that only the best were left for the actual competition. Besides which, many had come long distances by boat and sea-legs needed time to adjust to dry land before the runners could give of their best.

The trainer's commands no longer applied in Elis, though Ageus was allowed to watch the training sessions. There was little else to do than train, eat, rest and sleep in what was neither a town nor a village: Elis was simply the residence of the priests who watched over the shrines and managed the cultic and sporting festivals. All these hopefuls were faced with a hard regime in this camp, where the weakest were rejected until only the best were left in each discipline. It took a special something to qualify for this great event held every four years, and hundreds of highly trained men did not make the cut. The competitions were restricted to Greek men born of free Greek citizens. Ageus knew that this did not tally with reality and that the competition from North Africa, Egypt and other areas around the Mediterranean was strong – and that there were competitors who used to be slaves and who, because of their sporting talents, had been given citizenship by city-states to which they would bring prestige.

Two days before the games Ageus and the remaining competitors were called before the ten judges. They were invited to participate in the games and then the procession left Elis and headed for the ancient cult-site Olympia, a distance of some eighteen miles, which they had to walk as a group. The remarkable procession began to move, with the judges at the front dressed in violet clothes and with garlands of flowers around their necks. Next came the athletes, surrounded by their trainers and relations. Carriages, horses and sacrificial animals – among them a hundred oxen bred in the neighbourhood – brought up the rear. Right at the back walked the spectators who had been watching the training. The journey from Elis to Olympia took two days and there were animal sacrifices along the way, so it was hardly the ideal build-up for a top sporting performance.

Spectators arrived in droves on foot along paths and poor roads through the hilly countryside. Those from far away had been travelling for weeks by land and sea to enjoy the atmosphere at Olympia. In Ageus' day the whole Greek world from Marseille to the Black Sea was represented. There were dark-skinned North Africans, Arabs and fair-haired races, and they included people who spent much of the year travelling around athletics meetings to cheer on the favourites from their home city.

The spectators looked out over Olympia, where the arrivals were preparing for the celebrations. It was bustling with people, prostitutes all dressed up and ready to earn a year's wages in a few days, merchants erecting their stalls and philosophers engaged in intense debate. They saw the temples, the baths, the stadium and the great horse-racing track, and the sacred olive tree whose leaves would be picked to make victory wreaths for the winners. Historians were reading their works aloud like heralds and the poets were there ready to compose new verses about new winners. All kinds of people were crowded together to make a profit from the events or to watch or to take part. They formed a motley and expectant gathering of people who slept in tents or under the open sky but, apart from the prostitutes, who were here to work, married women were not allowed in the stadium. It is said that married women caught trying to sneak in were hurled from a nearby cliff. Ideally there should be peace and a state of truce in the whole of Hellas during the games – they were, after all, an occasion for all Greeks, and every city state wanted to preserve them.

For Ageus, things could not be more serious. In Ancient Greece victory counted for everything and the competitors from Sparta, in particular, scorned defeat. If a runner beat a Spartan it was because he was faster, not because he had a greater will to win. The solemnity of the occasion was intensified on the first day, when Ageus and his helpers swore an oath before the judges and a statue of Zeus that they would obey the rules.

Magic and spells were part of the runners' tactics and some of them were unbelievably cunning.

On the fourth of the five days of the games the time came for the men's races. There were also boxing and wrestling matches, horse-races, a pentathlon and other disciplines.

Ageus was taking part in the long-distance race, the first of the three distances run that day, and it started immediately after dawn in order to avoid the baking heat. He rose early, received advice and a massage from his trainer, swore oaths according to ritual forms and composed promises to the gods. The huge camp came awake, tired faces peered out of the tents, and the thousands of bodies lying on the ground all round began to stir. Thirty to forty thousand people rubbed the sleep from their eyes and took their places in the stadium at Olympia as the first rays of the morning sun rose above the mountain ridges. The first spectators arrived during the night to make sure of the best seats.

Ageus and over twenty other competitors oiled their bodies and waited to be summoned through the gate into the stadium. In accordance with Greek tradition they were competing naked. In war, too, nakedness had been used as a shock tactic. The odour of olive oil hung around the men as they performed their stretching and warm-up exercises.

Ageus heard the sound of the trumpet calling them to the *dolikos*, the long-distance race, which at Olympia was run over 24 lengths of the stadium, equivalent to 2.9 miles. The judge called 'Step forward!' and each man was led round while the herald shouted his name and city and asked whether anyone present could vouch for his free status and good repute. Ageus was given a good testimonial and thus cleared the final hurdle. They all went to the sacred silver urn and drew lots to decide their starting positions. After the lots were drawn the herald called: 'Let the contest begin, put yourselves to the test and victory is in the hands of Zeus'. The wait was nerve-racking, with tens of thousands of enthusiastic spectators at close quarters – and getting a good start was all-important.

The *hysplex*, the rope that marked the start, falls, and the field set off in a great knot to the end of the stadium and then back, as the Greeks did not run round a circuit. Ageus slotted into his regular rhythm, kept a good position and spurted home to victory.

His trainer, his relations and his fellow citizens roared with joy. They carried him around in triumph and were the happiest people in the world. Later in the day they walked proudly among the tents inviting people to a celebratory party in Ageus' name, with wine and grilled meat on the menu. They celebrated through the night, singing, dancing and praising Zeus, who had presented them with a winner. Olympia was lively on nights like this, with flickering fires and the buzz of thousands of voices in many languages and dialects. But this time the winner was not present in their midst.

Ageus wanted to demonstrate how vigorous he was and immediately after the victory ceremony he continued to run. He raced through woods and over rivers, along paths and up over mountaineer's terrain, the whole 62 miles to Argos, entering the gates of the city the same evening, sweating and happy. The surprise led to uproar in the city, celebrations in the streets with speeches and toasts, congratulations and parties. Since he was such a good runner and had shown such consideration for the people of his city, they planned a statue of Ageus – but this time there would be two, the customary one in the stadium at Olympia and another in his home city.[4]

In Honour of Zeus

The Olympic Games were the first and greatest of the games that existed among the 1,000 or more Greek city-states. Running was important, particularly the shortest race, and the games were named after the winner of that race. The Olympic Games traditionally began with one event – the *stade*, a sprint over one length of the stadium. It was a race in honour of Zeus, with the runners carrying torches to light the flame on the altar of Zeus. In 776 BC the Greek cook Corobeus was the first winner and his prize was an apple. It is impossible to say for certain when and why these games originated but it has been suggested that the inspiration came from Crete, from the Phoenicians in Lebanon and Syria, from the steppes of Central Asia and from Indo-European immigrants. There is an Irish claim that they were modelled on the Tailteann Games in Ireland, which are supposed to have started in 1829 BC, although that is impossible to prove.[5]

Running was one of the oldest events in Greek sport. Sources such as Homer's *Iliad* and *Odyssey* from the eighth century BC describe 'Achilles, the fleet-footed hero' competing at the funeral games in honour of a distinguished man. The goddess Atalanta, his female counterpart in Greek mythology, is also mentioned in stories about legendary runs. Greek sport and running grew out of a cult of ancestors and gods in which physical strength was vital for self-defence.[6]

Running and sport were practised in many places before the Olympic Games but these games have retained their significance because they provided the model for the Ancient Greeks and, consequently, for Western civilization over two millennia later.

The Olympic Games expanded to include other running events as well as the sprint; there were races over two lengths, a long-distance race, a race in armour and a short-distance race for boys. These became the norm for Greek games, the best of which – what were called the 'wreath games' – ran in cycles at fixed intervals. Around 500 BC the programme was as follows:

Olympic Games, July/August 500
Nemian Games
Istmian Games, August/September 499
Pythian Games, April/May or May/June 497

Nemian Games, August/September 497
Istmian Games, April/May 497.[7]

Each city-state arranged its own annual athletics meeting in addition
to these, and in Athens and Sparta they were more frequent. There were over
200 major competitions in Greece, with good prizes, around the year 150
BC. The best athletes earned a fortune and could live well for the rest of their
lives. The winners would roll through the streets of their city in a horse-
drawn carriage to wild acclaim – almost 300 carriages, drawn by white
horses, are named. The athletes might get olive oil for the rest of their lives,
amphorae of olive oil being very common items of barter and as good as
money. They often received a pension, were exempted from taxes and had
a free house. The winners would be invited to splendid dinners, eat free in
the city chambers and have a set seat at the front in the theatre. They
could earn a great deal by simply appearing at later sporting events and they
might use their status as the springboard for a political career.

Reckoned at 2008 values, a total of $570,000 was paid out in prizes at
the Panathenian Games between 350 and 400 BC for competitions that included song, running, throwing, jumping and chariot racing. The biggest
prize went to the winner of the men's sprint – 100 amphorae of olive oil,
$40,000 worth at 2008 prices.

The stars lived on money from rich benefactors or from the city-state
and they had their own trade association. There was no word for 'amateur',
the nearest being *idiotes*, an unskilled and ignorant individual.[8]

Homage to Hera

Greek women ran, too. Usually the runners were young girls, who then
stopped running after having children. Spartan women were accused of
exposing themselves and of provocative behaviour – and also of being boyish and coarse. According to one play, 'They leave home and go out with
young men with their thighs bare and their skirts open. They run races and
they wrestle with boys.'[9]

The young girls in Sparta pushed themselves hard, doing all-round
training at their training ground, the *dromos*, which means 'race track'.
There were no hardier people than the citizens of this city-state, in which free
citizens were in a considerable minority and existence depended on their
phenomenal skills in war. Boys and girls were taken from their parents at
seven years old in order to become warriors, live simply and become strong
and hard – they scorned weakness and considered themselves invincible.
Spartan girls learned all the sporting disciplines, including wrestling, and
were muscular and well-built. They had no choice. The function of the girls
was to bear good warriors in a society which hurled weak babies down into
a chasm without mercy and where boys were whipped so that they might
sacrifice their blood to the gods and show strength – if they did not die

from the whipping. The boys watched when the girls were training, commented on their bodies and chose a fit spouse. Athletics even had marital significance in Sparta, as when the girls sprinted in an important race dedicated to the god Dionysus.

Spartan women were notorious for running naked whereas Greek women avoided doing so, at least once they had grown pubic hair. There was, however, a fertility ritual for young girls that involved a naked run across sacred ground: the fertile powers of the earth would pass across into the body and ensure offspring.

Girls and women also travelled as a group in order to compete and their greatest race also took place at Olympia. Every fourth year, one month before the men, the girls came to Olympia to run the 175 yard Hera Race – Hera being the Queen of Heaven and the wife of Zeus.[10]

In the villages near Elis sixteen chosen women planned the coming Hera Race. They went to a chosen building nine months in advance in order to weave a fine robe for the goddess and it is noteworthy that the ritual was the same length of time as a pregnancy. It was a laborious and important task and fashion played no part in the garment they were weaving, since the robe woven for the Hera Race remained the same for 900 years from 580 BC, the whole time the race existed.

The girls were divided into three age groups, ranging from the underthirteens up to the oldest in the race, who were between eighteen and twenty, and only unmarried girls could take part in this rite of passage. There was less fuss than at the Olympic Games, fewer spectators and less prestige, but it was a great and important event nevertheless. It did not degenerate into several days of celebration but remained a simple sprint, and in that respect the Hera Race remained more untouched than the Olympic Games and was less affected by corruption and competitive egos.

There was a feminine charm about the place on the day of the race. Women of all ages watched and helped their protégées. They dressed as Amazons, the mythical race of superb female warriors, with short skirts and the right shoulder and breast bare.

Important Professions and Critical Philosophers

Running had more than just symbolic and athletic functions in Hellas since the skills involved were of just as valuable in everyday life. Specially trained messengers or 'day runners' could cover long distances in 24 hours. The postal system in Hellas was poor and depended on running messengers who carried oral or written communications. They worked over the whole of Hellas and all of the armies had many of them. Day runners were forbidden to use horses because it was more difficult for the enemy to find a runner than a horseman. Runners could travel easily along paths and tracks through hilly country or dense forests and over ravines and mountains that horses were unable to cope with. There were also professional scouts positioned on ridges and mountain tops, whose only job was to run and give warning of the approach of enemies.

Alexander the Great discovered Philonides in Crete and employed him as a messenger. Philonides also worked as a surveyor, working out the distance between important towns by counting the number of paces. The Greeks often used slaves for tasks such as these, when accuracy and reliability counted for more than speed. Two of Alexander the Great's generals transported a 200-metre-long goatskin tent with them on campaign and it was erected in bad weather. Philonides and his colleagues trained in it when it was windy or raining.[11]

Alexander, who recruited all the best runners from a very wide area into his army, was fleet-footed himself and believed that he descended directly from the mythical runner Achilles. According to legend, Alexander stopped running because someone let him win – which he took as a great insult. He recognized the social and political value of sports and of the Olympic Games and when invited to participate at Olympia he replied: 'Yes, if I might have kings to compete against.'[12]

Writing about 430 BC, the historian Herodotus, in his description of the battle between the Athenians and the Persians on the plain of Marathon in 490 BC, names the messenger Phidippides or Phillipides,[13] who ran from Athens to Sparta to summon help, arriving there the following day. He then probably ran home again, in which case he would have covered just under 290 miles. Herodotus does not mention the return trip, nor does he make much of the distance – this was simply what was to be expected from day runners.

There is a myth that Phidippides was also the man who carried the news of the Greek victory at Marathon to Athens, whereupon he collapsed and died. This is rather improbable since Phidippides, as an experienced messenger whose profession was running, is hardly likely to have died of exhaustion, the 25 miles from Marathon to Athens being an easy task compared to many of the missions carried out by him or his colleagues.

Famous Greek doctors, authors and philosophers wrote about running. Socrates complained that runners had 'overdeveloped legs'.[14] Aristotle (384–322 BC) mentioned running at least eighteen times, describing technique and training methods and warning against excess. Plato (429–347 BC) did the same; he was a good wrestler in his younger days and was given his name by his trainer because he was so broad in the shoulders – *platys* is Greek for both 'flat' and 'broad'.[15] In Plato's ideal state a stadium race of 60 lengths (about eight miles or 13 km) and a cross-country of 100 lengths (twelve and a half miles or 20 km) were a part of his conception.

Solon of Athens, a respected statesman in the years around 590 BC, also applauded the fastest boys in his city:

We should also train our young people in running, from which – when the course is a long one – the most important thing they can learn is to save their breath and strength so that they can hold out to the finish. If, however, they are only running a short distance, it should be covered at the greatest speed possible. It is just as important that they practise leaping over ditches or anything blocking the road, and they should do it with heavy balls of lead in their hands.[16]

Not even Athens, however, could be immune to the negative effects of affluence. The comic playwright Aristophanes (447–385 BC) saw the alarming changes in Athens when young men could no longer manage the torch race. Rich young men gave up training to live a life of milk and honey in the market squares and luxurious bath-houses, becoming spectators rather than active participants in sport. Among ordinary citizens, physical fitness declined when their military responsibilities were taken over by a professional army. Young people had fewer demands placed on them and less to strive for. [17]

Like all Greek sports running was closely connected to warfare. The *hoplite* race, in particular, in which the runners wore armour over two or four lengths of the stadium, was an imitation of war. At the Eleutheria Games at Plataea, where the Greeks were celebrating a victory for freedom won in 479 BC, fully armoured athletes ran fifteen lengths and the winner was acclaimed as 'the best Greek'.

The victory symbolized Greek unity. The race started at the altar of Zeus and in its course it passed the graves of dead heroes and thus formed a link between the dead, the living and the unborn. If the winner took part on a later occasion and lost there was a risk that the Greeks would also lose their good fortune so, to discourage winners from entering again, they had a harsh rule that any winner who subsequently lost was immediately killed.

The Fleet-footed Crotons

This would not have frightened the people of Croton, a coastal city in the far south of what is now Italy. The city produced the fastest runners in the Greek world for a long period. Between 588 and 488 BC eleven of the 26 winners of the sprint at Olympia came from Croton and there was a proverb, 'The last of the men from Croton is the first among other Greeks'.[18] When they were at their best, seven of the eight finalists at Olympia were from Croton and by the time of their last victory in 476 BC hundreds of the city's athletes had been successful in the great competitions in the Greek world during its two most glorious centuries.

A tradition was established in Croton that was passed down through many generations. Running offered a route to fame and social success. Young people watched the fastest men in the city training, were given good advice and were proud to come from a city with such widespread fame.

The saying 'healthy as a man from Croton' pointed to their way of life outside the sporting arena and demonstrated the connection between physical welfare and sporting achievement. The physicians in Croton were considered excellent, which was important for the runners, and Croton attracted young runners as well as serious intellectuals of a practical turn of mind from all over the Hellenic world.[19]

The mathematician Pythagoras moved to Croton around 530 BC, at a stage when the people of the city had slipped into decadence. Pythagoras was a vegetarian, a believer in fasting as a cure, and emphasized harmony in the individual. Milo, perhaps the greatest athlete of the ancient world, was one of his pupils. During Milo's youth Croton had been defeated in a major battle and Pythagoras' teachings about simplicity and manly virtues came to the people's aid: they flocked to him and were influenced by the teachings of a wise man.

The school of Pythagoras was exclusive and highly regarded, not something for people who wanted to lead dissolute lives or to moderate his demands to their own advantage. Kylon, a powerful man who passionately desired to be accepted as one of the Pythagoreans, was rejected because of his immoderate behaviour and then led an attack on the Pythagoreans in Milo's house, killing him and his friends and driving the rest of the Pythagoreans out of Croton. The physical decline of the Croton population followed and Croton won its last Olympic victory twenty years later.

Astylus was one of Croton's great runners during this critical phase and he won the double victory at Olympia three times in succession in the years after 488 BC; he also won the armoured race. Given his achievements, he should have had the place of honour in the Croton statue park but he had been tempted into representing the city of Syracuse in Sicily at the Olympics in 480 and 484 BC. The citizens of Croton tore down his statue, put him under house arrest, refused to acknowledge his achievements and cut off all his ancient privileges. Even his family turned their backs on him and Astylus died alone, poor and exiled, rejected by his own people.

Greek Records?

The Greeks never recorded running times. They estimated speed symbolically and compared it to animals: was it fast enough to catch a hare or to beat horses over long distances?

There were water and sun clocks in ancient Greece but they were insufficiently accurate for use either for sprints or for longer distances. The Greeks divided the day into forenoon and afternoon; they observed the sun and organized the rhythm of the day according to light and dark. 'Cock crow' was early morning and 'lamplighting' early evening. Sundials measured the hours but were dependent on the sun to function. Water clocks, in which the water ran from one container into another, like sand in an hourglass, were used when a man was speaking in court: he could speak for as long as the water ran.

It is possible that the Greeks did without effective chronometers for sport because time and distance were unimportant to them; they could, for example, easily have measured out the running tracks with a rope.[20] What mattered in the Hellenic world was to win in as many designated sports as possible, preferably one after another, and after a series of such victories the sportsman would pronounce himself to be the only one to have done anything comparable. As far as running was concerned, the number of victories in the great games counted most. Someone who won three races in a day was given the title of honour *Triastes* and was admired for it. It was no mere accident that people said of Leonidas of Rhodes, perhaps the greatest runner of the ancient world, that 'he ran like a god'. He was a triple winner at the 164 BC Olympics and he repeated that achievement three times, as well as being victorious in innumerable other places.[21]

Taking running as his theme, Zeno of Elea (490–430 BC) devised one of the great paradoxes of the ancient world. The unbeatably swift Achilles was to run a race against a tortoise, a ridiculously unfair competition since the standard of the two was so unequal. To give the tortoise a chance Achilles allowed it a start, let us say ten metres, and Achilles ran ten times as fast as the tortoise. If they set off like this the tortoise would have moved forward a metre to the eleven metre mark when Achilles passed the ten metre mark. So Achilles would have to run one more metre to get in front, by which stage the tortoise has crawled a further ten centimetres. Zeno argued that they could continue like this *ad infinitum*, with the tortoise always in front but with an ever smaller lead. Achilles would have to cover an infinite number of ever smaller distances but would always remain a little behind the tortoise.

Everyone knows, of course, that Achilles would rapidly overtake the tortoise, but Zeno had nevertheless proposed a sound argument even if it was one that led to a false conclusion.

This paradox has occupied mathematicians and philosophers for centuries: there is a flaw in the logic somewhere in it but no one has yet been able to point to it. Gilbert Pyle, one of the great philosophers of the twentieth century, thought that the tale of Achilles and the tortoise was the ultimate example of a philosophical riddle.[22]

4
Roman Games

It is rare for God to allow a man to run life's race from
start to finish without stumbling or falling.

—Philo (20 BC–AD 50)

The philosopher Seneca (4 BC–AD 65) noticed that old age was creeping up on him – the Roman Stoic felt that he was no longer so light on his feet when out running. The Stoics believed that the body should be taken care of and that was particularly true of Seneca, who had long suffered from poor health and tried all sorts of remedies, including all-round exercise. Even though he was a philanderer and had been exiled to Corsica for treason, he did not shirk his running. To the Stoics and to Seneca reason was the highest authority and it told him to keep running even if his suppleness and endurance were less than before. He got his exercise by running and he was not alone in that during his time, though he was hardly representative of normal citizens. Educated Romans knew that running and walking trimmed off the fat and made a man vigorous.

In AD 50 Seneca had a young slave, Pharius, who trained together with him.[1] We see Seneca waking early one morning. The only light in the dark bedroom is the flickering flame of a wax wick. He sleeps with his clothes on at night so he only needs to lace on his sandals and put on his cloak to be ready for his run. He drinks a little water and walks with his slave to the nearest bath-house – the streets are no place for Roman runners so they go to bath-houses, which also provide parks and tracks. There they meet acquaintances, philosophers out for their morning walk, alone or in conversation with others. Seneca is a proud man and dislikes being beaten, so the slave Pharius stays behind him in spite of the great difference in age: it is the good behaviour appropriate to a slave and also fear of insulting his owner.

But on this day they come in equal. Seneca has to push himself and feels his position threatened. As a stoic he views the situation with common sense and humour: 'I'll have to get a slave who is less physically fit. A great and well-known man can't have an anonymous slave running away from him.' He is being ironic, for Seneca argues strongly for the human dignity of slaves and has helped them to get their conditions improved.

Seneca, like many wise men and philosophers, saw the value of training without necessarily applauding competition. He did not consider a race against his slave meaningful training since it would be too much of a strain.

He was expressing a view common among cultivated Romans in the first century AD. He hated gladiatorial contests and preferred to sit in his quiet study while the applause and cheering from the arena echoed around. The efforts of sportsmen went to waste and the public were blinded by that sort of bloody spectacle and hero worship: a man should not *only* train his body, he should train his mind.

That did not prevent running providing a philosopher with ideas. In one of Seneca's metaphors he suggests that a man with a moral dilemma should take a deep breath and run to the top of a hill, where the decision would become crystal clear to him.[2]

Whereas there are numerous heroes and an abundance of sources about sports in Ancient Greece, history suggests a life without sports for a considerable period among the Romans. These enterprising empire-builders founded their city in 750 BC and then entered a long struggle with the Etruscans to be the most powerful state in what is now Italy. The Romans learned a great deal from the Etruscans, including gladiatorial contests, but they also looked to and visited Hellas to see Greek sports, particularly after they conquered that country in 146 BC.

After 186 BC important Romans brought Greek sportsmen to perform in Rome. Their ulterior motive was to win the goodwill of the people and to spice up the animal fights and battles between groups of warriors in the arena with exotic activities like running, jumping and discus throwing. The politicians were willing to pay out of their own pockets and attached much importance to being seen by the public when the entertainments started. It sent out a signal that they were on the side of the people and shared the same interests and preferences in terms of entertainment. Sport in Rome was an imported phenomenon and part of its fascination lay in its otherness.

The Roman power elite had an ambivalent attitude to Greek culture. They admired the Greeks for many things but scorned what they called Greek foolishness, such as the naked participation in sport recommended by Greek intellectuals, tutors, philosophers and rhetoricians resident in Rome. Sport never achieved the same widespread support as an activity and civic duty in the Roman Empire as in Greece. The Romans were more often spectators than active participants, although they did build thousands of multi-functional bath-houses in the manner of the Greeks.

According to the writer Pliny the Elder, the Romans were the first to record times for long-distance running but we know little more about it. The Romans made great progress in the development of clocks. Sun clocks and water clocks became accurate devices and their size was reduced so that by the first century AD there were models – *solaria* – down to an inch and a half (3.8 cm) in size that were used like modern pocket watches. Water clocks were more accurate and did not depend on sunshine, though, as Seneca remarked, it was easier for philosophers to reach agreement than for the clocks in Rome to agree. By modern standards Roman measurement of time was approximate – hours, for instance, varied in length depending on the time of year – but it was possible to know the time fairly accurately over long distances.

They would count the circuits or lengths of the track completed in an hour or a day. One man ran 160 miles in the Circus Maximus, the great arena that held 250,000 spectators, and an eight-year-old ran between 70 and 75 miles for fun. Apart from these two occasions, however, very few other feats of endurance are known of.[3]

There are very few traces of women runners in the Roman Empire. The most complete surviving mosaic is that of the so-called bikini girls at the Piazza Armerina in Sicily, which shows scantily dressed girls running, dancing and playing ball. Women had a short youth, marrying between the ages of twelve and fourteen, at the time of their first menstruation.[4]

Roman emperors established games in honour of the gods or mortal heroes. In AD 80 Sulla moved the Olympic Games to Rome to celebrate a great military victory and he built the city's first Greek stadium. Apart from the sprint, which remained in Olympia that year, everything else took place in Rome. This demonstrated Roman power and their stranglehold on the Greeks, but also their admiration for Greek traditions. When the Romans conquered new lands they insisted on the setting up of Greek games in one place and their abolition in another, for no apparent consistent reason.

More and more Roman festivals and games of various kinds included sport. The Emperor Marcus Aurelius loved running and promoted it, along with other sports, during the AD 170s, and it became more popular without becoming particularly deep-rooted and without competing with gladiatorial contests and chariot races in terms of public popularity. The sport seemed too tame and lacking in drama, and it lacked historical foundations.

The Romans had no heroic golden age to look back on, no sporting heroes to worship as demi-gods. Italy was not composed of city-states desiring to compete with one another but of different tribes, among which the daily toil for bread and frequent wars against their neighbours took up most of the time. Unlike those leisured Greek citizens they did not have the chance to train and to worship physical ideals, even though the Roman system was based on slavery. The Romans imposed many things on their subjects but not the duty to practise organized sport.

Many did recognise the value of training and both Julius Caesar and Augustus frequented the *Campus* where recruits trained and competed with one another – it was a model for similar localities across the empire. Caesar and other military leaders did, of course, have messengers, who had a 24-hour radius of 150 miles and were well paid. To spend days and months, however, jumping, running and throwing in order to strip naked in front of thousands of spectators and risk making a fool of oneself, that was beneath the dignity of a Roman. The Greek ideal that sporting victory was a proof of manhood never caught on to the same extent in Rome.

There is an important respect in which Roman games, *ludi*, are quite distinct from Greek games. Few nations have celebrated as lavishly and passionately as the Romans, whether in honour of Jupiter or of successful military campaigns, when plundered treasures were shown off and victorious soldiers marched through the streets to the acclaim of the population. *Ludi* offered a break from everyday toil and the numbers of them increased century by century. The Roman desire for *ludi* seemed insatiable and by the middle of the fourth century there were no fewer than 176 official *ludi* in the calendar annually.

Greek games were competitive, whether poetic, musical or athletic, whereas the Roman *ludi* were more entertainments and diversions, often performed by men brought in for the purpose. Greek sportsmen found a new market in the Roman Empire as the number of games increased throughout the second and third centuries and when the Romans attempted to revitalize the Olympic Games. Athletes were used to travelling a long way and would go where the money and the prestige beckoned. They met Romans in gymnasia all over the empire and they met young aristocrats in *Iventus* – clubs that trained young men for military service or other important functions.[5]

Sportsmen who competed in the Roman Empire, whether in Tunis, Austria or France, shared little of the glory of the gladiator, around whom there was an aura that was frequently attractive to women, who were known to dip a spear in the blood of dead gladiators and use it in their hair before their marriage in order to gain magical and charismatic powers.

Galen, the most famous doctor of antiquity apart from Hippocrates, worked with gladiators and recommended running to combat obesity. Moderation was the catchword and the most common method of slimming in his time – he lived a century and a half after Seneca and the need for slimming had increased among the gluttonous Romans. Galen recommended other exercises as well as running, which he thought too one-sided to achieve optimal muscular harmony. He believed, moreover, that running would damage the veins, and he did not think that running would of itself help develop a manly character.

Runners in Rome never achieved the same divine status as in Hellas, as we can see from the absence of the names of good Roman runners in surviving sources or in the archaeological material. Whereas the Greeks recorded their sportsmen's names and dedicated any number of statues to them, the Romans did not bother to pay homage to or even name their champions.

The World of Paul

Sometime between the years 5 BC and 10 BC a boy was born in Tarsus in Turkey, an old town at the crossroads of important trade routes. The boy's father was a Jew of the tribe of Benjamin and also a Roman citizen. He ensured that Saul, later known as the apostle Paul, was given a strict Pharisaic upbringing. But the boy did not just sit bent over his books: he was sent to a rabbi in Jerusalem, he learnt the trade of tent-making and he developed a lasting interest in sports by frequenting the stadium in Tarsus and training there. There were regular sporting events there and a great deal to interest an inquisitive young mind and to give him an insight into Greek, Roman and Jewish culture.

Around about the year of Paul's birth King Herod travelled to Rome, a city he knew well and where he was on good terms with the top social groups in the republic. On his way there he called in at the Olympic Games and found to his sorrow that they were in decline. Herod was the founder of many gymnasia and was keen to spread Greek sports.

So this was the age in which Paul was growing up. Herod had begun to organize games in Jerusalem and Caesarea in 12 BC and, even though there were strong protests from the rabbis because the body was considered sinful in ancient Jewish belief, the games in Caesarea continued for at least a century and a half. Competitors came from 'the whole world' and the Jews were shocked, particularly by the images of the Roman ruler Augustus, in whose honour the games were held.

There are several references to running in the writings of Paul. In one of his letters to the Corinthians he writes: 'Do you not know that those who run in a race all run, but only one receives the prize? Run in such a way that you may win.'[6]

Running is frequently referred to in the Bible, particularly in the Old Testament. Two long-distance runs, one of around 25 miles and the other 35 miles, are mentioned around 1000 BC in connection with war. Whereas Paul was influenced by the ideals of Greek competition and used them metaphorically, most of the Biblical references are to the carrying of messages and running for practical purposes.[7]

According to the Bible King Solomon ruled a kingdom centred on Israel and lived c. 1000 BC. He had 40,000 horses and 10,000 runners and arranged contests between his horses and his men. These figures may be exaggerated but he certainly arranged betting races for 'the wise, the priests and the Levites'.[8]

The philosopher Philo of Alexandria (20 BC–AD 50), a contemporary of Paul, was the Jewish writer who wrote most about running. In passage after passage he used the literary image of running to explain the dilemmas and everyday concerns of life. A runner on the starting line was like a Roman army ready to march, impatient, nervy and subdued. The rushed and usually turbulent race over two lengths of the stadium symbolized life: 'It is rare for God to allow a man to run life's race from start to finish without stumbling or falling, or for him to successfully avoid both accidental and intentional misfortune by sprinting past the others with a great burst of speed'.[9]

Distance was like life itself. When a man reaches his prime he no longer goes forward but may, like the runners in a race over two lengths of the stadium, turn and go back in the same direction. The runner weakens as he approaches his goal and the old man grows ever weaker as he approaches death – his goal. Philo also uttered a prophecy about the Jews: 'They will weep and wail over their injustices but then turn and run the *diaulos* back to the welfare of their forefathers'.[10]

The references by Paul and Philo to stadium running show the acknowledged status of running even among the learned Jewish writers. The English historian H. A. Harris has studied Jewish attitudes to ancient Greek sport. He is of the view that Jewish historians underestimated Jewish interest and participation in sport because it was seen as 'unjewish'. According to Harris there is no evidence that orthodox Jews shunned the games either in Egypt or in Palestine. Harris' view seems probable, given that Paul, who spent twelve years travelling in Asia Minor, Greece and Macedonia to spread the message of Jesus, used his experience of running as a way of explaining things. Paul was beheaded by the Romans in *c.* AD 67 for spreading false doctrines.

Christianity became the official religion of Rome in AD 381, and in 393 the Emperor Theodosius I banned the Olympic Games.

The Christians banned sport, as it was seen as a homage to the heathen gods. Christianity taught that mankind's thoughts should concentrate on eternal life, not on the development and worship of the body, especially not in its naked state. The human body was sinful even if the soul was saved: the body could be tempted into sin, drunkenness and lechery and thus lead the thoughts away from God. Sport thus became an enemy of God. Even Paul writes, in his Second Epistle to Timothy, that there is little value in physical exercise, whereas fear of the Lord is useful in all things since it concerns both this life and the life to come. The emperor also banned gladiatorial contests, since they too were seen as heathen.

In AD 420 Theodosius II ordered the demolition of the Temple of Zeus. Germanic tribes plundered the temples in Olympia, and in 522 and again in 551 the region was covered by a fifteen- to fifty-foot-deep (4.5 to 15 m) layer of ash and mud after the volcanic eruptions at the Kronion hill. Flooding by a river made the area virtually unrecognizable. Greek games continued to be held at Antioch in Syria until 510 and those are the last games we know of.

There are both similarities and differences between running in Mesopotamia, Egypt, the Roman Empire and Ancient Greece. Running had a sacred function everywhere, but winning was also of great importance.

5
Elephant Races and Chinese Tales

He tied ten metres of rope to his head and ran so fast that it streamed
straight out in the air behind him – his speed was faster than a horse.
—*On the Chinese Soldier*, Yang Dayan

Once upon a time there was a tribe in northern China who thought the
sun went down too quickly – it gave too little heat and was not as useful
as people thought it ought to be. They therefore sent a young runner to
the sky to catch the sun so that it would remain present in the sky perpet-
ually. The boy chased the sun from morning to evening and, worn out and
thirsty, he caught up with it at the valley. He drank up the whole of the
River Wei and also the Yellow River and wanted to move on to another
river to drink that, but before he could he died of exhaustion. Then, to the
great good of mankind, a metamorphosis occurred: his hair turned into
grass and plants, his blood became a river, and his staff became a peach
garden. He had not succeeded with his tribe's mission but he gave everything to the earth so that his tribe's descendants could fulfil mankind's
plan to cultivate the earth and get food.

The Chinese folk-tale *Kuafu's Chase after the Sun* described a mythic
time 5,000 years before Christ when China was at a stage of transition to a
more civilized society. There, as in many cultures, a runner was the main
character in a narrative that explained the origin of natural elements – those
things that created order and provided the basis of existence. The runner
was an ambulatory figure with unusual talents and special insights. People
told the story about Kuafu solemnly and respectfully, certain of the bravery of his effort and of the importance of his creative role.[1]

The Chinese state came together in 221 BC and its history is linked to
dynasties in which power passed from father to son. The Han dynasty from
206 BC to AD 220 was China's first period of greatness and it coincided
with the period that the Roman Empire was flourishing. The Han Empire,
however, was even bigger, the biggest empire in the world, though little
known by Europeans (here we can see the beginnings of the European
undervaluing of Chinese culture – Europe is always thought of as being the
centre of the world). Buried in Chinese history there are treasures of inconceivable richness, early technological progress and a mentality different
from that of the West. The principles of *yin*, the earthly, and *yang*, the
heavenly, were key concepts and symbolized opposites such as cold-hot

and active-passive. Yin and yang must complement one another otherwise balance cannot be achieved. The aim of ancient Chinese physical exercises was the achievement of balance, whether in breathing exercises, defence techniques, ball games or running.[2]

There is a well-known Chinese painting, *Ling's Cooking Pot*, which shows an emperor in the Zhou dynasty (1100–771 BC) leading his subjects and slaves to the spring ploughing and sowing. On the way back to the palace he promises a rich reward to two guards, Ling and Fen, if they can run as fast as the horse-drawn carriages. The men, the horses and the coachmen sped along the rough road in a frantic race and the guards, who usually ran in front and behind the emperor, brought all their experience to bear. The runners arrived first and were proud both of themselves and for their employer, who liked to have agile men under him – even though the emperor also wanted his carriages to travel as fast as possible. The two sweating guards were the heroes of the day and the emperor stuck to his promise and rewarded them. Ling used his reward to make a cooking pot on which the story of the race was engraved.

Chinese sources tell mainly of running for practical military purposes. A plentiful supply of fit infantrymen was vital, men who could use the crossbow and spear. Runners had an important function in Chinese military theory which, in the wake of many wars, had developed into an advanced art.

Sun Wuoi, a counsellor in the army, was for some years in the service of the Emperor Wu, one of the rulers in the period 722–481 BC. Sun Wuoi ordered the soldiers to run 90 miles in full kit before they moved into their quarters. He promised to select the 3,000 best for a special force, a troop in permanent readiness, in which running would be an important skill. Sun Wuoi surveyed the soldiers who were training and saw a magnificent sight: tens of thousands of committed young men running. Rarely had so many been brought together for a race as for this selection procedure, even in this, the most populous country in the world, where there were armies of several hundred thousand men.

After their selection into the special troop these three thousand men provided the force that attacked the Chu Empire quickly and unexpectedly, taking the enemy by surprise. In a short time they occupied far-distant areas and, since all of them were highly trained men, they did so without rapidly losing all their strength. The mounted units took care of the long-distance objectives while the foot-soldiers undertook shorter surprise attacks because they were more flexible than transport animals, which needed fodder, drink and rest. The runners, of course, needed that too but they lived an ascetic life, carrying only the most vital things with them, including several days' rations. They drank water from streams and allowed no physical obstacles to hold them back. They pushed on through all kinds of terrain, climbed when necessary, and poured onwards like a swarm of human bees. The running technique of these soldiers was influenced by the fact that they wore mail on their chests, stomachs and legs, had protective headgear and carried swords, bows and arrows. In later dynasties we hear of men having to run 30 miles in order to be accepted into the army.

China was the location for one of the world's first annual ultra-marathons – distances longer than the 26 miles of the marathon. In the Yuan Dynasty (1271–1368), also known as the Mongol Dynasty since its founding father was Genghis Khan, a special unit – 'the rapid runner unit' – met in Beijing every year to run the 55 mile *Gui You Chi* (Mongolian for 'fast runner') run. Another race over the same distance was started in the same period in Inner Mongolia. The frontrunners took six hours for that distance, roughly the same standard as in modern long-distance running.

The demands on military runners were exacting and enshrined in writing. They were handed on from commander to commander, adjusted or newly written by new dynasties, and they applied to both long- and short-distance runners. Sprinting ability was important on the battlefield, but the ideal was a combination of speed and endurance. Warriors trained wearing double equipment to improve their capacity over short distances, and they tied sacks of sand and weights to their legs. Afterwards they would feel light as a feather and virtually fly, not unlike the soldier Yang Dayan, who demanded a sprint test after having been declared unfit for service. He tied ten metres of rope to his head and ran so fast that it streamed straight out in the air behind him – his speed was faster than a horse. He was afterwards appointed as an officer of the vanguard.

On the Starting Line against Elephants

Long ago drummers went from village to village in India spreading the king's or a nobleman's message about an event due to take place the following week: the elephant run, a race between men and elephants. People knew that the winner would gain honour and cash prizes, as well as the special notice of the king. Crowds turned up and took their places on benches in the square in front of the palace where sports and plays were presented. It was an event popular with both the aristocracy and the common people. Beautiful pennants waved in the wind, marking out the course, and the elephant handlers prepared their animals, ensuring that the blindfolds were in place. The handlers had great responsibility, since bolting elephants are likely to trample people to death, so the start for the elephants and the runners had to be synchronized.

The participants made their solemn entry to the square, introduced themselves to the public by running and jumping, shouted and clapped their hands to bolster their courage and win the favour of the spectators. Meanwhile an orchestra was whipping up the mood and ensuring a jolly atmosphere, since this was a mixed entertainment that included acrobats, wrestlers, dancers and singers.

Men and elephants were divided into three classes depending on speed. The runners and the animals were positioned at different points around the arena based on their earlier performances. The aim was to stay ahead of the elephant and the man who increased his lead by the longest distance had beaten the animal and won the race. Anyone who fled the arena because of fear or anyone caught up by the elephant was a loser and had to endure the shame. Giving up was far from the minds of these tough participants and they were ready for some robust action. Nevertheless their hearts were pounding nervously in the moments before the start.

The elephant was held at the starting line with a cloth over its head and the horse and elephant keepers took care of it. Then the runner was led in front of the elephant and the cloth was taken off the elephant's head. As soon as the elephant saw the runner it went wild and chased him angrily. If the elephant went completely out of control they used a herd of cow elephants to regain control of the wild beast.[3]

The elephant race was a risky sport, with elements of a test of manhood, accompanied by the echoes of thundering feet and the screams of the elephant. It was essential not to be panicked, not to lose speed by looking nervously over your shoulder. Even though an elephant can weigh six or seven tons and looks clumsy, it can reach a speed of 15 miles an hour (24 km/h) when it gallops.

There have been tame elephants in India for several thousand years and Indians credit then with supernatural powers. They have a higher status than horses and are the bearers of *Indra*, the king of the gods; they were both religious symbols and important tools in warfare. But elephants can also lose their tempers and have killed many people. The certainty that the animals could easily kill the puny runners, and the belief that they are divine creatures, were important factors when men raced against elephants: it was a holy act, like so much else in that country.

India extends from latitude 37° N to 8° N, that is the distance from Seville in Spain to Sierra Leone in Africa. Climatic and geographical conditions range from eternal snows to humid jungles and over 200 languages are spoken. The existence of so many peoples suggests early settlement and many waves of immigrants moving into the valleys of the Indus and the Ganges, where the true culture of the country developed. The best-known Indian contribution to physical and spiritual well-being is *yoga*, which is Sanskrit for 'uniting' or 'union'. Various branches of yoga developed, emphasising physical and mental control and harmony and with the particular aim of reinforcing *prana* or *ki*, the life energy that keeps the body healthy.

Even though yoga and prana were important, many of the country's mythic figures – Prince Siddhartha Gautama (565–485 BC), for instance – are also connected with running. Like many of his class, the prince was put through an all-round physical education as he grew up, and it included running. According to the story he left his wife and newborn child to dedicate his life to isolation and meditation. Later he gathered together disciples and was given the name Buddha, the Enlightened One. Krishna, too, one of the most worshipped of India's gods, ran in his youth.

The physical ideals of Vedic civilisation, 2000–1000 BC, are reminiscent of those of Ancient Greece. Indian physical culture, however, developed over a longer period and also held a popular sports festival, *Samana*, with a religious theme. In Vedic times the upper class was absorbed by diet and personal hygiene, by training and the correction of physical deformities. The body should be tempered, man should strive for perfection and care for the temple of his body.[4]

According to Indian Ayurvedic medicine (*ayur* means 'life' and *veda* means 'knowledge') – one of the oldest extant medical systems in the world – running on a full stomach leads to inner imbalance. But running while hunting was to be recommended. It improves the digestion, slims the body and makes it more robust.

Training started early for those involved. Play was followed by physical education, even for girls. Trainers educated the youth of the warrior class – running was the training, particularly for soldiers with throwing weapons or for fist-fighters, boxers and wrestlers. Being fast on your feet could make the difference between life and death in battle.

The period from 1000 BC to AD 200 was the epic age in India. During this time there were sports stadia, amphitheatres, theatres, parade grounds, training centres, games parks, swimming pools and other facilities for the development of sports. *Samajja*, a sporting festival, was organised by the king to entertain the people, and sports were also a part of the religious festivals held at harvest time and at the full moon.

At certain sporting events the daughter of some powerful man would choose her husband among the princes who were meeting to compete in the amphitheatre. The Greek historian Arian described something similar: 'When the ladies are at a marriageable age their fathers will present them in public so that they may be chosen by the winner at wrestling or boxing or running or by someone who has distinguished himself in manly activity'.[5]

During this period the system for physical well-being was regulated according to the seasons and to people's stage in life. Running was recommended for boys and girls of between sixteen and twenty-four in order to develop their competitive instincts, to increase fitness and to satisfy the need for movement – it should preferably be undertaken in the morning. Walking was ideal for men over seventy, as it was for women over fifty.

Messengers, on the other hand, pushed themselves hard all the year round. *Dak Harkara*, one of the world's most extensive messenger systems, was developed in India.

Dak is Hindi for 'post' or 'letter' and *Harkara* was a runner who transported the post in India. It resembles the systems in other countries, with huts along the tracks and roads where the men passed on the post to each other, rested and waited for the next mission. The post-sack was carried in a cleft stick and the post runner had this stick and a spear as defensive weapons. The post-runners in India had the mystique and status of heroes and poems and stories about these brave men were told in many languages and dialects.

The *dak* runners were characterized by endurance, courage and honesty and they lived dangerous lives. From the earliest days on they were accompanied by a man beating a drum to alert the people and to scare off dangerous animals – frequently the man also carried a torch. At other times bells were carried and could be heard at long distances. On dangerous stretches the post-runner might be escorted by two torch-bearers and two bowmen. They had to push on through jungles, thick forests and mountains irrespective of the weather, even during the monsoon, and there were *dak* runners who were taken by tigers, drowned in rivers they had to cross, bitten by snakes or killed by snowslides. Highway robbers and criminals robbed and murdered *dak* runners, since they also transported money. The postal system in Marwar even functioned in wartime and the king received letters by runner even on the battlefield.

From 1584 the Mirdha family organized the postal system in Marwar in Rajastan, one of India's princely states. On long runs the *dak* runners covered daily stages of varying length depending on the terrain and the urgency of the message. Fourteen to twenty miles was a minimum on paths in hilly country with necessary stops and errands on the way. There was much rivalry to get important commissions and the ability to cover the longest distances gave status. In this respect the post-runners resembled ambitious sportsmen.

Datine from Nagaur was young when he started training for the *dak* life and he became both the fastest runner of his time and the one with the most stamina. Fifty to 55 miles a day was normal but on one occasion with urgent mail he covered 66 miles between dawn and dusk. His employer was so impressed that he gave Datine the right to ride a horse, a right normally restricted to the upper classes.

Runners and riders were stationed at permanent staging posts and letters had to be delivered within a set time for a fixed payment that varied depending on the distance. Between Delhi and Lahore the time taken was five days. Runners between Jodphur and Mount Abu earned 180 rupees a year – the camel postman, however, earned 718 rupees a year because animals carried heavier loads.[6]

Neither in China nor in India was running as common as in Ancient Greece and the Mediterranean area, but it was one of a number of ways for ordinary people to keep fit in civilian life. Doctors and experts in China and India recognized from earliest times the good and health-giving effects of running, with allowance made for age and ability. Those who ran simply for the exercise are rarely mentioned in old historical sources, but such people did exist in Asia, running to improve their lives with the blessing of experts.

6

The Running Monks

> One of those initiated into the sacred teaching claims that after many
> years of practice the feet of the *lung-gom-pa* – once they have covered
> a certain distance – no longer touch the ground and they glide
> through the air with utter lightness and speed.
> —Alexandra David-Néel, Belgian-French traveller and explorer in Tibet

Can all those stories about the mystics and ascetics in Asia really be true?
All those wise men who have themselves buried alive, those hermits who
live in holes for years, isolated from their fellow men with only mountains
and loneliness for companionship?

Of course not, but some of them *do* hold true – such as the stories of
the *lung-gom-pa*, the tireless runners in Tibet. The Belgian-French author
Alexandra David-Néel, who travelled in Tibet for more than twenty years
at the beginning of the twentieth century, claimed to have seen these legendary runners at close quarters.[1]

On the Northern Plain, Chang Thang, in northern Tibet, a wild, grassy
and thinly populated area, no one lived but nomads in tents when David-
Néel travelled through on horseback. She became aware of something
moving far away on the plain and her telescope showed it was a man.
They had not seen any other people for ten days and people rarely ventured
alone and on foot in these regions. Perhaps it was a refugee from a caravan
that had been robbed, someone in need of food and help?

The man was moving both quickly and in a peculiar way. 'It looks like a
lama *lung-gom-pa*', said one of the Tibetan servants in her group, and no one
doubted that when the ragged man came closer.[2] His impassive face and
wide-open eyes were fixed on a point on the horizon. He was not running but
leaping with long, regular strides as if his legs were on springs and his body
was air. He was carrying a dagger in his right hand and he passed close to the
six riders, apparently unaware that he was being watched, but the Tibetans
dismounted and bowed low to the earth to show respect.

David-Néel was excited and wanted to talk to the man but her servants
advised against it. The runner must not be disturbed because he might die
if the god dwelling within him were to suddenly desert him. David-Néel followed him for two miles until he turned off the path and climbed a steep
slope before disappearing into the mountains, still in a trance and still with
strange movements.

Four days later they came across a group of shepherds who had also met
the runner. They believed he had come from a monastery in the province

of Tsang where the monks trained in *lung-gom-pa*. There was a legend telling how this monastery, Shalu Gompa, had originally become the centre for this kind of training.

The magician Yungtön and the historian Bu-ston were two lamas who lived in the fourteenth century. Yungtön decided to perform a solemn ritual every twelfth year to gain control over Shinjed, the Lord of Death, and if it was not carried out at the correct time the divinity would slaughter one creature each day to satisfy his hunger. This ritual, together with daily prayers, gave the magician control over the Lord of Death for twelve years.

Bu-ston heard about this and visited the god's temple accompanied by three lamas. The god was demanding more food and Yungtön suggested that one of the lamas should sacrifice himself. All three refused point-blank and disappeared but Bu-ston was prepared to die. The magician, however, ensured that there was a happy outcome to the ritual and there was no loss of life.

Afterwards Bu-ston and his followers were appointed to carry out the ritual every twelfth year and since then the reincarnations of Lama Bu-ston, masters of Shalu Gompa, have maintained the ritual. The number of demons increased, however, and in order to gather them all up it was necessary to find a capable runner – known as 'a calling buffalo' – who was chosen from among the monks of two monasteries after strict training.

The training lasted three years and three months. One important exercise in particular, which like all the others was performed in complete darkness, seems impossible. The monk would sit cross-legged on a cushion and breathe in slowly to fill his body with air, then he held his breath and shot straight upwards, legs still crossed and without using his hands, before falling back into the same position. The exercise was repeated time after time, not to turn the monks into acrobats but to make them light and capable of floating.

For the final test the monk sat in a grave in the ground as deep as a man was tall, and over this they built a cupola of the same height from ground level to its top point. So a man who was five feet six inches (167 cm) tall was sitting eleven feet (335 cm) below the small hole in the cupola. The test consisted of jumping out through the opening in the cupola with crossed legs, a jump from a sitting position. David-Néel heard of such feats but never saw them herself, perhaps because they are physically impossible.

There was another variation of this last exercise. After three years isolated in pitch darkness the monks were walled into a small hut. Seven days later they were to climb out of the side of the hut through a small square hole. Anyone who managed to wriggle his way out became a 'calling buffalo'.

Only the monasteries in Shalu used methods like this and some of them also used marching exercises in mountainous terrain. *Lung-gom-pa*, moreover, was not so much aimed at strengthening the muscles as at building the mental powers necessary to make the strange running style possible. A 'calling buffalo' would start his mission on the 11 November and travel for a month without stopping in order to round up demons.

David-Néel also met two other runners in Tibet. The first of these sat and meditated naked on a knoll with iron chains around his body. When he saw people he leapt up and disappeared. The natives said that the man used the chains because he was so light that there was a risk of him floating in the air, just as is recounted in stories from several other parts of the world. The Tibetans believed that the best runners had bodies of a supernatural lightness and that they were able to float.

The other runner had the appearance of a poor pilgrim, of which there are hordes in Tibet. The man climbed up a slope at great speed, using the typical springing run, and then he stopped, still in a trance. He slowly came to himself and began to speak. He had practised *lung-gom-pa* training in a monastery but his teacher had disappeared and he had been forced to go to Shalu Gompa to continue his training. As the speed of the caravan increased, he shifted automatically into the springing gait, helped by secret words and the formulae of his master, which regulated his breathing in a particular rhythm and easily led to a state of trance. He got bored with the leisurely pace of the caravan and disappeared silently one night, springing off into the darkness.

The runners concentrated on repeating their formula silently to themselves while breathing and striding rhythmically. They looked neither to the side nor behind, did not speak, kept their eyes fixed on a distant point and were capable of keeping direction and seeing obstacles even in their trance. Wide-open plains were ideal for training and they quickly entered a trance, particularly at dusk. In the darkness the runners would continue for hours with their gaze fixed on a star. Beginners would stop when the star disappeared but the more experienced could still see it within them and could continue.

In Tibet Alexandra David-Néel met runners and walkers who had trained in advanced exercises. She did not believe everything the Tibetans told her but accepted that the most advanced followers of *lung-gom-pa* felt a great lightness in their bodies and were capable of extreme endurance.

Holy Mountains and Holy Men

On Hiei, the sacred mountain in Japan, lives an order of monks – known as the marathon monks – who have to walk and run farther than the circumference of the globe in order to achieve purification and a Buddha status.

The rituals originate from AD 831 when So-o – 'he who serves others' – was born. At a young age he refused to eat meat and fish and preferred the ascetic and hermit life. At the age of fifteen he moved into a small hut on Hiei to live a holy life and there he was noticed by the abbot Ennin. The abbot initiated So-o into tantric mysticism and described to him the tradition of making pilgrimages to mountains, a tradition from Chinese Buddhism. In a dream So-o heard a voice saying: 'All the peaks of this mountain are holy. Follow the instructions of the gods of the mountain and go to the mountain's holy places. Practise this hard every day. And you shall be respectful to all things, then you will understand the true Dharma.'[3] He should view everything as a manifestation of Buddha and worship nature with his body and soul.

After his formal ordination as a Buddhist monk in 856, he built a one-man hut in the Mudoji valley. So-o's powers of judgement grew and his prayers cured diseases, helped women in childbirth, drove away demons and eased toothache. After a thousand days of solitude he and his assistants built a house on Hiei which became the residence of the Kaihogyo monks (*kaihogyo* means 'the custom of walking round the mountain'). The monks would visit the holy places of the mountain and pray to them, a custom performed on many of the holy mountains in Japan.[4]

So-o died in 918 and according to the story the mountain played divine music that day. His successors continued the pilgrimages to Hiei, though it is uncertain exactly how, since the accounts disappeared when the temples were plundered in 1571. But as early as 1310 people had already begun to visit the holy places for 100, 700 or 1,000 days. 'The History of the Wandering Saint' of 1387 described a 25-mile (40 km) run which was to be completed daily for 700 days, followed by nine days of fasting. In 1585 Koun completed 1,000 days of this trial, thereby setting a demanding standard which still applies.

The monks at Hiei are Tendai Buddhists. The practice of pilgrimages on foot incorporates all the aspects of Tendai Buddhism: meditation, initiated knowledge, self-sacrifice, nature worship and good deeds. To become an abbot in one of the under-temples on Hiei a monk must complete 100 days in succession.

Beginners are first accompanied on a tour and given a handbook and secret oral instructions, necessary information about the terrain and paths before they are ready to travel alone.

Dressed in white clothing, with a rope around his waist and with a knife – a reminder to commit suicide if he fails to complete the test – the monk rises at midnight so as to start his first stage an hour and a half later. He puts on straw sandals, knowing that they wear out quickly and will have to be changed up to five times a day: in dry weather they last for several days but when the rain is pouring down they crumble in a couple of hours, so the monk carries several spare pairs. Rain and snow are the monk's worst enemies – they destroy his footwear, reduce his speed, wash away the paths and extinguish his lanterns. In the worst rainy periods his clothing is never dry. The clothing and the oblong hat must not be removed, the route must be followed slavishly and it is forbidden to stop to eat and rest. Prayers and songs have to be performed properly.

The routes are from 18 to 25 miles (29–40 km) in length and the monk stops for a few seconds or minutes in front of stone images of the Buddha, sacred trees, rocks, ridges, waterfalls or pools, makes the correct hand movements, prays and hurries on. Progress is not rapid as there are 255 stopping places and the rugged terrain slows the pace of the tour, which lasts until seven or eight o'clock in the morning depending on the weather. Older monks criticize young ones who rush through the run – it is excellent to be fit and light on your feet but correct ritual practice is just as important.

After prayers, bathing, lunch, temple duties and supper, the monk goes to bed at around eight. This rhythm is repeated for a hundred days, apart from between the 65th and 75th days, when the run is 35 miles (56 km) long and goes through the city of Kyoto with its million inhabitants. That is so the monks may understand that their endeavour is also for the benefit of the outside world.

The first two or three weeks are the worst for beginners. They not only have to remember a great deal and find their way through hilly country where mist often makes visibility difficult, they get sores on their feet, become stiff and feverish, suffer from diarrhoea and pains in their hips and legs. After a month the body begins to become accustomed to the rhythm and after about two months the monk has an easy and relaxed style.

A hundred days is merely a warm-up for the most ambitious of them: some want to carry on for a thousand days and covenant themselves to a seven-year, sacred marathon. The first five years contain seven periods of 100 days, each involving 25 miles a day. In the sixth year the stages are increased to 38 miles. The climax is reached in the final year, which has 52 miles (84 km) a day for 100 days before finishing with a 'mere' 25 miles. By that stage the monks have covered 29,107 miles (46,843 km).[5]

The most demanding test comes after 700 days: they must fast for nine days without food, drink, sleep or rest. Under the watchful eye of two monks, the monk must sit still, the only interruptions being simple rituals involving little movement. The older monks in the temple keep watch and touch his shoulder should he doze off or fall out of the sitting position.

The monk has already reduced his food intake in advance so the fasting is no great burden at the start, but after five days dehydration has become so extreme that he tastes blood in his mouth. He is allowed to rinse out his mouth with water but must spit it all out. He is allowed to go outdoors and he notices that his skin absorbs damp in rainy weather. The time without food, sleep and drink – the fast is actually seven and a half days (182 hours) in total but they refer to it as nine days since the starting and finishing days are included – is to give the monk a glimpse into death. According to the report, the monks originally fasted for ten days but since almost all of them died the period was reduced. Damp months like August are unsuitable and two monks in modern times have suffered internal decomposition and died in that month.

The absence of food and drink is, however, not the worst part, which is having to hold the head in the same position without resting. The monk becomes extra sensitive, can smell food at long distances and all his senses become more acute.

Finally on the ninth day the monk sits before the altar in the presence of up to three hundred Tendai priests and is given a special drink to stimulate him. Many of them faint when they step out on to the veranda and symbolically turn their back on life. Physiologists have examined the monks at this point and they confirm that their condition resembles a pre-death stage. The monk has been purified in body and mind and views the world with new, utterly clear eyes.

After some weeks of eating they recover and regain the lost pounds, becoming full of energy and life and they are eager to continue.

To complete 52 miles every day for 100 days takes courage and drive. They receive plenty of help from fellow monks and the local population, including from so-called 'shovers' who prod them carefully from behind with padded poles, although some refuse such assistance. The monks hurry on for 52 miles through the residential areas in Kyoto, blessing thousands of people, going over traffic crossings and along streets, keeping going for sixteen or seventeen hours and with hardly any time to sleep. 'Ten minutes sleep for a marathon monk is worth five hours of normal rest', so the saying goes.[6] Good helpers are important at this stage. They take care of food and clean clothes, carrying equipment and directing traffic when the monk in his old-fashioned clothing enters the city traffic and has to watch out for cars. The role of the helpers is a hereditary one.

A total of 46 men have completed the 1,000 days since 1885. Two monks have managed it twice and one man committed suicide on his 2,500th day. One monk, Okuno Genjun, has done it three times but without running every day of his last session, when he was carried. The majority of the men were in their thirties, though Sakai did his 2,000th day when he was 61. It is not known how many have died or committed suicide along the way, but along the paths there are the anonymous graves of monks who collapsed and died.

These monks are not highly trained sportsmen but are inured to and strengthened by physical work such as chopping wood, heavy lifting and carrying and by a simple, modest way of life with a vegetarian diet. Breakfast is eaten at 1.30 a.m. and the preferred choice is noodles, rice, potatoes, soya, green vegetables, herbs, honey and nuts. Five small meals provide sufficient calories and energy to achieve a daily marathon. Sakai, one of the veterans at Hiei, only ate 1,450 calories a day when he ran 25 miles and he nevertheless retained a robust physique. Their spiritual disposition endows them with endurance. Those who complete the 1,000 days join the highest ranks of Buddhist saints.

These laborious rituals have to be understood in the light of Buddhist teachings, which cannot be realized through the intellect alone but must also be experienced physically. 'Learn through your sight, train with your legs.'[7] The monks' training produces what is called *innen* in Japanese – *in* refers to those characteristics relevant to the Buddha mentality that arise from within one, *en* are the circumstances in which this takes place.

Of all the tough figures from Hiei, the toughest of all was perhaps Hakozaki Bunno, the son of a poor fishing family. He roamed around taking casual jobs from his earliest years and lacked any direction in life until he had a spiritual awakening in a prison cell after a binge. In another version of the story he had tried to hang himself in a park but was cut down by a Tendai priest who then led him to Hiei. He left his wife and children in the care of relatives and begged his way to the mountain.

The priests were unwilling to accept this unknown man dressed in rags but one monk showed him goodwill. Hakozaki began as a bearer for Okuno Genjun, a cripple who was carried round the mountain on his daily route, but when the bearers took a corner too quickly and the crippled man tumbled out of his chair and down a slope Hakozaki was blamed and had to move to a different temple. But the doors were closed to him there, too. 'Either they let me in or I will die!' Hakozaki said and sat down in front of the entrance. He remained there for four days without food and water, was hit with brooms and had buckets of icy water poured over him. On the fifth day they took him in and he began a monastic life of frenetic activity.

No one walked and trotted so far, no one worked or prayed so much as Hakozaki. He sought out isolation in mountain hollows and sat for days in the lotus position, paying no attention to his surroundings, before returning strengthened and inspired to continue his activities.

A young mountaineer sought shelter in a cave during a cloudburst and found himself suddenly looking into the face of Hakozaki, who had been fasting for nine days and looked like a statue. The young man got the shock of his life, crept out of the cave and ran back to the village, terrified by the experience. Hakozaki performed the nine-day fast without food, drink or sleep no fewer than 36 times, often at the end of a year in order to purify his body.

The monks in white have been striding over Hiei in the spirit of Buddhism ever since the ninth century and they resemble sportsmen in their asceticism, self-denial and membership of a brotherhood with defined rituals. They are still active. In many ways they are more extreme than top athletes – monks, like other people, go to extremes when trying to outdo others. It seems likely that some of the same human motivations, such as the urge to distinguish themselves and to perform outstanding feats, are shared by the best runners in the world and the most dogged of the Japanese marathon monks.

7
Racing against Horses

Young people today behave differently from when I was young.
In those days we were eager to perform great feats, nowadays young
people are just stay-at-homes who want to sit there chilling their
bellies with mead and ale.
—Elderly Viking in the tenth century

'It's a lie!' Magnus Sigurdsson said.

'No,' Harald Gille answered, 'in Ireland there are men who can run faster than horses.'

This quarrel between two heirs apparent took place at a drinking feast in Oslo at the beginning of the twelfth century. The men were sitting in the hall eating and drinking, telling tall tales mixed with true stories – and honour and pride were at stake. Harald Gille had grown up in Ireland but come to Norway claiming to be the son of the Norwegian king Magnus Barefoot, who had campaigned in Ireland and left several sons behind.

Then Magnus Sigurdsson said: 'Now you shall make a wager with me that you can run as fast as I can ride on my horse, and you shall stake your head and I shall stake my gold ring against it.'

The next morning he summoned Harald to a race. Harald came dressed in a shirt, short cloak, Irish hat and with a spear-shaft in his hand. Magnus marked out a course but Harald said it was too long, so his opponent made it even longer and said that it was nevertheless too short. In front of a great crowd the race began, Harald equipped with a staff – a shepherd's tool and weapon.

Harald ran the whole time at the horse's shoulder and when they came to the end of the course Magnus said: 'You held on to the saddle-girth and the horse dragged you.' Magnus had an unusually fast horse from Götaland. Then they ran another race and this time Harald ran in front of the horse the whole way. When they came to the finish, Harald said: 'Did I hold the saddle-girth that time?' 'No,' said Magnus, 'This time you were holding the horse back instead.'

Now Magnus let the horse get its breath back. When it was ready, he put the spurs to it and it set off immediately. Harald stood still. Then Magnus looked back and yelled 'Run now!' Then Harald began to run and soon passed the horse and reached the finish far ahead. He reached the finish so far ahead that he lay down and then jumped up and greeted Magnus when he arrived. Then they went back to the town.[1]

Harald Gille and Magnus Sigurdsson later fought for the throne and Gille had his rival blinded, chopped off his feet and castrated him.

Horses in the Viking Age were a short-legged Icelandic breed of pony, probably of the same origin as the Norwegian Fjording and later crossed with breeds from Shetland and the Orkneys. Icelandic horses move with an ambling gait or use a characteristic gait similar to both the amble and the pure trot. They are not the fastest breed of horse but they can cover 430 to 490 yards (390–450 m) a minute, carrying a twelve stone (76 kg) man. It is hardly accidental that most of the sources in which men race horses and win originate in Iceland.[2]

We should, however, be sceptical about accepting stories with a markedly legendary stamp as fact since a good story rather than a slavishly factual account was what mattered most to the creative imagination of the *skald*. But the Vikings were undoubtedly influenced by sporting impulses from Ireland.

There was a great sporting festival in Ireland, the Tailteann Games, which existed for several centuries in the Middle Ages and only ceased after the Norman invasion of 1168. According to legend, the Tailteann Games had existed for three thousand years and were originally held in honour of the dead Queen Tailté, a beautiful, cultured queen familiar with the knowledge and secret lore of Europe and the East. She was thought worthy of the description: 'one of the best female druids in the western world'.[3]

The queen chose her own burial place, a picturesque, sunny spot in the woods twelve miles from her favourite palace at Teltown. She commanded that the *Aonach* (festival) be held there. The first games were organized for the queen's funeral and they continued annually on the same dates, starting on the first day of August and lasting for 30 days.

There was a great variety of activities: running, long jump, high jump, steeplechase, spear-thowing, fencing, wrestling, boxing, swimming, horse-racing, chariot racing, pole jump and archery, as well as many other physical tests. There were also competitions in music, singing, dancing, storytelling and handicrafts. There was even a market with numerous wares for sale and animals on show – a real piece of everyday life where local people mixed with those from far away and picked up ideas and influences.

Similar festivals were held at many places in Ireland but the Tailteann was the oldest, the most important and the biggest – and they were also a model for other peoples, such as the Vikings. Even if running was not the most important Viking skill, Scandinavia did produce famous runners in the ninth century.

In the sagas there are many traces of Viking sports. 'They all learnt sports from Odin', it was said.[4] Sport also included various kinds of mental knowledge and a true chieftain was one who combined good mental abilities with sporting competence. King Olav Tryggvason was 'foremost in all sports' and a good runner.[5]

A boy in the Viking Age would play on the farm and soon get toughened up. He ran racing games in the courtyard or on the games field, a flat grassy area where the local people played ball games, danced and met together. The young lads lifted stones, swam in the fjords, developed their imagination and were eager to shoot with the crossbow, ride, fence and wrestle, as well as to ski and skate.

Ambitions were, of course, stirred when the lads heard stories of the adult men's travels: their fathers were often away on expeditions and had selected substitute fathers – *fostri* – to train the lads in various sports. The aim of the education, as with the Spartans in ancient Hellas, was to produce good warriors, but it was to be done not by legal compulsion but by guidance, encouragement and by inspiration drawn from the great honour in which warriors were held. The sportsmen we know of began at an early age – Olav Tryggvason began as a nine-year-old and by the age of ten was often competing with adults. Viking running-tracks were called *skeið* and were on a field or a plain. The name was also used for the competition itself, whether it involved horse-fighting, horse-racing or men running.

Childhood ended at the age of twelve and a boy's next test was a Viking expedition. Around the year 1000 the age of majority was raised to sixteen in Iceland and fifteen in the rest of Scandinavia, and the same ages were valid for sporting activities. It was shameful to try to avoid sports: 'All young men go to the games but you are the sort of wretch who just lies by the hearth so that your mother trips over your feet.'[6]

As early as the tenth century some older people were pouring scorn on the lethargy of youth: 'Young people today behave differently from when I was young. In those days we were eager to perform great feats, nowadays young people are just stay-at-homes who want to sit there chilling their bellies with mead and ale'.[7]

The period from roughly 800 to 1100 in Scandinavia is usually called the Viking Age. The attack on Lindisfarne in England in AD 793 is the first Viking raid that can be dated securely. Long-distance expeditions led to permanent settlement abroad, but the Vikings also went on seasonal raids to England, Ireland, France, Turkey, the rivers deep in Russia and the Black Sea.

When the Norwegian king Sigurd Jorsalfare arrived in Miklagard (Istanbul), the emperor asked whether he would rather receive six ship-pounds (2,400 lbs or around 1 ton) of gold or whether he would like the emperor to arrange games as he usually did. Sigurd chose the games and had his men take part in the sports.[8]

Even during a voyage it was essential to keep muscles in condition and not lose pace – all skills must be kept intact. It might have looked idyllic when a shouting and laughing band of warriors was absorbed in playing games on land or in the water but there was also a very serious side to it:

> We see a Viking fleet lying in the harbour. They have pitched camp
> on the shore and now they are holding games on the greensward
> – for the moment they are free of serious activity. This is the

scene of the first meeting between Hjalmar and Orvar-Odd. Erik Målspage's band is waiting on the shore while he and his brother are away bidding farewell to their father. Some are practising jumping, some running, some are hurling huge stones and others shooting arrows from their bows.[9]

The Scandinavians lived according to a world-view governed by the Norse gods. The most important duty of a free man was to fight bravely and achieve a place of honour in Valhalla, the realm of the dead. The highest form of death was to fall in battle, otherwise one would not be remembered either by gods or by men. The gods of war were the mentors in a society such as this, where people exacted blood-vengeance.

Every third year the Vikings would come together at a market on Brännö in the island group off Gothenburg in Sweden. Huge crowds came there and drank and took part in the entertainments: wrestling, swimming, weight-lifting, ball-games, archery and running.[10]

The Swede Bertil Wahlqvist, who has studied 106 sagas, scaldic poetry and prose texts, has found references to sporting activities in about half of these. Out of over 300 references swimming came top with 41, followed by wrestling (30), weight-lifting (29) and sword fighting (19). Running was mentioned thirteen times.[11]

Sport was also the popular entertainment after meetings, feasts, Yule-visits and weddings, and even thralls and kings might meet in competition on these occasions. The courts of kings and chieftains were the main centres for sports as they were the places of residence for active and competitive men, for the warrior band of the chieftain and for local fighters. Games held outside the hall or house functioned as military exercise for the warrior band in peacetime and saga literature frequently depicts such scenes, with the chieftain himself as either a spectator or a participant. Great men put up a brave fight against 'Elle', as the Vikings called old age, and even 60 year olds took part in the games. Old men had a particular need for massage and warm baths before the games and there were specially trained people to help motivate them.

In his *Younger Edda* Snorri writes of the length of a running course. When Thor travelled to meet Utgard-Loki he was accompanied by Tjalvi, 'the most fleet-footed of men', but Tjalvi was easily beaten by the boy Hugi in three races across a flat field.[12] According to Snorri's account Hugi beat Tjalvi by an arrow shot and half the course. An arrow shot was equivalent to 240 fathoms and a fathom was about 5ft 6in (168 cm), so the course would have been approximately 440 yards (400 m). The Vikings ran back and forth between two marks and Tjalvi and Hugi probably ran one and a quarter miles (2 km).

Hugi was a phantasmagorical figure, a thought-product of Utgard-Loki's arts of illusion in the form of a boy. Even though Tjalvi was the fastest runner known he was outclassed by Hugi, whose name means 'thought'.

Running had a lower status than many other activities because fleeing from an enemy was considered cowardly. Riding ability rated much more highly and prominent men preferred the horse as a means of land transport. Members of the royal vanguard, who rode at the front of the army, had a boy running alongside holding on to a strap. There are accounts of men running up steep slopes: this skill was particularly useful at sieges, for instance, when it was necessary to attack a fortified town with protective ramparts. The most skilled men could run almost vertically.

One particular trick was to run back and forth along the oars as the ship was being rowed along. Olav Tryggvason could do this, simultaneously juggling with three objects into the bargain. Harald Gille, too, had good balance and ran forward along the oars while the boat was at full tilt, jumped across to the other side and ran back to his starting point.[13]

A number of authors outside Scandinavia, Italian geographers among them, referred to fleet-footed Scandinavians: 'Denmark produces the fastest men of all nations'. Thietmar of Mereburg states that the inhabitants of Kitawa (Kiev) consist mainly of 'fleet-footed Danes'.[14] Harald Harefoot got his nickname because of his good running skills. In Irish sources Vikings are referred to as fast runners and the Irish cut all the hair off the back of their heads so that Scandinavian hands had nothing to catch hold of when the Irish fled.

Nevertheless, as the story of Harald Gille suggests, the Scandinavians did not consider themselves particularly fast: the Vikings thought that the fastest men were to be found in Ireland and Scotland. In the *Saga of Eirik the Red* there is a description of Hake and the woman Hekja. They were two Scottish thralls who could run faster than deer. Olav Tryggvason gave them to Leif Eiriksson and he took the Scots with him to Vinland (America). The two Scots were sent to reconnoitre the land to the south and returned after 36 hours. They wore special running clothes that left their arms, legs and feet bare and on their return they brought grapes, wild wheat and a description of the terrain. So this Scottish couple were perhaps the first Europeans to run in America.[15]

The Vikings did not only run on tracks and over short distances; there are also accounts of some legendary long runs. Grettir Asmundsson (997–1031), 'Grettir the Strong', was one of the great athletes of his age and is commemorated in his own dramatic saga. He ran and swam fast but was particularly outstanding in feats of strength. He became a renowned athlete but did not handle life outside sport well. He was a complex character, both quick-tempered and friendly, naive and crafty. Grettir was an outlaw and lived on Drangøy, a small island off the north coast of Iceland, surrounded by vertical cliffs and with just one route up to the plateau 500 feet (150 m) above sea-level.

On one occasion Grettir met Gisli and they began to fight with swords but it was not long before Gisli threw away his sword and fled down the mountain:

Grettir gave him time to throw away anything he wanted to and every time Gisli had a chance he threw off more clothing. Grettir ran just fast enough to leave a space between them. Gisli ran over the whole mountain and was now left with nothing but his linen undershirt on, and he was beginning to feel terribly tired.

Grettir ran behind him, always close enough to catch hold of him. Gisli did not stop until he had come right to the edge of the water but the ice had opened up and it was difficult to get over it. Gisli was nevertheless going to leap straight into the water but then Grettir grabbed him and now one could see how much stronger Grettir was.[16]

After they had run eight miles Grettir gave Gisli a thrashing with a bundle of brushwood.

As sportsmen the Vikings surpassed many of the European peoples of their day. The chronicles of those they attacked curse them in harsh terms but also express amazement at their courage, strength and sporting prowess. The Scandinavians were better trained from childhood on and they were often well-built. Without pushing comparisons too far we could argue that they were the Greeks of their time in terms of athleticism.

Up and Down Mountains in the Highlands

Scotland is rich in ancient running traditions. The clan chieftains in the Scottish Highlands organized competitions in running, throwing and lifting in order to find good bodyguards and fast messengers. King Malcolm Canmore arranged one such selection process and he also promised a purse of gold and a fine sword to the first man to reach the top of the mountain Craig Coinnich and come back:

All the participants set off and the two MacGregor brothers – the favourites – were in the lead. At the last moment the third Mac-Gregor brother joined the group and the youngest overtook his older brothers at the top and asked 'Shall we share the prize?' 'Each man for himself,' came the answer. As they raced down he lay in second place and then he passed his eldest brother. As he passed him his eldest brother grabbed him by the kilt but the younger brother stripped off his kilt and managed to win – kiltless.[17]

Thus ended the first recorded hill-race in Scotland.

Ever since the thirteenth century the Scots have come together for Highland Games to compete in caber-tossing, hammer-throwing, running and other sports. There are few other countries in which the tradition of gatherings of this kind has survived into the modern period. After the Battle of Bannockburn in 1314 when the Scots defeated the English in the Wars of Liberation, the Scottish victor got the population of Ceres in Fife to organize games to commemorate the victory. The sixteenth-century English chronicler Raphael Holinshed refers to the Scottish clans and their training: 'They kept themselves fit and fast on their feet either by hunting or by running from the ridges down into the valleys, or from the valleys up onto the ridges.'[18]

Italian Running Festivals

In Verona in Italy the inhabitants used to gather for an annual race – the *Corsa del Palio*, 'the run of the green cloth' – in which the runners ran naked and the winner was presented with a green cloth. The man who came last also received a trophy, a humiliating rooster that anyone could take from him as he made his compulsory circuit of the town to receive the scorn of the citizens. The race began around AD 1207 to celebrate the victory of the city-state of Verona over the Counts of San Bonifazio and the Montecchi family. It is mentioned by Dante (1265–1321) in *The Divine Comedy*, Canto xv, lines 121–4:

> Then he turned back and looked like one of those
> who race for the green cloth in Verona
> across the plain, and he looked like one of those
> who wins, not one who loses.

Dante also describes running in Hell, an eternal ring-dance with nothing but pain and torment and no chance to rest, urged onwards by stinging insects. He describes the devil as a fast runner who beats his wings at full speed.

The Verona race took place on the first Sunday in Lent and was a celebration for the whole city, one of the citizens' annual festivals and not a sporting event in the modern sense. We know what the course of the race was and that it was subject to change by the city administrator. It first started from the Tombo quarter, and then later from the neighbouring Santa Lucia, and it wound its way along the southern walls of the city past the Porta al Palio and across flat ground. Then it cut back diagonally, went inside the walls, into the main street and so to the palace of San Fermo.

In 1393 a second race was added and the first prize was changed to a red cloth, the same as for the winner of the horse-race held the same day. Women now ran for a green cloth, and they had to be 'respectable women' – but if no respectable women wanted to take part prostitutes were allowed to run. Immediately after 1450 the date was changed to the last Thursday before Shrovetide, which is usually in February.

There are no reports of the Verona races, no detailed descriptions of the preparations and celebrations afterwards, but we know that the prize-giving was an important event and that the public congratulated the winners and shouted at the losers during the joint lap of honour. The tradition survived until the nineteenth century, with the runners training beforehand in order to avoid that shameful last place. Great efforts were made in the narrow streets and the event was packed with cheering spectators, anxious about who would win. As time passed the race became more and more of a sporting event.[19]

During the thirteenth, fourteenth and fifteenth centuries, cities over the whole of Italy established annual races for men, women, children, horses and asses. The most special of the women's races was the one held in Ferrara in northern Italy where the fastest received a red cloth but even those farther back in the field received prizes. In these Italian cities, surrounded by walls and ramparts, where noble families barricaded themselves in towers during times of war, there was a culture of running ultimately traceable back to the *ludi* of the Romans.

During the Middle Ages Italy was also an important European guardian of classical Greek learning. Having read ancient Greek texts, Professor Pietro-Paulo Vergera (1348–1419) in Padua argued that people needed games and training and that they ought to respect their bodies. Such statements sounded radical to many people but among the philosophers at the courts of the Italian city-states the concept of *l'uomo universale* – the whole, rounded man – became an important motto at a time when the ideas of humanism were finding the soil fertile. And during the same period the princely houses were attacking one another and needed soldiers in good physical condition.

During the fourteenth and fifteenth centuries many Greek intellectuals fled the Byzantine Empire and took refuge in Italy. They brought with them a renewed interest in the culture and history of classical antiquity. In 1430 the politican and author Mateo Palmieri wrote his *Book Concerning Civil Life*, the third volume of which takes Olympia as its topic.[20]

The Italian humanist Virgilius Polydorus described the four great athletic games of ancient Greece in his 1491 encyclopaedia *Concerning the Origin of Things*. The work went through twenty editions in Latin and there were almost as many translations, the first of them into German in 1537. Book publishing in Italy, particularly in Venice, led to a growing interest in Greek history all over Europe. Affluent readers in Italy, France, Germany, Holland and England began to recognize the athletic traditions of the Greeks.

In 1530 Cardinal Sadoleto published his *De Libris Recte Instituendis*, in which he recommended running rather than military-based exercise. The centuries before the publication of the book had seen the flowering of the Age of Chivalry in Europe but in a quotation referring to the Italian province of Lombardy the author speculates whether the great men of the future might find merit in games in the open air: 'One sees young gentlemen spending their time wrestling, running and jumping with village people. I do not believe it will do them any harm.'[21]

Women's races were a typical feature of the Italy of this period.[22] At carnivals, such as those held in Florence and other Italian cities, women's races were part of the festivities and races for prostitutes took place in several other

European countries as well, both in and outside carnival time – in 1501 no less a figure than Pope Alexander IV invited people to such a race in Rome.

When Castruccio Castracani from the city-state of Lucca wanted to humiliate the inhabitants of Florence, which he was besieging at the time, he organized a whores' race, along with other sporting events, outside the city walls. After his death the Florentines took their revenge by sending their own prostitutes to compete in front of the walls of Lucca as a symbolic insult to its honour.

Prostitutes were mocked as they ran. When a competition was for money rather than clothes it was considered acceptable for the spectators to trip the women, causing them to fall down for the amusement of the onlookers. The women, however, showed their business acumen and, bearing potential future customers in mind, sometimes ran completely naked. After the races the prostitutes distributed prizes – clothes and fabrics in colours that symbolized the city's prostitutes, who were recognizable by the special, brightly coloured clothes they wore.

Prostitutes lived in particular streets and made up their faces in a different way. This guild-like community, for which the women had to pass entrance tests, ate communally and shared the daily expenses, creating a sense of solidarity and professional pride. The prostitutes' races continued for decade after decade and satisfied people's desire to see something brazen and out of the ordinary. The prostitutes may have enjoyed more freedom than most women, but they were also stigmatized.

Even ordinary women took part in races, sometimes with troughs of water on their heads or buckets in their hands, and the aim was not to spill them. One false step was enough to get soaked and be the butt of much laughter. Sometimes women in races encouraged each other to fight, like the shepherd girls in Würtemberg in Germany. The alderman of the town rode behind them to keep control and prevent cheating, scratching, hair-pulling and hitting, but even then quarrels broke out and resulted in bumping, tripping and wrestling in the grass. Men liked watching this crowd of angry, bare-legged shepherd girls: they were fascinated by girls and women fighting, perhaps because they were putting all inhibitions aside and behaving in an unseemly fashion.

Naked for the Sake of God

The Adamite sect arose in Bohemia in 1419 as a movement critical of the corruption of the Roman Catholic church. The Adamites protested against the disintegrating morality of the church by running naked through the streets, thereby causing a sensation in a society in which nakedness and the body were perceived as sinful. A naked group running at full tilt through narrow streets and crowded squares was like a demonic invasion and it caused shock and anger. It broke all the accepted norms of people who went quietly around in shifts and capes and hoods, and it was made all the more shocking by the ritual nakedness of the Adamites during their religious services.

The fifteenth-century Adamites were merely a new variant of an old sect that had sprung up in the second, third and fourth centuries in parts of North Africa and Egypt and which had practised holy nudism during community worship. The sect had adherents in the Netherlands in the fourteenth century and also in Bohemia and Germany a century later. Many of its members settled on an island in the river Nezarka in Bohemia before being expelled in 1421.

The Adamites called themselves 'the holy ones of the last days' and like other doomsday sects they believed that God spoke directly to them and to no one else, giving them one last warning about the moral disintegration of humanity. They admonished the whole of society – a society that was structured around the church and in which government by priests was often the rule.

They were protesting against many things, including marriage. They believed in relationships of free love, love by attraction and spontaneous joy rather than arranged marriages with erotic relationships on the side. They quoted Jesus's views on publicans and sinners and took the line that even the virtuous and respectable people of the fifteenth century would have difficulty getting into the Kingdom of God. By running naked they were trying to pass on to the common people their message about a state of innocence and purity. They achieved notoriety and were described as madmen. According to one medieval chronicle the Adamites were burned as witches.[23]

Laughter and Popular Entertainment

The German historian and cultural sociologist Henning Eichberg has pointed out that popular sport, including running, in sixteenth- and seventeenth-century Europe belonged to a 'culture of laughter': it offered a laughter-arousing spectacle that brought people together.[24] It took place in everyday surroundings, in the streets and in areas normally given over to other activities, not in specially demarcated sporting arenas. Situation comedy and laughter were important ingredients. If the race involved obstacles, if it was a hunt that depended on catching or being caught, or was a sack-race with betting, it was popular and created amusing situations. Popular sport had more strategies than its modern descendants.[25]

The fool was central to popular sport and popular games in the Middle Ages. He wandered around playing pranks, poking people with his wooden sword if they broke with normal customs, and spread laughter around him. He rewarded the silliest aspects of sporting competition and the audience laughed.

Jugglers and acrobats were part of the scene when runners, jumpers, throwers and stone-lifters met in combat. These experts in comedy created a jolly atmosphere and the laughter and mockery was also directed at outsiders or the nobility or the upper classes, whose arrogance provoked the common people. Running belonged to a carnival tradition in which the usual norms were not operative and forbidden things could go unpunished.

The nobility and churchmen of Central Europe took part in these amusements up until the sixteenth century and, since the common people could laugh and boo at them, they provided a release as well as entertainment. Priests and noblemen felt thoroughly uncomfortable when they found themselves surrounded by hundreds or thousands of drunken, excited spectators. They rarely had the chance to win running or lifting competitions and, because they were made fools of during the few hours the common people were in control, noblemen and churchmen stopped attending games of that sort. From the sixteenth century many local authorities in Central Europe banned such amusements, fearful that they would lead to a breakdown of authority and undermine the morality of the inhabitants. This 'culture of laughter and strength' was repressed in many places during the eighteenth and nineteenth centuries – not, however, in Britain.

8
Wagers, Clocks and Brooms

The roads were blocked and people fought until their knuckles
bled and teeth snapped. There was so much drinking and so many
injured that the sheriff had to arrest the woman and put her in gaol
to restore order.
—On the occasion of the attempt by a 70-year-old woman from Scotland
to walk and run 96 miles in 24 hours in 1830

He was called 'The Flying Butcher from Leeds' and he earned more money
from running than from chopping meat. Butcher Preston was one of the
best long-distance runners in England in the 1680s, a cunning tactician
capable of fooling and bluffing almost anyone when the need arose. In
1688 Preston was matched against the king's favourite at court in a contest
watched by 6,000 spectators. Few people gave the butcher a chance because they knew the quality of the king's lackey – he had been selected from
keen candidates and his only occupation was to run around obeying his
master's orders. An anonymous butcher had little to offer – or so the spectators thought, turning their pockets inside out for betting money. And
some of them put excessive amounts of money on the king's man.

As it turned out Preston reached the finish a couple of steps in front and
a goodly number of people trudged home that day having wagered away
horse and carriage, richer in experience but poorer in pocket. It was not the
first time the words bankrupt and broke were mentioned after a betting
race, but Preston and his assistants could count their winnings and plan
their next coup elsewhere in the country.

But rumours travelled faster than the butcher ran. Wherever he tried
to set up a new competition the answer was no, because no one was prepared
to risk their money against a talent of that kind. Preston moved to London
in order to disappear into the crowd and he adopted a new identity as a
miller. In the service of a nobleman, with a new name and an ever-changing
appearance, new clothes and a beard – and in the clothes of a different trade
– Preston bluffed his way through wager races without being uncovered. For
Preston was active at a time when, as a result of better measurement and
better clocks, betting on races was on the increase in England.[1]

Queen Elizabeth had standardized the English mile to its present length
of 5,280 feet (1,609 metres) in 1588. The mile, however, had originated in the
Roman Empire when the Romans measured distances in double paces. A
thousand double paces for a Roman soldier (*mille passus*) came to roughly
1,479 metres. They set up milestones (*millarium*) along Roman roads at
every thousand paces to mark the distance from Rome. When the Roman

Empire fell, the milestones remained and new rulers applied different length systems to them.

During the seventeenth century an Englishman, Edmund Gunter, made an iron measuring chain 66 feet long (20 metres) which was used in the setting up of milestones along the toll-roads.[2] This preceded an epoch-making advance in the technology of clocks.

The need for clocks had arisen in monasteries in order to announce the hours of prayer – the word clock derives from the Latin *clocca*, meaning 'church bell'. Monasteries used them to proclaim the times of the day reserved for regular rituals, rather than measuring time for its own sake, but in the course of the fourteenth century more and more churches and town-halls also got bells to ring out every passing hour. The residents could now 'hear' the time and gradually a new consciousness of time developed. Mechanical clocks came into use from about 1330 and there was a new and significant advance when the German Peter Henlein invented the spring-driven clock just after 1500.

Between 1556 and 1580 the Turk Taqi-al-Din, who was an amazing all-round scientist, invented the first clocks capable of measuring the time in minutes and seconds. He used them as astronomical clocks to determine, for instance, the positions of the stars.

The pendulum spring was invented in 1670 and soon the best clocks were accurate to within ten seconds a day. Seconds could be measured from 1721 and the stopwatch came ten years later.[3] Timekeeping in horse-racing increased the certainty of accurate times, and accurate measurement became possible for anyone who owned or could borrow a clock, in cooperation with a clockmaker to supervise the timekeeping.

The English were probably the first to record exact times for running. Horse-riding with betting against the clock had begun as early as 1606 and we know of some instances of pedestrian runners being timed after 1661. Along with betting came the idea of 'matches against time' and it became more common to keep records of times over specific distances.

Betting on sport was hardly new in Britain but henceforth the British began to bet on sports which were *only* practised for the sake of the betting, which were organized by betting men and bookmakers, who would pay a share of the profits to the sportsman. The 'match against time' also coincided with and to some extent symbolized the arrival of the Industrial Age, in which Britain led the way.

It was in Britain, then, that the recording of times originated and horse-racing records were kept as early as the eighteenth century, largely in order to inform the breeding of new winners. Although running times for both men and women were measured in Britain in the eighteenth century, no record lists were published in book form until the following century.

The British would bet on almost anything, including such things as races between disabled people or between old people and children. They bet on times, lap times, the order the participants would be in at a given point – anything at all relating to the runners and the times. There were races on stilts and races on crutches, men with a wooden leg against others with the same handicap, fat men competing with a thin man carrying someone on his back and so on. In 1763 a fishmonger tried to run from Hyde Park to the seventh milestone in Brentford with a 56 lb (25 kg) load on his head. It took him 45 minutes and he won his bet, which was to do it in less than an hour. To make results less predictable races could be run with the best man wearing heavy boots and the slowest in light shoes or barefoot. Betting was not solely a British phenomenon, it also occurred in other countries, often for payment in kind such as beer and spirits.[4]

A French priest called Le Blanc lived in England from 1737 to 1747. A young nobleman of his acquaintance was doing everything possible to become the champion runner of England in keen competition with men from the lower orders who needed to run to earn a living. Driven by a desire for fame not money – the family had plenty of the latter – the young aristocrat lived a frugal life and pushed his body to the limit. It seemed unlikely that he would ever reach the level of the highly motivated workmen and farmhands but after training tenaciously he beat all the professional 'footmen' – and their standard of performance was high in the middle of the eighteenth century. The young nobleman made a lot of money from wagers, particularly by betting on himself. The French priest simply could not understand why he was willing to forsake all the pleasures in life, live on a diet, drink witch's brew, torment himself until the sweat poured off him, and take massages and sweat baths. Le Blanc was certain that diets and exertions of that sort were harmful, at least in the long term. He believed that the desire for sporting fame could only arise in a sick mind and he warned against it.[5]

Most sports historians are agreed that timekeeping is one of the criteria of modern sport as distinct from folk sport. Allen Guttmann in the USA, however, emphasizes that it is impossible to draw a line and say that this is where the modern begins – historical processes are too complicated and difficult to trace for that to be possible. He argues that modern sport is characterized by being secular, that is, having no religious component, and being open to all: 'Modern sport is also specialized, rationalized, bureaucratically organized and obviously characterized by a sort of mania for quantification and the records that make quantification possible.'[6]

Dover's Olimpicks

Among the oddest sporting events of the seventeenth century were 'Mr Robert Dovers Olimpick Games', held in the Cotswold Hills in England between 1604 and 1612 on the initiative of the said Robert Dover. King James I gave permission for the games and they were held on the Thursday and Friday of Whit Week.

Robert Dover was born in Norfolk in 1582, son of John Dover, Gentleman, and he studied at Cambridge, tried the priesthood, read law and tried his hand at many things before this became his career. In 1611, as a married man with children, he moved to Saintbury in the Cotswolds.[7]

There he became involved in the games that carry his name, although we do not know whether he invented them or revived them. The best contemporary source about the games – the 1636 book *Annalia Dubrensia*, which is in verse form – praises Dover's work, and the 33 contributions the book contains in support of Dover's initiative are something of a political statement.[8]

The contributors were well-known poets and they viewed the games as a revitalization of English folk life, a harmless and positive occasion that was in no sense as morally deleterious as the Puritans asserted. The book also brought the games to the attention of the nation, since the local aristocracy attended and the king supported the event.

The games were a protest against the Puritans' strict views on sports and amusements. The Puritans recognized the importance of recreation and did not condemn all sports, but they were against those that led to betting and drinking, considering these to be all too reminiscent of pagan festivals. They also objected to the killing of animals for entertainment – cock-fighting, for instance – and to breaches of the Sabbath. The Puritans believed that even minor activities on the day of rest would lead to eternal perdition and that the sinners would burn in Hell for eternity. The fear of sin and Hell pervaded life and there were some Puritan landowners who barred their servants and farm-workers from participating in sport on Sundays.

Thousands of people of all social classes travelled up to 60 miles on foot and by carriage to attend the Cotswold games. From a grassy natural amphitheatre they could watch Robert Dover, on horseback and ceremonially dressed in a cloak and plumed hat from the royal wardrobe, lead in the parade. The horses and men were all decorated with yellow ribbons and they all paid homage to Dover as King of the Games. He was respected and admired, noble and jovial, and had friends in all social classes.

Tents had been erected for the nobility while ordinary people sat on the ground and ate and drank as they watched. The sounds of a hunting horn and a cannon opened the proceedings. Horse-racing, hunting, wrestling, fencing, dancing, hammer-throwing and running were just some of the activities, with hundreds of participants competing for silver trophies and honour. It was unique and spectacular, an event to attend year after year, a memory for life.

Robert Dover upset the Puritans in many ways. The big resplendent feather in his hat announced that he was not a Puritan: they did not wear feathers in their hats and some of them even objected to elegant hats. Dovers Olimpicks had the good sense to avoid the Sabbath but the Puritans disliked it being held in Whit Week, and they were concerned that the festivities would get out of control and lead to drinking and fighting.

While making a royal tour in 1617, King James I heard that Puritans were preventing the people of Lancashire from playing legal games and sports after church on Sunday evenings. He issued *The Book of Sports*, which proclaimed the people's right to amuse themselves – even on Sundays – and stated that recreation was good for them. This proclamation was to be read out in all the parish churches in England and anyone refusing to do so would be prosecuted.

Dover himself never did state any particular reason for starting his games but it seems likely it was simply for pleasure. In *Annalia Dubrensia* Dover and his friends refer to the Olympic Games in Hellas and compare the Cotswold games with them. It is unlikely, however, that the idea originated in a desire to recreate the Greek games: they preferred an event in the English spirit and suitable for the conditions of the age.

Dovers Olimpicks was held annually, as were various other events. There were, however, no oiled naked bodies on show in the arena and the English competitors wore heavy clothing. Everything passed off in the English manner, in line with the climate and the moral prohibitions of the country. The soul was more important than the body and salvation and the certainty of eternal life counted for more than self-assertion. There were certainly books around that recommended the nurture of the body but such ideas had not yet achieved any wide circulation.

Dover had a feel for spectacle and entertainment. Dover's Castle, a small, mobile imitation of three of the royal residences, attracted many curious visitors. The castle was big enough for people to go inside and strong enough to carry small cannon with real ammunition. The cannon were sufficiently powerful for Dover to need royal permission to fire them from his castle during the games – one of the high points for the spectators.

Robert Dover died in 1652, the same year that the last of his games for some years was held. But when the Stuarts were restored to the throne in 1660 after the Commonwealth interlude, the Olimpick Games were revived by Dover's family and they continued until 1852. Later they were revived yet again and are still in existence, some four hundred years after they began.

It is quite possible that William Shakespeare may have been one of the seventeenth-century spectators since popular productions of that kind interested him. He knew about running and referred to it in several plays. In the first scene of *Henry IV Part 2*, the rebel Morton comes to the Earl of Northumberland at Warkworth Castle and informs him that the rebels have lost the Battle of Shrewsbury:

'Say, Morton, didst thou come from Shrewsbury?'
'I ran from Shrewsbury, my noble lord.'

The distance is 350 kilometres and feasible for a fit soldier. Morton had been on the losing side and ran to announce the defeat.

'But I would give a thousand pound I could run as fast as thou canst', says Falstaff to Poins in *Henry IV Part 1*. In *Henry VI Part 3*, the Earl of Warwick is resting after a battle: 'Forspent with toil, as runners with a race, I lay me down a little while to breathe'.[9]

Women Runners

Shakespeare was also familiar with what were called the 'smock races' for women, which were common in England and Scotland for two hundred years or so from the seventeenth century on. They were usually over short distances. The name comes from the prize, which was often a smock, although petticoats, skirts, hats, skirting material, aprons, legs of mutton, sugar, tea and money are all listed as prizes by Peter Radford, the authority on smock races and himself a world-class sprinter in the 1960s.[10]

The women, usually between two and six of them, ran on saints' days, church festivals, local feast days, at horse races, market days, weddings, cricket matches and other occasions. And there were different classes for under-15s, under-20s and 25s, or over-35s and so on.

Smock races occurred at fixed places and fixed times year after year. Prizes were announced and displayed on a pole or a tree during the days before the competition. Money prizes were donated by affluent local people and collected by a committee, whose job it was also to ensure that the women decorated their brooms. The season lasted from April to October and peaked in May and June.

Peter Radford has uncovered most smock races in the county of Kent – there were at least 20 races there annually during the eighteenth century. The earliest and most important of them began in 1639 when the rich judge and multi-talented civil servant Sir Dudley Digges died and left £20 annually (£2,300 in 2008 terms) to the young man and the young woman who won a race, which became known as 'The Running Lands race', on 19 May. It was held at Old Wives Lees, which is also where the qualifying run for the main race was held on 1 May. Another qualifying run was held in Sheldwich about five miles away. To enter the main race, participants had to win the qualifying round.

The Running Lands Race continued well into the nineteenth century. Girls and women set their sights on the competition just as their mothers and grandmothers had done, for fun, for prestige and for the prize. Even though the prize varied during the eighteenth century and the winner did not always receive £10, it was still a considerable sum of money. A young servant girl would earn £2 a year plus her food, clothes and lodgings, so a victory would increase her income fivefold. We do not know the distance run at Old Wives Lees, but on Midsummer's Day a month later races were also arranged there and they were 220 yards (200 m) for women and 440 (400 m) for men.

The competitions in Kent were organized on a pattern that had Old Wives Lees at its centre. Some two miles away in Brabourne Lees earlier winners were not allowed to participate, nor was anyone who had won at Old Wives Lees. The exclusion was to give others a chance and this rule also applied at other places in Kent. The winner of the biggest race in the county had to accept that there would be fewer future opportunities to compete and might perhaps give up racing. But it seems that earlier winners wanted to race again and were happy to walk for four or five hours to run in villages where the exclusion rules did not apply. According to Peter Radford this is the oldest known network of races for women in the world.[11]

Ordinary smock races were most commonly part of a larger programme of entertainment in which men might climb slippery poles or young men wrestle while the spectators laughed at them – as they did at the women running.

Visitors from other parts of Europe remarked on such races. Women might even be weighed, like jockeys, for betting purposes, even if weight counted for little. An episode in the 1778 novel *Evelina* shows the grotesque forms this could take: two very elderly women are depicted as racing against each other to the great amusement of the upper-class organizer. The women are puffing and struggling and they trip over each other and fall, but the people in charge of the betting demand a restart since there is £100 at stake. It was acceptable to exploit the elderly poor for entertainment and the women made fools of themselves because they needed the money.[12]

English women's clothing in the eighteenth and nineteenth centuries was hardly conducive to running. The long skirts and underskirts prevented a woman from taking full-length strides, flapping against her legs and those of other competitors. Sometimes scantily clad women would be advertised to pull in the crowds, such as at a cricket match on Walworth Common in 1744 when, as an extra attraction, two of the city's streetwalkers turned out in their underwear. The organizer prepared for a huge influx of people because of this – it was titillating, just as exotic runners were.

In 1740 William Somerville described Fusca, a gypsy woman in Gloucestershire, who 'view[ed] the grand prize with greedy eyes', and whose filthy legs disgusted the spectators. She slipped and fell down, to the amusement of the onlookers, but got up and strode off.

Fusca would have been little concerned by the laughter and shame since gypsies were outside any social norms and used this fact to their advantage. They were quite prepared to do jobs that ordinary people considered beneath them and it was generally believed that gypsies were unclean. They were thought of as primitive, outside the community of the church and carriers of a contagious immorality. Running was not an unclean occupation but gypsies walked a lot and were often fleet-footed – and it was easy to combine smock races with a rootless way of life.

Dogs could cause chaos in these competitions and there are illustrations from the eighteenth century showing women being tripped up by them. A notice in Sandwich in 1739 states that 'any dog that comes near will be shot'. Eleven years later we read 'Leave your dogs at home, or they will be shot'.[13]

British women also ran long distances for bets from early in the eighteenth century and even more frequently in the century that followed. There were even families who travelled around with running as their occupation. Emma Mathilda Freeman was eight years old in 1823 but did not live like most children of her age: her father and mother arranged wagers on their daughter and in that year she completed one run of over 30 miles and another of over 40 miles. The little girl was impressive – a cute little sensation who did her best for her parents and showed what stamina a small girl was capable of.

Female runners and competitive pedestrians in early nineteenth-century Britain ranged from the very young up to those in their seventies. Married or unmarried, spinsters or widows, they all came from the lower social classes. At the bottom of the scale were itinerant individuals and families who collected money and payment in kind from the spectators and arranged bets on the spot.

'Do you want to bet on what this woman can do over long distances?', the man shouted, pointing to his mother, Mary Motulullen, a woman of over 60 from Ireland. Her hollow wrinkled face and slight build were guaranteed to encourage men to bet against her and, like a circus owner with an exotic animal on show, her son would point to his mother and egg his listeners on with a brazen commentary.

'Easy money!' thought the men in England, looking at her bare feet and tattered clothes, seeing the ravages of age and a creature submerged in poverty. Mother and son, apparently indigent and foreign, would stand on the square or outside the drinking dens of England, ready to take on any challenges over distances from 20 to 92 miles.

Mary Motutullen travelled round with her two sons in the 1820s. People who met them in October 1826 and heard them talk of 90 miles (144 km) inside 24 hours doubted if it was possible. Mary set off, barefoot as usual, but encountered difficulties other and worse than the distance. Those who had bet against her tried to get her to give up, offering her bribes so they could win their bets. It simply made her more determined and she made the deadline. On another occasion, when doing 92 miles (148 km) in 24 hours in Lincolnshire, she arrived eight minutes late because a gang of young louts had blocked the road, spat at her and delayed her.

The throngs of people, the drunkenness, the uproar, narrow roads in enclosed villages could all make Mary's job a walk to Canossa. On other days her surroundings could smile on her as, for instance, when 6,000 people watched her cross the line wearing a fine new hat with bows on it – donated by a well-wisher – to the sound of fiddles and tambourines. She had a special charisma, was an eccentric and a folk hero at the same time, and she proved that old age was no hindrance to long and strenuous pedestrian performances when the driving force was to escape deep poverty.[14]

In 1833 a 70-year-old Scotswoman caused an uproar when she attempted to do 96 miles (154 km) in 24 hours on the road between Paisley and Renfrew. The roads were blocked and people fought until their knuckles bled and teeth snapped. There was so much drinking and so many injured that the sheriff had to arrest the woman and put her in gaol to restore order.

At the beginning of the nineteenth century the support for fairs and markets in British villages began to diminish. Old customs changed as people moved into the towns and British society was transformed by industrialization. But even though smock races disappeared in many places the interest in women's wager races increased and peaked in the 1820s. With the Victorian age two decades later, however, a new view of women prevailed. Women came to be regarded as weak creatures, unsuited to strenuous physical exertion, and after the 1840s running or pedestrianism by women came to an end or, at least, the newspapers ceased writing about it.

Fact or Fabrication?

Who was the first to run a mile in under four minutes? It is common knowledge among those interested in running that the Englishman Roger Bannister broke the mythic barrier with his 3 minutes 59.4 seconds at Oxford on 6 May 1954.

Professor Peter Radford tells a different version. He has studied British running before 1800 more thoroughly than anyone else and thinks he has evidence that this barrier was broken as early as the eighteenth century. In London on 9 May 1770 the street-seller James Parrott set off from Charterhouse Wall in Goswell Road, crossed the road, turned right and continued along Old Street at a terrific pace, urged on by onlookers and watchmen, for a wager of fifteen guineas to five that he would do the mile inside four minutes.[15]

And, indeed, according to the timekeepers he did it. The condition and the runner's form were so good that he achieved his goal and won a healthy sum of money.

We might ask why James Parrott is so little known in the history of running. In the first place, the man and his feat have only recently been rediscovered by Radford. Secondly, modern statisticians, understandably enough, refuse to believe his time. They are of the view that no runner as far back as 1770 could have achieved such a high standard. Furthermore, neither time nor distance was ratified in accordance with modern criteria, even though it was all reported as fact in a newspaper that same week. To the ears of the sceptics this sounds like an untruth from the age of unorganized sport. They think the same about a man called Powell who ran a mile in four minutes in 1787 for a wager of 1,000 guineas (about £780,000 in 2008 values).

In 1796 a third man, by the name of Weller, excited the punters when he offered to run the mile in four minutes. He had plenty of experience of racing commercially in and around Oxford and he challenged any three men from anywhere in England to a contest. According to the papers he sprinted home in 3 minutes 58 seconds and thus provides the first accurately reported mile in four minutes noted by the press. The date was 10 October 1796.

Eighteenth-century newspapers also reported on distances of between 20 and 30 miles (32–48 km) and Peter Radford has recalculated them to the modern marathon length of 26 miles 385 yards. According to his calculations a Swiss runner did the marathon in under 2 hours 10 minutes in 1769. Another staunch fellow, probably an Italian, finished in 2 hours 11 minutes in 1753. In terms of absolute distances, the newspapers reported James Appleby as taking 57 minutes for 12 miles (19,108 metres) in 1730. In this race Thomas Phillips came in 15 seconds behind him. Both of them later ran four miles (6,436 metres) in 18 minutes – times that are still of a high standard 200 years later.

Modern experts are right to ask questions about distances and time-keeping but not everything was left to chance. In England in 1770 the distances were measured with equipment used in agriculture and were correct to the nearest inch. And unlike countries with regional measures of distance, England had a national standard. The races, moreover, often involved a wager between two parties and everything, including timekeeping, had to be done properly: each side would appoint an arbitrator, and if they could not agree about practical things like time and distance a judge would be appointed.

As Peter Radford rightly points out, however, they did not always measure time and distance exactly in the eighteenth century even if they had the means of doing so. Both sides might agree that a certain discrepancy in the number of yards or seconds were of no relevance to the wager. Radford found, nevertheless, that the performances of particular runners over different distances and at different places matched one another and he concluded that there was little inconsistency either in terms of measurement or timekeeping in the races he studied. In the case of Pinwire, for example, who won 102 races between 1729 and 1732, we have times for two of his runs: 52 minutes 3 seconds for 10 miles (16 km) in 1733 and 64 minutes for 12 miles (19 km) in 1738. These two times correspond very closely: if distance or time or both were wrong for the first race, they must have been wrong by approximately the same amount for the second one in 1738.

Radford found specific individuals with up to twenty consistent results and thinks we should reconsider our attitude to the sportsmen of the eighteenth century. Perhaps they performed at a higher level than previously thought. It is assumed that racehorses 250 years ago ran as fast as those today, so it is possible that sportsmen did the same, particularly since we know that the best of them took running very seriously and they were competing for large sums of money. Wager racing in England threw up great stars.

It is hard to believe, however, that Radford's discoveries give us the whole picture and he would agree with that, saying: 'I'm only reporting what I find.'[16] We know that records have steadily been improved on since the end of the nineteenth century and it seems illogical that the best competitors a hundred years before *that* had attained a much higher standard.

We have been brought up to believe that sporting progress is linear, not that there are periods of stagnation and decline followed by new success.

Before industrialization, however, the population of eighteenth-century Britain frequently enjoyed good physical conditions. Records of the diet in the British navy during that century show that the food was adequate and it seems probable that the average eighteenth-century diet in Britain was good until industrialization really took off.

Many grew up and lived in rural areas. They walked a lot and performed physically heavy work from a young age. In a relatively poor society where it was possible to earn many years' wages in a single race, there was a group of good runners and competitive pedestrians – an elite that invested that bit more and raised the level. Their basic physique was much better than that of their successors who moved to the cities and grew up there in the nineteenth century working in industry. Dreadful living conditions, poor diet and hygiene combined with gruelling work in an unhealthy environment undermined the health of the city-dwellers. The population of the towns had worse preconditions and lower reserves than were necessary for good runners, as well as less open land to run in and fresh air to breathe.

It is impossible to know for sure whether anyone ran a mile in under four minutes during the 1790s, but it is important to point out that even the history of running *may* contain great surprises. History *always* contains surprises if one digs deep enough and in unfamiliar places. New historical knowledge that challenges established views is easy to brush aside as fabrication, even when it is about something as concrete as running. Human beings at all periods have liked to consider themselves better than those who went before and it is difficult for us to imagine that our predecessors, with simpler technology and lower scientific development, performed many things just as well as later generations.

Peter Radford presented his research findings in 2004 in connection with the 50th anniversary celebrations of Roger Bannister's record. Reaction to his findings was divided. Dr Greg Whyte, Director of Science at the English Institute of Sport said:

> Sport at that time was more open than when the Victorians intro-
> duced the amateur ethic, thereby making it more difficult for the
> working class to participate and also making sport something for
> the upper classes.[17]

Nor did Bob Phillips, author of the book *3.59.4* about Roger Bannister's 1954 record, rule out early eighteenth century 'Superman' times. But Mel Watman, one of the leading statisticians in British athletics, had doubts both about timekeeping and distance as far as Parrot's 1770 run was concerned. He thought it was something the papers reported but which did not stand up to scrutiny. Watman's great hero for the mile was Walter George, who set the world record for the distance with his 4 minutes 12.75 seconds in 1886.

Walter George (GB), left, and Lon Myers (USA); the intense middle-distance rivalry between these two during the 1880s was regarded by many observers as one of the highlights of late-nineteenth-century athletics. George's 1886 world record for the mile (4:12.75) was to stand for 37 years.

That record stood for 37 years and Watman thought it unlikely that some-one living a century earlier could have run so much faster.

Without Clothes and Without Shame

Naked runners made an appearance in England in the middle of the seven-teenth century – newspapers referred to them as *in puris naturalibus*. Philip Kinder described a two or three mile race between 'a naked boy' and 'two opponents who were stark naked' in the middle of the winter in Derbyshire.[18]

In 1681 three or four ladies ran naked apart from a cloth that covered their private parts. Although several thousand people were watching we cannot say with certainty how many clothes the ladies were wearing because observers and writers through the ages have differing interpretations of nakedness and scanty clothing.

It seems likely there is a gradation of nakedness in the nineteen cases from the north of England and the London area that Peter Radford has investigated. The boy in 1681 is simply stated to be 'naked' whereas the other two boys are said to be 'stark naked', which can hardly mean other than completely naked.

We are not here dealing with spontaneous acts of self-exposure like, for example, the 'streaking' phenomenon that occurred in the USA, Canada, England, Australia, Italy, France and elsewhere during the 1970s in connection with football and rugby matches. These streakers took advantage of the element of surprise to throw off their clothes and run out on the pitch in large arenas when the occasion was being televized.

In eighteenth-century England naked running was often announced in advance and attracted hundreds or even thousands of spectators. The participants did not try to hide their identity, nor did they seem to be embarrassed: in fact, they actually wanted attention, just as the scantily dressed do in modern days. But unlike now, not all the naked runners were arrested, although there were both warnings and arrests following these events, which tended to take place early in the morning.

Women were often warned against taking their clothes off and, moreover, men and women did not run naked together. In 1725 in London two women planned to appear *in puris naturalibus* but were told to wear white underpants and vests. Ten years later two almost naked women in London were reprimanded and told that in future they must retain their underpants and vests for the sake of decency. Men had rather more freedom and aroused different reactions in the male part of the audience.

Peter Radford believes that English Puritanism, which was particularly powerful in the first half of the seventeenth century, provoked this public nakedness. The undressed runners were perhaps consciously doing something the Puritans disapproved of and thought sinful.

In the case of the seventeenth-century Derbyshire incident Radford thinks that both the boys and the writer Philip Kinder were aware that sportsmen in Ancient Greece raced naked. Kinder's term *Gymnipaida* for two of the boys suggests that he knew Greek history and tradition. By throwing off their clothes the boys were paying homage to an age that was familiar at least to the upper classes. People were fascinated by the classical style in art and in the years between 1720 and 1770 it is estimated that 50,000 paintings and 500,000 etchings and engravings entered England from Italy, France and the Netherlands alone. Those with the means to purchase art and hang it on their walls were surrounded by depictions of the naked body. This influenced the taste of the British upper class in matters of art, literature and architecture and if authors and painters could look to classical times sportsmen could do the same.

The custom of running naked disappeared from England in the nineteenth century. The dress norms of that period meant that naked runners risked arrest, heavy fines or incarceration in an asylum.

9
French Enlightenment and German Health Education

Women were not meant to run; they flee that they may be overtaken.
—Jean-Jacques Rousseau

In 1762 the French philosopher Jean-Jacques Rousseau completed his book *Emile, or On Education*. It was part of a lifetime's work that was to have huge significance for the development of Western culture.

Rousseau understood that childhood was different from adult life, that it was a separate stage and not just a preparation for maturity. As an educator he recommended freedom and wildness – as a philosopher he believed that civilization had destroyed mankind's 'naturalness'. He wanted to allow children to gain experience and be cared for but not to be pampered. They should be allowed to play away their early years before beginning a more structured regime from the age of twelve. The education of Emile was an intellectual experiment and a pedagogical utopia in which a boy is separated from his parents and brought up by a private tutor: 'Once I set about training a listless and lazy boy to run. He would not of his own accord have become involved in exercise of this kind or, indeed, any other physical exertion even though he was destined for a military career'.[1]

The challenge was to turn an arrogant scamp into a 'fleet-footed Achilles' and, moreover, to do it without nagging since an aristocrat could not be given orders. It was a case of finding the pedagogical element in running.

Rousseau always carried two cakes in his pocket when he and the boy went for a walk in the afternoon. One day the boy found an extra cake in Rousseau's pocket and asked for it. He was not allowed to have it – Rousseau wanted it himself or intended to give it as a prize to whichever of two boys playing nearby won a race. He showed them the cake and suggested a race; the course was marked out and the boys set off at the given signal. One of them won, grabbed the cake and devoured it.

This made no impact on Rousseau's lazy walking companion. The education of children takes a great deal of time and demands patience so they continued their walks, always taking cakes with them. On each occasion the little lads got a piece or two of cake as a prize after their race and on each occasion Rousseau and his pupil sat and watched. Passers-by stopped and watched, cheered and clapped, since the news had spread and made the event a much-discussed affair in the neighbourhood. The aristocratic boy also began to be caught up in the contest and would jump up and shout enthusiastically.[2]

He eventually tired of seeing the tasty pieces of cake disappearing into the mouths of the other boys and saw that racing was good for *something*. He began training in secret and jokingly asked to be given a cake. No, came the answer, at which the boy became angry: 'Put the cake on a stone, mark out the track and we'll see!'[3]

Exasperated by Rousseau, he ran and won and got his reward, after which the aristocratic lad became keen on running and needed neither praise nor encouragement. He shared his cake with the others since running had made him noble and generous, but Rousseau had guided the outcome by influencing him in his choice of distance. He wanted the boy to become aware of the difference made by the length of the course.[4]

The boy gradually came to understand that it was advantageous to select the shortest route. He looked at the length of the course and paced it out, but a child is too impatient to do this for long. He preferred to be training, so he practised judging distances by eye and became capable of defining the distance to a piece of cake with the precision of a surveyor. Thus Rousseau had moved him on to a different topic: human sight and the ability to quickly judge distances in everyday life, which can also be developed by running.

Emile became a young man and was eating cakes at a social gathering and remembering his childhood games. Could he still run? Of course he could! They set up a marker for the finish and put a cake on it while Emile and three other young men prepared to join in. Emile shot off and reached the finish before the others were even properly under way. He received the prize from his friend Sophie and treated the other competitors to it.

'I'll challenge you!' Sophie said to Emile, hitching up her skirts to make them short enough and taking as much care to show her pretty legs as to run. She flew off at the starting signal whereas Emile remained standing.

Her lead became so great that he had to give his all to catch up with her but, to be chivalrous, 'he allows Sophie to touch the goal first and shouts "Sophie is the winner"'. Rousseau then, however, makes disparaging remarks about women:

> Women were not meant to run; they flee that they may be over-taken. Running is not the only thing they do ill, but it is the only thing they do awkwardly; their elbows glued to their sides and pointed backwards look ridiculous, and the high heels on which they are perched make them look like so many grasshoppers trying to run instead of to jump.[5]

Rousseau had novel ideas in many areas but little faith in women as runners. They were, of course, hindered by their clothes: the fashion for girls and ladies in the France of his day, with its underskirts and overskirts and even corsets, allowed them little movement. The posture and physical development of growing girls was affected by their clothing.

It was in France in 1796 that the world's first measured and timed 100-metre sprint was held, the metre (Greek *metron* = 'measure') having been defined in France in 1791. The unit had been proposed for modern use by the Italian scientist Tito Livio Burattini in 1675, inspired by the Englishman John Wilkins, who had described a universal unit of measurement seven years earlier.

In 1791 the National Assembly in France accepted a proposal from the Academy of Science that a metre should be equivalent to one ten-millionth of the length of the meridian from the Equator to the North Pole running through Paris. Later measurements showed that the definition was not absolutely exact. In the meantime, however, they had cast the first prototype bronze metre in France in 1795 and it deviated from the exact measure by one-fifth of a millimetre. In 1812 France then became the first nation to introduce the metric system.

The Metre Convention of 20 May 1875 was an international scientific treaty by which many countries agreed to go over to the metric system and new prototype bars of platinum and indium were cast in 1889. The standardization was, of course, significant for all those people, including runners, who wanted to measure time and distance exactly.

German Philanthropists

Rousseau's Emile and his natural education inspired thinkers in many countries, not least in Germany where Johan C.F. GutsMuths wrote the following in his 1793 book *Gymnastik für die Jugend*: 'Almost all day is spent sitting still; how can young people's energy be developed?'[6]

School attendance had become obligatory in a number of countries during the eighteenth century though far from every child was included in it.

The Philanthropists in Germany, a group of men with education as their life's work, established several schools where 'natural education' was practised – once again, the influence of the Greeks is evident.

There is a historical line of development which, though sometimes interrupted, runs from Ancient Greek wisdom about sport. Many people became aware of it from their reading of the classics and, indeed, it should really be self-evident: with all our spirituality and religiosity, how have we come to forget the care of our bodies? Reformers through the centuries have seen the value of our heritage from Hellas and have presented the ancient ideas – which frequently appeared to be pioneering, since the knowledge had almost disappeared.

The first school in modern Europe known to have had daily physical exercise on its timetable opened in Dessau in 1774, its founder being the pedagogical reformer Johann B. Basedow (1723–1790). One of the teachers at this school, Christian G. Salzmann, left there in 1784 and started a similar school at Schnepfenthal in the Duchy of Gotha.

That is where GutsMuths worked from 1785 and the following year started his first gymnastics class from eleven to twelve in the morning, outdoors in the fresh air, surrounded by a grove of oak trees. He recommended running, which should be performed in a planned way so that the runner knew the times he had achieved and could thus later attempt to better them. GutsMuths believed that nothing offered more encouragement than success. He was one of the first to focus on timekeeping and measurement in running for young people but he recognized that this could be problematical since the pocket watches of the time only registered minutes, if that.

GutsMuths developed and perfected natural education, training and outdoor play and his message spread far beyond Germany through his books, translations and other works.[7]

GutsMuths lived in a central part of Europe at a time of upheaval. The American and French Revolutions had placed the individual at the centre of things; future development was pointing to liberty, equality and fraternity and away from feudalism and apathy; in theory, anyway, every man had individual value and dignity and could influence his own life and well-being through gymnastics. The states of Germany were still under the thumb of feudalism in GutsMuth's day and when his day of awakening came he saw the vast class distinctions in society.

He criticized clothing fashions that hindered physical development, particularly for girls and women. 'Let them come out into the fresh air, care for their bodies, expose them to all kinds of weather without being afraid of it. Swimming and bathing are good and every school should have a swimming pool', he wrote in 1793, sounding amazingly radical. GutsMuths was dismayed to see poor families sending their children into full-time work at the age of ten or eleven, long before they were physically ready; and, moreover, the jobs they took were often hard and repetitive and could easily destroy them physically.[8]

He stressed that play was a vital and valuable learning process, an important part of an individual's development. Other, rather more military, reformers are more familiar to posterity than GutsMuths, particularly his fellow-countryman Friedrich Ludwig Jahn (1778–1852), who was an important pioneer in turn-gymnastics but was also interested in short-distance and relay running. After many setbacks in his youth he became an honoured German folk hero credited with the strong position of turn-gymnastics in Germany throughout the nineteenth century. This form of gymnastics spread to other countries and the newly started turn associations also included sprinting. Jahn preached the message 'free sky, air and light'. German turn gymnastics and a variant form of Swedish gymnastics represented by Pehr Henrik Ling (1776–1839) became widely known.[9]

Thomas Arnold (1795–1842), who in 1828 became headmaster of Rugby, a traditional English public school, also became a well-known figure. Arnold had studied Classics at Oxford and is known as a pioneer of sport at English public schools. Arnold was mainly interested in sport as part of his project to educate Christian gentlemen so, for him, sport was a means of achieving more than just physical attributes.

At Rugby and the other English public schools the boys had already organized activities for themselves before Arnold's time. The pupils played football, ran or rowed, and cross-country running was particularly important. In the popular 1857 novel *Tom Brown's Schooldays* the author Thomas Hughes painted a rosy picture of his own experiences at Rugby in the 1830s. The author believed passionately in upbringing, daring and effort – the latter was necessary at Rugby, where the boys might do cross-country runs of up to ten miles. This story of life at Rugby was read in many countries and the ideas contained in it took root, as did the reforms in gymnastics, education and sport at school level in many European countries in the first half of the nineteenth century.[10]

10
Mensen Ernst and Captain Barclay

*People who saw him rushing along the highways and through
the countryside considered him an eccentric, as a madman even,
or possessed by the devil.*

—On Mensen Ernst during his run from Paris to Moscow in 1832

The Norwegian Mensen Ernst (1795–1843) was born into a crofting family at
Fresvik in Sogn as the youngest of seven children. He was christened Mons
Monsen Øhren but, like many others, changed his name in the course of his
life. The name change was natural enough for a man who went to sea and
moved abroad: Monsen Øhren became Mensen Ernst on British ships.[1]

He went to sea around 1812. He sailed the world's oceans on the *Cale-
donia*, visiting distant ports in India, Australia and China. In South Africa
he won a race – not all seamen could handle the transition from the rolling
motion of a ship to the solidity of land. When Ernst was paid off in London
in 1818 he was used to the ways of the world and a good linguist.

Now he began to run. London was the perfect place for an aspirant runner to live and foreigners came there to compete. Ernst could earn more from
racing bets than from a seaman's pay and he had found his metier.

He left London in 1820 and moved to the Annenrode (Anroda) manor
estate between Mühlhausen and Dingelstadt in Germany: during his time as
a seaman Ernst had saved the life of the father-in-law of the estate's owner.
After four happy years there, he was out on the road again, but Annenrode
remained a place to which he loved to return.

He was prepared to race anywhere for small or large sums of money, in
Switzerland, Italy, Austria and so back to Germany, living frugally, with fruit,
bread and wine as his basic diet. He rarely ate hot food, and meat was not
part of his regular diet, but wine was a favourite. He was an adventurer and
his running talents made it possible for him to see and experience Europe
as a sporting tourist, and one who was eager to learn. He read a great deal
and moved in learned circles, had access to good libraries and new maps for
the planning of his trips. He never returned to Norway but paid a visit to
Denmark in the winter of 1826, giving performances that drew thousands
of spectators, including the king in Copenhagen. His feats as a runner made
the crofter's son a celebrity whom even the nobility wanted to meet.

In front of audiences of princes, great men and the general public, Ernst
put on his performances – 'productions' – in over seventy towns, promoting them with posters he ordered from the printers and stuck up himself.

Mensen Ernst,
Norwegian long-
distance runner
and globetrotter.

His visits to the great men and dignitaries of an area, and the fact that those with power were among the spectators, made for good advertising and eased his way with the authorities. He lived on his reputation and it spread through the aristocracy and royal families of Europe, whose family bonds crossed all the frontiers. In October 1830 he visited Odense:

> The famous Norwegian runner, familiar to us from last year, has visited England and France, including Paris at the beginning of July, since he was last here. Last week he gave us a demonstration of his skill at a particularly elevated level in that he ran with stilts approximately two feet high attached to his feet. On Wednesday the 6th, the third day of the market, he ran the length of Odense town from the post office to the Vesterport four times in 26 minutes on stilts, and then did the same on foot in an even shorter time. He is said to be a fairly wealthy man who could easily dispense with this way of earning a living but who continues with it partly because his constitution is accustomed to it and needs such exercise and partly, no doubt, because he has developed a taste for the travelling life.[2]

Runs of this kind in small towns became routine but he also had ambitions to perform what seemed to be an impossible feat.

On 11 July 1832 he left Paris to run the 1,600 miles to Moscow in fifteen days. Betting men speculated whether it was achievable. Immediately after the start he was stopped by some drunken peasants who tied him up and threw him on a cart. He tricked his way out of this difficulty by offering to run a race against their fastest horse. He continued through Germany and on into Poland towards Krakow: 'People who saw him rushing along the highways and through the countryside considered him an eccentric, as a madman even, or possessed by the devil'.[3]

What people saw was a small, thin, grey-haired fellow with a weather-beaten face, for the effort soon sets its mark on the face. He was not going particularly quickly, six miles an hour and even slower in hilly terrain, but the miles soon built up because Ernst did not waste much time sleeping: he preferred to sleep outside, straight on the ground, which allowed him to get the most rest in the shortest time. His ability to do with little sleep or rest meant he could run extra distances with the moon and the stars keeping him on the right track in the dark. The navigational knowledge gained during his years at sea was vital as he romped through unknown country with his compass, wooden quadrant and map. In the evening of 19 June he reached Russian soil near Chelm, with long stretches of flat country still left between him and Moscow. Five days later he plodded into Borodino, where twenty years earlier Napoleon had fought his battle against the Russians. Moscow lay one day away and he had 48 hours before his time ran out. Feeling pleased with himself, he booked into an inn to enjoy the moment. But, what with the obvious signs of being a traveller in a hurry and his eccentric and outlandish appearance, people were suspicious; nor did it help when he showed his pass and tried to make himself understood. His pass was confiscated and Mensen Ernst ended up in a cell, desperate but still self-possessed. The chimney pipe offered the only possibility of escape: he loosened some stones, crept up the chimney and out onto the roof – where he was discovered. Fortunately there was a ladder down from the roof and he shot down it and sprinted away. The villagers were unable to keep pace with him and Mensen Ernst was once more on the road to Moscow, where he was expected at 11 p.m. on 26 June. At 10 a.m., one day early, an unknown and sweating man came to a halt in front of the guard at the gates of the Kremlin. Once the Russians had understood the situation and he had handed over the French papers he was travelling with, Mensen Ernst was greeted cordially in upper-class French. After cheers from the crowd and toasts to welcome him, Ernst retired to a tavern with a large, newly acquired sum of money in his pocket. He had no desire, however, to sleep in a fine bed and preferred a wooden bench for the whole week he was in Moscow. A message announcing his arrival was sent to Paris by semaphore telegraph, the fastest means of communication at the time.

1,600 miles (2,575 km) in fourteen days means about 115 miles (185 km) a day. It does not sound humanly possible to keep up this mileage for such a long period but Ernst was in his best years, well trained, fully experienced and he needed little sleep. He had to keep going for at least eighteen to twenty hours a day to cover stages of that length, but that is not physically impossible for some people. The roads, however, were not always straight and flat and it took time and skill to navigate his way through unknown country even though he had planned his route in advance. If there was any-one in the 1830s who *could* run from Paris to Moscow in two weeks, that someone was Mensen Ernst.

An 1844 German biography of Ernst by Gustav Rieck lists some of the places he passed and the dates:[4]

> Chalons-sur-Marne: 11 June, evening
> Kaiserlautern: 13 June, morning
> Mainz: 13 June, midday
> Tinz: 16 June
> Sandimierz: 18 June, evening
> Chelm: 19 June, night
> Mogilov: 21 June, afternoon
> Smolensk: 23 June, morning
> Moscow: 25 June, morning

Rieck's biography, written to order for its main character, contains some gross errors and some free imagination in order to spice up the story and make it more readable, but it also provides demonstrable facts. Ernst's tour from Munich to Nauplion in Greece the following year is well-documented in contemporary sources. Ernst took 24 days, 42 minutes and 30 seconds for almost 1,700 miles between 7 June and 1 July 1833 – an average of 95 miles (153 km) a day. With him he carried letters from King Ludwig to his son King Otto of Greece. In view of the mountainous nature of the country this feat is at least the equal of the run to Moscow.

It was not only long distances Mensen Ernst had to contend with, however: he had to cross rivers and face dangers such as highway brigands, wild animals and infectious diseases. On occasion he was able to avoid towns afflicted by cholera or plague because there was a man at the gates of the town warning people of the danger. His documents, stamped with well-known seals, made it easier for him to pass through border posts, and there was something exotic about this polyglot courier with gold coins and travel permits from the aristocracy in his pocket even though he himself was un-prepossessing to look at – Queen Therese of Bavaria, for instance, was amazed at how small the famous runner was.

It is difficult to decide what his greatest feat was, though his longest run was in 1836 when he ran from Istanbul to Calcutta in four weeks – and then back. The whole trip took 59 days and he covered almost 5,200 miles (8,370 km), or 95 miles a day. There is some question as to whether he got all the way to Calcutta. A signed letter from Teheran confirms that, on the return journey, it took him eight days from there to reach the Swedish envoy in Istanbul. What motivated the run was the desire of the Englishmen of the

East India Company to send despatches from Turkey to India. The idea caught Ernst's imagination and he offered to complete the task in six weeks, which he achieved with plenty of time to spare. When he studied a new map of Asia before setting off, he recognized the dangers of the route and his own limitations: no one knew better than him how much planning and effort these runs demanded.

But in spite of the difficulties he dreamt of crossing Africa or running to China. In 1842 he entered the service of Prince Hermann von Pückler-Muskau, a German nobleman and enthusiast for long-distance running and Greek history. Ernst arrived at the prince's estate and in February 1842 the prince wrote to a friend: 'Everything here is as usual except that I have taken the runner Mensen Ernst into my service as a two-legged trotting horse in a Turkish costume'.[5]

In consultation with the prince Ernst agreed to go to Africa to seek the sources of the Nile, unknown territory for Europeans at that time. The journey took him via Jerusalem and Cairo and from there far up the Nile, where Ernst caught dysentery and died on the banks of the river on 22 January 1843 at the age of 47. Some tourists buried him on the spot and he probably lies buried under the great lake later formed by the Aswan Dam.

The following notice appeared in the German newspaper *Allgemeine Zeitung* in Augsburg on 21 March 1843: 'The famous pedestrian Mensen Ernst, who had set himself the goal of discovering the source of the White Nile, caught dysentery and died in Syene at the end of January. Travellers familiar with his great talents arranged for him to be buried by the first rapids on the Nile'.[6]

Mensen Ernst lived before official records, measured tracks and championships and consequently his achievements are not recorded in formal lists. He was certainly impressive over short distances in the streets of towns but what distinguished him from most nineteenth-century professional runners was his ability to run at a steady pace for weeks on end. Ambition and the urge to test his own ability were powerful motives and he was keen to ensure his position as the best of his kind and as the one with the most staying power. It is naive to assume that he was only driven by money and applause. He was the fastest courier in the Europe of his day, faster than horses over long distances, and capable of quite unique feats.[7]

Captain Barclay

He was a giant of a man, a primeval force that hated sitting still and who preferred to be roving round testing his strength and endurance. Robert Barclay Allardice (1779–1854) was one of the most active men in Britain, fast, tough and strong as a bear – a sprinter, long-distance runner, competitive walker, weightlifter and boxer rolled into one.

His most famous achievement came in 1809 when he set out to walk 1,000 miles (1,609 km) in 1,000 hours. It was the biggest sporting event in

England in living memory and attracted tens of thousands of spectators to Newmarket, 65 miles north of London.

Barclay wagered that he would walk one mile every hour for the next six weeks, Sundays included, and the initial wager was 1,000 guineas against James Wedderburn-Webster. But the stakes increased very considerably, eventually reaching 16,000 guineas, equivalent to 320 years' wages for a farmworker. Over and above that, a number of rich men – including the Prince of Wales – had laid bets of £100,000 between themselves, the equivalent to some £40,000,000 in modern terms. So there was a huge amount of money at stake in addition to the apparently impossible physical demands since, according to the doctors, Barclay risked overheating of the blood, which would either kill or permanently cripple him.

In the early stages there were few spectators at the half-mile course along which Barclay was walking back and forth. The news soon spread, however, and they came streaming in, including fashionable ladies and gentlemen who would normally have avoided popular spectacles but who now arrived in their carriages. They came from all over, all dressed in their best: servant girls, workmen, lords and dukes.

Barclay and Wedderburn-Webster's supporters, timekeepers and assistants were stationed respectively at opposite ends of the course, sleeping in tents and sometimes joining in. Shortly before 2.30 p.m. on Wednesday, 12 July 1809, Barclay emerged from a tavern full of enthusiastic supporters. He had lost weight and looked worn after six weeks of little sleep and a great deal of exercise. Nevertheless, his massive physique was visible under his clothes as he removed the bandages from his legs and prepared for his 999th mile on the flat, grassy course, illuminated by gaslights. The lamps were the latest novelty to provide better visibility when he walked in the dark and they were an attraction that drew even more spectators. Some of the lamps had been smashed and an armed bodyguard, the boxer Big John Cully, walked with Barclay during the hours of darkness.

He had walked in his sleep, slept while standing at the starting line, had knee problems and toothache, trudged on in the pouring rain and sweated in the heat. He had limped so badly that reporters had written of a man ready to drop, wrestling with death. He had followed the advice of Dr Sandiver about rubbing himself with oil and using hot cloths, he had experimented with old wives' advice, irrespective of the source. His race plan, however, was a success: he walked a mile at the close of an hour, took a short break and walked the next mile at the start of the hour. That gave him an hour and a half's rest between each lap.

At 3.37 Barclay stepped across the finishing line at the end of his 1,000 miles. Jubilation broke out, the church bells of Newmarket rang and newspaper men hurried to deliver the latest news of the event. Barclay got into a hot bath and immediately fell asleep, his first real sleep for 42 days.

The following morning he felt in good shape and walked the streets of Newmarket – 28 pounds lighter – receiving congratulations and applause.[8]

Robert Barclay Allardice was born in Ury in Scotland in 1779, a member of the noble family Barclay, which could trace its ancestry back 700 years. He grew up in the countryside knowing that he belonged to a tough breed in which his grandfather Robert 'the Strong' was just one of many renowned ancestors. The family home did not have a door at ground level in case of enemy attack and guests had to climb up a rope to get into the house. Whether it was by swinging on a rope or by racing against other youngsters, young Barclay laid the foundations of a phenomenal physique. From the time he made his first wager in 1796, a 100-guinea bet that he could walk six miles in under an hour, he enjoyed competition. He won the money and learnt he could make a good profit by betting.

Barclay's father died in 1797 at a particularly unfortunate moment for the family. He was deeply in debt but Robert was assured of an income of £400 a year as well as certain rights to the estate. He became the sixth laird of Ury and it was up to him to straighten out the finances. The situation became even worse in 1801 when Barclay lost four bets with 'the Daft Laird' in five months, losing a total of £6,175, four times the family's annual income. He had to recoup the money and running and walking offered the best chances. He went for a big win and in the autumn of 1801 made a new wager against the same man for a total of 10,000 guineas. At the suggestion of Lord Panmure Barclay visited the experienced trainer and tenant farmer Jackey Smith, who knew how to motivate sportsmen and build up their confidence, but he made strict demands: they could only sleep five hours a night, had to hang in a hammock for two hours and were woken at four o'clock in the morning.

Smith sent him out at six o'clock for the first of the day's two running sessions.

'Lean forward,' Smith said, 'shorten the length of your pace and stay in contact with the ground.'[9]

That took the weight off his knees and protected his back, particularly when Barclay set off on eighteen-mile runs carrying a heavy load of butter and cheese with orders to be back within 90 minutes. That was, of course, impossible but his training sessions were particularly demanding in the autumn of 1801 and were interspersed with frequent sweat baths.

In the middle of October 1801 Barclay was ready for his last test run: 110 miles (177 km), starting just before midnight on a wet night. Oil lamps shone over the track and a rope had been stretched as a guide in case all visibility was lost. Barclay tramped out a path and by dawn he was wading up to his ankles in mud. His trainer cut a notch in a plank for each circuit and checked the clock; three times he ordered Barclay into a hut to eat bread and chicken and to drink old ale. Following his trainer's instructions he dried off and lay in the darkness for ten minutes in a specially constructed hut, insulated so that all light and noise were excluded. The idea was to concentrate as much mental energy as possible during the short breaks. Barclay took 19 hours 27 minutes for the 110 miles, the best time for the distance in

England and particularly impressive given the bad weather conditions. He was ready to win his bet with the Daft Laird, who had chosen November because it meant there was a good chance of bad weather, wind, heavy rain and fog. He also believed that the human physique was at its weakest in November. Barclay, however, swept all doubts aside and won the 10,000 guineas in foul weather: that day ten times the sum of his earlier bet changed hands and Barclay, who was only 22, was already a legend, a master of all distances. He became obsessed with pushing his body to the absolute and painful limit by walking the longest day stages possible. Barclay was not like other gentlemen – rather than sleep in a warm, peaceful bed he was happy to leave a roadside hostelry and walk the whole night.

He frightened off many challengers, but not all. Abraham Wood lived in Manchester and in 1807, in spite of a bandaged leg, he had shown his fantastic form over nine miles on the horse-racing course at Doncaster. It was said that no one in England could beat Wood and he had challenged anyone in the world, irrespective of the size of the bet. Barclay heard the news but preferred to run 440 yards (400 m) against another challenger and won in 60 seconds.

Abraham was the leading runner, just as Barclay was the top walker, and a duel became inevitable. The date was set for 12 October 1807 and the challenge was to cover the longest distance in 24 hours. Barclay was to be given a 20-mile start since he was walking.

During the eight weeks of preparation Barclay lived on the south coast of England and trained with boxers while Abraham Wood and his supporters had a training camp close by. Barclay ran, walked and boxed from morning to night, eating two pounds of beef or more for breakfast. He easily jogged 80 miles (129 km) in 12 hours, but Wood covered 53 miles (85 km) in seven hours.

The duel took place in Newmarket, where they were used to crowds flocking in, but not on this scale. Among the many spectators was the nineteen-year-old poet Lord Byron. Those who had put money on a cancellation lost because the two men set off energetically on Monday, 12 October, after having marked out a new course. Earlier they had demanded separate courses, Barclay preferring a mile-long course, illuminated and with connected awnings in case of rain, whereas Wood had measured out a three-mile course in the neighbourhood. Right up to the last minute the two sides intended to continue separately with their sophisticated arrangements, which included night lights, rest tents and flags to mark the course. Finally, however, they selected a new course along the London road and everything was set up there, along with stewards, functionaries and the timekeepers, who were equipped with two clocks selected and adjusted by Mr Bramble, a renowned London clockmaker.

Wood went straight into the lead and was well ahead after an hour. While the two men were resting and consuming boiled chicken, rumours spread that the race was fixed and that Barclay would win even though Wood was ahead. Wood seemed tired after a couple of hours, took off his shoes and ran barefoot, only for his feet to be cut up by the rough surface. After six hours he began to lose speed and consulted his helpers, the surgeon and other specialists in his tent. Then the news was released that Wood had dropped out.

The betting men scented cheating and a planned withdrawal. The bets were not paid out and the atmosphere became restless while the rumours grew and became ever wilder. It was stated that Wood had complained of stomach pains during the race, which accounted for his withdrawal. He disappeared abruptly and two days later his life was apparently in danger – Barclay was said to be sitting by his sick-bed and the two men had shaken hands. Immediately afterwards Abraham Wood died – or so said the rumours.

There was, therefore, great astonishment two days later when Wood was seen at a boxing match, alive and well and none the worse for wear: the crowd booed and reacted loudly and vociferously.

According to the rumours the whole thing had been fixed. Those who had laid bets on it were enraged and pointed the finger at Wood as the scape-goat, which was unjust since if it was a fix Barclay must have been involved too. Later, at a tavern in Cambridge, the beer drinkers plunged the place into darkness on discovering that Wood was among the customers – and then they threw him out.

Barclay was the great hero, but there were still discussions as to which of the two was the better man since their big meeting had not been a fair contest. Sabotage was suggested and one eyewitness said that Wood had appeared dazed when he left his tent after 22 miles. Someone had slipped poison into his drink, probably opium drops, and no one knew who was the perpetrator, but it was not like either Barclay or Wood to resort to dishonest tactics since both of them behaved decently.

Unofficially Barclay became a national champion among the pedestrians but the *Sporting Magazine* refused to recognize the title, arguing that such an honour would have to be won in a fairer and more rigorous manner.

A new candidate, Lieutenant Fairman of the Royal Lancashire Militia, was the best challenger. The little man challenged Barclay and offered to give him a 20-mile advantage over 24 hours but Barclay refused. They corresponded for three months, arguing about the conditions for their duel. Fairman suggested a race of 500 miles (804 km) whereas Barclay preferred a meeting on a course chosen by himself at his residence at Ury. Fairman rejected this and, frustrated by Barclay's unwillingness to meet in neutral surroundings, Fairman's backers arranged an exhibition race of 20 miles (32 km) from Marble Arch in London to Harrow and back. Fairman won by four minutes and challenged anyone in the kingdom, indeed anyone in the world, to a competition in which the aim would be to walk or run the longest distance without eating or drinking.

Barclay felt insulted and ignored the challenge – the whippersnapper Fairman was not an experienced pedestrian and lacked all serious qualifications. It was all about ego, pride and being the best in the country, and Barclay planned to capture the crown and demonstrate his lasting superiority.

It was this that led to the great 1,000-mile wager in 1809. Barclay's achievement of this feat stirred up a national fever in England and inspired others to attempt the impossible. One overweight man failed before he had started; another, John Bull, proposed walking a mile and a half every hour for 1,000 hours; a Scot dreamed of reading six chapters of the Bible every hour for six weeks; a glutton wanted to eat a sausage an hour for a thousand hours but gave up after three. All Barclay's imitators failed and he alone ruled supreme in 1809.

In the years that followed he did a lot of boxing and he also trained boxers (who did a lot of running), teaching some of the nation's most hard-hitting pugilists new tricks in that bare-knuckle age. The famous English boxer Tom Cribb stayed at Ury in 1811 to get into shape for a match against the black American champion, Tom Molineux, a freed slave. Cribb came into Barclay's hands overweight and short of breath but, under a strict regime, he lost weight by the week, particularly by uphill runs, which Cribb proved unusually good at. Barclay would fill his pockets with sharp stones and hurl them at his pupil's legs as he ran uphill. Cribb lost his temper, threw them back and then had to chase him. Barclay also tied Cribb's best punching arm to a carriage to train him to hold it up: he then drove the carriage for 30 miles with Cribb being dragged along behind for several hours. On top of that he had to work hard on the estate, humping sacks of corn, digging ditches and chopping down trees, all on a meagre four pints of liquid (beer) a day and a monotonous diet of beef, pork and chicken legs.

Cribb won the fight in front of a crowd of 20,000 and he gave much of the honour to Barclay, his trainer, who won £10,000 in bets.

As to these strict rules about diet and drinking, it is questionable whether they were really adhered to or whether they were an ideal to strive for. Later in the nineteenth century good runners liked to keep their preparations secret and would lie about diet and training in order to confuse the opposition: they preferred not to shout their training methods and trade secrets from the rooftops.

A Lot of Training and Little to Drink

A carefully worked-out buildup lay behind Barclay's achievements and it is one of the first modern training programmes for running we know about. He prescribed three substantial doses of Glauber's salt over a period of eight days to purge the body and make it receptive to training.

Barclay got up at five o'clock and ran a half-mile flat out uphill, followed by six miles of walking at a moderate pace, before going back for a break-fast of beef or mutton chops, dry bread and beer. Then came another gentle six miles and at twelve o'clock it was time for a half-hour's rest, naked in bed.

After that the programme required a four-mile walk before dinner, which consisted of more beef, chops, bread and beer. Immediately after the meal he would sprint for a half mile and follow it with a fast walk of six miles. Barclay then went to bed at 8 p.m. having covered well over 20 miles, most of it at a gentle pace, apart from the one mile at full speed.

After three or four weeks of this routine the body demanded a 'sweat run', that is to say, a four-mile run at full speed dressed in heavy, warm clothes. After the run he drank a specially-concocted, hot 'sweat drink', consisting of caraway, coriander seeds, liquorice and brown sugar, then lay down fully dressed and covered with six to eight plaids in order to sweat even more. After half an hour it was time to get up, undress and dry off. Barclay would then stroll for two miles wearing a heavy overcoat before breakfasting on roast chicken and returning to normal training. The sweat treatment would be repeated several times. If the stomach played up it would be dosed with an emetic one week before the race. Over and above that Barclay recommended light physical activity to keep oneself in form all day – sitting still was both forbidden and debilitating.

The trainer should ensure that the diet was appropriate, that is to say, almost exclusively meat, apart from bread and dry biscuits. Veal and lamb were not good, nor was pork or anything fatty. Barclay preferred lean meat. Carrots, turnips and potatoes contained too much water and caused digestive problems, as did fish. Butter, cheese, spices and salt should also be avoided. Eggs were also unsuitable, apart from raw egg-yolks on an empty stomach in the morning.

All liquids, especially home-brewed ale, should be consumed cold, but too much liquid caused the stomach to swell and impeded the breathing. Three pints of beer a day was the maximum, and any alcoholic drink stronger than wine was not permitted. Barclay did not drink either milk or water and recommended as little liquid as possible in order to avoid digestive upsets.

This diet has to be seen in the context of the British diet at the start of the nineteenth century. Drinking water was often impure and there was little fruit outside the season. In comparison with many people Barclay ate sensibly, particularly by avoiding heavily salted food and by 'only' drinking two and a half pints of beer a day.[10]

Barclay was not cut out for marriage though he was happy to enjoy an abundance of sexual pleasures and in 1816 had a child by Mary Dalgarno, a serving girl. He put off marriage, however, and Mary died in 1820 giving birth to their third child, a son who did not survive long. Barclay settled on his estate with his two daughters, and ran the farm. He became a judge of races and competitions and an adviser and trainer.

Even when he was over fifty he remained an enthusiastic pedestrian and open-air man, an eccentric, tobacco-spitting old fellow who refused to allow increasing age to limit his activities. Not even all-night drinking and feasting curbed his desire to keep fit: two miles on foot after breakfast and then a couple of hours on horseback was the norm – even without a night's sleep.

He employed close to eighty people and managed the sheep and other beasts. Barclay valued freedom and practised free upbringing: his daughter Margaret refused to wear shoes at her boarding school in Edinburgh, running around barefoot just as at home.

As a 70-year-old Barclay still had the strength of a bear and liked to impress his guests with it. At a dinner party he put his hand on the ground and told Darwin Galton, a fully grown man weighing twelve stone (76 kg), to stand on it. Then Barclay lifted him right up and placed him on the table, just as he had done 45 years earlier when he lifted an eighteen-stone (114 kg) man with one mighty heave. This time the 70-year-old Barclay impressed his guests – but he did strain his shoulder.

In 1854 he had several mild strokes and was partially paralysed, but he got out as soon as his body permitted and pushed himself hard with both work and exercise. Exercise, that was always his prescription against ailments and troubles, exercise all day, even with a limp and a temperature. On 1 May 1854, after being kicked in the head by a pony, he was suddenly taken ill and died.

Both Mensen Ernst and Captain Barclay were driven by ambition and a sense of adventure. They were artists and sportsmen, commercially acute and capable of generating large sums of money and a great deal of attention. for the whole of their adult lives they were at the centre of entertainments that drew great crowds and they were acclaimed as supermen. They both had a lasting urge to prove that they still counted for something in their field.

But unlike the primitive peoples of their age Ernst and Barclay were not running in order to uphold law and order or to communicate with the gods. The Native Americans, for example, could match these two in terms of endurance but their running had quite different origins and motivations.

11
Buffalo Heart for Breakfast

As I ran, my whole body was covered in a thin layer of ice and it
crackled all over over, even my penis. It was completely frozen.
—Young Navajo runner

When the Milky Way was formed, it was laid out as a running track, which is why the Apaches used to run every autumn. This was the explanation they gave for the origin of their relay race for young men – the race was revealed to mankind as an inspiration to help them in both everyday and ceremonial life. By repeating the race they ensured stability and bound the past and the present together. They were imitating creation and communing with the gods and the powers of the universe.[1]

Many of the indigenous tribes in California believed that the Milky Way was created from the dust kicked up in a race between the Prairie Wolf and the Wildcat – two well-known figures in Native American mythology who were fierce competitors at running. The Prairie Wolf was the representative of the first people, a mythical race that first populated the world and lived here before us.

Native American myths contained many accounts of running. The gods told men to run and the animals showed them how. Accounts of mythical and sacred races explained the origin of things and taught mankind about the world. Running races defined the nature and physical characteristics of individual species. Mythical runners were the progenitors of clans that reflected the social organization of mankind.[2]

There are few groups for whom running has been as important as it was for the Native Americans. Without horses and without wheeled vehicles in this huge land, they had to rely on their feet and this has left traces in the stories and customs of the tribes. Researchers have been investigating this since the nineteenth century and have uncovered a rich tradition which lived on even after the native peoples came into contact with the white man. Runners could, in fact, be used effectively in the struggle against the settlers.

Messengers and chiefs from the Pueblo tribes of northern New Mexico met in Red Willow in the spring of 1680 to listen to their religious leader Po'pay – 'Ripe Squash'. They had much to avenge on the Spaniards, who had ruled them since the 1590s, compelled them to accept Christianity, suppressed their beliefs and ridiculed their way of life. In 1660 a Franciscan

Native American
running in the forest,
c. 1903, painting by
Frederick Remington.

priest burned hundreds of sacred masks and in 1675 the Spanish had
flogged their religious leaders, including Po'pay, in the square in Santa Fe.

The Native Americans had planned an uprising to coincide with when
the maize was ripe in August. Messengers were to spread the news to 70
Pueblo and Hopi villages up to 300 miles away by means of symbols inscribed
on deerskin. The runners set off on foot to spread the word, each in a different direction.

As August approached the messengers met again and each was given a
piece of rope with knots in it to mark the days left. The villagers were to cut
off one knot every day until they were all gone and then they were to attack.
The situation was tense. The Spaniards suspected something was afoot and
hanged two runners. The Native Americans responded by bringing forward
the attack to 10 August 1680.

Little is known about the actual uprising except that the Native
Americans demolished Spanish churches, killed priests and burned church
documents and that 380 Spaniards and Native Americans were killed. On
the ruins of the square in Santa Fe the Native Americans raised a *kiva*, a
sacred place, as a symbol of their dominance.[3]

Toughening up the Young

The Navajo were fast and serious runners. 'Talking God' would wake the young people in the morning: 'Rise, grandchildren, it is time to run for your health and your well-being'.[4] He was 'the grandfather of the gods' to the Navajo, a guide who travelled on rainbows and sunbeams and who communicated by mimicry. He gave advice and he assessed initiative, courage and intelligence – qualities that were reinforced by running. The old people said that the gods rewarded those who ran in the morning since that was particularly beneficial.

Rex Lee Jim grew up in Canyon de Chelly in a family that was firmly loyal to traditional ways. From the age of four his grandfather woke him at 4.30 a.m. to go running – it was a matter of stealing a march on the sunrise and of going in an easterly direction. Over long distances Rex Lee Jim sang about the puma, the antelope and the deer – what were called leg-songs – in order to run faster and more nimbly.

Grandfather boiled up sage leaves and the boys drank the potion before running to make them throw up and thus cleanse the body. At the halfway point of their morning run Rex and his companion rounded a bush and stopped. Rex pummelled his skin, kneaded his muscles – 'moulded his body' – and massaged his companion. One of them pushed an eagle's feather far down his throat to make himself vomit again. They put sand in their shoes to harden their feet and they held icicles in their mouths. The young men took a mouthful of water and ran with it in their mouths while breathing through their noses to strengthen their breathing – after four miles they spat out the water.

In the winter they rolled in the snow. After the second snowfall of the winter they set off in the cold, wearing only moccasins and nether garments while sprinting and shaking snow down from the trees onto their naked bodies. Toughening-up practices of this sort made them immune to cold as adults, and banished indolence, strengthened the body and gave them keen sight, just like the ice-baths another Navajo tells of: 'I stayed in the icy water as long as I could bear it, roaring and screaming to develop my voice. Then I got out, put on my moccasins and ran home, taking great strides. As I ran my whole body was covered in a thin layer of ice, which crackled all over me, even my penis. It was completely frozen. That was the worst thing. Before I got home I rolled in the snow again.'[5]

The Apache made even sterner demands on their young men. Their sons were indoctrinated in youth that endurance, a high pain threshold and courage were the most important things in life's struggle. Running was part of a regime that created characters that were physically and mentally tough. A father would say to his son: 'Rise before dawn and run to the mountain. Come back before it is light. You must do it and I shall force you to do it. I shall train you so you are good when you have grown into a man. It will develop your will. And your legs will be so well-developed that no one will out-run you.'[6]

They ran with heavy loads, they hurled themselves into icy waters, they fought one another and suffered with little or no food. The men who led the training egged their pupils on against each other like angry steers. It is told how one trainer shot at the legs of a pupil running downhill to demonstrate the boy's ability to avoid bullets. The Apaches laughed brutally at such incidents and it was humiliating for a young man to be afraid. The hardening-up period ended with a two-day run without food or rest. After that the sixteen-year-olds were ready to be fully-fledged braves.

The Apaches specialized in surprise attacks and rapid withdrawal. They moved at night at a run and rested in long grass during the day. Food was eaten cold: this strengthened their teeth and prevented them becoming loose in later life but it also meant there were no fires to give them away. During their first attacks young men ran extra distances in the mornings and evenings, sprinted up hills, pissed against trees and howled like prairie wolves to bring themselves success. To carry out ambushes and raids for plunder young braves would be sent to run long distances at night by the light of the full moon and their enemies were astonished at the range the Apaches could cover. Geronimo (1829–1909), the famous Apache chief who refused for many years to bow to the white man's laws, used surprise tactics in Mexico. His small bands of braves could range up to 75 miles (120 km) in 24 hours over extremely rugged terrain.

Once they had reached puberty but before they married, Apache boys had to take part in a relay race in the autumn. The Apaches believed that the fastest runners were unmarried boys with no sexual experience. Once he had sexual contact with a woman a boy would never again achieve the same speed and vitality. Those who did not run the relay would become sickly and contemptible. According to tradition the race had its origins in a mythical ancient past and taking part brought blessings and strength to the young. This is the story they told:

> Once upon a time long ago there was too much of all kinds of food simultaneously, both meat and plants. Crops did not have fixed seasons and the people could not handle the situation. The Sun and the Moon decided to divide the year in order to provide varied food at different times of the year.
>
> The Moon said: 'I wager all my fruits against you.'
>
> The Sun said: 'I wager all my animals.'[7]
>
> The Sun and the Moon agreed to run this race every fourth year. They took it in turns to win so that people would not have to eat only meat or only plants, and so they ensured a varied diet for mankind. The race was then passed down to the Apaches, who had witnessed it and learnt from it. If they did not carry out the ceremony they would starve.[8]
>
> They were divided into two teams – *Ollero* (potters) and *Llanero* (plains people). The former represented the Sun and the

animals, the latter the Moon and the plants. The Apache believed that the Moon ruled over the water, determined the seasons and produced fruits, just as a woman bears children. The Moon represented the feminine side whereas the Sun, being male, was linked to animals.[9]

At first the relay race was fitted in around hunting and harvesting but later the three-day long ritual began on 13 September.

Before the race the participants abstained from meat, did not smoke and avoided women. They trained and rubbed the ashes of sunflower stalks into their insteps in order to run faster and to have more supple joints. They also chewed sunflower root and then rubbed it into their legs. The two enclosures in which the race was to be run symbolized the location of creation: the track was where the plants and animals had first run round the earth.

As the first day of races approached, crowds of onlookers began to arrive and pitch camp. The men levelled out any uneven parts of the track and built two sacred structures to the east and to the west. The rectangular track lay between them and was marked out with four stones of different colours, under each of which were placed the fresh feathers of fast-flying birds. However, if a menstruating woman crossed the track, the boys' running skills would be diminished.[10]

After an intense selection process the ceremonial relay race took place on the third morning. The man responsible for body painting smoked and blew smoke in all directions, strewed pollen and muttered prayers. Other men brought dead birds, the feathers of which were used to decorate the runners to help them be victorious. The leader and three assistants knelt, sang and cast pollen and paint at set points, where they drew four figures on the slope. The painting of the runners took place immediately before the start and the two best in each team were painted identically and given identical clothing.

After they were all decorated with paint to resemble birds, the men sang while the young men danced down across the running field, led by two girls who were to be given in marriage. These unions were part of the fertility ritual and it was propitious for the girls to be given a husband after the relay.

The dancing teams met in the middle, surrounded by happy onlookers. Four older men would test-run the course slowly, symbolizing the four supernatural powers and forces. When two of the old men passed one another at the western end, two young runners set off at full speed – the start of the race itself – and when they had passed the stones the next set off. Then the competition was fierce until one team gained a half-length's advantage – the winning margin. The relay would continue until that happened or until one side conceded defeat; it might last for many hours since the will to win was strong and the boys did not give up easily.

Afterwards everyone was in a mild and gentle mood and in the evening they settled down to a feast of gluttonous proportions with all-night dancing. The three days of the ceremony came to an end the following morning.

Navajo and Apache girls also ran initiation runs when they entered puberty. In the Navajo ritual, *Kinaalda*, the run symbolized the girl's future willpower and beauty. The family would celebrate a girl's first menstruation for four days and she would run three times a day, each time longer than the last: this was to lengthen her life-span, to strengthen her body and to bring her good fortune in life.

Among the Yorok tribe in California running was part of a more wide-ranging process for young people, which included all-round training, wrestling, swimming and much else. One legendary young man had sped over the hills from Terwer Creek all the way to the top of Red Mountain, a climb of 3,000 feet (914 m). In the beginning he carried light stones with him but gradually increased them to large rocks. By then the young man was in his mid-twenties and he left a sizeable cairn as a lasting memorial to the hundreds of training runs of his youth.[11]

More advanced boys and girls of the Yorok tribe carried out esoteric training practices – *hohkep* – in order to communicate with the invisible powers and to gain insight and self-control. A special kind of running was important here: a gliding, utterly effortless style, which came after much contact with the spirit world. The runners flowed easily over bushes and became a part of the flow of nature. Aspirant runners developed a close relationship with the trails, singing and talking to them and letting them be the masters. The trail passed beneath them of its own accord, so to speak, and they ran swiftly with their eyes closed, relying on the trail to guide them. Gradually they tried out even more difficult forms of running, such as running blindfold down steep hills.

Visualization was of great importance. The energy used belonged to the world, not to the runner, and instead of feeling how the foot struck the hill, one should feel how the hill pressed back up against the foot. Bit by bit they came to rely on the hill and everything became quite natural. The pupils were taught how to 'see' the air as a rope they could pull themselves along by means of breathing technique and arm movements. The final test in this esoteric training consisted of a three-day run in the mountains, running only in the dark and resting and meditating during the day. Running was a means of spiritual growth and also a tool for medicine men, for whom it had important functions.

The Hopi ran in order to call down rain – a practice called sympathetic magic. The chief went barefoot and almost naked to warn the rulers of the clouds, and he ran quickly so that the clouds arrived immediately:

He runs in a wide circle on the first day because the chiefs of the clouds dwell far away. He goes to the north-west, south-west, north-east and south-east in order to catch the attention of all the rulers of the clouds. Each day he runs a circle with a smaller radius. We want to bring the clouds closer and closer so that on the day of the ceremony they are above us and will pour down their rain on our houses and on the earth around.[12]

The Initiation of a Fox Runner

Runners were also important in the myths of the Fox Indians. One account of the tribe's origins tells how the tribe was unhappy and confused and, in order to achieve wisdom, some men began to fast: they were given knowledge of how life in Meskwakis, the chief's village, should be organized and what they should do to become a tightly knit tribe. This was the origin of the rituals of the ceremonial runners.

God placed three men – runners – on the earth and endowed them with special talents. People consulted them and they were able to settle quarrels. They took part in negotiations and discussed the most vital questions of existence with the religious leaders. These runners foretold deaths and visited the villages seeking tasks for themselves:

> Those called to be ceremonial runners had a hard life. They watched over everything, they watched over the Indian villages and where the villages should be located. They also had a duty to be present on battlefields since they understood the mystical powers. They had been blessed by Manitou in that they had been permitted to have this understanding, which is why they were strong men and why they were fast runners, as well as being wise. They could be sent on assignments however great the distance, and however far they had run they must still pass on the news to the Indians or call on people who lived far away. The runners must not refuse.[13]

The Fox Indians told of three ceremonial runners: a leader, a successor and a number three. The last ceremonial runner of the Fox tribe was born a little before 1810: we do not know his name but we do, however, know a little about him, such as the fact that he fasted for ten days to purify himself for his initiation.

The next winter he fasted for twelve days and dreamed that he was told to go to a river in order to be blessed.[14] The lad went to the river, waited and heard a whistling, at which a tiny but handsome man appeared:

> I run round and round. Did you see how fast I move? Yes, I shall bless you, even though I can do nothing special and am not fit for any job. But who is to take over from me?

You will be very, very fast. You will call yourself 'ceremony runner' and that is what wise people will call you. They will be proud of you as long as you are a mortal man.

You will continue to help people in all possible ways. They will send you on difficult assignments, far from home, and you may not refuse. I shall give you the ability to be happy and courageous.[15]

This Fox runner was also given the ability to be invisible.

He lost his voice and began to behave differently. Then came a stream of instructions about how he should only follow the good and not think evil thoughts or dislike his running duties even if the errands were long and difficult. He should always start a journey from a southerly point and he should cast tobacco into the rivers and sing in honour of the gods, and this would bring him great strength and make him immune to bullets and arrows. Women were dangerous because they were infected by bad *manitou* – this meant menstruation. If there was a menstruating woman living close to the runner's residence, she would destroy him. Nevertheless, he should not speak badly of women.

The runner should neither gorge on meat nor leave food behind on the wooden plate he carried with him. If he desired meat on long trips, turtle dove and quail were best, since they could fly fast. He should bathe every evening, respect his elders and take care of his parents. He must always sleep outdoors on the south side of the huts and lie on the hide of a speckled deer he had shot himself. He was forbidden to wear anything red when he was carrying news of a death, since the blood had stopped flowing in a dead man. The runner should never jest on his journeys and he should pass on his information in a low voice even when fulfilling a herald's role – all Indian councils would pay heed to him anyway. He should never say anything negative or use bad words, nor should he speak ill of people or mock them. Theft was forbidden and he should treat children kindly.

This man, the last of the Fox ceremonial runners, remained unmarried all his life and became an important and respected individual. Around 1865 he carried out the task of warning of an approaching war and he died the following winter, at 56 years of age, after prophesying that the Fox Indians would be destroyed and wiped out, not by Indians but by white men. 'When the ceremonial runners are no more, there will be no one to tell you what is happening to you. You will find life difficult. Even when someone dies, there will be no one to pass on the news. Hold fast to your religion and do not desert your traditions or the white men will take advantage of it', the ceremonial runner said.

Half a century later the prophecy had almost reached fulfilment. None of the tribe fasted any more, none of them was fleet of foot and none of them had divine knowledge. A few ran errands but they were less caring than their predecessors. Even in the 1920s there were still those who were in charge of the ceremonial life among the Fox, but they were lazy and the traditions became hollow and disappeared. The young ignored their inheritance from the past and adopted the customs of the white men. Earlier, the Indians had been careful and vigilant because the runners gave them a direction and linked villages and families together.

That was also the case among the Chemehuevi tribe in the desert in the south of California, where there was a guild of runners who worked for the chieftains in war and in peace. They referred to each other as 'cousins', bound by a common occupation. When the anthropologist Carobeth Lairds studied them between the wars there was only one runner still working in the traditional way. He was called 'Rat Penis' and he was taciturn and modest. When he ran for fun with his friends, he did as they did, but when he ran alone he followed the traditions of the tribe and went into a trance.

One morning he left his friends at Cottonwood Island in Nevada and ran towards the Gila River in Arizona. His friends followed his tracks and they soon saw that his strides were becaming longer and longer and his footprints less and less visible in the sand: it was as if he was floating over it and scarcely touching the ground. When his friends reached Fort Yuma they heard that Rat Penis had long since passed through.

Typically enough, no one saw his special running technique: Rat Penis was not the recipient of supernatural assistance, he ran like that because he had the 'old knowledge'.[16]

Running for His Life

There are accounts of the settlers and the indigenous peoples running peaceful races when they met at markets but John Colter ended up in a much more serious situation in 1808 when he and his companion John Potts were paddling along the Jefferson River close to where the small town of Three Forks in Montana was later founded. The two trappers were stopping and checking their traps, then paddling on along their regular circuit, when 500 Blackfoot unexpectedly appeared on the river bank.

The trappers simply wanted to hunt but a misunderstanding arose and suddenly both Potts and one of the Blackfoot lay there dead, the trapper with several arrows in his body. Colter was captured and then watched how the Blackfoot hacked his companion's body to pieces.

They removed Colter's clothes and discussed how to put him to death. The first idea was to use him as a live target for their bows and arrows but then the chief asked whether Colter could run fast. He was 35 years old, strong and agile, an open-air man who had lived out in the wild and was generally tough.

'No', he answered tactically – he could not run *that* fast.

The Blackfoot gave the trapper a chance. Accounts differ as to whether they gave him a start of 100 or 400 yards. Whichever it was, with his life at stake he ran naked and barefoot in front of six chasing Blackfoot across eight miles of flat prairie, heading for the nearest woods that grew along the Madison River.

Colter ran faster than he had ever run before, keeping in front of the Blackfoot, who had reckoned on catching their prey. His pursuers were catching up and halfway across the prairie Colter's feet were slashed open by sharp stones. Exhausted and despairing he saw one man immediately behind him catching up fast. He stopped suddenly, turned round and killed the man.

He reached the Madison River on the point of passing out with exhaustion, leapt in and hid under a floating island, and there he lay motionless while his pursuers searched for him. After dark he moved quietly on, heading for a trading post a good 200 miles away at the confluence of the Bighorn and Yellowstone Rivers. He crossed Lost Trail Pass in snow, drank spring water and lived on wild roots for the whole week that his journey took.

The look-out at Fort Lisa saw a horrific sight approaching; naked, bloody and impossible to recognize, Colter collapsed in the arms of the men sent out to meet him.

Few people believed the story but Colter was no braggart. He lived for two more years in the wilderness before moving to St Louis, getting married and then buying a farm near Dundee in Montana. Before he died of Yellow Fever at the age of forty in 1813, he gave an account of this run, the most dramatic event of his life, to the naturalist John Bradbury. In Bradbury's 1819 book *Travels in the Interior of North America*, there is a version of the story based on Colter's own account. At the end of the 1970s, 'Colter's Run' was organized, an eight-mile race in memory of the event.[17]

On Ice-floes and in the Rainforest

The original inhabitants of all the Americas ran. During the 'Bladder Festival' in January, the Nunivak Eskimo in the coldest regions held sprint competitions on the ice and snow in honour of their dead. They paddled first and then ran immediately afterwards in a double exercise that trained the whole body,

In a totally different environment, the Payacú people lived at the mouth of the Amazon in Brazil.[18] More than twenty tribes in this damp, hot climate ran races and carried logs – all other sport was unimportant compared with the timber-log run. Even women ran, although less frequently and carrying lighter logs. But the men competed all year round, either on impulse or at fixed festivals. They needed no encouragement to chop down a log and challenge one another.

European explorers and researchers have referred to the custom ever since the sixteenth century but it is much older than that. The Kraho believe that their progenitors, the Sun and the Moon, performed it and passed it down to their human descendants.[19]

The log race was held on cleared tracks, a mile or so in length and running to the four points of the heavens - the main tracks. They would cut angles in logs three feet long and weighing from 100–200 lb (45–90 kg) so as to get a better grip on them and to provide better balance on their shoulders. When they could not manage to go any farther, the log was passed on to the next man in the chain.

In Sherente every boy was assigned to one of two tribal teams, and in Apinaye the teams depended on where one's hut was in the village. In other cases the composition of teams varied with the season of the year and the purpose of the race. Tribes would challenge each other and it could easily end in quarrels.

The ethnographer Curt Numuendaju witnessed a race in which the teams sang good-luck songs the evening before while whipping up team spirit as a group. On the day of the competition, they first of all inspected the track and then prepared the logs, laying them out neatly at the side. The opposition announced their arrival by blowing a horn and the teams began to sing and stamp to warm up. Four men lifted a log up onto the shoulders of the first bearer and he set off quickly in the direction of the village, accompanied by a shouting crowd of slim, naked men who kept to their own half of the track.

> To ensure a good start, the first man was always fast: a headlong chase then begins. Screaming encouragement at the runners, blowing on trumpets and other instruments, the Indians leap to the right and left of the log-carrier's path, waving grass decorations and jumping over grass and bushes. After 150 yards someone runs up to the log-carrier who, without stopping, twists his body so that he can pass over the burden to his team-mate's shoulders and the race continues without interruption. And so it goes on, desperately, down hilly paths in baking sunshine, over streams and uphill again, through burning, loose sand that gives way beneath the feet.[20]

Women, the old and the men who had been at the start soon fell behind. Only the most vigorous could keep pace and ensure that new men took over the burden when the last man was so exhausted that the pace dropped. Desperate to stay in front, each man gave his all for a few seconds and gave a signal when he was ready to hand over. After a half a mile or so it was back to the most vigorous in the village again. The shouting was no longer so loud, the stages became shorter and more painful and it was good to be doused with water by the women along the course. But no one would throw the log to the ground, however far in front they were.

At last the village was in sight. In one last great effort the runners forced themselves on and carried the log 30 or 40 yards (27–36 m) before their legs went stiff, but then there were always new hands and new shoulders to take the relay on towards the finishing point in the village, where the log was dropped to the ground.

There were no scenes of triumph or sighs of disappointment afterwards. Neither the winners nor the losers received praise or blame. The angry mood, the yells and mad rush along the course a few moments earlier came to a sudden end and they were all friends again. The English anthropologist David Maybury-Lewis, encouraged by the tribesmen, took part in a race of this kind during the 1950s. In this case the winners made fun of the losers at the end, but the losers did not respond and merely went indoors to eat. The winning team belonged to the Kraho tribe from 150 miles away and they mocked their hosts' running abilities: they were incompetent, did not know how to celebrate feasts properly, were all talk and so on. When they heard it, the losers simply grinned. The following day the teams challenged each other again. Now the tables were turned: 'the Kraho don't know how to run', commented one of the Sherente with a sneer, even though the opposite had been proved true the day before. 'Fit for nothing but talk – that's all the Kraho can do. They don't work. They don't plant their vegetable plots. All they do is run log-races at home and yet they can't do it properly when they come here.'[21]

One can wonder why the attitudes changed so quickly. This time the Kraho could not care less whereas the Sherente were racing not just for fun but to prove something. Maybury-Lewis, however, failed to come up with an explanation. The next morning the tribes ran another race, this time starting many miles from the village.

The symbolic and practical meanings of the custom are not clear. A number of researchers believed that the tribes were competing to improve their chances in the marriage market, but the participants were anything from fifteen to fifty and many were already married. In the 1930s the ethnographer Curt Nimuendaju rejected the suggestions that it was a marriage ritual. Another theory argued that the log symbolized a human being and that the Kraho were attempting to protect themselves against evil influences. The tribes themselves responded to questions about the symbolism with very vague answers: it seems likely it was a combination of symbolic act and sport – with the main emphasis on the latter.

Tarahumara

Sport was also an important activity among the Tarahumara in Mexico. Of all the Native American tribes they were the most famous for running. They refer to themselves as *raràmuri* – 'those who run', 'those who are light on their feet'. Tarahumara is the Spanish form of the name of the tribe that lives in the federal state of Chihuahua in the north of Mexico. The Norwegian explorer Carl Lumholtz studied them at close quarters in the 1890s. The Tarahumara knew nothing of sporting arenas and stopwatches, knew nothing of modern athletics – they simply ran, as they had done for hundreds of years. 'There can be no doubt that the Tarahumara are world champions when it comes to running, not because of speed but because of endurance. A Tarahumara can easily run 160 miles continuously. If one of them is sent off with a message, he lopes off at a slow trot and neither stops nor takes a break.'

Lumholtz heard of men who had carried letters from Guazapares to Chihuahua in five days, a distance of 625 miles (1,000 km) by road, during which they only drank water and ate plants they picked along the way. When they worked for the Mexicans they were often given the job of catching horses, which they would bring in in two or three days. They would also chase deer, whether it was raining or snowing, until the animals were so exhausted that they became easy targets for their arrows.[22]

They were particularly fond of races between teams consisting of four to twenty runners, who kicked a small ball along in front of them. It could go on for hours, all day and all night sometimes, back and forth along a course that was often laid out on a flat mountain ridge. They might run a fifteen-mile (24-km) course anything up to twelve times, so a total distance of 165 miles (265 km).

These men were trained up to performances of this kind from a very young age and the hilly, rough terrain of the Sierra Tarahumara fostered tough and tireless men who ran long distances as a matter of course. Special dietary rules, celibacy, good luck rituals and magic were practised among them when it came to important races. Shamans helped the team captains, offered sacrifices to their ancestors and buried human bones under the track to impair the opposition. If a runner passed over these bones he would lose strength and energy. Every weapon in the tribe's arsenal of magic would be used to weaken their opponents and achieve victory.

The onlookers bet heavily on the result. Even though the Indians had few possessions they would wager clothes, tools and even valuable domestic livestock. After all the bets were laid and a stone set out for each circuit to be completed in each round, they were ready to start. The organizer of the race then made a speech warning them against cheating or touching the ball with their hands – a hand ball would lead straight to Hell.

Once the starting signal was given the runners dropped their blankets and ran after the ball that had been thrown ahead of them. It was a noisy field, with animal skulls and other things clattering on their belts to prevent them falling asleep. They did not sprint away from the start, everything was done at a steady, gentle pace of seven or eight miles an hour (11–13 k/ph, though fast teams might cover eighteen miles (29 km) in two hours.

Rarely in world history can there have been such active spectators. They followed along the course, pointing out the ball when it disappeared, particularly in the dark, and happily ran long distances in order to get a good view of the competition. Women would heat water and give it to the men as they passed and, when darkness fell, the spectators lit torches and carried them in front of the runners to light up the trails and the terrain.

As time passed many of the runners gave up but the number of spectators and the cheering increased until there was only one man left or the leader was very far in front of the others. There was no prize for the winner apart from honour and praise, but he often received gifts from people who had won their bets.[23]

Why Did the Native Americans Run?

The Native Americans ran for many reasons. Running was sacred and mythic, a thread that linked people and that linked the tribes and the gods. But it was also an important practical skill: 'Long ago the Hopi did not have horses and had to hunt on foot. They had to train their legs, think hard and pray hard to make their legs fast. Men tried as hard as they could to out-do one another in running, that's why they ran.'[24]

Another Hopi said that they had always run far and fast and the clouds rejoiced to see the development of young people, and they heard the prayers for rain. The Hopi knew that running improved the health, elimi-nated sadness, firmed up the body and increased vitality – basically the same arguments as those of a modern jogger.

Running for the Native Americans was an intrinsic part of everyday life and was something they had to master for both serious and pleasura-ble purposes; and it was a good way of getting on in the world. Some tribes retained the running tradition long after the white settlers had forced them into reservations, but even those tribes lapsed into indolence.

Many theories have been proposed to explain what running meant to the Indians. Stewart Culin, who travelled the world studying sport and games among aboriginal people as his main field of research, published *Games of the North American Indians* in 1905.[25] He argued that both secular and religious games and practices had their origins in 'extremely ancient *idées fixes*' and were performed to stave off disease, to make rain and to increase crops. The competitions arose as part of the struggle to survive and to give the tribal peoples identity – sporting traditions demonstrate that. In the practice and accounts of Native American athletics and games he found reflexions of creation and origin myths. They reflected the beliefs the Native Americans held about their own past.

But many Native Americans also ran in order to win fame and earn money in the white man's world.

12
Bluffing and Handicapping

He trained on a box of cigars, his pipe and tobacco – and copious
amounts of sherry.
—On Sambo Cobo, Australian Aborigine and professional
runner in the 1880s

In the late summer of 1861 the Native American Lewis Bennett, 'Deerfoot',
went aboard a ship sailing from New York City to England. The English running promoter George Martin had discovered the 30-year-old running star
and promised him success and affluence if he accompanied him to England.

He saw the potential in Deerfoot – he had a good figure and he was
bold and charismatic, qualities that would feed the European stereotypes
and romantic perception of Native Americans. Novels and reports had given
rise to vivid fantasies about Native Americans and letters home from
friends and relations who had emigrated told of the settlers' conflict with them,
of scalpings, torture and savagery in a part of the world where the native
inhabitants lived in a covenant with nature.

Deerfoot had competed against a type of runner common in the
United States in the 1860s – the bluffer, who sprinted for bets. They were
called 'Ringers' and the name has spread to all four corners of the world.[1]
A ringer disguised himself as an ordinary man or as a drunk or vagrant. He
would arrive at a town or a village, preferably one where no one knew him,
and visit the drinking dens or wherever men gathered. He would mutter
about his achievements and boast about his ability as a runner. If the man
knew what he was doing, it would not be long before someone was provoked into challenging him and willing to lay money on it: they were eager
to see an outsider lose face and money – and even more eager to win both
for themselves.

If the fastest man in the town was not already present, they would send
for him, and then it was often just a case of going outside, roping off the
street at each end and getting going. Friends of the local sprinter were
happy to bet on their man.

So there they stood, a stranger and a local lad, neither of them knowing
the standard of the other. Looking down the street they would see expectant
spectators, hear the shouting and feel the pre-race tension and excitement.

There was a crack as the pistol fired into the air and they were off in a
cloud of dust while the spectators roared enthusiastically – after all, their
investments were at stake.

The ringer had everything to lose, even if – as far as the crowd was concerned – he was the one who had made a fool of himself by whipping up the betting. The best of the ringers knew exactly what they were up to, made sure there was some drama along the way, adjusted their winning margins and acted surprised when they won – as if it was the first time it had happened.

For the ringer it was all about bluffing, running and staying calm before moving on promptly. If he was a real expert no one suspected the confidence trick and he could move on to the saloon in the next town, pull up a bar-stool and lie his way into his next job. If the fiddle and his true identity were uncovered, however, the ringer really did need his speed since there were likely to be threats and violence from an angry crowd: then it was time to move on rapidly, to avoid trying any more tricks in that area and even to change his hairstyle, grow a beard and buy new clothes.

Henry Crandell from Niles in Michigan was one of the smartest ringers of the 1860s. He targeted California, the goldrush state, sparsely populated but with busy and rich districts around the diggings. He won so many challenges and wagers under his assumed name of Grainger that he was pitted against the fastest man on the west coast – and beat him by a clear 75 yards (69 m).

The usual prize was gold-dust. In Colorado Springs he beat Milliard Stone and left there a wealthy man. Immediately after that, in Pueblo in the same state, he set up a new contest. Crandell wrote to Colorado Springs inviting people there to come to Pueblo and bet on him in an easy race – he claimed he had a bad conscience because they had lost so much by betting on him earlier.

Excited by his gesture and the tip he had given them people laid money and possessions on him and many of them actually went to Pueblo. But Crandell, who had no equal as a sprinter in any of the surrounding states, deliberately came second so that his 'friends' lost and were cleaned out. It was a straight swindle.

Henry Crandell had conned the citizens of Colorado Springs for the second time and now he was in danger of being lynched. According to the newspaper *The Mountaineer* Crandell left the town by train, taking his luggage and his new wealth with him. The paper commented that if he had sprinted half as fast in the race as he ran to the train he would have won the race. The visitors from Colorado Springs were both disappointed and broke – and unable to pay for either food or lodgings. They were given a free meal and lodgings before being sent home by train (at Pueblo's expense) the following day, by now aware of their own incredible gullibility.[2]

Similar tactics were used by George Seward, who was born in New Haven, Connecticut, in 1817. He revealed his unusual speed and agility while still a boy by jumping over a standing horse. Running under his professional name, 'Down East Yankee', he beat William Belden, one of the fastest men in the country, in 1841 and after that no one would take on Seward in a wager race.

He looked towards England and signed on under a false name as a seaman on a ship bound for Liverpool. When he went ashore he went to an
inn where wager races were organized. Many inns had laid out running
tracks close by, thus increasing their trade when the thirsty spectators frequented the bar before and after the races. Anyone wanting to start out as
a runner would come to such a place and the owner would organize things,
send out invitations and advertise in the paper.

Seward knew the set-up when he arrived at an inn in Liverpool. He
kept his ears and eyes open and asked to meet no one less than Jack Fowler.

What! Did this stranger really intend to take on Jack Fowler, known to
be the fastest man in England outside London, over a hundred yards?

'Yes,' answered Seward, but only if he was given a short lead at the start.

He could certainly have his lead, this greenhorn from America, and it
looked like being easy money for the Englishmen.

Seward hung around the inn in the days before the race. He was dressed
in his seaman's clothes, talked in a broad, foreign accent and he listened to
the laughter and teasing of the Englishmen who were having some fun at
the expense of this naive American. The grins got wider when Seward strut-
ted around the track on the day of the race dressed in an elegant hat, big
boots and trousers as if that was suitable attire for sprinting. Then Seward
stripped off his shirt and heavy boots and trotted round in silk tights and
running shoes, suddenly transformed into a full-blooded runner. He started
– and won – in front of a crowd that was gaping in amazement.

Seward did not get any more races in Liverpool but he toured England,
competing with great success over distances from a hundred yards to a mile
and sometimes in steeplechases and hurdles. In order to encourage re-
matches he won by as little as possible, more interested in victory and profit
than in times. His record of 9¼ seconds for the 100 yards (91.4 m) was set in
Hammersmith in the autumn of 1844 and attests to his enormous ability,
as do his best times over 120 yards (110 m, 11 1/8 seconds) and 200 yards (183
m, 19½ seconds).[3] When converted into metres these times remained at an
international elite level well into the twentieth century in spite of the fact
that Seward was competing in primitive conditions, with a standing start,
no spikes in his shoes and running on uneven, badly prepared tracks. After
more than 25 years as a professional he settled in Liverpool and returned to
his old trade as a silversmith.[4]

Seward made a good living out of athletics because the tradition of
wager races was firmly rooted in both the United States and Great Britain.

An 'Indian' in the City

It was these stars that Deerfoot was going to challenge when he disem-
barked in England in the late summer of 1861, having been well-drilled by
his manager George Martin in how to behave in what was regarded as 'the
Indian manner'.

Deerfoot was a sensation in England and, according to Martin, had never competed before, having only run when hunting his prey in the wilderness. He was supposed not to understand English and his trainer Jack MacDonald communicated using sign language. Martin leaked stories and anecdotes to the press which, given its power to create and sustain myths, added some itself. Deerfoot's image as a child of nature stirred up interest in the polluted, noisy city of London and his manager's sense of theatre meant that everything was inflated even more.

Deerfoot appealed to a wider public than just the sporting men. He was part of the European tradition of exhibiting 'wild natives', whether they were Africans, Aborigines or Pygmies. There was a worldwide industry in the exotic and the unfamiliar in the middle of the nineteenth century and whenever anything spectacular turned up anywhere in the world, whether live animals or dead fossils, the American impresario P. T. Barnum and others like him would collect them. So the visit of a Native American to England during the American Civil War (1861–5) fitted in very well.

When Deerfoot made his debut at the Metropolitan Ground he started by walking round the circuit cloaked in wolfskin and wearing a headband and feathers, an exact replica of the spectators' stereotype of a 'fine Indian'. In this first run of six miles (9,654 m) Deerfoot demonstrated his usual fartlek tactics. He was flirting with the spectators and the cheering and admiration for the noble savage grew with every sprint. He continued in this uneven tempo and lost in a time a little over 32 minutes 30 seconds.

The British spectators and journalists were ecstatic. A journalist from the *New York Clipper*, however, saw through the deception in Deerfoot's performance more easily than the English – to an American he was less exotic. On the orders of his trainer Deerfoot competed according to a plan by which he would win and lose alternate races in order to keep interest high.

Deerfoot ran with a bare torso, wearing thick rings on his fingers and bells on his ankles. He screamed victorious war-cries during his final spurt and his face was daubed with war-paint. He lied in answer to questions about food and sleep and did everything Martin asked in order to reinforce his marketable myth.

Artists painted him and sold lithographs by the thousand, which people hung on their walls. Deerfoot met the Prince of Wales and other members of the nobility, and he was the centre of receptions and guest of honour at great houses. When ladies started surrounding the arena in order to admire his brown torso, he began to cover himself up. By 16 December 1861, his last appearance of the autumn, Deerfoot was worn out and he was getting some criticism in the British press.

Following various claims about race-fixing and rumours that Deerfoot had an alcohol problem and was homesick, he went on the offensive in 1862 and set an unofficial world record of 11 miles 729 yards (18,412 metres) for a one-hour run. By the time he left England in 1863 after a stay of twenty months, he was popular and had inspired many people to take up running.

The name Deerfoot nourished all the fantasies about his glorious race – it had the same aura and potency as Hiawatha, the Indian boy in Henry W. Longfellow's poem who could run at superhuman speeds. In a strange way Deerfoot found a niche in the English national consciousness and stimulated their curiosity about so-called primitive peoples.

Imaginative Tricks

In the second half of the nineteenth century professional running was particularly strong in Britain, the United States, South Africa and New Zealand – with the exception of the United States, all members of the British Empire.

Major meetings, mostly for sprinters, were held in London, Sheffield, Manchester, Birmingham and Newcastle. An enduring sprint tradition began in 1870 at the Powderhall Grounds in Edinburgh in Scotland and still continues – it is now in its third century. And the Stawell Gift in Stawell, Victoria, Australia, which began in 1879 as a fun-run among the gold-diggers, is still an annual event. The most colourful professional running culture of the latter part of the nineteenth century grew up in Australia, which by 1868 had received close to 100,000 British convicts.

The discovery of gold in Australia in 1850 attracted fortune-seekers from all over the world. The gold-diggers were soon challenging one another to races for gold dust or nuggets, with their cheering mates as spectators. In a typical male society of this kind, with its strong pioneering spirit, athletics and running became one of many measures of a man's strength.

Both professional and amateur running in Australia and elsewhere during this period often took the form of handicap starts. They hardly exist at all nowadays though they were common everywhere in professional races and sometimes in amateur races up to the Second World War – and even later in some places.

The principle is both simple and complicated. Slower runners start first and run shorter distances than the best runners. They are given a handicap, that is, an advantage. Theoretically it means that any inequalities in standard are levelled out at the start in order to make the result and the betting less predictable. The peculiar thing about this kind of professional running was that its practitioners did not try to win every competition or even aim for the best possible time: they targeted particular races, often years ahead, and trained and competed with them in mind. Trainers guided the process and taught the runners how to build up the necessary resources for the great occasions and thus enhance their chances of winning. It was a crafty kind of under-achievement but always with the ultimate bull's-eye in mind.

There were at least a hundred professional runners making a living at this sport in Sydney and Melbourne between 1885 and 1890. A trainer might have up to six or seven men in his stable, all competing simultaneously. Since the sport revolved almost exclusively around sprinting, it was dominated by naturally talented runners who did not need a great deal of training. The Aborigine Sambo Combo, who ran the 100 yards in 9.1 seconds in 1888, was a runner of this kind. He was said to train on 'a box of cigars, his pipe and tobacco and copious amounts of sherry'.[5]

The competitions were often dramatic as, for instance, when the Irish-man Matt Higgins met the Australian Tom Cusack in the latter's home-town of Wangaratta in 1869. The local patriots went for him with sabotage in mind when he arrived two weeks in advance with his trainer and two assis-tants. When Higgins showed himself to be in stunning form, the inhabitants of Wangaratta grew concerned and there is some suspicion that poisoning was the cause of him being horribly sick the day before the race. The spec-tators even hurled stones and threats through the window when he was changing in the cloakroom.

Higgins was still pushing his way through the crowd when the starting pistol for the 100 yards went off too early, but the men were about equal at the finish. One spectator punched Higgins. In the next race Cusack false-started again and won – and once again Higgins was laid flat on his back by a punch. When Higgins won the 300 yards and they were equal in terms of points, Cusack's supporters went berserk and hurled more stones through the cloakroom window.

Higgins lined up for the final race, the 200 yards, apparently unmoved by the cheating, the threats and the crowd pressing in on him. A local chim-ney-sweep had climbed up in a tree and crashed down close to Higgins on the track but Higgins carried on and, to the great annoyance of the mob, won. After the finish Higgins ran as fast as he could and barricaded himself in his hotel, fearing for his life and with good reason to keep well away from the crowd. Cusack's financial backers lost £3,000 that day, in addition to two other defeats immediately before.[6]

This lawless running culture led to epoch-making news stories that benefited the rest of the sport.

It was at Carrington Ground, Sydney, Australia in 1887 that the abori-ginal runner Bobby McDonald leapt up from a crouching position and took a clear lead in a sprint race. The onlookers and competitors were astonished: what sort of starting style was this supposed to be? In the next round, which was the semi-final, McDonald recognized that he had an advantage and once again took a clear lead and won easily. After some serious discus-sion and suggestions of cheating and unfair advantage, the judge banned the new starting style for the final.

In his next race McDonald once again took up a crouching stance, shot away and took first place. His opponents protested and the judges refused him permission to use the technique.

McDonald had discovered this starting position by chance. He tended to feel cold before the start of a race and crouched down to shelter from the wind in what later became the 'on-your-marks' position. One evening, while he was still in this position, the starter fired his pistol unexpectedly,

McDonald instinctively started and noticed that his acceleration was faster and his balance better than from an upright start. But he had to cease using it when the judges brought in a ban.

Harry Bushell, a white Australian runner, was experimenting with this stance at about the same time. He dug two small holes to give him a kick start and noticed that he reached his maximum speed faster this way. When he threw away the pieces of cork that runners of that time squeezed in their fists when they were pushing themselves extra hard, he found he relaxed more and achieved a better flow.

After a lot of practice Bushell tried out the crouching position in the Carrington Handicap and won. The public clearly saw the advantage of the method but one of the competitors protested. The jury dismissed the protest and from then on the crouching start spread across Australia and the rest of the world.[7]

We cannot be sure whether he was the first to do it, but there was an Aborigine in the 1890s who entered a sprint at Carrington Ground. He was given a good handicap and turned up in the evening ready to give his all under the gas-lamps – though the start and the finish of the course were in complete darkness. The men managing the Aborigine painted a white runner black so that people took him for the Aborigine. On the starter's command, the painted runner shot out of the darkness and won, but then continued at full speed back into the dark. He quickly donned a heavy coat and was led away on the quiet while the Aborigine, who had meantime been hiding dressed in identical running kit, jogged back to the judges and was proclaimed the winner. His supporters won a good deal of money.[8]

Big-time Australian runners from the towns also travelled out to the country districts to challenge local heroes. A bookmaker would accompany them, the amount of ready cash in his wallet governing the sums that could be wagered in this unscrupulous business.

A party arrived at a meeting in Hungerford, New South Wales, and entered their sprinter under a false name. As usual, people at the hotel were discussing the race and whether the visitors would beat the local boys.

'Our man is unbeatable', the Hungerford men said.

'There's a woman in our party good enough to beat him', one of the visitors said sarcastically.

The locals immediately accepted the challenge to run their man against the woman.

'OK, but only in the evening and on the main street', the visitors said, knowing that the lighting was bad.

That evening the course was paced out, the public came in droves and all eyes were on the woman. She stormed away and won sensationally, then disappeared just as rapidly into the hotel before quickly moving on to a neighbouring town.

There the nimble lady decided to appear in a charity concert. Some Hungerford men recognized her on the stage and addressed her brusquely, at which she jumped down and disappeared again: here, as elsewhere, the confidence trickster had to move fast. This smooth-chinned male sprinter was an expert at donning women's clothing and playing the woman in women's clothes.[9]

Entertaining hoaxes of this kind angered those people who, by the end of the nineteenth century and the start of the twentieth, were calling for pure and clean amateur athletics.

To understand amateur athletics, in this case running, it is not enough just to be familiar with the rules of amateurism, it is also necessary to know what the amateurs were against – to know how the professional form of running worked. By examining the latter, the attitudes of the amateurs become more understandable. 'We don't want it to be like that!' they said. No one was more familiar with professional running than the British, which is why they took centre stage in the international amateur associations for many years.

Amateurs disliked the way professionals would cheat in order to fix handicapping decisions and ensure that they would be given an advantageous starting position at big meetings. They objected, too, to participants betting on their own races and thus making money. Professionals also learned to run 'dead', that is to say, to produce a worse performance than they were capable of in order to fool the opposition. This could be done in a number of ways, such as training hard on the morning of or immediately before a meeting so that the runner was unable to produce his best performance – to slow down during the race itself was, of course, too easy to detect. And even if those setting the handicaps knew that fixing was going on, it was still better to cheat discreetly. The Australian Roger Best explained his method of slowing himself down when he was on top form: 'I would go to Monash University on the way to the meeting and run two 400-metre runs flat out, one straight after the other so that I felt sick. Then I would go to the meeting.' In the course of two years he was never accused of cheating or of performing below his best.[10]

Others were less competent at bluffing. The Australian John Whitson lessened his chances of winning at big meetings because he was unable to lower his pace in races that would decide his handicap without it being too obvious. After one training session a friend's coach brought him a pair of insoles to go in his running shoes:

> He had coated the underside of the insoles with lead and each of them weighed nearly ten ounces. For the whole of that season I ran with these lead weights. The only way to be caught was if someone was nearby when you took off your shoes and then you'd have to pick them up yourself since they looked like other running shoes with insoles. But you couldn't let anyone else lift your training bag because it was the heaviest in town. I got through the whole season without being talked to by the judges.[11]

Middle and long-distance runners had a wider choice of tricks than sprinters. The runners could run on the outside of the track or position themselves so they were boxed in and blocked in the final sprint. They might drink fizzy drinks and eat hamburgers or other inappropriate food before the start, or a crowd of them might go out on a hard training run immediately before an important race. The idea was to dupe the judges, who travelled around checking on participants' performances with a view to setting future handicaps.[12]

In Australia in the 1920s all of this became positively mafia-like thanks to the 'Black Hand Gang' – a group that recruited runners and fixed races systematically. The activities of the gang caused ripples far beyond the Commonwealth of Australia and they became so powerful that they challenged the official authorities. The young men recruited by the gang were under strict orders not to inform on it and it took ten years of investigations, endless hearings and a lot of detective work to put an end to the conspiracy.

Six Days at a Stretch

These races lasted for six days because on the seventh day God and man should rest. Six-day races were most popular in the United States and England during the 1880s. The races were held indoors in warehouses or in the newly built rinks for roller-skating and the spectators spent the long hours gaping, eating, smoking and betting. The competitions were called 'Go as you please', and that is exactly what the participants did, walking, jogging or staggering with exhaustion.

The first six-day race for bicycles was organized in Birmingham in 1875 and the six-day races on foot were inspired by this; pedestrian races also played their part in the new development, but the six-day races were much more commercial. Participants could move in any way they chose: they often ran at the start, walked later and staggered at the end of these bizarre endurance events. It all took place in carefully regulated conditions, yards and miles being carefully counted. To us it may seem unbearably tedious to run and plod around short, badly ventilated indoor tracks with anything up to 50 laps a mile – the tracks could be as short as 35 yards (32 m) – with spectators at very close quarters, but six-day races were novel spectacles, even if boringly protracted.

The American Edward Payson Weston (1839–1929) was an important figure in the origin and popularity of six-day events. He was a pedestrian racer and entertainer, not a runner, whose walking feats from 1861 on were given huge coverage in the press. Even though he walked alone rather than risk defeat, his feats intensified the rivalry between pedestrians and long-distance runners in Britain. In the years following 1877 he visited Britain a number of times and made a name for himself there, too.[13]

The 1870s and '80s witnessed a great flurry of tough challenges over 12 hours, 24 hours, 48 hours and 72 hours, or over 25 miles, 50 miles or 100 miles.[14] One purely betting exercise in the United States was called 'walking the plank' and entailed walking along a plank or bench between five and fifteen yards (4.5–14m) long for as many hours as possible – 100 hours was not out of the question either for men or women.[15]

Many of those taking part in the six-day races in New York in the 1880s came from the poor potato farms of Ireland and were prepared to make any sacrifice necessary to win, but as well as the Irish there were Scandinavians, Germans and Italians. They were competitors with international ambitions who had crossed the Atlantic to meet new opponents and to find new markets. Just as Americans in Europe stirred up interest, fresh European arrivals were welcome in the United States. They were known by smart nicknames and their careers rarely lasted long in this ruthless business with its cheating, its fixed races and short-lived fame.

By the end of the 1880s the interest in six-day races tailed off in New York and other American cities, but what had started out as a city phenomenon spread to small towns, lumberjack camps and mining communities – anywhere with a big male population. The tightly knit cohort of distance runners, just like a circus troupe, moved on to Nevada, Michigan, Wisconsin and other states. The Alaska gold-rush at the end of the 1890s attracted runners looking for a new market. Just like capitalists, they moved wherever fortunes were being made and money was easy. At Nome in Alaska they competed in huge log-cabins in front of an audience of rough golddiggers who defied the cold to live in a settlement that grew from nothing to 18,000 in two or three years.

Women too, particularly from Britain and the United States, competed in six-day and long-distance races. The men tended to alternate between jogging and walking whereas the women almost always walked, partly because it was unseemly for them to run but also because of their clothes: long skirts and petticoats were the only socially acceptable woman's clothing.

It was an entertainment business, pure and simple, just as among men, but it was also a part of the struggle for more exercise for women, in the same period as women were being given the right to higher education in several countries. High schools specifically for girls were opened in Britain, the United States and elsewhere in the 1860s and '70s and women began to achieve rights in what had been male domains. They did exercise at their boarding schools and walked a great deal but were advised to avoid overexerting themselves physically so as not to impair their fertility. The possibility that exercise might impair childbearing ability was a cause of fear among women, husbands and fathers for many years.

Tests of endurance were part of the spirit of the age. Two English women swam six miles (9.6 km) in the Thames in London in the middle of the 1870s while thousands watched them from the river-banks. Men and women marched against each other around circus rings as a test of women's endurance – this made the newspaper headlines on both sides of the Atlantic.

Bertha von Hillern came from Germany originally but in the second half of the 1870s she was matched in several hard-fought duels in the United States against the American-born Mary Marshall. When they walked against each other for six days in Chicago and in New York in 1875 and 1876 thousands of spectators had to stand outside the ground since all the tickets were sold out.

At two performances in the Music Hall in Boston in 1876 over 10,000 people paid to get a glimpse of this elegant, well-dressed woman whose picture sold by the thousand and whose hat was declared to be the latest fashion. Von Hillern was a fine example for women who wanted to take exercise. This modest and deeply religious young woman was concerned about what Christian people thought of her and she feared the wrath of the Lord: although barely twenty years old, unlike many female sports stars she was not presented as a sex object.

Her main public in the United States was made up of respectable citizens, churchmen, lawyers, fine ladies and doctors. The medical men applauded her achievements and pointed to her as the female model for exercise and care of the body. In spite of her popularity, or perhaps because of it, she gave up appearing and settled to a respectable life in Boston. Long-distance walking was one way of going up in the world and, in her case, earning money, making a name for herself and making a good marriage.

Madam Anderson from England was a complete contrast to von Hillern: a muscular, outspoken and middle-aged woman who had been an actress and a clown before she entered the competitive walking business in her home country in 1877. Whereas von Hillern had usually completed her performances within 24 hours, Madam Anderson would continue for days and weeks and came close to the best of the men in terms of the miles she covered. She trained with William Gale, one of the best endurance trainers of the time, and sang, tumbled and gave short speeches. She had several helpers on her road to success: her husband, her manager and a medical assistant. Behind Anderson's performances, which were spiced up by a masculine intake of alcohol during the competitions, there was concealed a smart, well-trained businesswoman who considered herself ethical in everything she did.

Anderson was more of a challenge to the ideals of the age than von Hillern. She was a twice-married, half-Jewish working-class woman who set about making her own fortune quite systematically. Many in Britain were angered both by the fact that she would compete on the Sabbath and that she went to the United States in 1878 to make more money and win more fame. The American reaction was similar when, in San Francisco in 1879, she wrapped herself in the American flag during the final lap and thanked God for the tens of thousands of dollars she had earned.[16]

There were over a hundred professional woman pedestrians competing in the cities of the United States in the year that Anderson arrived in New York. Women boxers and trapeze artists tried their hand at this business, along with young women straight off the immigrant ships from Europe.

The interest in women's six-day races died away quickly during the 1880s and it is worth speculating why. Warnings from religious and medical quarters had an effect on the women, as did the arrest of competitors and local bans. After the initial novelty, interest had calmed down and the cramped, unhygienic and fire-hazardous venues gave the performances a bad name. There was also the fact that entertainment phenomena had a short shelf-life in the United States, a society in constant change in the hunt for money, but the six-day runs for women in the 1870s and '80s were, nevertheless, a first flush of physical pride by women and an interesting pointer to the future.[17]

The Beginnings of Modern Track Sports

Developments in Britain in the second half of the nineteenth century had enormous significance for sport and athletics. One important source of inspiration came from the Highland Games in Scotland. These all-round games, which featured the first hill-race in Scotland, have roots going back to the eleventh century and have survived through the centuries to celebrate Celtic and Scottish culture. The tradition was strong in the Scottish Highlands, the homeland of the clans, and the games, including log-carrying, throwing heavy weights and running, spread in the nineteenth century to England, the United States, Canada and the many British colonies with Scottish immigrants. They are a way of paying homage to the home country and of celebrating solidarity with one's countrymen. Modern athletics are partly modelled on the disciplines in the Highland Games.

The world was looking to Great Britain in this period and Scots and Englishmen took the lead in many sporting activities that later became Olympic simply because the British were engaged in them. To understand the rise of modern sport and running it is essential to know what was happening in Britain in the nineteenth century. It is also important to bear in mind the flourishing tradition of professional running, which drew in all social classes and which therefore forced the English upper classes to define their own sports – without cash prizes and, ideally, free from corruption and cheating.

Pedestrianism, which in Britain covered both walking and running races but here refers only to the latter, was mainly a sport for the working classes in a country where class-consciousness was very strong. English gentlemen, with plenty of leisure time, estates and fortunes, belonged to a totally different social level to the majority of runners in the middle of the nineteenth century. There were a few, like Sir John Astley (1828–1894), who was an officer, who entered races in the company of men of the lower classes and referred to themselves as amateurs. When he was in his prime in the 1850s, 'amateur' implied a gentleman, whether or not he was competing for money, and a gentleman did not *need* to win money from sport, which in turn implied a degree of superiority. Strictly speaking, a gentleman did not work but lived on the interest from his fortune or income from his property.

What was happening at the main English universities, Oxford and Cambridge, had major knock-on effects. These were places where men from the upper classes spent important formative years and entered long-lasting friendships. In 1850 Exeter College, Oxford, organized a race and other colleges at Oxford and Cambridge later followed suit and began to develop an appreciation for athletics, in which running was a core activity.

This interest was related to what became known as Muscular Christianity, an education for young men in which athletics was a tool for creating Christian gentlemen. This spread to other countries, firstly to boarding schools but then via Young Men's Christian Associations.

A number of athletics associations were founded in England at the beginning of the 1860s, the most important of which was the Amateur Athletics Club (AAC), founded in London in 1866 by John Chambers, who had graduated from Cambridge that year. The invitations to the first meeting the following year stated that it was open to 'any gentleman amateur'.[18] But even gentlemen who had participated in open meetings or handicap meetings were not permitted to take part in anything organized by the Amateur Athletics Club: it was, then, an exclusive group from the start.

Chambers is called the architect of modern athletics and his aim was to bring together from universities round the country, including Scotland and Ireland, all the athletic talent interested in following the principles of amateurism.

The French word *amateur*, derived from Latin *amatorem* = 'lover', was first used in France towards the end of the eighteenth century to denote a person with an interest in art, architecture or anything else but with no expectation of economic advantage. It was, in fact, a term of praise in many languages. The word 'amateur' in English had been used in rowing and cricket since the eighteenth century. In the magazine *Bell's Life in London, and Sporting Chronicle* in 1835, an amateur was someone who rowed but did not work at sea or row for a living. Those who received free training and drew profit from the activity were not considered amateurs. *The Rowing Almanac* of 1861 defined an amateur by listing the universities, schools and institutions that had fostered such 'superior' individuals. Tradesmen, workmen and craftsmen were excluded.

The Amateur Athletic Club gave its own definition in 1866: 'An amateur is a person who has never competed in an open competition, nor to win money, nor has received money for appearing, and who has never had athletics as a means of earning a living.' They did not, however, mention private competitions or betting. In 1867 they made an important additional exclusion: 'nor be a craftsman nor a workman'. The following year they changed the opening phrase to read: 'An amateur is any gentleman who . . .'[19]

Like any other gentleman's club, their aim was to be self-selecting and to set their own conditions, and they wanted to exclude working men whose work provided them with training. Blacksmiths and masons, for instance, were enormously strong and tended to be good at throwing events whereas shepherds and other men in outdoor jobs that involved walking had an advantage when it came to running.

At the end of the 1870s different groups quarrelled about the future of sport. It all revolved around the need to agree on a common championship for the whole country, the inclusion of occupational groups that were excluded, and the removal of the word 'gentleman' from the membership criteria.

In 1880 three young men – Clement N. Jackson, Montague Shearman and Bernhard R. Wise – proposed the formation of the Amateur Athletic Association (AAA) to bring an end to the disagreements and to bring together the whole country in the first national association of its kind in the world. The definition of the word 'amateur' was an important topic when the delegates met for the inaugural meeting in the banqueting hall of the Randolph Hotel in Oxford on 24 April 1880. Even the most conservative accepted the inclusion of occupational groups previously excluded. Although more groups were now included than permitted by earlier statutes, many were still excluded and arguments about who was in breach of the rules of amateurism and what those rules meant would mark athletics and other branches of sport for a century or more. But this new organization also set in motion the enduring process of standardizing records.

The keeping of running records does not have a long history. The first official athletics records were recorded in 1864 during a meeting between university teams from Oxford and Cambridge, and there is an 1868 athletics training manual that mentions the best performances in England. The *Oxford English Dictionary* names 1883 and 1884 as the first years when 'record' was specifically used about exceptional sports performances. Montague Shearman, the English sports historian, used the word in his 1887 book *Athletics and Football* and knew that his readers would be familiar with it; he was, however, distressed by the American obsession with records. In no other country was there such a fixation with records and Shearman was greatly concerned that such an obsession would lead athletics in the wrong direction and break with the ideals of English amateur sport.

The introduction of national records in running necessitated a standardization of tracks, the marking of exact distances and the existence of reliable timekeepers – a process that took many years to complete in different countries. Records in running are not as 'natural' or obvious as one might believe. They demand technology, standardization and an attitude of mind that only became common from the end of the nineteenth century under the influence of social developments in Europe.[20] The norms of industrial society were transferred to and became dominant in sport, the aim being to produce quantifiable results. This, of course, undermined the circus and carnivalesque traditions in sport.

The development of regulated sport was gradual. To a latter-day observer the serious sport of earlier times is frequently a cause of amusement in that it seems so innocent and comical, even though its practitioners were deeply serious. Victorian England idealized restrained behaviour and playing 'for the sake of the game'. In the view of the upper classes this was a more cultured and civilized attitude than the lower classes' boorish approaches to sport.

Professional running counted as one of the boorish approaches. It is underrated in history books because amateur ideals had become dominant and because it was amateurs who wrote the history – without leaving sufficient or, indeed, any room for the professionals. The concept of the amateur in sport only became widespread with the growth of modern sport at the end of the nineteenth and beginning of the twentieth centuries. Earlier it had not been an issue: now, however, it became important because of the arrival of a great, international sporting event – the Olympic Games.

13
The Revival of the Olympic Games

The runners were spitting out dust, coughing and vomiting. William
Garcia from California almost died of poisoning and ended up in
hospital with stomach bleeds caused by the dust.
—After the marathon on a particularly hot day during the 1904
St Louis Olympic Games

It is a myth that it was solely the Frenchman Pierre Frédy, Baron de Coubertin,
who rediscovered the Olympic Games and revived them in 1896. A very long
period of development preceded this. By the end of the nineteenth century
the stadium at Olympia lay revealed for all to see after more than a millen-
nium of obscurity and a great deal of archaeological effort.

French, German and English archaeologists had been visiting and pro-
posing to excavate Olympia since the eighteenth century. At the beginning
of the nineteenth century the Olympic Games were well known to European
antiquarians and a number of English expeditions went to Olympia, which
the local population was using as a quarry for stone. One of the Englishmen,
William Martin Leake, arrived there in the winter of 1805 with the intention
of 'acquiring more knowledge of this important and interesting country for
the British authorities'. The French undertook the first extensive excavations
at Olympia in 1829, the same year as Greece declared its independence from
the Turks.[1]

In 1838, overjoyed by the recent achievement of independence and by
the classical heritage rising from the earth, the town of Pyrgos proposed
the reintroduction of the Olympic Games. A rich Greek, Evangelios Zappa,
enthusiastically offered to pay all the costs and bequeathed all his fortune
to that end. Funds from that source financed the Olympic Games in Athens
in 1859, 1870, 1875, 1877 and 1888/9.

In 1874 Kaiser Wilhelm I made an agreement with Greece that all the
archaeological finds at Olympia should belong to the Greeks but that the
Germans should have the right to publish the results of the excavations.
The excavation was led from 1875–80 by the German archaeologist Ernst
Curtius. His books sold in large numbers all over Europe and stimulated
interest in the classical era.

The French were envious that their arch-enemy Germany was systematically excavating and reconstructing this magnificent era in European
history. If the Germans were uncovering some of the splendours of antiquity, the French would have to come up with some weighty contribution
in the same field.

This was what inspired the aristocratic Pierre de Coubertin, born in Paris on 1 January 1863. His father was an artist and his mother a highly trained musician and both parents were genuinely engrossed in history. His mother instilled a respect for the past in her children and Coubertin also acquired a great insight into the classical world at the Jesuit school he attended in Paris. As a matter of family duty Coubertin studied law but important impulses from his upbringing remained with him as an adult. When he took up various sports such as fencing, riding, boxing and rowing during his time as a student he found they provided a balance to his existence. Coubertin's project grew out of these experiences and out of his strong desire to revitalize the French education system so that it would consist of more than sitting still and learning by rote. And in Paris he could see that times were changing at an ever greater speed, with railways, rapid industrialization and a faster pace of life.

Coubertin went to England in 1883 with the intention of learning and taking home anything useful he might learn to France, where the development of sport was now a topic of vigorous debate. He visited English and Irish boarding schools and asked both pupils and teachers about their daily lives, in which sport played a significant part. He wrote extensively about his enquiries in articles, letters and books in order to spread the word as effectively as possible.[2] In 1888 he was appointed general secretary of the Committee for the Promotion of Physical Education in Schools in France, an ideal position for him. After a study visit to the United States two years later he came to the conclusion that, unlike the many 'games' that had been arranged in the modern period between 1612 and 1880, the Olympic Games should become truly international. Games with 'Olympic' in the title had been organized in at least thirteen different places but whether they had taken place in Sweden, Canada, the United States, Germany, Greece, Yugoslavia, France or England they had all been essentially local in character.

In 1890 Coubertin attended an English model, the Much Wenlock Olympian Games in Shropshire, and these provided him with the decisive stimulus. Full of enthusiasm, he mounted the rostrum at the Sorbonne later that year and at the end of a lecture on modern sport he declared that 'the Olympic Games must be reinstated – for the whole world!'[3]

He launched the idea that the modern reintroduction of the ancient Greek ideals was not only about the cultivation of the body but also about harmony between mind and body. The achievement of peace between the nations was a further argument, with participants in the games being ambassadors for peace.

Most of the audience at the Sorbonne considered his proposal impossible but he had a more favourable opportunity to promote it at the 1894 Paris sports congress, the purpose of which was to standardize the rules of international amateur sport. In spite of much lobbying the delegates from the nine countries represented there seemed sceptical when the issue was addressed but, when put to the vote, the proposal gained a majority.

Coubertin won the vote because he was persistent, had good contacts and because the age itself was in his favour: increased internationalization, improved means of transport and press interest were making organized international sport an inevitability. The dissemination of European civilization and of particular sporting disciplines was in the spirit of the colonial age; all countries, of course, had their own local variants of sport that did not fit in with the Olympic programme. The existence of the Olympic Games was, however, an uncertain one during their first decade and it was to take time for them to find their form.

An Epoch-making Proposal

Why not organize a race in memory of the messenger who ran from Marathon to Athens with the news of the victory over the Persians in 490 BC and then died of exhaustion?

This was the suggestion made by the Frenchman Michel Bréal in 1892 when plans were being made to revive the Olympic Games in Athens. Coubertin was rather sceptical about such a long distance. 'I'll donate a cup for the race', Bréal said before the vote on his proposal.[4] He suggested a course from Marathon to the Pnyx, a hill in Athens – from a plain outside the town to the traditional meeting place in ancient Athens. It would be a test of will with historical echoes.[5]

The idea was received with enthusiasm in Greece, where it struck patriotic sparks. The Plain of Marathon would be the start of the long run and the runners would enter the newly built Olympic stadium in Athens, a distance of 25 miles (40 km). So it was a scholar's love of history that lay behind this first marathon race and no one in the 1890s worried about whether the myth was historically accurate.

Organized races of 25 miles and more are not mentioned in ancient sources from either Greece or Rome – the longest races referred to are a tenth of that. The marathon as a sporting event had no historical roots, it was an *idée fixe*. The myth concerns a messenger called Phillipides and *he*, anyway, is not a figure of fantasy. What is doubtful is any connection between him and the myth.[6]

In 490 BC the Persian army planned to take Athens and waded ashore near the Plain of Marathon, a strategically important location for landings. Two or three hundred shiploads of soldiers, a thousand horses and a mighty war machine made ready. The Athenians left their city in order to attack the enemy and they despatched Phillipides, an experienced messenger, the 150 miles to Sparta to ask for help. Even though he arrived there and delivered the message the following day the Spartans could not send help until after the full moon, some six days later, because they were celebrating a religious festival. The messenger set off back for Athens and on the way the god Pan promised to help.

It seemed foolhardy for the Athenians to attack: the Athenian forces numbered 10,000 men against the 25,000 Persian warriors. But cunning, courage and surprise worked to the Athenian advantage. They formed up before dawn and ran a mile to make a lightning attack, fearless and determined to crush the enemy. Once within range of the Persian arrows the Athenians speeded up, causing the Persians to retreat; the sudden appearance of this horde struck panic into the hearts of the Persians, who believed the Athenians were possessed by the devil. The battle came to hand-to-hand fighting with swords, bows, arrows and fists before the Persians fled towards the sea and back to their ships. During the few hours the battle lasted the Persians lost 6,400 men compared with Athenian losses of 192.[7]

The victory at Marathon was a huge triumph for the Athenians. This was the first real military defeat the Persians had suffered and the battle was consequently of great importance in Athenian and Greek history.

The Greek historian Herodotus (c. 484–425 BC) talked to soldiers who had fought there and based his account on contemporary sources. He does not mention Phillipides or anyone else running from Marathon to Athens and announcing the victory before dropping down dead. No doubt someone carried out that important task and one can imagine the joy and pride with which he informed the tense and anxious citizens who had been expecting the worst. Messengers like Phillipides were regularly used to carry such despatches but he is not known to have been present at the battle and, given his long experience as a runner, it seems unlikely that he would die after such a relatively short distance.

The Greek satirist Lucian (c. AD 125–after 180) was the first to state that Phillipides was the messenger of victory,[8] but this, the only source to suggest that it was Phillipides, was written over six hundred years after the event. Plutarch (c. AD 46–120) names a different messenger, Eucles, who had returned from abroad and marched to Marathon in time to take part in the battle. He then ran back to the city in full kit and dropped down dead after announcing the news to the Athenian authorities. According to Plutarch the majority of Greek historians of his day thought that Eucles was the name of the messenger, although there were those who believed it was Tersippus. What the debate does show, however, is that the myths lived on for centuries after the battle; and long after that again the myth concerning Phillipides became known in academic circles in the rest of Europe.

The Greek struggle for independence at the beginning of the nineteenth century led to renewed interest in Greek studies and delighted enthusiasts of Greek history. The English poet Lord Byron (1788–1824) travelled around Greece and fought alongside the Greek revolutionaries. He visited the Plain of Marathon, which made a powerful poetic impression on him:

> The mountains look on Marathon/ And Marathon looks on the sea;/ And musing there an hour alone,/ I dream'd that Greece might yet be free/ For, standing on the Persians' grave,/ I could not deem myself a slave.[9]

The poet Robert Browning (1812–1889) also dreamt of the Golden Age of Greece and in his poetic eulogy 'Pheidippides' he gives the messenger the honour of having brought the warning to the Spartans and then making the fatal run from Marathon to Athens.[10]

Many poets took their source material from the same mythological landscape and their literary contributions, in conjunction with the blossoming of Greek studies and the strength of Greek patriotism – particularly the latter in the case of the organizer of the 1896 Olympics – meant that Bréal's proposal for a long race was accepted. It was what Pierre de Coubertin needed, the final link in the chain between the ancient and the modern Olympic Games. The Greeks themselves took particular note of the marathon race: it was something to be talked about, something on which expectations could be built, including those of prospective participants. In contrast to the short track events in which the English and Americans excelled, the Greeks saw the marathon as a chance to assert themselves.

The Water Bearer

In 1895 Spiridon Louis was doing his military service as a stable-boy for General Mavromichalis. As they were passing the building site of the new Olympic stadium one day the general told him about the glorious race from Marathon which would involve runners from many countries.

'I'd like to be among them. I'm a good runner, General', Louis said to him.[11]

'You, Spiridon? You? And running?' the general answered, tapping Louis's head gently with his finger as if to help the message sink in.

When Louis finished his military service and went home there were already several runners and a wrestler in his home village training for the Olympic Games. The Greeks were best prepared for the marathon. Smitten by the Olympic bug and further inspired by donations by wealthy Greeks such as Georgios Averoff and Ionnis Lambros who, hoping for a Greek victory, had donated an antique vase as an extra prize for the winner, poor, barefoot Greek boys had been training for weeks beforehand. The word had gone out all over Greece that the search was on for men of endurance, for shepherds, for natural prodigies. Miles away from Athens peasant boys and labourers were in training and according to rumour three young men died from excessive training.[12]

The Greeks held two trial runs. In the first of them, on 10 March 1896, twelve men competed. An experienced competitive walker, Karilahos Vasilakos, won this first marathon in history in a time of 3 hours 18 minutes. In a second trial, only five days before the actual Olympic event, 38 men took part and the best time was 3 hours 11 minutes. The unknown Spiridon Louis came in fifth.

Carlo Airoldi, a good Italian long-distance runner, wanted to take part in the Olympic Games. He left Milan for Greece on foot on 12 March 1896 and twenty days later had reached Ragusa (Dubrovnik) in Croatia, from where he took a boat to Corfu and so on to Patrasso in Greece. He then walked the rest of the way to Athens – a total walking distance of 830 miles (1,336 km). He asked to take part, but the Greek judges refused because the Italian had competed for money in road races and because he had raced against horses and cyclists in Buffalo Bill's Circus. He had to walk home disappointed, one of the first victims in Olympic history of the principle of amateurism.[13]

On 9 April 1896, the day before the race, the runners were transported from Athens to the village of Marathon, a slow, bumpy, four-hour journey. The mayor of Marathon welcomed them and exhorted them all to eat and drink well to prepare for their exertions.

'Is there anything more you need?'

'Bring us some more wine, Mr Mayor', the runners said and ate, laughed, sang and feasted away the evening until fairly late.[14]

Of the eighteen entered for the race one unidentified German pulled out. No fewer than thirteen of the rest represented Greece and the remaining four were Edwin 'Teddy' Flack from Australia, Albin Lermusiaux from France, Gyula Kellner from Hungary and the American Arthur Blake. Of the foreigners on the starting line only the Hungarian had ever run a distance of 25 miles before. Flack had actually won the 800 metres on the same day as the journey to Marathon, and three days before that Flack, Blake and Lermusiaux had respectively taken gold, silver and bronze in the 1,500 metres. It was a case of strong middle-distance legs against Greek grit, patriotism and prayers to the Almighty. During a service in Marathon church on the morning of the race, the congregation had whispered prayers for a Greek victory and several of the runners had knelt and made the sign of the cross.

Spiridon Louis and the three others from his village laced up the fine shoes their friends had taken up a collection to buy and did a few circuits in the neighbourhood to loosen up. Back at the inn the race doctor carefully tapped their knees three times with a hammer – four in the case of Louis – and commented 'He'll maybe make it', when the knee reacted positively.

Each man was served with milk and two beers at 11 a.m. The starting pistol was fired at 2 p.m. on 10 April 1896 and off went a carnivalesque field of lightly dressed runners, cyclists, mounted soldiers to clear the road and finally, some distance behind, carriages full of watchful doctors. The whole local population along the route turned out and for the majority of them it was the first athletic competition they had seen. They cheered and clapped everyone and offered them food and drink.

The fleet-footed foreigners went straight to the front, each man accompanied by a cyclist. The Frenchman was well in the lead and when he passed through the village of Pikermi, roughly the halfway point, he was leading the Australian, the American and the Hungarian. Spiridon Louis seemed in fine fettle, accepted a beaker of wine from his stepfather and asked how far ahead the leaders were. 'I'll catch up with them', he promised.[15]

The Frenchman reached the village of Harvati, the 15-mile (24-km) mark, in 1 hour 34 minutes, the Australian in 1 hour 35 and the American in 1 hour 38. Vasilakos and Louis, the two best Greeks, came through immediately behind them.[16]

At a hilly section a little later the Frenchman shouted to his assistant, who rushed up to massage him and rub him with spirits and, while they were standing there surrounded by curious onlookers, the Australian passed him and took the lead for the first time. At 20 miles (32 km) the Frenchman collapsed and was helped into a carriage. The Australian Flack was also shaky on his legs and ready to drop out when Spiridon Louis came up alongside him.

This was the point at which the winning instinct seriously took hold of Louis for the first time. An officer fired into the air with joy and called out 'Long Live Hellas!' as the Greek and the Australian ran shoulder to shoulder. Louis watched out of the corner of his eye to make sure his rival did not gain an advantage before his own spurt. A little later the Australian began to stagger and had to give up and topple into a carriage.

General Papadiamantopoulos, the starter of the race, came riding up alongside Louis:

'Do you want something to drink?'

'Water.'[17]

They gave him cognac, however, and he spat it straight out. The general offered him his handkerchief and Louis wiped the sweat from his face but dropped the handkerchief. He was about to pick it up when the general called 'Save your strength!' Louis was still feeling in good shape and rallied even more when an acquaintance from his home village gave him a glass of wine. A symbolic shot was fired at the city limits. The noise was thunderous as the spectators in the streets let off rockets and Louis was given segments of orange and proposals of marriage.

Rumours about how the race was going were buzzing around the 70,000 spectators in the stadium and when the German cyclist August Goedrich pedalled in and announced that the Australian was in the lead, a wave of disappointed sighs spread around the stadium. But just a little later the starter entered on horseback, covered in dust from his ride, and went straight to King Georgios on the royal podium.

A few minutes later a roar of triumph went up as a sweating and sunburnt figure dressed in white passed through the stadium gate. Hats flew in the air and people screamed and embraced. The past and the present became one in the figure of Spiridon Louis, who was bearing on his shoulders the proud inheritance of Greece's classical past and who received the greatest and most triumphal roar heard in Hellas since the days of Olympia's greatness. The Greek king and the prince leapt down and ran alongside him, deeply moved, like the other spectators, when Louis, confused by the stadium, asked a spectator where the finishing line was. Happy and exhausted he completed the race in 2 hours, 58 minutes and 50 seconds and then collapsed.

He was hungry and was given milk and biscuits, as were the others who staggered through to the finish. Nine men completed the race, the last man taking 3 hours, 58 minutes and 50 seconds. The only foreigner was Gyula Kellner and he submitted a protest that Belokas, the third man in, had been given a lift in a carriage on the way. An inquiry upheld the protest and the Hungarian moved up to third place behind two Greeks.

Louis was 23 years old and came from the village of Amaroussion near Athens. He was not a hard-training athlete; he was an industrious working man who collected spring water near his home and took it by horse and cart the nine miles to Athens, he himself walking quickly or trotting alongside the cart.

Louis received his gold medal, a winner's diploma and an offer from King Georgios – 'You can have whatever you want!' Louis, however, said no to everything apart from the offer of a better cart and a livelier horse for transporting water. He also received offers of marriage and good jobs, and a chocolate factory had promised the winner free chocolate for life. Louis remained in the same social station and never competed again. There are few athletes who have achieved so much by only taking part in two races in their lives, and both of them within the space of one week.[18]

A Tough Woman

The 1896 marathon was restricted to men but there was also a woman who wanted to take part. In the weeks before the Olympic Games Stamata Revithi left her home in Piraeus and walked to Athens, determined to try her luck in the city after the cruel loss of a child of seven. The poor woman was 30 years old but looked older as she walked along carrying her few possessions and a seventeen-month-old baby.[19]

On the road she met a runner who enquired why she was walking so slowly and alone. He encouraged her, gave her money and advised her to appear in the men's race from Marathon.

Stamata liked the suggestion. She was strong and tenacious and could certainly complete the run. But she was embarrassed – it would not be proper for a woman to run alone. It would nevertheless be an achievement and might lead to celebrity and other advantages for her child.

Stamata arrived in Marathon the day before the men's start and told the journalists that she was indeed going to run to Athens whatever the committee of judges might say.

'You'll arrive in Athens after all the spectators have gone home', one man remarked.

'No, I won't', Stamata answered stubbornly.

It was risky for women to run through the streets in scanty clothes since the sight of too much leg or too much bare skin would cause offence, so Stamata wore a knee-length skirt and hid her arms in a sling. On the morning of the day of the race she asked for a blessing from the aged priest in Marathon and he refused her because the judges had not given her permission to run.

No one knows exactly what happened, apart from the fact that Stamata Revithi was not allowed to take part. She did, however, run the day after the men's race and she got the mayor to witness the time and place and to sign a handwritten document.

She arrived in Athens five and a half hours later, having been slowed down by several long breaks. She was interested in boats and had stopped to look at them, and she had met someone who would confirm the time of day.

'Why are you running so far and wearing yourself out?'

'So that the king might possibly give my child some kind of position in the future. And now I'm going direct to the general secretary of the Greek Olympic Committee to tell him how many hours I took to run from Marathon to Athens and that anyone who wants can race against me.'[20]

She removed her wooden-soled sandals and ran on barefoot. Nothing is known about her later fate – but she has not been forgotten.

The Continuation of the Marathon

Bréal's original suggestion had been for just one marathon race since it pertained to a myth with a fixed and particular location. The race lacked any historical anchorage in other countries. But the success of Spiridon Louis and the aura around him, together with the articles in the world press after the games, created a lasting enthusiasm and provided fertile ground for more of the same. The marathon acquired a life of its own and spread to Paris in the summer of 1896 and thence to the United States, Hungary, Norway and Denmark by the autumn of that same Olympic year. Two years later Germany and Italy organized their first marathons and in 1899 Sweden became the ninth country to arrange a race.

The American athletics squad in Athens had had many members from Boston and they too were inspired by the marathon. In Boston they dug into their own history and in 1897 arranged a marathon in memory of Paul Revere and William Dawes who, during the American War of Independence in the 1770s, had undertaken a long night ride to warn the Massachusetts farmers that British troops were advancing. Naturally enough the race in their memory was arranged for 19 April, Patriots' Day.[21]

Much of the reason for the success of the Boston Marathon comes from this link with an important national event. It caught on immediately and by 1902 it was attracting crowds of at least 100,000, making it the world's most spectated sporting event. Now, 110 years later, it is the world's oldest race of its kind and still popular.

Even though the marathon achieved an independent life for itself outside the Olympics, within the Olympic Games there was some trial and error before the event found its final form. The Games in Paris in 1900 were held in conjunction with the World's Fair from 14 May to 28 October, the athletic events taking place in the middle of July, and spectators were not always aware that these actually were the Olympics. The Paris Games lacked both opening and closing ceremonies and Coubertin's revival of the games had not really been expected to have either a long life or high status.[22]

Professional stars such as Len Hurst from England, the fastest marathon man of the day, were not allowed to take part. Consequently, those who set off on 19 July 1900 were not the best marathon runners in the world: there were sixteen men from seven nations with handkerchiefs on their heads or peaked caps or anything else to protect them from the sun. The temperature reached 39°C.[23]

A number of them dropped out early because of the heat, in addition to which bad route-marking and a shortage of stewards made it difficult for those who did not know the area. The Frenchman Touquet-Denis took a wrong turn and stopped at a café for a drink: they only served beer and he drank two glasses before dropping out. After nine miles the runners came across sheep and cows wandering on the road, and motorcycles, cars and pedestrians crossing the roads made the race difficult through the streets and back-streets of Paris. Michel Théato won in 2 hours 59 minutes 45 seconds, five minutes in front of Emile Champion, thus giving France first and second places. Some 90 years later it emerged that Théato was born in Luxembourg and had been representing the wrong country.

The 1904 St Louis Olympics in the United States also coincided with a World's Fair. The first two black competitors from Africa, Len Tau and Jan Mashiani, appeared in the marathon,[24] as did Felix Carvajal de Soto, a postman from Cuba who paid for his boat ticket to New Orleans by giving exhibition runs at home. From New Orleans he hitchhiked to St Louis, learning English as he went.

The day of the 1904 race was also hot and the runners suffered badly from thirst. The only points at which water was easily available were a water tower after six miles and a well near the road a little farther on. Dehydrated runners were stopped by cramps or dropped out, unable to endure any more. Meanwhile they were surrounded by cars, both those escorting them and general passing traffic, which stirred up dust and aggravated the effects of water shortage. The runners were spitting out dust, coughing and vomiting. William Garcia from California almost died of poisoning and ended up in hospital with stomach bleeding caused by the dust.

The different levels of support and assistance for the runners made the competition unfair. The winner, Thomas Hicks from the United States, was certainly not the best in the field but he had help. At one point along the route he encountered a group out for a walk eating peaches. 'Can I have some, please?' Hicks asked in vain before snatching two and eating them as he went. His support car also cooled him down with sponges and provided him with water and artificial stimulants. At eighteen miles he took a concoction of strychnine – a white, bitter-tasting substance – and egg-white.

Strychnine, which stimulated the central nervous system, was also used in rat-poison and the dosage had to be exact to avoid poisoning. The substance could, in the worst case, prove fatal.[25]

Hicks had a clear lead but wanted to drop out, so his helpers topped him up with the concoction. He turned pale after the first dose of strychnine and then took another, along with two egg-whites and spirits. He limped on and was given more eggs, spirits and sponge-downs before entering the stadium, where the prize-giving was already underway.

The American Fred Lorz had actually arrived a quarter of an hour earlier and people thought he was the winner. Lorz had given up after nine miles and had gone in a car until about three miles from the finish, when the car had broken down. Rather than sit in the baking sun and wait for breakdown assistance he had continued on foot, passing Hicks on the way. He finished in 3 hours 13 minutes and accepted the acclamation of the crowd. He kept the joke going until Hicks arrived, at which point he admitted his deception.

The greatest performance of the day was that of the Frenchman Albert Corey, who took second place without having received any help. Felix Carvajal de Soto, who came in fourth, went scrumping apples on the way and had to ask people which way the route went.

The following Olympic marathon, London in 1908, was important in a number of ways. The exact distance, 26 miles and 385 yards (42,195 metres) was established, the reason for the distance being that the Princess of Wales wished to let her children watch the start and so the starting line was moved inside the grounds of Windsor Castle. They then measured the distance from there to the Royal Box in the White City Stadium, the largest sports arena in the world, with a capacity of 90,000. This became the official standard marathon distance from the Olympic Games of 1924, although the roughly 40 kilometre (25 miles) length was the norm for many years.

Disaster

The 1908 marathon also witnessed the drama of the little Italian Dorando Pietri staggering his way into the history books. Over the last six miles he gnawed away at the lead of the South African Charles Hefferson. Hefferson accepted a glass of champagne from a spectator, hoping it would fortify him, but instead he suffered stomach cramps. Catching up with him had sapped Pietri's strength but he continued, needing all of his iron will to stay on his feet. Once inside the White City Stadium he turned right instead of left, then staggered around to the left and collapsed. Making a superhuman effort he got back to his feet and continued. He tried to run but could not. He tried to walk but fell, got up again and fell again several times like a drunk. They poured water on him, massaged him and shouted to him while the whole stadium was roaring like a storm at sea. When he had 50 yards to go to the finish, the second man entered the stadium.

On seeing his opponent closing in, Dorando sort of pulls himself together, gets back on his feet and makes a terrifying effort to run to the finish. Hayes is struggling behind him, hardly 50 yards back. And Dorando really does run for the finish. He is finally going to take the laurels!

But no, not yet! Two or three yards from the finish he collapses. The Italians are screaming like madmen at their fallen hero. They lift him up and he struggles on and across the line. He is received immediately into the arms of jubilant friends, who treat him like a child, lay him on a stretcher and carry him to an ambulance. Just 32 seconds behind Hayes arrives – but without any help – crosses the line and throws himself down. Helping hands catch him as he falls and he too is taken to the ambulance.[26]

The runners were suffering from dehydration and carbohydrate depletion. They had eaten a good steak for breakfast, followed by two raw eggs and toast and tea. The official food stations provided rice pudding, raisins, bananas, mineral water and milk – and artificial stimulants where necessary. But the assistants accompanying the runners on bicycles were not permitted to provide stimulants such as brandy and arsenic.

The United States lodged a complaint that Pietri had received help at the finish and the complaint was correctly upheld. Pietri was disqualified for accepting help and the American John Hayes was the winner.

The rumour that evening was that Pietri was dead. His condition was critical for a few hours but he recovered and went to the stadium the next day for the medal ceremony, apparently unconcerned. He was like a new man, ready to receive both the acclaim of the crowd and a special prize from the queen. Hayes won the gold medal without winning the hearts of the crowd. Pietri was the moral victor.

Pietri's staggering and collapse changed people's perception of the marathon. Until then most people had felt positive about the event, even if the participants were regarded as ascetic eccentrics with an urge to torment themselves. In the wake of the Spiridon worship that followed the Athens Olympics of 1896 the marathon had become a Herculean feat, something new, something not fully studied, but with a historical basis.

When the first man home in 1908 seemed about to imitate the original myth and die at the finish, it sparked off an international debate about whether the event could be justified. Was the Italian the fool in some barbaric drama? Was the marathon harmful?

Pietri said that the jubilation of the crowd at the finish confused him and caused a mental short-circuit at a stage when his body was already at breaking point. It has also been suggested that Pietri may have taken stimulants, which may, of course, have had the opposite effect to that intended and caused sudden and unforeseen reactions of a debilitating kind.

Is the Marathon Harmful?

Critics believed that the 1908 race symbolized a kind of sporting fanaticism that was being fostered by the Olympic Games, an excessive eagerness to stretch the limits of human performance in front of tens of thousands of spectators. Prominent sports writers in Britain, Germany, the United States, Scandinavia and elsewhere held the same view. The marathon had become a diseased branch on the sporting tree. But few of the commentators had any experience of marathon running and what the participants thought counted for nothing.

The 1908 race also had a political sequel. The American president Theodore Roosevelt was sceptical about a form of competition that led to so much fuss and disunity but he was nevertheless happy to use sporting achievements as markers of national strength. And he liked to shake hands with the stars of sport and to have them around him. In private letters he expressed his annoyance at the behaviour of the officials in the White City Stadium and in his patriotic mind he believed that the British had been trying to prevent an American victory.[27]

During the summer and autumn of 1908 Dorando Pietri was the most famous sportsman in the world. His disqualification had merely reinforced the world's sympathy for this little man with his big eyes and elegant moustache. A collection for him in London brought in £300 and at home in Italy the collecting tins were full. In London immediately after the games Pietri could fill theatres – people rose and applauded him wherever he showed his face. There was something gallant about Dorando Pietri. His conduct was modest and honourable and he was charming to media and entertainment people: the writers of revues and cartoonists in many countries transformed the events into sellable art, with Americans humming Irving Berlin's melody 'Dorando' and the Olympic film filling the cinemas of Europe and the United States throughout the autumn.

The public demanded further races between Hayes and Dorando, but both of them had left the ranks of the amateurs, Dorando as a result of the flood of gifts he received after the Olympics, Hayes because of his employment at the Bloomingdale Department Store in New York, where he spent his time training on the roof of the tall building rather than working.

American promoters wanted to profit from the events in London, but to ensure good takings any event would have to be held in an arena so that the public would pay a good price for their tickets and watch at close quarters. In the United States, that meant an indoor arena. About four months after the London games Dorando and Hayes appeared before a crowd of 12,000 in New York. They were led in like boxers to an arena that was thick with cigarette smoke and where betting had added some extra excitement. Both were dressed in the same clothes as in London, apart from the cigar advertisement on Dorando's vest. There were generous sponsors at that kind of level. In these chaotic surroundings the Italian took his revenge, urged on by Italian immigrants who leapt onto the track and ran the last two laps with him.

A wave of marathons swept across the United States, with individuals challenging one another for considerable sums of money and backers milking the business for all it was worth. The lure of profit drove good long-distance runners into the marathon circus. Between 1908 and 1911 the public demand was so great that the press christened it 'Marathon Mania' or the 'Marathon Craze'.

The critics of professional sport and particularly of the marathon regarded these lucrative contests in the wake of the 1908 Olympics as an undesirable development. But the critics could not deny that the growth of organized sport produced new heroes: men who were flesh and blood but who were elevated to a hallowed status that satisfied mankind's primeval need for heroes. Heroes provide certainty and inspiration, they act as waymarkers in a vast and unpredictable world. There was something simultaneously recognizable and superhuman about the achievements of marathon runners, a kind of breathless mystique in the air when Dorando Pietri and his opponents strode out as if in a classical drama. There was something reminiscent of religious devotees about marathon runners, something reminiscent of the monastic life. Did they achieve an insight that was denied to others?

The drama of Dorando led to the medical examination of many long-distance runners and to debate among doctors as to whether marathon running could be justified. The death from sunstroke of the Portuguese runner Francisco Lazaro in the Stockholm Olympics of 1912 added to the debate. He collapsed after eighteen miles and, although he received medical treatment very quickly, died after being unconscious for fourteen hours.

Given the events of 1908 and 1912 it is easy to see why the interest in marathon running tailed off over the following years. The discussion about whether running was bad for the heart continued for years and doctors misinterpreted a low pulse rate at rest and a large heart as being injurious. They believed that the blood pumped by an excessively large heart exerted dangerous levels of stress on the arterial walls and that 'hammering' shortens a runner's life.

The marathon was the discipline at risk, in spite of research at the Boston Marathon that showed that the heart could tolerate such loads. It was much less harmful than many other young men's activities.

The most thorough investigation was carried out in the United States in 1909. A doctor organized a marathon in Pittsburgh that year and all 55 entrants filled out forms documenting their medical history, diet, training and consumption of tobacco and alcohol. Doctors measured the size and sound of their hearts, checked their pulses and took urine tests before and after the race. In spite of a hard and hilly course the doctors could find no permanent damage to the runners' organs.

Doubts about hard endurance events did not, however, disappear quickly. Both experts and the public remained sceptical because these events were new. They symbolized the restless new age at the end of the nineteenth century and throughout the twentieth century – an age that demanded increased efficiency in industrial productivity and in which the clock became the mighty arbiter of working life.[28]

14
Running Round a Track

He was leading the whole way round and winning easily when a stray
sheep found its way onto the track and stopped, probably confused by
the runner's great speed. The runner collided with the sheep, broke
its leg and completed his quarter mile in just over 50 seconds.
—At the English Running Championship in 1868

The development of the Olympic Games, organized athletics and national
championships led to a break with what had been the main arenas for running in the past – markets and festivals, exhibitions and betting matches,
all independent of clubs and sports associations. Not all of these traditions
disappeared, however, even though the organization of running adopted
new and more fixed forms.

In Central Europe traditional women's races, with the women carrying
buckets on their heads or eggs in spoons, symbolized the everyday activities of women. The bull runs in Pamplona and other towns in the Basque
country demonstrated the courage of young men. The animals were driven
through the streets on the morning of the bullfights in the ring in the afternoon and the young men ran in front of them in danger of being impaled
on the horns.

Cross-country running on the British model appeared in several continents from the end of the nineteenth century and was particularly strong
in Britain and Belgium. Orienteering, however, a Norwegian-Swedish
invention that started in 1895, and fell-running, with its long and rich
tradition, both failed to put down roots in many countries. Running as a
form of exercise was of little significance around 1900, though a moderate
amount of it was recommended, particularly in English training manuals.
Walking was considered to be the healthy form of relaxation for those who
did not walk enough in the course of their everyday activities.

The runner is a well-known type and legendary figure in the storytelling
tradition of many countries – a man who, in folk-tales, runs to the end of the
world to fetch water and who performs superhuman feats. In New Zealand
they told the legend of the Maori runner Te Houtaewa, who ran a hundred
miles along the beach to fetch food. In Wales the best-known runner in folk
memory was the shepherd Guto Nythbran Morgan in the eighteenth century:
in his youth he overtook a hare and plucked a flying bird from the air but
later collapsed and died after a legendary run. In Ireland Finn McCool organized a women's race to find himself a wife, only to see the winner abscond
with a younger kinsman: a mountain was named after the event.

In many of these stories fact and myth merge into each other: the three referred to all deal with real people who have become shrouded in the aura of folk-tale. The same is true of the stories about Alexis Lapointe from Canada, a country with a rich tradition of snowshoe racing.

Lapointe was born in 1860 in the Charlevoix region of French-speaking Quebec. He was one of a family of fourteen. While growing up he was quite unable to sit still and spent the whole day running around. Legend tells us that in his boyhood he built wooden figures of horses and played with them, utterly fascinated by the animals and sure that he was a horse that had been born in a human body by mistake. He whipped himself in his youth to stimulate his muscles and he went off on long walking and running tours. Thus began a restless life, in which he revealed unusual endurance.

On one occasion he and his father were standing on the landing-stage in La Malbaie waiting to take the eleven o'clock boat to Bagotville. His father refused to take him along and Alexis became animated: 'When you arrive in Bagotville I'll be standing there waiting to take the mooring rope!'[1] He whipped himself and ran off, all 90 miles (145 km), and was waiting on the quay when his father's boat docked in Bagotville that evening.

He earned many nicknames as a result of his innumerable appearances at markets all over Quebec: *le Surcheval* ('Superhorse'), *le Cheval du Nord* ('the horse of the north') or 'the flying horse from Saguenay'. His most famous race was against a well-known stallion, Seigneur Duggan de La Malbaie, which he beat over a long distance.

Lapointe was a simple man but smart enough to profit from his eccentric nature. He could dance the whole night without tiring, liked to impress women and was quick to pay court to them, though he always got no for an answer. He simply had too much masculine force and it was hard for such an energetic fellow to be laughed at and rejected by women.

His strength and endurance declined in his fifties, as noted by one of his workmates on a construction site in Matapédia: 'He was still well spoken of, but like a faded star. They said he could no longer run any faster than a regular horse'.[2]

The legend of Alexis Lapointe became the subject of books and comic books. Streets were named after him and songs and even a ballet were written about him.

Metres and Miles

One defining feature of modern athletics is the fixed and measured length of tracks and arenas. The setting for competitive running is regulated and reflects the industrial age that constructed arenas for measurable performance. Measured metres, measured yards and stopwatches became necessary in modern running, otherwise a competition would not be taken seriously by the judges and organizers of the sport, who would consider it inferior and incomplete. The international standardization of measurements and time at the end of the nineteenth century also spread to sport.

The motto of the Olympic movement is *citius, altius, fortius* – faster, higher, stronger – and it pushed developments forward at an unexpected rate. Records and the thought of new records at different levels, constant improvement and a refusal to accept stagnation, and a fascination with the idea that just a *little* faster was always possible – these are the characteristics of modern sport. According to Pierre de Coubertin the idea of records holds the same position in the Olympic ideology as the force of gravity occupies in Newtonian mechanics. The thought of records was an infinite basic principle, a driving force and a goal. It entailed both a constant and a romantic notion about progress for mankind and for the individual.[3]

'Time is what you measure with a clock', Albert Einstein stated, saying much about the mentality of people in the twentieth century, while knowing well that time is not always perceived in the same way. But given accurate clocks, no one could doubt running performances, and they could then be recorded in a system that made comparison possible. Timekeeping to the second was a precondition for the development of modern competitive running.

Few branches of sport are as brutally measurable as running round a track. You start, you run, you finish, while times are clicked off and placings recorded. But to do so there has to be a standardized, checkable system for guaranteeing track length and timekeeping.

At the end of the nineteenth century running tracks were of different sizes and different shapes. There were short ones and long ones, or even u-shaped as at the 1896 Olympics, where the long sides were over 200 metres. In the 1880s the Englishman Montague Shearman argued that a running track should be as straight as possible and the bends should be short: an equilateral, right-angled shape was the ideal, not the rectangular shape which eventually became the norm.

Modern athletics began on trotting tracks, fields, meadows, plains or roads – flat areas that had a reasonably even surface and were fenced off from grazing animals. In the 1868 English national championship at Beaufort House Grounds in London the sprinter Edward Colbeck was sprinting for the finishing line in a quarter-mile race: 'He was leading the whole way round and winning easily when a stray sheep found its way onto the track and stopped, probably confused by the runner's great speed. The runner collided with the sheep, broke its leg and completed his quarter mile in a clear 50 and two fifths seconds.'[4]

Many European tracks outside Britain measured 500 metres, as did the track at the 1900 Paris Olympics, which made 1,500 metres a natural distance for an event. At the London Olympics eight years later the track measured one-third of a mile, or 536.45 metres. It is hardly strange that the world elite became confused when, in Stockholm in 1912, they found themselves competing in a stadium where the laps measured 383 metres.

After the 1920 and 1924 Olympics had been run on 500-metre tracks, the track in Amsterdam in 1928 was 400 metres and that became the norm.[5] It was a compromise between metres and miles – a quarter of a mile is just under 402 metres. During the twentieth century this standard spread over the whole world.

For records to be ratified the surface must be even and the track must not rise or fall too much. The Astor Ground in Birmingham had an incline of two metres over a lap and was not extreme. Runners at the beginning of the twentieth century and for several decades afterwards competed on surfaces with hollows and bumps and with cambers going in all directions. Tracks at the greatest arenas, however, were being levelled and smoothed.

Record times were not always ratified, sometimes because of suspicions about wind conditions or irregularities to do with the track, sometimes because cheating was suspected. Running was dominated by Europeans and Americans and they had a tendency to be slightly sceptical about time-keeping and conditions in other parts of the world.

In Tokyo in 1902, for example, the Japanese runner Minoru Fujii ran 100 metres in 10.24 seconds – 0.36 of a second better than the world's best. Judges and officials in Japan wrote in vain to the athletics associations in the United States and Britain to have the time accepted as the best. They described the electronic timekeeping system used and its accuracy and reliability, but it did not help. Their system was similar to the one invented by Professor C. H. McCloud in Montreal and first used in 1883: it was set off by a switch on the starting pistol and stopped when the winner broke a thin cord or wire. The electrical starting and finishing impulses were recorded on a tape, which was regulated by a chronometer. In principle, times could be measured to an accuracy of one hundredth of a second.

In the case of Fujii in 1902, however, there was a lack of accurate information about wind conditions and the length and gradient of the track. Fujii never competed in Europe or the United States but had he done so successfully it is possible that his time would have been ratified as the world record.

Shoes for Comfort, Shoes for Pain

After a long period of development, running shoes, too, were specially adapted and standardized. Sandals, which were perhaps running shoes used for hunting 10,000 years ago, have been discovered in Fort Rock Cave in Oregon. Over the following millennia many peoples developed the skills and technology to sew clothes, sandals and more robust footwear but we know little about running shoes as such.

Among the Ancient Greeks only messengers wore shoes and many simply did without. The Roman Emperor Diocletian (AD 244–311) enjoined runners to use *Gallicae Cursuriae*, leather shoes with a single sole and straps around the ankles, unlike the double-soled shoes of farmworkers. The

Romans were concerned that running shoes should be functional and as light as possible.[6]

Special running shoes did not appear in England until the nineteenth century. In 1839 Charles Goodyear discovered a method of converting rubber into a practical raw material – it had not been in common use earlier because of its low tolerance of both heat and cold. Goodyear heated raw rubber and sulphur until it melted and when it cooled he found he had a stable and elastic substance suitable for a wider ranges of uses than previously possible. This process was called vulcanization and led to the growth of the rubber industry.

In the following decades rubber was used for many purposes, including running shoes. The Englishman Sir John Astley, who raced in the middle years of the nineteenth century, wrote of having 'rubber shoes that fitted him like gloves'.[7] Astley also referred to a competitor in 1852 as using 'an excellent pair of spiked shoes'. Shoemakers had long been trying to satisfy the demands of discriminating runners.

Spiked shoes were patented in England for cricket in 1861. Four years later Lord Spencer ordered a pair of spiked shoes for running – rather like cricket boots but weighing no more than 280 grams. Three spikes at the front and one in the heel made them suitable for long-distance and cross-country running.

Running shoes, with and without spikes, were used in many countries from the 1890s on. Particularly in marathon running it was extremely important to have comfortable and suitable footwear – sores and blisters were the bane of marathon runners wearing stiff and heavy shoes.

Jock Semple, who competed in the Boston Marathon in the 1920s, soaked his feet in salt-beef brine for a half-hour every evening to make them more resistant to the friction of his shoes. People greased their feet with foot oil and many other home remedies and Semple belonged to a group of men who discussed foot problems as much as they talked of training. Desperate marathon runners experimented with tennis shoes, bowling shoes or made their own with soles cut from car tyres.

Adolf 'Adi' Dassler, a German sportsman, saw the growing need for special models and began to make shoes for the different athletic disciplines. He made the first pair by hand, using sail-cloth as the main material, in his mother's washroom in 1920. In these years immediately after the First World War Dassler made his shoes of parachute silk and the leather from helmets: light shoes with spikes became Dassler's speciality.

His brother Rudolf 'Rudi' joined him in 1924 and they founded the Gebrüder Dassler Schuhfabrik (Dassler Brothers' Shoe Factory) in their home town, Herzogenaurach, twelve miles north-east of Nuremberg. They were manufacturing 50 pairs a day at this stage and saw a much bigger potential. This enterprising pair distributed their shoes free to elite sportsmen, made long-lasting international contacts and recognized the value of great sporting events as the shop window for their products. The Dassler dominance in the

Olympic Games began when Jesse Owens used their shoes in the 1936 Olympics and they sold 200,000 pairs in the year before the outbreak of the Second World War.

In spite of their success the brothers found it difficult to cooperate and in 1948 they went their separate ways. Rudi Dassler set up Puma whereas Adi Dassler's company traded under the name of Adidas – the first syllables of his name. The rivalry between them was fierce but Adidas took the lead and became the best-known trademark in the sporting world for many years.[8]

Sport as Imperialism

Great Britain consciously used sport to spread its customs and it culture. Kenya, later famous as a country that produced good long-distance runners, provides one example.

There are no written sources about running before the British took over the country in 1888, and there are no newspapers before 1901. But running was an important skill for many of life's activities, including games and races. As early as 1876 the French geographer Elisée Reclus noted that the tall, slim Masai were built for running. They were happy to run 60 miles to deliver a message.[9]

From 1901 on there were running competitions in Kenya on the British model, with different classes for Europeans, Africans and Asians. Championships were organized under the aegis of the military and the races attracted thousands of spectators.

Many of the British officers in the colonial administration had come through the universities of Oxford and Cambridge, both of which had a strong athletic tradition. As ambassadors of British civilization they went out to many parts of the world and spread British ideals, including those of sport. The introduction of organized British sport, in this case running in Kenya, did not only raise the physical fitness of the sportsmen and the soldiers, it also functioned as a form of social control. Kenya was not a natural nation; it was divided for the convenience of the colonial power into a multiplicity of groupings that cut across tribal areas. In a 'constructed' nation of this kind it was necessary for the Africans to try to imitate the living and thinking patterns of their white rulers: they were to put aside any anti-imperialist attitudes and adopt more 'civilized' customs. In Kenya during the 1920s athletics became more common in schools, in the prison system, in the police and in the army. The national championships in these institutions came to be significant in the long term. The Masai were sceptical about participating in British athletics, believing them to be a devious form of recruitment into the army, and their sporting behaviour was not of the gentlemanly kind the British desired.

In 1922 the African and Arab Sports Association (AASA) was founded in Kenya on the initiative of the British and two years later an athletics section was formed. From 1924 sport in Kenya was divided along ethnic lines.

The British wished to control the leisure activities of Africans in order to distance them from any political activism that might undermine the colonial power. The European colonial rulers across the whole of Africa viewed the continent with ethnocentric eyes and the methods used by the British in Kenya were well-recognized. They deprived the Kenyans of their own culture and introduced European models instead. European sport gradually marginalized traditional African practices and disciplines by means of the educational system of the public and mission schools, the army, the police and the prison service. In Kenya it was athletics, particularly running, that was most widespread, although the runners did not achieve a notably high standard before the Second World War: the tradition of aiming for the top international level had not yet been established. On his first excursion outside Kenya, to Uganda in 1934, the best Kenyan runner produced the pretty ordinary times of 30 minutes 57 seconds for six miles and 4 minutes 35 seconds for one mile.[10]

In their own eyes the colonists' reasons for encouraging sport were rather high-minded: they desired to promote the same character traits as in Britain, where sport was assumed to build character and develop loyalty, reliability and contentment. Their aims were not unlike those of the Christian missionaries. To the British mind, building 'character' was more important than fostering the intellectual development of the Africans. Too much education could be a threat to the colonial power and there was no wish to encourage educated Africans who might criticize the system.

The Women Arrive

Women, too, were very soon accepted into the family of track runners. In the 1890s there were significant developments at American women's colleges, where a daily walk had already been on the timetable for decades.

The women of Vassar College in New York State were pioneers in athletics and running, and the sports field was the school's most popular meeting place. The women began taking part in athletics in the 1890s, with the 220-yard (201 m) race as their longest distance. The Vassar women sprinted in the lightest clothing of the day, whereas the woman with the starting pistol wore a long skirt and an enormous hat. Pictures from Vassar show happy women, laughing and embracing after relay races and hurdles. The women were capable of all the sports although it would be ridiculous to compare the standards with those of the men – they needed to set their own standards.[11]

In 1903 Agnes Wood was recorded as doing the 220 yards in 30.3 seconds. She was running in a circle and her time is not too bad for a track with bends that was not favourable to sprinting. There were few if any men present, only women students and teachers, and everything proceeded according to the women's understanding of the dictates of propriety. They were respectably dressed even though bare legs could be glimpsed below skirts that were gradually becoming shorter as fashions changed.

Athletics and running for young American women at the start of the twentieth century was a white, upper-class phenomenon. Running was also recommended for women in several other countries, particularly England and France, by the experts of the day – who were usually men.

This was the age of the suffragette. Women in the United States, Britain and elsewhere were demanding the right to vote, as well as other rights in the field of work. In 1893 New Zealand was the first country to introduce the vote for women and other countries followed. Women factory workers went on strike, to the annoyance of factory owners. In Chicago on 3 May 1908 they organized the first women's day and there was a growing consciousness among many upper-class and working-class women of the rights of their sex. The most extreme of them resorted to militant action. In London crowds of angry women marched through the streets, shouting slogans, smashing windows, breaking into shops and calling for equal rights. Their leaders ended up in gaol, went on hunger strike and achieved the status of martyrs.[12]

Feminist agitators contributed to the increased rate of development within women's sport. Why should they be excluded from these new activities? Were they not also created to grow and flourish vigorously? The pioneers within the women's movement met with resistance and ridicule, as is often the case with pioneers, but they also had their male supporters.

One supporter, Dr Harry Eaton Stewart, together with several other authoritative figures, pointed the young American women in the direction of an international women's meeting being organized in Paris in 1922 by the International Association for Women's Athletics, which had been founded there a year earlier. Pioneers from five nations participated in Paris in August 1922 in front of 20,000 spectators.[13]

Women at the beginning of the twentieth century mainly ran in sprint races. In the English-speaking countries 200 yards was counted as long-distance but in Germany 500 and 1,000 metres were also included in the women's programme. The many international women's meetings of the 1920s, along with vigorous lobbying, opened the way for other distances and for women's inclusion in the Olympic Games, though Pierre de Coubertin himself disapproved of elite level sport for women.

In 1928 women's athletics were included in the Olympics for the first time. The first of the golds for running was taken by an inexperienced American seventeen-year-old, Elizabeth 'Betty' Robinson, who ran the 100 metres in 12.2 seconds.

Her home town, Riverdale in Illinois, was so small she had to take the train to go to school in Harvey, two stations away. The station in Harvey was on a hill and one day a train was puffing to the top when Betty was still at the bottom. A teacher standing on the platform saw the girl and thought she was going to miss the train since the guard was already blowing his whistle. Betty ran as fast as she could, leapt up the steps to the platform with long strides and flopped into the seat beside the surprised teacher.

'We'll have to time you over fifty yards', he said.[14]

They did so in the corridor at the end of the school day. When the teacher saw her time he realized the girl should be entered in major competitions, which was something Betty had never reckoned on or indeed known about – she had quite simply always enjoyed running and been the fastest among her schoolmates. Her teachers helped out, got her spiked shoes and entered her for meetings. In her second race she set a world record of 100 metres in 12 seconds flat. Her third meeting was the qualifier for the Olympics. That spontaneous sprint for the train had had unexpected consequences.

The next Olympic Games four years later were to be held in Los Angeles, home ground for Betty, and she was the favourite. On a training day in 1931 the weather was so hot the women could not manage any training and, as runners, they were not permitted to swim. In order to cool off Betty asked her cousin, who was part-owner of an aeroplane, to take her for a cooling flight in the open cockpit.

The plane climbed to 400 feet, suddenly went into a spin, quickly lost height and crashed into soft ground. Betty suffered multiple injuries, a broken legs and hips. Her knee was left stiff and the doctors said she would have to walk with a stick and would never compete again. Expensive medical bills and long-term rehabilitation put an end to her training.

Three years later she tried running for fun. It worked: she joined her old club again and qualified for the 1936 Olympics in spite of a stiff knee. In Berlin she ran in the American team that won the 4 x 100 metres relay.

Even in Betty Robinson's day sprinters would try any fad that might help them achieve better results. The American sprinter Eddie Tolan chewed gum in the 100 metres and found it increased his running cadence and speed – his legs kept pace with the cadence of chewing. His friend Jesse Owens tested himself against one of the great physical phenomena of the inter-war years, the American tap-dancer and film star Bill 'Bojangles' Robinson (1878–1949), who could do 100 yards (91 m) backwards in an unbelievable 13.5 seconds. Owens ran 75 yards (69 m) forwards and Robinson 50 yards backwards and the 22-year-old star only just beat the 57-year-old dancer: the secret was to watch the track markings so as to avoid looking over your shoulder.

In the film *Little Colonel* Bojangles danced down a staircase with the child star Shirley Temple. The most spectacular part was when Robinson tap-danced backwards up the staircase.

Some people used running backwards as a form of training – boxers, in particular. In 1926 the heavyweight Gene Tunney prepared for his fight against the legendary Jack Dempsey by running between four and eight miles on the road backwards every morning, shadow-boxing as he went. When fighting at close quarters boxers spend a lot of time moving backwards and it soon tires them. Tunney beat Dempsey and gave much of the credit to these backwards sessions. Muhammad Ali did the same thing decades later, tiring out his opponent by dancing away backwards.

The Greeks and other experts in ancient times knew that running backwards builds up stamina, strengthens the leg and thigh muscles and improves speed and balance. The Chinese have walked and run in that manner for thousands of years and the Taoists crawled backwards – there was both a philosophical and a muscular theory underpinning the monks' exercises. Later research has shown that running backwards burns up 20 per cent more calories than running the normal way.[15]

In the first decades of the twentieth century running and track racing became established sports in many countries, but there were still prejudices to be overcome and new attitudes to be created before they could achieve universal acceptance.

15
Finnish *Sisu*

Nurmi and those like him are like animals in the forest. They began to
run because of a profound compulsion, because a strange dreamlike
landscape called them with its enchanting mysteries.
—Jack Schuhmacher on Finnish runners

The three young Kolehmainen brothers set out for a run, dressed in overcoats and long trousers. The superintendents of a local mental hospital
have told them to dress like that so that they do not frighten the people
they meet or look as if they are absconding patients. If taken for patients
they risk being reported and arrested.

In Finland in 1906 many people walk, both far and frequently, but few
people run. A runner is breaking the socially acceptable speed-limit for
pedestrian travel. A runner is overdoing things, is rushing, and no sensible, law-abiding person needs to be in such a hurry. To break from a walk
into a run is undignified and only children do it.

The Kolehmainen brothers from Kuopio knew this. A training run is
also an exercise in self-control, in not breathing too heavily, in not waving
their arms around, in not looking exhausted. When they meet people on
the road or in the forest it is important to appear normal and at ease so as
not to arouse suspicions. Which is why they go out training when there are
very few people around to see them, in the dark and in the morning, and
they go where the chances of being seen are least. There is something
slightly criminal about the way they sneak off hoping, as far as possible,
to be unseen. 'Come and have a look at someone running naked!' is what
people say when they see sportsmen wearing short trousers and short
sleeves. At that time 'naked' did not necessarily mean wearing no clothes
at all.[1]

There was a general feeling, too, that able-bodied people, whether
young or adult, should not be wasting time and energy on unproductive
activities. 'You're lazy!' was what the small clique of runners heard from
people, because sport was taking the place of rest and many other things.
When men worked 60 or more hours a week, often in heavy physical labour,
rest and sleep were the sensible things to do with the rest of the time. It was
easy for runners to suffer a bad conscience when their exhaustion came
from training and competition.

The Kolehmainen brothers are really cross-country skiers but they
are getting more and more of a feel for running. Johannes in particular is

Hannes Kolehmainen wearing the Winged Fist of the Irish American Athletic Club, in the *New York Times*, 1919.

talented and athletics will soon be more important than skiing – and the 1912 Olympics in Sweden are beckoning.

At the 1912 Games Johannes 'Hannes' Kolehmainen takes gold in the 5,000 metres, the 10,000 metres and the cross-country. He also sets world records. He is angry when the Russian flag is hoisted as he stands on the victor's rostrum, angry that Russia will receive the honour for the Finnish gold medals since Finland – after centuries of Swedish and Russian rule – has set its heart on independence.

Johannes Kolehmainen became a Finnish folk hero and long-distance running soon became a Finnish national sport: the age of hero worship had arrived and a few years had passed since the Kolehmainen brothers had to train in overcoats and long trousers. How did an activity once criticized as being only for eccentrics suddenly become common property?

The 1912 Olympic Games were an epoch-making event.

Immediately after the 1912 Olympics Laura Pikhala described the close relationship between long-distance running and cross-country skiing. In fact it was not true that these two disciplines had a parallel history with roots in ancient Finnish culture, but this became the accepted view and a part of the myth. Long-distance running was thus cloaked in Finnish national colours and, like cross-country skiing, was viewed in a greater national context.

This happened at a stage when Finland had few heroes and needed to bolster its identity. Runners with *sisu* ('strength of will', derived from the Finnish word *sisus*, 'something within', 'something internal') expressed the heart and the thrust of the young nation and became symbols of Finnishness after the country had achieved independence from Russia in 1917. The cultural concept of *sisu* was transferred to the sporting arena and became the distinguishing mark of the Finns, providing that extra bit of willpower that could be called on when the going got tough.

Long-distance running was a late arrival in Finland compared to the other Scandinavian countries. The first Finnish marathon was held in 1906, ten years later than in the neighbouring countries. It was won in a time of 3 hours 15 minutes by the stonemason Kaarlo Nieminen, who had begun serious long-distance training a year earlier – the first Finn to do so.[2]

Long-distance races were unusual in traditional Finnish peasant society. In 1883 the Finnish carpenter K. J. Johansson accepted a challenge made by Adolf Dibbels from Vienna to run a one-hour race near the railway station in Helsinki. The Finn started too late to be eligible for the prize money but he kept up a higher average speed than Dibbels. This race has sometimes been claimed as the start of the miracle of Finnish running but according to the researcher Erkki Vettenniemi there is no real link between it and later long-distance running.[3] It is true that the introduction of modern sport into Finland can be dated to the 1880s, but that involved cross-country skiing, cycling and gymnastics. To find the decisive impulses that led to long-distance running in Finland, it is necessary to look south.

The Finn Emil Karlsson studied bookbinding in Germany and Denmark and was part of the running scene in Copenhagen. On his return home in 1897 he founded the Helsingfors Pedestrian Sports Club, which lasted for three years and organized races on roads, in parks, on trotting tracks and in velodromes.

But they were just a small clique. Finns were more attracted to other sports, such as cycling and cross-country skiing. Cross-country skiing was quickly accepted by all social classes, mainly because it was recognizably traditional. The national epic poem *Kalevala* describes ski-running and good cross-country skiers became national figures in the 1890s. Whole families went out on ski-tours in the cold of winter and skiing was said to be morally beneficial. Many Finns who started out in cross-country skiing converted to running with considerable success.

An article in a Finnish sporting paper of 1898 listed sports in order of their benefits and their importance. Typically enough, running is not mentioned in the survey since in 1898 it was still virtually unknown. Running was a activity that humorous magazines still poked fun at as a stupid fad, youthful madness, or something done by health fanatics at spas. As far as organized athletics were concerned, no distances longer than six miles were run in Finland up until the autumn of 1899.

The advocates of physical education in Finland had been recommending short runs as part of their gymnastic philosophy for several decades, and sack-races and sprints had been common at fairs since the 1860s. The first race we know the results of was organized in 1871 by Viktor Heikel, who had studied gymnastics in Sweden and Germany.[4] In the so-called Achilles meetings between 1882 and 1884, which also included gymnastics and where a stop-watch was used, children ran 70 metres and students 356 metres – one third of a Russian *verst*. Heikel emphasized technique and posture and he warned against overexploiting the body by running distances longer than one or two miles – precisely the distances that became the heart and soul of the Finnish running miracle.

Stoneface

There is a picture of Paavo Nurmi in a suit and tie, leaning slightly forward as if at the ready, accompanied by an elegantly dressed man and woman who both resemble the pistol-brandishing starters of the race. The photograph was taken in Hollywood in 1924 and Nurmi is smiling enigmatically, his eyes angled down to the ground. The photographer has managed to eavesdrop on and preserve the smile on that thin face – a smile caused perhaps by being with the married couple in the picture, the actors Douglas Fairbanks and Mary Pickford, two of the biggest and most entertaining stars of the silent screen. They, perhaps, were able to get Paavo Nurmi to drop the sphinx-like mask he usually wore. He was a mystery, this Finnish prodigy who set world records with the regularity of a machine throughout the 1920s.

Paavo Nurmi was born in Turku in Finland in 1897 as the oldest of four surviving children. They were a strictly Christian family, which lived in one room and rented out their kitchen to a working-class family. His father Johan Fredrik came from a peasant background but was a carpenter when he married Mathilda Wihelmina. He was in poor health, had a weak heart and was plagued by fainting fits. When he died at the age of 50 in 1910, Paavo – who was barely thirteen – became the main family breadwinner.

By that time he had already staked out the course of his life: he was going to be a runner, having inherited his talent and energetic constitution from his fleet-footed mother.

After the death of his father Paavo left school and went to work. He became an errand boy, strengthening both his legs and his will-power by dragging heavy hand-carts up the hills in Turku. He became a vegetarian for the sake of sport and he stopped drinking coffee. For six years Nurmi did not consume meat, coffee, tea, alcohol or tobacco, living a life of such discipline and asceticism that he was isolated from others of his age. While they hung around cafés he went running in the forests near home, always alone, always serious and always single-minded.

He took the long-term view. In the summer of 1912 thousands of Finnish boys began training, inspired by Johannes Kolehmainen's Olympic gold medal. Many of them burnt themselves out by over-training, but not Nurmi, who, during the coming years, portioned out his energies into three or four weekly sessions of between one and four miles. He began to compete seriously as a seventeen-year-old and in the following season achieved 3,000 metres in 9 minutes 30 seconds and 5,000 metres in 15 minutes 57 seconds, but he was sluggish and lacked a good final spurt. After a great deal of practice with intermittent sprints and speed training he was afraid of no one. Nurmi cut down on his skiing and began to live less ascetically – he started eating meat and drinking tea and coffee, although in small doses. Cereals and milk products remained his main diet, however.

As a nineteen-year-old Nurmi extended his training programme. He added a great deal of walking – up to fifteen miles a day – plus runs of between one and four miles five times a week with built-in spurts. These were followed by concentrated gymnastics. Paavo Nurmi started his military service in 1919 and stunned everyone by running in full kit on the long marches instead of marching, outclassing them all whether on the road or cross-country.[5]

The 1919 season marked his breakthrough. He began running with a stop-watch, both when training and in competitions, thus developing his fine sense of pace. The watch clutched in his fist became his hallmark and he tossed it to the inside of the track towards the finish, certain that his pace was the correct one. His competitors were irritated and the spectators fascinated when Nurmi glanced at the second-hand as he ran. What was he planning? The stop-watch added a mathematical element to his running and people sensed that it was possible to calculate races. Nurmi had no desire to smash records by big margins – small and frequent improvements were better suited to his style.

Nurmi used to go to the railway to increase his speed and the length of his stride. In 1920 he ran behind the train from Turku to Littois for a mile and a half at a faster pace than usual and taking longer strides – he ran on the right-hand side of the train with his left hand on the last carriage. He persisted in doing this behind slow-moving trains, stretching his stride and increasing his capacity while the passengers stared and pointed. On the flat and uphill everything went well; downhill, the speed really picked up, but that, too, helped.

Finland, by now independent, sent a team to the 1920 Antwerp Olympics. Their star and medal hope was Nurmi and he took the 10,000 metres gold and the 5,000 metres silver.

Throughout the 1920s Paavo Nurmi and his fellow Finnish runners shone like stars in the heavens. The miracle of Finnish running fascinated journalists, spectators and medical authorities alike. Finns were the fastest in the world at distances over 1,500 metres and they set over 70 world records between 1912 and 1940. They seemed virtually unbeatable, these three or four men running one behind the other, sinewy, hollow-cheeked, high cheek-bones, men apparently specially made for running.

After he had won the 1,500 and 5,000 metres in the course of little more than two hours at the 1924 Olympics Nurmi went out dancing at a night club. A Finnish journalist was amazed to see the champion on the dance-floor but Nurmi knew the value of dancing and relaxation after such a tight running programme.[6] He won five Olympic golds in six days, three for individual events and two for team events.

On completion of his military service Nurmi went on to a technician's course in Helsinki, where he lodged with an elderly woman. Early in the morning he would set off from his room on long training marches. A woman on a farm outside the city rushed to her barn to guard her animals when she saw this strange, fast-moving figure, dressed in a sheepskin coat and army boots and carrying a heavy pack. The walker would appear in the darkness at regular intervals and the woman assumed it was someone not quite right in the mind. She was wrong: it was Paavo Nurmi doing his twelve miles with a 66-lb (30 kg) pack on his back before going to college; by 8 a.m. every morning he would be at his desk listening to the lecture.[7]

By this stage Nurmi's running style had begun to settle into what would be his characteristic pattern. He ran with his arms working hard and quite far out from his sides, and his body seemed to be being driven forward by long, irresistible strides with much use of the hips. It was a running style that required strong hips and the ability to take long strides without inducing stiffness – many runners tried to copy it in an effort to keep up with him.

America, too, wanted its share of Nurmi. On the voyage across the Atlantic he ran round the deck and spent hours soaking in the bath to keep his muscles supple for his arrival in New York on 9 December 1924. Instead of moving into the luxury villa on offer he preferred to live with a fellow Finn in a simple basement on the outskirts of the city. His taciturnity caused even more of a stir in the United States than in Europe.

Nurmi trained and competed, running in three or four indoor events a week, often late in the evening on small, enclosed tracks with tight bends and cigarette-smoking spectators at close quarters. He was not used to the floodlighting and the fuss afterwards and the programme did not finish before midnight, when he – as the main attraction – had crossed the finishing line. Then there was the journey home so it was often 2 a.m. before he got to bed, but he still rose at 7 a.m. and did not take a nap during the day. The same routine continued week after week, with twelve races in each of January and February and fifteen in March. In addition to this there were the long car and train journeys, strangers' hands to be shaken, photo calls with prominent individuals, school visits, demonstration runs at army camps, visits to universities – always a new place and a new reason for him to demonstrate running. Nurmi had not planned to remain in the United States so long but his popularity delayed his return home.

Indoor athletics drew big crowds in the United States. In every city and every university there were arenas or sports halls of various kinds and with every sort of floor – boards or concrete or tiles or just earth. They could be quickly converted into circus-rings or boxing arenas or running tracks with short straights and sharp bends. Rather like trotting tracks, indoor athletics provided the perfect stage for duels and heavy betting. Assisted by Hugo Quist, his manager and interpreter, Nurmi became king of this arena and between them they conquered virtually the whole continent.

As a cure for travel fatigue Nurmi would hop off the train when it stopped and run the length of the platform. Here he comes, this Scandinavian who never rests and never shirks his training – even in his suit and tie he can really get up steam! In between bouts in the sauna at the kind of heat and humidity only a Finn could tolerate, he took Quist's hard pummelling on the massage table; and even when travelling he stuck to the routine of cold showers and whipping with birch twigs after his sauna.

The newspapers revelled in him as a character made for the hall of fame. The newspaper mogul Randolph Hearst could destroy a man for life with a piece of gossip but he could turn others into demi-gods if it would sell more papers. Nurmi was a primeval force from Europe, a breed of winner good for Hearst's business.

Nurmi represented a part of the world the Americans romanticized. Many of them were recent immigrants with a longing for the old country – or, rather, for their perception of the old country. Nurmi's mystique was reinforced by the fact that he did not give interviews. When the journalists pressed in close and the photographers were taking shots from all angles they got nothing out of Nurmi, so they went away and wrote their own versions, praising or blaming on the basis – at best – of information from his manager. Taciturnity can be taken as arrogance, no matter that Nurmi needed an interpreter. It was this mixture of closeness and distance that was so effective in creating the Nurmi myth: no other foreign runner before or since has been so celebrated by Americans and yet been such a mystery to them. Nurmi quickly became a legend.

Nurmi was enormously important to Finland and his immediate publicity value has been estimated as many million dollars. Without being asked, an American banker telegraphed a Geneva businessman and offered favourable new loans to Finland: if a country could produce such a unique phenomenon it deserved credit. Immigrant Finnish shopkeepers in the United States advertised their wares using Nurmi's name, just as the unemployed got jobs on the basis of claiming they knew the hero from the home country. The Finns came to be seen as a dogged, tenacious race.

Indoor records fell like dominoes. The unusual distances – yards, miles, half miles, quarter miles, eighths of a mile – meant that Nurmi broke more than 30 records in about 50 races. And because the public liked to see times improved, races were arranged over unusual distances so that the organizers could announce a new record at the end of the meeting. Nurmi only lost one race and only failed to finish once.

There were few white runners capable of beating Nurmi but on the West Coast of America there were stories of Native Americans who were unbeatable over long distances. At the end of April Nurmi competed against Native Americans in a three-mile (4.8 km) race held at the Los Angeles stadium. In front of a crowd of 40,000 he easily drew away from the best of the Hopi Indians in a contest between the white man and the original inhabitants of the country.

A photograph was taken afterwards showing a dour-looking Nurmi standing holding his cup and flowers between two of the organizers. The two plump-cheeked functionaries, standing there in collars and ties, are bursting with pride, just as if they had found a large nugget of gold. The viewer senses a profound feeling of satisfaction in the thin and ascetic-looking Nurmi – he looks like a man from another planet who is thinking, 'I am the winner. I am the best runner in the world and no one can take that away.' Many years of discipline and effort are revealed in that enigmatic expression. It is the compensation and small revenge of the outsider while the masses applaud. He often stood like that in front of a rapturous audience, satisfied but determined to improve and hold on to his place at the top, painfully aware that there was always someone at his shoulder.

The usual accusations of professionalism were made against Nurmi during this 1925 American tour. A number of promoters tried to tempt him with illegal extra payments, knowing full well that it could lead to the loss of his amateur status. Some athletes suggested that the Americans were trying to embroil European competitors in financial fixes in order to weed them out before the Olympic Games.[8]

Nurmi frequently received and rejected professional offers, such as $60,000 to appear at a circus for five months and film offers worth almost $25,000. A New York theatre owner wanted to hire the Finn to run on a treadmill in order to demonstrate the speed a human being could achieve with his legs.[9]

Paavo Nurmi did, however, often compete for illegal payment. The reasons are understandable enough: he came from a poor background, bore the burden of being the family breadwinner and, after all the self-sacrifices he had made, he was in a position to secure his future. Being a financially acute man he later invested in property in Helsinki and became more affluent than the majority of top sportsmen.

The vagueness of the amateur rules left the way open for alternative methods of payment. Let us say that a major star demanded illegal appearance money – $800 seems to have been the going rate for the biggest stars in the United States at major meetings in the 1920s.[10] After the meeting the promoter would appear in the competitor's hotel room with his pockets stuffed with notes or with an agreed sum in an envelope, all depending on whether records had been broken that day. 'I bet you $800 that you can't jump over that chair', the promoter might say. 'I bet I can', the competitor would answer before jumping over the chair. The forbidden payment had thus been converted into an unimpeachable bet.

All those involved knew the score but few considered reporting things because they were often guilty themselves. Bribes could buy long term silence for several generations. Sportsmen who were accused denied the allegations because they knew of the sins of their opponents. There were, of course, also genuine amateurs at the top level who did not break the rules.

His tour of the United States in 1925 took its toll on Nurmi's iron constitution. Over the Olympic distances of 1,500, 5,000 and 10,000 metres he never beat his 1924 records of 3 minutes 52.6 seconds, 14 minutes 28.2 seconds and 30 minutes 6.2 seconds respectively. He entered a slow downward spiral in which his margins of victory became narrower and his defeats more frequent.

He intended the 1928 season to be his last but set off instead on another, shorter tour of the United States in the following winter and was soon back on top form, stronger than ever over the longest distances and keen to climax his career with a gold for the marathon at the 1932 Los Angeles Olympics.

That dream was crushed. In the spring of 1932 he was disqualified by the International Amateur Athletic Federation after allegations of professionalism. He went to Los Angeles and continued pushing himself hard in the hope of being allowed to compete. Angered by his exclusion and with an injured foot, Nurmi could hardly walk, far less run, but he struggled on against the injury and hoped for a reprieve right to the end.

Nurmi was not allowed to take part and could not bring himself to watch the 10,000 metres and the marathon: according to him he would have won the latter by five minutes.

The Finnish Athletics Federation refused to accept the international ban. The athletics authorities in Finland were well aware of the double morality at many levels of sport and were not about to cut the legs off of the nation's greatest hero, so to speak. Nurmi carried on competing in his homeland and won his last victory at 10,000 metres in the autumn of 1934 when he was 37 years old.

'Running is in the blood of every Finn'

Many people have tried to explain the miracle of Finnish running. Were the Finns better suited to running than other races as a result of their *sisu*?

Helsingen Sanomat, Finland's biggest newspaper, fed the myth of the country's sportsmen standing there alongside the peasant farmers because of their hard work and physical toil. In Finland, as in many countries, the socio-economic elite propagated national myths by elevating aspects drawn from among the common people and making them national property. The social elite in Finland basked in the glow of what was created by the toils of the lower classes.

Many local communities in Finland were dependent on agriculture and forestry. *Helsingen Sanomat* and other newspapers regarded the lack of industry and of a modern infrastructure as a strength when it came to achievements in the athletics arena: what was actually an economic handicap and the cause of the great emigration to the United States and Sweden – the virtual absence of industry and diversified employment – was held to be Finland's trump card in the field of world-class running.

Hard work was a Finnish virtue. The image of the Finns as a hardy forest people spread around the world. When Finns were called 'natural' sportsmen, the men being referred to came from a peasant farming background and the lower social strata. It is not surprising that the Finns were astonished to discover that sport in many other countries was linked to academic study.

The top Finnish sportsmen often spoke of having done hard physical work from the time they were six or seven years old. For hard-working farming lads, whether they came from Finland or elsewhere, frittering away whole days on sport as they did at representational events was something they were unused to.

In the 1930s the German Jack Schuhmacher resorted to the landscape and physical conditions of the country to account for the miracle of Finnish running. The climate and the topography endowed the Finns with tenacity and *sisu*:

> Running is in the blood of every Finn. When you see these pure, deep forests, these fertile wide-open fields with their typical red-painted workers' houses, these ridges with their clusters of trees, the endless blue horizon that shades over into lakes, then you are overwhelmed by excitement and you feel the urge to run – because we have no wings to fly. Just to run on light feet through this Nordic landscape for mile after mile and hour after hour. Nurmi and those like him are like animals in the forest. They began to run because of a profound compulsion, because a strange dreamlike landscape called them with its enchanting mysteries.
>
> It is not only the hunt for records, for praise and for honour that spurs on the sons of Scandinavia to almost superhuman achievements. Their awe-inspiring times are a way of giving thanks to Mother Earth.[11]

But if climate was the reason for success Sweden and Norway ought to have produced equally good runners between the wars. Sweden attained a good standard but Norway – more like Finland in population numbers – lay far behind. There was no widespread culture of long-distance running in Norway, Norwegians trained less, and Norwegian training experts warned against over-training and burnout.

The Finns were best because they trained hardest and trained most intelligently at the time. They had the best supporting structures and put in most effort. Many Finns between the wars and in the decades before that grew up in simple circumstances and developed the physical and mental toughness necessary in long-distance running. They lived on small farms in the forest, did a great deal of walking as they were growing up, worked in the fields and bent over the chopping block. The forces of nature gave them an edge. But this was hardly unique to Finland: in countries all over Europe people worked hard to survive, and long walks to school and child labour were common. Schuhmacher's views were formed by the reputation of the Finns and all the stories about them: at international championships they were shy, they were renowned for their taciturn nature and their downcast eyes – a kind of humility that became self-confidence in the great running arenas. There was an aura around Finnish runners that was re-inforced by their silence and lack of linguistic skill and, of course, because it is easy to be tempted into speculating about the unknown and the exotic. In the case of the Finns the myths that arose and existed abroad also became the building blocks that major Finnish authors used in the construction of a national identity.

The widespread culture of running in Finland was the determining factor in their success, but no one can deny that running over the longer distances appealed to something in the Finnish national character. It was a modern variant of the hard slog of logging in the forests – something to show the rest of the world before bringing home the laurels. Distance was like time spent in the sauna, where what mattered was holding out for the longest possible time at the highest possible temperature. It hurt at the time but felt sweet afterwards. And with practice one could learn to put up with a lot.

It is impossible to choose the greatest single moment in Finnish running. What *feels*, perhaps, like the greatest moment came in 1952 when Finland hosted the summer Olympics in Helsinki.

The stadium is packed with spectators for the opening ceremony and Finland is the focus of the world's attention. The teams march in and file past until all of them are drawn up behind their banners.

Then comes what they have all been waiting for – the Olympic torch arrives, held aloft in the hand of a small man, running easily. The style and the long strides are familiar, the runner is solemn and self-composed. The jubilant roar that greets him fills the heavens in this light Finnish summer: 'Paavo Nurmi!' The name rings round the stadium and the voices of radio reporters send the scene to every corner of the world. It is the man himself, the symbol of Finnish *sisu*, still impudently vigorous and mysterious even if his hair is thinner. Tens of thousands of spectators feel the prickle of gooseflesh and grown men have tears in their eyes as they rise to their feet and clap and roar.

Paavo Nurmi and Finland merge into one. He is the nation's prize exemplar of *sisu* and he reminds them of the independence they longed for and achieved after centuries of foreign rule. He is a strange and wonderful example of what something as simple as running can do for a man and a nation.

16

Ultrarunning as Nation-building

I considered the Indians to be the worst of human parasites,
but I have seen the light.
—Jacobo Dalevuelta on the Tarahumara in Mexico after
they had run far and fast in the 1920s

Two enduring traditions of long-distance running, the *ekiden* in Japan and
the 'Comrades' in South Africa, originated during the First World War.

The first *ekiden* between the ancient and modern capitals of Japan,
Kyoto and Tokyo, was organized in 1917 to celebrate Tokyo's fiftieth anniversary. The distance was 315 miles in 23 stages and the race took three days on
ordinary roads.

The name *ekiden* is a compound of the words *eki*, 'a station', and *den*,
'to convey', and the name was made up in 1917 by the poet Toki Zemmaro
who worked for *Yomiuri Shimbun*, the newspaper that sponsored the race
from the start. Thus, rather like the Tour de France cycle race, the race was
the creation of the national press: in Japan as in France newspapers recognized the possibility of increasing circulation by having their own sporting
events.

The idea did, however, have roots in Japanese culture. The old horse-
drawn transport system had worked on a relay principle with stations along
the main roads where travellers could have their horses changed while remaining in the same coach. People, letters and important packages were
transported in this way and the thought behind *ekiden* was to imitate and
commemorate the ancient transport system. By using runners the race also
symbolized the new, modern and efficient Japan.

The newspaper ran a big advertising campaign in 1917 to attract participants. 46 men were chosen and formed into two teams, with 23 students
from Tokyo in one and 23 teachers and students from the prefecture of Aichi
in the other.

The race caught on immediately, whipping up excitement over the
whole of Japan, and as the runners approached the finish in Tokyo they
were cheered on by 100,000 spectators. *Ekiden* became the Japanese sporting event with the biggest following and it inspired similar races all over
the country.

Shizo Kanaguri, who ran in the marathon at the 1912 Stockholm
Olympics and was the father of Japanese marathon running, wanted to
train world-class runners. He saw the success of the first *ekiden* and urged

the universities in the city to start one. In 1920 four universities cooperated in the Hakone *ekiden*, which ran from Tokyo to the Hakone mountain region and back. New projects of this kind also reflected the increasing attention being paid to Western sports in Japan.

In its early days the Hakone *ekiden* was run in a rather happy-go-lucky fashion. The runners started in the afternoon because the students had lectures in the morning and they could choose their own route: all that mattered was getting from start to finish.

When the 78th Hakone *ekiden* was run between 15 student teams in 2002 a quarter of the TV viewers in the country watched the direct transmissions and hundreds of thousands lined the roads. The race consisted of ten stages, five in each direction, totalling 134 miles (216 km) with a winning time of about eleven hours. The desire to take part in this race has encouraged many Japanese into higher education.

In an *ekiden* each runner runs from one station to the next carrying a piece of cloth, *tasuki*, which is then passed on. Each piece represents the runner, the team, the company or the region the team belongs to and any changes in the position of the teams is greeted with joy or disappointment by the onlookers. It all appeals to the Japanese sense of local patriotism or company loyalty – loyalty which during the twentieth century could often last for the whole of an employee's working life. Superficially *tasuki* are the same as the batons in relay races but they have a deeper symbolic significance. What makes *ekiden* so special and so popular is the combination of traditional competitiveness with a uniquely Japanese spirit.

The fact that the participants are contributing to a team effort, joining forces and demonstrating group loyalty explains why the *ekiden* has caught on, since these attitudes are highly regarded in Japan and were even stronger at the time such races started.

The longest *ekiden* is the 'Prince Takamatsu Cup Nishinippon Round-Kyushu Ekiden' which, with its 661 miles (1,064 km) and 72 stages, is probably the world's longest relay race.[1]

Comrades

Vic Clapham from London emigrated as a boy with his parents to Cape Colony in South Africa. He enlisted as an ambulance man at the outbreak of the Boer War (1899–1902) when he was only thirteen. In the First World War he joined the 8th South African Infantry and marched about 1,700 miles across the East African savannah in pursuit of Glen Paul von Lettow-Vorbeck's battalion – a German general who employed guerrilla tactics. There were German colonies in German East Africa (now Tanzania) and the general's force wanted to avoid meeting the South Africans in battle.

During these difficult times Clapham saw suffering, death and destruction but he also saw a solidarity that he valued. After the war ended in 1918 he wanted to commemorate the long march and his fallen comrades with a race that would reflect some of the hardships. He turned to the athletics authorities in South Africa and also to the League of Comrades, an old soldiers' association, the comrades being military colleagues, friends or allies.

Inspired by a march from Brighton to London Clapham proposed a 56-mile (90-km) race from Pietermaritzburg to Durban but the soldiers' association protested on the grounds that the idea was unrealistic – who would be capable of completing it? Clapham believed, however, that if ordinary citizens plucked from the street and put in uniform could march across half of Africa carrying 55 lb (25 kg) on their backs as he and his comrades had done, then well-trained runners could run 56 miles without a load. In 1919 and 1920 his proposal was rejected but in 1921 the association agreed to the event and it started from the town-hall in Pietermaritzburg on the 24 May – Commonwealth Day – that year. 34 white entrants were brave enough to enter and W. Rowan won in 8 hours 59 minutes.

The following year the race was run in the opposite direction, which is how it has continued since. The first woman – Frances Hayward – completed it as early as 1923 and in 1931 a schoolteacher called Geraldine Watson entered after only six weeks training and completed it three years in succession, taking 9 hours 31 minutes for her last run after six months' preparation. Over the following decades the Comrades Race was a contributing factor to South Africa producing the world's top ultra runners – those who seek out longer distances than the marathon.

News of the Comrades Race reached many parts of the world.[2] In Sweden it helped inspire *Vasaloppet*, a 56-mile ski-race founded in 1922 in memory of an heroic Swedish historical exploit.

The Comrades also led to new arguments in the debate about whether alcohol and running go together. This debate lasted for several decades with some amusing results, such as the compulsory serving of beer at the end of long-distance runs to restore the liquid balance – this was a period when drinking-water in the cities was impure. Exhausted runners were given bottles of beer and swallowed the contents, this being the best available alternative. The air around the finishing line was filled with an aroma of sweat and alcohol and runners of an international standard considered a rapid intake of alcohol as necessary for health.

Arthur F. H. Newton was born in England but lived in South Africa, where he was a farmer in the 1920s. He probably ran farther than anyone else in that decade and he experimented with many things, including alcohol, even though its use had a bad reputation among sportsmen by that time, in connection with competitions, anyway. There were stories, for instance, about the South African Charles Hefferson who missed the Olympic marathon gold in 1908 after accepting champagne from a spectator, as well as about other runners who had passed out from consuming more alcohol than was sensible.

Newton believed that alcohol had a positive effect if used in the right way, as with drugs, when the body was utterly exhausted. He carried out an experiment in which he reduced his daily training from his usual twelve miles, the aim being to induce overload and unusual levels of exhaustion on a 40-mile run when he was going to test the effects of alcohol.[3]

After doing 35 miles (56 km) Newton took a mixture of one dessert-spoon of brandy to six parts of water, brought along for him by his neighbour who was also his training assistant. He then continued, refreshed and at a faster pace, and the effect lasted for three or four miles, almost all the way to the finish. This prompted him to further experimentation.

The next time, running a marathon distance, he increased the amount of alcohol by 50 per cent and drank it before the same downhill sections. It was as if someone had punched him: the alcohol paralysed his legs and he could hardly run. He recovered slowly and dragged himself home, absolutely certain that the dose had been too big.

Newton then repeated the first experiment and found the same positive effect: a small alcoholic top-up might be helpful towards the end of the Comrades, his great goal of that season.

He did indeed take a measured dose after 48 miles and won by half an hour, not, of course, only because of the alcohol. He later concluded that alcohol was unnecessary and cut it out when competing. He did, however, stick to his conviction that a drop of alcohol had a good effect on the final run home – shocking the body, almost, into delivering even more.

For the Salvation of the Nation

Many people rose unusually early in the Mexican town of Pachuca on 7 November 1926. Even the mayor of the town and the governor of the state of Hidalgo were present among the spectators at 3.05 a.m. as three Tarahumara began their run to Mexico City 60 miles (97 km) away to the sound of exploding fireworks while the road was illuminated by the lights of cars and motor-cycles. The runners had bells hanging from their belts as an audible indication that they were members of the Tarahumara tribe, although they were clad in the Mexican colours of red, green and white.[4]

The runners attracted much attention. The bells in local churches pealed along the way, calling out spectators who saw one of them drop out halfway. As they approached Mexico City the caravan of cars following them caused a traffic jam. The Tarahumara arrived at the national stadium, having taken 9 hours and 37 minutes for the 60 miles.

Tomás Zaffiro and Leoncio San Miguel became national heroes after having set an unofficial world record for the unusual distance of 60 miles. The two only spoke a little Spanish and were unable to understand everything when the Mexican authorities handed out the prizes: two red silk handkerchiefs, a lot of white cotton and two ploughs.

The organizers had several ulterior motives for using an Indian tribe to demonstrate Mexican stamina and athletic skills. They were hoping that 60 miles would become an Olympic distance, preferably in Amsterdam in

1928, in which case the Tarahumara might win and bring honour to Mexico. An Olympic gold would help to sweep away the stereotype of the lazy Mexican.

Mexico was at the stage of rebuilding after a bloody revolution and considerable strife in the decade up to 1921. The two Tarahumara runners symbolized an effort to include all the native groups in the country in a new, proud Mexico, one in which there would be less discrimination. The Tarahumara were ideally suited to the role of athletic supermen.

By enlisting the Tarahumara the Mexicans were pursuing the ideas of one of the country's best-known artists and cultural figures, known as 'Dr Atl'. In the run-up to the 1924 Olympics, the first in which Mexico participated, he demanded that the country be represented by robust indigenous peoples rather than by 'civilized-effeminate', upper-class citizens. If they wanted to win the prestigious running events at the Olympics they would have to rely on the Tarahumara.

The aim of this plan was to bring together primitive strength and modernity. The two Tarahumara who set the 1926 60-mile record did so on a new road that had just opened to motorized traffic from all over the country and their run signified that even the poorest in the country could be included in the modernization process. Running might also contribute to a solution of the country's so-called 'Indian problem', since illiteracy and lack of schooling held poor local indigenous communities in a merciless grip.

All this would benefit the Mexican Revolution and the president, General Plutarco Elías Calles, who believed in advancement for the native peoples.[5]

The news of the two Tarahumara reached the world's press and created a great sensation, particularly in the United States, where Mexicans were held to be lazy and unsuited to top-level athletics.

The Tarahumara received a great deal of attention for several other long runs at the end of the 1920s, particularly after they brought the 60 mile time down to 7.30. But the IOC (International Olympic Committee) would not accept the proposed distance as an Olympic event – nor did they accept the women's marathon. José Torres appeared for Mexico in the 1928 Amsterdam Olympics and finished in what, for Mexico, was a disappointing 21st place. Runners from the Tarahumara tribe, however, retained their mythical status in Mexico in spite of their uneven performances in the developed world. The poet Alfonso Reyes wrote a famous poem as a homage to them:

> The finest marathon runners in the world,
> nourished on the bitter flesh of deer,
> they will be the first to bring the triumphant news
> the day we leap the wall
> with our five senses.[6]

These Tarahumara were the new Mexico's contribution to a world in which sport was becoming more and more significant as a means of self-assertion.

The Tarahumara reinforced prejudices when, as children of nature, they showed a childish fascination for inventions like the gramophone and films. After the run from Pachuca to Mexico City one of them said: 'We are strong because we live outdoors. Veneration gives our feet wings. Only then can a man be happy'.[7]

This campaign in Mexico, using the Tarahumara as mascots of tenacity, took place at about the same time as one of the most colourful events in the history of the world running.

17
Race across America

But the Englishman was unable to consume solid food because of an
inflamed tooth. He lived on a liquid diet for several weeks and suffered
terribly. He should have listened to his dentist at home who advised
him before he left to have all his teeth out to avoid problems.
—On Peter Gavuzzi from England, participant in the race across
America in 1928

The businessman C. C. Pyle foresaw enormous profits when, in the spring
of 1928, he announced a foot-race right across the USA in the same spirit as
the Tour de France in cycling. It was to be an event that engaged the whole
nation. No one had ever organized a comparable race, certainly not with
$25,000 as the first prize and a total of $48,000 dollars in prize-money. A
doctor pronounced that the race would shorten participants' lives by
between five and ten years and there was the possibility that no one would
complete it even if the runners were the handpicked iron men of the world.

It was mainly about money. Pyle's critics asserted that he was selling the
personalities of the runners and a constructed image rather than promoting real sport. But that is the way things were in the USA in the 1920s, with
bizarre tests of endurance such as dance marathons, daredevil swimming
stunts and the sailor Shipwreck Kelly earning a living by sitting on the top
of flagpoles for days at a time. It was all about going one farther than the
last man.

The runners would be advertising signed shoes, hair tonic, foot cream,
roller-skates and many other things and the coffee company Maxwell House
would be serving free drinks from a van shaped like the biggest coffee pot
in the world. Pyle signed a contract with all the participants that entitled
him to half of any of their earnings that could be attributed directly to his
organization of the run. He was hoping to create new stars who would be
offered film and theatre contracts or have new products named after them.

Pyle also made an appeal to local patriotism. All the small towns the
runners passed through would be covered in the national media and journalists and photographers would spread the news to all corners of the globe.
This was his main argument when he demanded that towns pay *him* to
have the caravan stop in them. Like an auctioneer Pyle called for bids from
the towns along Route 66 from Los Angeles to Chicago, one of the first US
Highways, only one third of which had a hard surface. If people could run
this route, it would reassure motorists and open the way to more traffic.[1]

Newspapers the world over wrote about this crazy race across a continent, starting in the film city of Los Angeles and finishing in New York

with its skyscrapers. It attracted adventurers, competitive walkers and the stars of running, all of whom saw fame and major earnings beckoning. The competition stirred up national sentiments: 'This is for us to win', thought Americans, Finns, Italians, Britons, Germans, Greeks and many other nationalities. Many of the toughest male runners and walkers in the world took leave from their jobs for months, others simply gave them up. Some of them were unemployed but they all hastily scraped together money for tickets and the entry fee, often by holding local collections, and set off for California as if they were joining the gold-rush.

By the beginning of 1928 close to 300 men had expressed an interest, including a number of international stars. In January 1928 they gathered from afar, the best of them with their coaches, to train in the hills around Hollywood. An organized training camp opened on the 12 February, three weeks before the start, in a tented village on Old Ascott Raceway in Los Angeles. At 6 a.m. every day the men left the village in droves to jog for a couple of miles or so.

Several favourites emerged. Willie Kolehmainen, one of the three legendary Finnish brothers, had ambitions and the support of two nations behind him since he had become an American citizen. Arthur Newton was looking strong after his world record for the 100 miles. He swore by his own training and dietary arrangements and by his typical short long-distance stride – which looked rather like mincing but used a minimum amount of energy. To top up his energy he took swigs of a special concoction of his own, consisting of half a litre of lemon juice, masses of sugar and half a teaspoon of salt. Newton happily smoked a cigar every morning before training and had another puff afterwards as his regular masseur kneaded his thin legs.

Newton was eccentric but not to the same extent as Lucien Frost, one of the greatest mascots of the race. This 43-year-old actor was a long-haired, bearded member of a religious sect and he turned out in a long shift: he had played in the film *King of Kings* and he ran in the same garb as he had worn for the part of Moses. When the wind was behind him his hair and beard blew into his eyes and blinded him; when the wind was against him they slowed him down. Frost found one solution – when the wind was at his back he spread his beard like a sail.

The race started on 4 March from Old Ascott Raceway. In typical Pyle style, a small bomb was detonated, causing tremors in the surrounding areas, and off went 199 men between the ages of 16 and 63.

100,000 spectators lined the road on the first day and watched the running carnival pass at different speeds. Behind the skinny marathon experts and hip-wriggling competitive walkers came an old gentleman with a walking-stick, who nevertheless completed the stage faster than a boy playing a Hawaiian guitar and shuffling along with two dogs. There were men in long underpants, everyday clothes and unsuitable shoes; there were former cyclists, boxers and the one-armed Roy McMurtry. From England there was Charles

W. Hart, who had beaten two horses in a six-day race. The German marathon swimmer Fred Kamler had crawled ashore to give it a try and he was one of those in the field who had never run competitively before. Rarely had such an ill-assorted band of runners appeared on the same starting-line.

The rules were simple. All the participants started at the same time and when they came to the finishing line of that day's stage their times were taken and the aggregate worked out. Anyone who did not finish before midnight was disqualified. The competitor with the best aggregate time on reaching New York would be the winner.

On the fifth day they arrived at Mojave Wells in the desert, a place with only one water-pump. The following day there were checkpoints set up at the water-holes along the road but Pyle could not provide enough to drink on the stretches between the pumps. Many of the runners suffered from thirst and sunburn. In some places oil had been poured over the road surface and had formed a sandy crust which broke under the runners' feet. It is easy to see why over a quarter of the competitors cracked that first week, among them Adam Ziolkowski, who trod on glass and received serious cuts. He stayed in the area and earned a living as a potato worker on a California farm before turning up in New York five months after the end of the race.

The evenings were occupied with food, massage and foot-baths. The runners had to sell the race programme or be interviewed by the only mobile radio station in the USA – radio was still in its infancy but Pyle took maximum advantage of it. Early in the competition the runners were annoyed that Pyle lived in high style in a specially built mobile home called 'America', advertised as being the best of its kind. It had hot and cold water, a shower, electric refrigerator, reading lights and was very luxurious.

Pyle also took a 'sideshow' along with him, a popular form of entertainment with deep roots in the USA. It consisted of fat ladies, fire-eaters, sword-swallowers, snakes and anything else that might cause a sensation in small towns, which included – in Pyle's case – a five-legged dog and the mummified corpse of an outlaw from Oklahoma. With these entertainers, who set up their booths wherever the daily stage was to finish, Pyle hoped to attract more spectators and increase his profits. It was not exactly a money machine but it caught on in some places and added a desirably exotic flavour to the caravan. Rather as Pyle had hoped, there was a mixture of confusion, entertainment and frustration day and night, although the reality was that he was not making enough money since the hundreds of thousands of spectators along the roads were seeing the runners without paying a penny. There were times when Pyle felt he was providing a free attraction.

After twelve days there were still 110 men holding out. Every day someone broke down along the way or at the finish, or announced in the morning they could not continue because of exhaustion, injury, infections or sore feet. Several were knocked down by cars or motor-cycles, one had a nervous breakdown and one suffered from irremediable homesickness. But there were others who dropped out in protest at Pyle's strict regime.

Before they started Pyle had been a strong believer in the endurance of the Native Americans but they proved unable to take weeks of road-running and gave up. Willie Kolehmainen dropped out after three days because of an injury and even Arthur Newton, who for a while was well in the lead, had to give up before the 600-mile mark. Newton had been the great international attraction and, in order to keep him involved, Pyle appointed him adviser to the runners: it was vital to have a big, well-known name involved.

With Newton out, the competition was more open. The new man in the lead was Andy Payne, a 20-year-old Cherokee Indian from Oklahoma who had advanced through the ranks when the stars dropped out.

Harry Gunn from Los Angeles, one of the walkers, accepted help from two private support cars and from his father, the wealthy F. F. 'Dick' Gunn, who had bet $75,000 that his son would finish. He had promised the boy a sum equivalent to the first prize if he did so. From the first day Harry walked deliberately at three and a half to four and a half miles an hour, avoiding injury and exhaustion, in contrast to many who trotted and soon got sore feet or dropped out. He changed his shoes often, slept in comfort-able hotel beds and ate tasty restaurant food. While the other competitors were trying to rest in noisy tents he was lying in a bathtub being massaged by his coach. But time would show that there was no way to buy victory or a top placing: the winner would have to run, not just walk.

After sixteen days the field was down to half. Andy Payne led by an hour from Arne Souminen, a Finnish-born masseur who had closed his practice in Chicago to take part – he was convinced that his professional experience and self-massage would give him a considerable advantage.

A few days after Payne took over the lead his tonsils swelled up. He eased his pace and continued bravely with a high temperature and pain when he swallowed. He gradually picked up and began to perform normally again after six days. By that time Souminen was three hours in front of Payne and just behind him was the Englishman Peter Gavuzzi, a particularly danger-ous challenger.

A storm hit them on a stage in New Mexico. Strong winds and whirling sand made it virtually impossible to run. The sand cut visibility for runners and drivers and motorists were bumping into exhausted men struggling to keep going in the right direction. Gavuzzi put on a spurt and saw his chance of moving up on the leader while the judges were warning oncom-ing traffic of what was happening. The men staggered in to the finish, thirsty, their mouths full of sand and their bodies covered in it. They had been run-ning for hours with their hands over their faces. Several of them got lost that day, but Gavuzzi moved up to second place overall.

At a general meeting the runners demanded better food and something more than tents with filthy bunks at night – the bedclothes were only washed once on the whole trip (in Texas). The feelings against Pyle were particularly bitter because, on top of everything else, there had been a day when the desert camp was completely without water. The runners were like a ship's crew planning mutiny but their threats came to nothing since they needed all their energy to run.

As the race went on fewer of the competitors slept in the tents. At the start different nationalities had shared tents but as numbers decreased, or when the caravan was late in arriving at the appointed stop, many of those who could afford to do so chose to sleep elsewhere. Apart from anything else, the tents offered no protection from the noise of the sideshows and all the other activities. It was not so easy for the black runners to escape the tents, however, even if they had money: racial segregation laws made it hard for them to find alternative accommodation.

The competitors had been promised fresh food, fresh fruit, vegetables and good meat dishes – and back in the training camp they had got them. But on the way across the USA the diet was monotonous, most often consisting of a strongly spiced hash-like dish, served on unwashed plates. The runners were even more annoyed because Pyle was eating fine food in his mobile home and generally living like a lord.

In Albuquerque in New Mexico the city authorities refused to pay a $5,000 contribution to host the race and the whole caravan camped in the desert outside the city. The combination of Pyle's uncompromising nature and suspicious local authorities meant that the route was forever being changed, sometimes in the course of a day after the stage had started, in which case the runners were passed messages and counter-messages by judges in cars. Pyle promised things would improve when they reached more populous areas but not everyone believed his promises.

Many competitors continued because they had nothing else to do and no job to go back to. That was particularly true of the rearguard of twenty to thirty men, who were taking the race less than seriously. When the vanguard set off at a steady pace in the morning, grimly determined to retain or improve their placings, the rearguard would wander into a cafeteria to eat breakfast. They were in no hurry. If they came to a lake they dived in and took a dip. They fished, slept and enjoyed their way across the country in the company of the dogs that had attached themselves to them. The best-known of the dogs plodded along with them for weeks from Arizona. Some of the rearguard were having their expenses covered by their home state and were living well on it. Mike Kelley was the leader of this gang of saboteurs of Pyle's conception: they used to hide in the dark close to the finishing line and cross it at five to twelve, just before the deadline.[2]

After 1,004 miles (1,616 km) Souminen had taken 167 hours and 55 minutes and was placed just four hours ahead of Patne and Gavuzzi, but Souminen fell on ice in Texas and suffered a badly strained ligament. When he was forced to drop out Johnny Salo, another Finnish emigrant to the USA, moved up to third place.

Life on the road was both varied and monotonous. The runners were subject to all the moods of nature, alone on long flat sections under wide skies and painfully aware that every little step only brought them a little closer to the finish. The alarm signal would sometimes ring at 4 a.m. so that they could start before 5 a.m. to avoid the worst of the heat. In Texas there was snow, wind and cold that led to split nails and frostbite and when the support vehicle with the food and sleeping gear stuck fast in mud on the way to Groom in Texas they were all forced to arrange their own food and lodgings. The Canadian competitive walker Philip Granville, who discovered that running was more efficient and won his first stage in Texas, telegraphed home for $1,000. This healthy financial top-up illustrates the class differences in the field. Those with most money lived most comfortably; those who were broke were more reminiscent of tramps than sportsmen, with ragged clothes and sunburn, prepared to eat and drink anything at all when they arrived at the finishing line late in the afternoon or evening.

One day in Texas there was a first prize of $500 for the stage winner. That caused some of them to push up the pace and Peter Gavuzzi walked off with the money. The authorities in Oklahoma offered $1,000 to whoever was first to cross the state line. That inspired Ed 'Sheikh' Gardner, who wore sheikh's headgear and was one of the few black runners in the race. He was a man of unpredictable tactics: he could suddenly strike and win a stage and the next day lie snoring by a ditch in between meals with strangers. Thanks to hospitable people Gardner put on weight along the way – he was an expert at finding ladies who fed him well. He was continually being invited to stay the night and there was often a local black band to welcome him home at the end of a stage. Parties in his honour went on until after midnight and he enjoyed being at the centre of things. But the hospitality slowed him down.

According to rumour the telegrams Gardner received contained instructions from bookmakers in Seattle telling him in what position he should finish the stages so that they could control the betting. In Texas the Ku Klux Klan grabbed him and held him back physically so that Andy Payne could cross the state line into Oklahoma first. They would tolerate a Native American winning the prize but not a black. When the Klan realized that black and white were competing together they set fire to Ed Gardner's support vehicle.

Oklahoma was a triumphal journey for Payne, who was involved in a close contest with Gavuzzi. The two of them shared the stage victories without giving away too much time: just half an hour separated them and they knew that the third man was about twenty hours behind them. In Oklahoma City, because of Payne's sensational lead there, the race got the kind of attention Pyle had dreamed of: spectators ran and cycled alongside and the motorcycle police blew their horns to clear away those who got too close.

Several other runners crossed the state line first in their home states and received a royal welcome even if their aggregate position was far back. The competitors would slacken off the pace and allow the home favourites to win. Pyle recognized the value of that kind of brouhaha. But when no one was prepared to pay enough for one stage in Missouri and Pyle ordered a diversion from Route 66, the population of Carthage felt cheated and reacted angrily. They pelted the lead car with rotten eggs and shouted at Pyle who was sitting safely behind the glass.

After 50 days they passed the 2,000 mile (3,219 km) mark and the field of 73 men was showing signs of strain and injuries. Many of them felt cheated by Pyle, feeling that he had conned them into an interminable nightmare that could do them long-term harm.

A steady stream of rumours soured the situation further. Were some of the competitors cheating by taking lifts? The front-runners' coaches kept a watchful eye on the runners closest to their own men in terms of aggregate time, but the suspicions were confirmed when one good runner hid under a pile of clothes in the back of his coach's car and stayed there for eight miles. He was disqualified, as were two men far back in the field who hitched lifts.

Many of the runners and judges suspected Lucien 'Moses' Frost of dishonest behaviour. He habitually came in last every evening but it was impossible to check everyone every single yard of the way. When, however, one of the judges noticed a long strand of beard fluttering out of the boot of a passing car he ordered the woman driver to stop; Frost was found curled up in the boot like an escaped prisoner. Full of shame and remorse, he made a tearful defence speech to the senior judge, offering to walk the stretch he had driven and receive a time penalty, but it did not help. Nor did his pleas that disqualification would ruin his film career. Frost was given back his $100 transport deposit and went home.

Just before St Louis in Missouri Gavuzzi took over the overall lead from Payne and in St Louis itself the two them finished the stage together for the twentieth time. The press noticed two things about Gavuzzi – his 'twin' runs with Payne and the beard he was growing. A beard on a young man was enough for a headline in a decade when beards were only for the elderly. Pyle encouraged the runners to do things to provide the journalists with fodder for their articles so he was enraged when, just before Chicago, Gavuzzi slipped into a barber's and had his beard shaved off. He also swore to remain clean-shaven for the rest of the race.

'Give me a false beard and I'll wear it into Chicago', Gavuzzi said.

But Pyle would have nothing to do with such obvious deception.

'All you are asked to do is to run and to grow a beard. Now you're shirking half your duty.'[3]

Coming into Chicago Pyle broke his principle of never running alongside the competitors, by running with the Finn Olli Wantinnen, who had been hit by a car and had several broken ribs. Pyle ran with the tiny, six-and-a-half stone Finn for a while to whip up the atmosphere.

By this stage, however, Pyle was in deep financial difficulties. He had invested heavily in a bank in Illinois and lost a great deal, and he had to talk to lawyers to avoid losing his mobile home 'America'. In Chicago the organization behind Route 66 would not pay up because the race had deviated from the route too often. Pyle was close to $200,000 in the red and risked having to call it all off with over 900 miles still to go. He was either going to have to run from his creditors or find something fast. Then F. F. 'Dick' Gunn came to his rescue. He promised to pay Pyle's most pressing debts and to cover the rest of the expenses to New York.

The competition was taking longer than planned so Pyle increased the length of the stages to at least 40 miles. He and others had underestimated the runners' stamina: the real sceptics had reckoned that no one would make it to New York whereas Pyle had believed that ten to twelve would succeed and now he wanted to weed out the slowest to save expenditure on food. Five more gave up soon after the stages were increased but that still left 65 stubborn characters hanging on.

There was now a real duel at the front. Through Indiana Peter Gavuzzi had increased his lead over Andy Payne to more than six hours. But the Englishman was unable to consume solid food because of an inflamed tooth. He lived on a liquid diet for several weeks and suffered terribly. He should have listened to his dentist at home who advised him before he left to have all his teeth out to avoid problems. Gavuzzi, whom the press had christened 'The Iron Man', would not give up voluntarily even though he was losing strength, but after a visit to the dentist he was pulled out of the race.

Andy Payne was now in the lead for the third time, 24 hours ahead of Johnny Salo, a longshoreman from New Jersey who had started the race in bad form and with no achievements behind him. He was ten hours in front of number three and almost 24 hours ahead of number four. Salo hoped to pull in the leader and he clipped an hour off here, an hour and a half there. But not even a superhuman effort on the longest stage was of any avail – 74 miles (119 km) through hilly country which Salo covered in twelve hours.

The race created great excitement in New Jersey, particularly when Johnny Salo passed through his home town of Passiac. He was immediately appointed as a policeman with a salary of $2,000 a year. When the runners lined up at the city stadium in the evening of 26 May to start the last stage to New York City, there were over 20,000 cheering spectators. A tail of motor vehicles followed Salo who, along with several others, set a terrific pace. All of them leapt on the same ferry, excited to be approaching the finish at last.

The cars of the runners' caravan left the ferry station first and drove to the finish. Pyle gave orders that the cars must not be washed and that everything must look dusty, muddy and authentic as proof they had crossed the continent. A sight like that driving along the New York streets would encourage more people to come to the finishing line at Madison Square Gardens. The metropolitan finish, however, was an anticlimax after the success in New Jersey and only 4,000 people were there to welcome the caravan, which managed to do one circuit before Salo and the fastest runners arrived after a nineteen-minute sprint from the ferry.

There were some strange scenes inside the Gardens. Pyle was shouting at the men to go for it, to sprint to the finish to make a fitting ending, but the runners wanted to shuffle and trot. To liven things up, $100 was offered to the fastest man over a mile and they all lined up, but after sprinting a few yards the majority fell back into a slow pace. Six men, however, pushed themselves hard to win and the winner grabbed his five $20 dollar bills as he passed.

George Jussick chain-smoked and trotted at the same time, just as he had done the whole trip. The Montreal competitor Eugene Germaine's lower left leg had swollen to twice the size of his other leg. The spectators saw men who were plodding and limping – over 40 participants had made it to the end even though they had no chance of winning. They saw T. 'Cotton' Josephs, at sixteen the youngest in the race, who was given a drink and congratulated by his younger brother. His lame and unemployed father, Henry Josephs, had been with him all the way after scraping together $50 to buy a car and accompany his son. Cotton was hoping to help his family not so much by winning the race but by finishing it and thus, perhaps, winning some fame that could be turned into earnings. A stone's throw from the finish the Josephs' car broke down and had to be pushed in.

Salo won the final stage but Andy Payne was overall winner with 573 hours 4 minutes and 34 seconds, a good fifteen hours ahead of Salo. Third place was taken by Philip Granville, the running walker.

Few people believed Pyle would be able to pay the prizes at the time agreed, one week after their arrival. For the most part the runners seemed satisfied to have finished and were happy to go into a hospital to be examined. Andy Payne, in fact, weighed a good two pounds more than at the start.

Andy Payne, a modest man, now had the attention of the whole country turned on him. He met politicians of all kinds, including the President of the USA. He married, studied law and was a popular man for the rest of his life – and was always remembered as the winner of the race of the century.

After the prize-giving Pyle was no longer the competitors' protector. He considered a future as a sports promoter and fought to avoid lawsuits and angry creditors. The demands were pouring in from all sides, even from those employed in the caravan, since they had received too little pay. Although he was on the brink of bankruptcy and plagued by angry enquiries, Pyle was still hatching commercial ideas: remedies for water blisters and care of the feet, a book on chiropody. Having studied foot problems for three months no one knew more about them than he did. Anyone who bought C. C. Pyle's Patent Foot Box would also receive the book he was planning to write about chiropody. Pyle prophesied that hundreds of thousands of Americans would begin to run marathons after his great race and there would be a demand for new products. The marathon did become a short-term fashion in the USA during these years and provided a good income for inventors. Pyle himself believed he was going to be made rich as Croesus by these crackpots who voluntarily wanted to run long distances.

Pyle's desires did not, however, come to fruition either in 1928 or in the following year, when he arranged another run across the USA, this time starting in New York City.

18
Dubious Race Theories

The Negro does well in certain disciplines because he is closer to primitive man than white people. It was not long ago that his ability to
sprint and jump was a life-and-death matter to him in the jungle.
—Dean Cromwell in 1941, track coach of the American
Olympic Team in Berlin in 1936

The term *eugenics* comes from Greek and means 'of good breeding'. It was
introduced into modern science by the English scientist Francis Galton
in 1882. Eugenics is the same as hereditary hygiene – teaching how a population can be improved through heredity, an idea that has been around since
antiquity. But eugenics is not the same as race hygiene even though the concepts are treated as if they are synonymous, since eugenics does not take as
its starting point the advancement of a particular race.

After white Europeans had conquered and colonized large areas of the
globe, racial theory was accepted at the beginning of the twentieth century
by recognized scholars in Europe and North America. Indigenous and black
races were considered to suffer from an inherited moral inferiority, partly because these peoples were at a different technological stage and partly because
they died in large numbers of diseases introduced by conquerors who had
greater resistance to them. Since they were often illiterate they were, to European thinking, at a lower cultural level. And they were not Christians.

Two weeks before the 1904 Olympics in St Louis in the USA an exhibition and series of tests were arranged – they called them 'Anthropological
Days' – in which non-western individuals were tested in Western branches
of sport. Those tested, defined by the organizers as 'savage' and 'uncultured',
were Africans, Asians and Native Americans specially selected for the purpose from people at the World's Fair that was taking place in St Louis at the
same time as the Olympic Games.[1]

The Africans were defined as a single group even though they were made
up of Zulus, Pygmies and Bushmen. The organizers divided all the 'natives'
into eight groups and these were then tested in the Olympic athletic disciplines but also given exercises that were thought more appropriate to them,
such as climbing up poles.

Apart from showing modern Americans examples of earlier stages of
human culture, the aim was to investigate the natives' competence in the
sports of the West. There was speculation as to whether they were advan-
taged by their lower cultural level, by their more primitive technology and
by the fact that they lived closer to natural conditions. This kind of research

was taken seriously by the great anthropological authorities of the day, and it was an age when European and American attitudes to many races were characterized by colonial ethnocentricity. Part of the spirit of that age was the exhibition of 'natives' at World Fairs.

The natives proved disappointing as runners. With a time of 5 minutes 38 seconds, the fastest of them over a mile was slow – far behind the best Olympic runners. Natives lacked the right attitude and approach to running on a track: 'Not unexpectedly the natives proved to know nothing about sprinting. With eight or ten of them on the starting line it was quite difficult to explain to them that they should run when the starting pistol was fired. When they reached the finishing tape some of them stopped and others ran under it rather than breasting the tape'.[2]

Even though Dr William J. McGee, president of the American Anthropological Association and one of the originators of the test, was sceptical about the scientific value of the event, his views were shouted down by those who wanted no doubts expressed about these newly confirmed results demonstrating the athletic inferiority of natives. The official report produced after the 'Anthropological Days' concluded that the results merited being utilized in lectures and in the literature for students.

Attitudes of this kind survived a long time and can be found in a Swedish encyclopaedia of sports as late as 1943. The writer refers to the 1904 tests and concludes that 'it is impossible to make sporting stars out of African Negroes'. In running, for example, they lacked the ability to exploit and apportion their own physical resources – so the weakness was also perceived as being on an intellectual plane.

Nordic races – so-called – were viewed as the mainspring of European civilization. Different characteristics were ascribed to different races and the adherents of these theories made a crude division of races into Caucasoid, Mongoloid and Negroid. The doctrine of the superiority of the Aryan race found fertile soil, particularly in Nazi Germany during the 1930s. The sterilization laws that many countries introduced in this period show a desire on the part of the authorities to prevent individuals classed as inferior from breeding. Against this background it is easy to see how a debate about running and race could come into being between the wars.

The black English sprinter Harry F. V. Edwards, who competed at the international elite level during the 1920s, stated with a heartfelt groan: 'For years it's been said that all negroes can sing and dance. From now on we'll be hearing the platitude that all negroes can run and jump.'[3]

Before the Second World War international running over all distances was dominated by whites. Black sprinters were very successful during the 1930s and the experts discussed whether race was of any significance in running, particularly after the 1936 Berlin Olympics. The question was whether black people originating from West Africa – that being where the slaves in the USA, Brazil and the Caribbean had come from – were better suited to sprinting than white people.

Adolf Hitler was of the opinion that blacks should not compete against whites over short distances because the blacks were superior. According to Hitler, the American sprinter and long-jumper James 'Jesse' Cleveland Owens should consequently be in a class of his own. Both black and white commentators poured praise on Owens as one of the greatest athletes of his time after he won four Olympic Golds in 1936 – at 100 metres, 200 metres, long-jump and 4 x 100 metre relay. Owens was not the first black American at the top level but was the first to receive international attention.

Whereas previously it had been said that blacks lacked aptitude, now their success was frequently ascribed to their natural, animal physique and talent. The American X-ray specialist E. Albert Kinley had predicted earlier that blacks would set records in many disciplines because they had longer heels than whites.[4]

Even black American eugenicists joined in the debate. The best known of these was William Montague Cobb, past professor at Howard University and the only black American before the Second World War with a doctorate in anthropology. He summoned the scientists of Case Western University in 1936 to measure the preserved skeletons of blacks and whites, the aim being to discover whether long heel bones, flat feet, longer sinews in the leg muscles and longer legs might lie behind the black successes.

The investigators examined Jesse Owens and Frank Wykoff, the fastest white American of the time and the man who came fourth in the 100 metres at the 1936 Olympics. Cobb decided that Owens had a typically Caucasoid leg musculature whereas Wykoff had what was considered to be the classic Negroid musculature.

Cobb's conclusion was as follows: 'Our Negro champions do not have a single characteristic in common, including their skin colour, which directly identifies them as Negroes.'[5] There was nothing, in his opinion, to suggest that blacks had certain physical characteristics that accounted for their success. It was consequently a mistake to classify blacks and whites according to their respective physiques or to explain black success as a result of physical advantage. He also rejected such pseudo-scientific notions as that blacks possessed 'an inner equanimity', 'thicker skin' or smaller organs such as heart, kidneys and liver. His very thorough investigations led Cobb to doubt whether any significant differences existed between black and whites.[6]

Cobb did not attach importance to all the tests. He measured, for example, Jesse Owens' reaction times and found him to be extremely fast with his right arm and above average with his left. Later tests suggest that blacks of West African origin have on average faster reflexes than whites.[7]

Dean Cromwell, leader of the American team at the Berlin Olympics, wrote in 1941: 'The Negro does well in certain disciplines because he is closer to primitive man than white people. It is not long since his ability to run and jump meant the difference between life and death in the jungle. He has supple muscles and his light-minded disposition is useful in the mental and physical relaxation necessary for someone who runs and jumps.'[8]

During the same period Francis Crookshank, a London doctor, was also speculating about the differences between blacks, whites and Asians when it came to sporting achievement and social behaviour. He suggested they could be traced to different ancestry: blacks had developed from gorillas, whites from chimpanzees and Mongoloids from orang-utans. Whites were the most intelligent because chimpanzees were the most intelligent of the apes.

In 1957 the French doctor Marcelle Geber examined children in Uganda and found there were differences from European children of the same age. The Ugandan children stood upright younger and moved better: 'Motor development was earlier than in European children of the same age'.[9]

The researchers also found other differences. Black children are born on average one week earlier than white or Asian babies. They are, however, more mature at birth in terms of skeletal development and other measurements.[10]

Robert Malina in the USA has been studying this topic since the 1960s. Black babies appear to have more muscular mobility, hand-eye coordination that is superior to white babies, learn to walk a month earlier and reach puberty a year earlier. This earlier maturation continues throughout the growing years even though black people are on average poorer than whites and eat fewer calories.[11]

Research carried out at the University of Colorado in the 1960s by Professor William Frankenburg showed up differences. It was based on thirty exercises to measure the motor development of babies and even at six months the black babies were developing faster than the white. These surprising results led to further investigations, which merely served to confirm them. White babies did nothing earlier than black babies during the first year of life, and even at the age of four black children were earlier in fifteen categories whereas whites were only earlier in three.[12]

Several studies show that black American children of five or six have a good aptitude for hurdles, long jump and high jump – all of which demand short, explosive bursts of effort. Teenage black boys have markedly faster knee reflexes and faster reaction times than white boys of the same age.[13]

A Man and a Myth

Certain sportsmen or individuals become linked to particular historical events because they have been associated with them in the collective historical consciousness through repetition in the press and in books, in films and in the school curriculum. Jesse Owens' outstanding performances are seen in the context of Nazism, a lunatic dictator and the machinery of the thousand-year *Reich* thundering its way to another world war.

Like no other runner in the first half of the twentieth century Jesse Owens came to represent the black man's entry into and success in the white man's arena. He had to suffer the racial prejudices of the USA and racial politics at close quarters but nevertheless he uniquely gained a ticket into the

Jesse Owens at the start of the record-breaking 200 metre race, summer Olympics, Berlin 1936.

uppermost social circles of a society in which his brothers and his sisters were considered to be inferior.

James Cleveland Owens was born in rural Alabama in 1913 as the tenth and last child of Henry and Mary Owens. His grandparents had been slaves and his father had progressed to being a tenant farmer before the family moved to Cleveland, Ohio, in 1923, where his father took a job in the steel-works. Young Owens stammered and spoke with a strong Southern accent: his teacher at school began calling him Jesse because she had misunderstood his name when he introduced himself.

The journalist Charles Riley saw Owens in a school gym class and advised him to concentrate on athletics. Owens worked as a shoeshine boy after school and had no time then, so they met for an hour's training before school. Riley took him along to the trotting races to study the horses' technique and Owens' very effective and relaxed later style was formed and fixed in his youth, as were the harmonious technique and special charisma which became his distinguishing marks and fascinated spectators everywhere. Victories in 75 of his 79 races at high school provided evidence of his great talent.

His real breakthrough came on 25 May 1935 in Ann Arbor, Michigan, when he set three world records in the course of one hour and came close to a fourth. After getting entangled in a case about professionalism in the same year, Owens qualified for the 1936 Olympic team. In the USA, where there were still separate leagues for black baseball and American football, they had begun to open up the national squads to a few black athletes. The US athletic squad at the 1928 Olympics had been all white but four years later there were four black athletes on the starting line. In the 1936 Games nineteen black athletes qualified for the American team.

The image of Berlin Owens saw in August 1936 was an idealized one. All Nazi activities had been forbidden, anti-Jewish slogans had been removed from walls and shop windows and public persecution of the Jews had been banned before and during the Olympic Games in order to show the world a shining example and win goodwill. The Propaganda Minister Joseph Goebbels instructed German newspapers to give a positive picture of black American athletes to avoid foreign criticism. But the journalists did not need encouragement: Jesse Owens was the great hero of the Games and quite unconsciously he played the role of superman.

An hour after his fourth Olympic gold Jesse was ordered by his association, the aau, to go to Cologne. The association was planning a European tour for the American athletics stars in exchange for 15 per cent of the ticket sales at each meeting. The agreement was that Owens would take part in the sprint and the long jump: the athletes did not know that the us Olympic Committee was $30,000 in debt and had to come up with the money immediately.

Owens competed in Cologne, Prague, Bochum and in England while lucrative offers were pouring in from the USA. On Saturday 15 August Owens ran at the White City Stadium in London but then, on the advice of his coach Larry Snyder, he refused to accept air tickets to Stockholm, which was to be the start of a week's tour of Scandinavia. They wanted to return home and milk money out of the Olympic golds.

The AAU reaction came at once. Jesse Owens was disqualified on grounds of professionalism. Avery Brundage and Daniel Ferris of the AAU called in the press on the last day of the Berlin Olympics and announced this dramatic piece of news to the world. Owens was forbidden from competing under the aegis of the AAU or at university level because he had broken the contract to complete the tour of meetings. Owens felt unjustly treated because his expulsion came *before* he had broken any amateur rules.

Jesse Owens was nevertheless given a grand welcome in New York. He was paraded in an open car down Broadway to the cheers of both black and white spectators. His old friend Bill Robinson masterminded the welcome ceremonies.

Owens soon wanted to get back on the track: 'I am not a professional. I have never received payment'.[14] The AAU considered that exclusion for one year was a minimum. But the money rolled in. Owens signed agreements with black-owned companies to appear at celebrations and balls in return for an honorarium. The press wrote in November 1936 that he had earned $50,000 since coming home – a sum that was exaggerated. Jesse Owens did, however, earn a great deal, certainly more than all the other runners in the world.

Was he bitter that his athletics career was finished? The AAU did not choose Jesse Owens as its best performer of 1936, it chose Glenn Morris, a white car salesman who won the decathlon in Berlin and played Tarzan, Lord of the Jungle, in a film. When Morris heard the result of the ballot he remarked 'Don't talk such nonsense': he was certain of Owens' sovereign status.[15]

Owens' first race after the Olympics took place in the half-time interval of a football match in Havana in Cuba in December 1936. He was matched against the racehorse Julio McCaw, which started forty yards behind him, and he won the 100-yard race in 9.9 seconds. It was the first of many professional races against horses, greyhounds, cars, buses, motorcycles and anything else that moved fast. As long as the horse was standing close to the starting pistol so that it was startled and hesitated a little, Owens won. He ran round baseball pitches and basketball courts, sometimes tripping over on purpose so that small boys could say that they had beaten the Olympic champion. His earnings made up for the lack of sporting challenges.

His last race against a horse took place in 1943 in Freemont in Ohio, a small town which had a handwritten sign as you entered – 'No dogs, no Japanese' – it might also have said 'No Negroes'. The USA was at war with Japan and Owens was meeting a horse he had already beaten six times. This time he lost and from then on he turned down similar events. He now preferred to take on more respectable tasks.

Owens was a good speaker once he had overcome his stammer and he became a builder of bridges between black and white people. His visit to and speech at the Olympic Stadium in Berlin in 1951 touched German hearts. He was happy to let himself be used as a representative of the oppressed in his own country. Avery Brundage had become president of the IOC by this stage and he saw Owens as his main spokesman when it came to spreading the Olympic idea. And the USA needed a black hero.

Owens' elegance and charm made him more than just a retired sportsman. He was a true example of the fact that sportsmen only become real heroes when they have something more to contribute than sport. He proved that great men achieve even greater stature when their greatness is nourished by their environment. His manner was impeccable, even after becoming a chain-smoker at the age of 30, and to do 100 yards in 9.7 seconds at the age of 42 is an incredible achievement.

Owens was a rare type – a rich black man who moved in all social circles and was respected virtually everywhere. He was master of all occasions, great and small. He lived on his own legend but he also lived up to it, partly because it paid him to do so and partly because that is the kind of man he was. The facade admittedly showed some cracks: he went bankrupt several times and there were cases of tax evasion and fines, but they never destroyed the myth. As a man he was far from perfect. He had trouble reading and for a long time he kept a flat specifically for extramarital sexual activities.

Jesse Owens' achievements in Berlin in 1936 were never shown on television in the USA. It was only with the showing of Bud Greenspan's documentary *Jesse Owens Returns to Berlin* on 180 stations nationwide as well as fifteen countries overseas on the 30 March 1968 that the nation finally saw clips from the Olympic Games. Owens' own deep voice provided the narrative and the film made an indelible impression on millions of Americans, not least because many of them saw parallels with the racial discrimination of 1960s America. Just five days after the showing of the film Martin Luther King was murdered.

It was in 1968, too, that Tommie Smith and John Carlos made their famous gesture of protest on the Olympic victors' rostrum after the 200 metres. Each of them raised a clenched fist clad in a black gauntlet, the symbol of the Black Panthers' liberation movement. A number of radical young runners thought that Jesse Owens overlooked the struggle for black rights, that he had been emasculated and exploited by powerful whites. But they came from a different generation and in his younger days Owens too had been the cause of turmoil and contributed to a greater acceptance of black people.

Jesse Owens died of lung cancer on 31 March 1980 at the age of 66. The news of his death and the obituaries that followed gave new life to the old scenes, and when the pictures of Owens running at top speed rolled across the television screens of the world his myth reached out to new generations. And from Vienna in Austria the high-profile Jewish Nazi-hunter Simon Wiesenthal announced that a main road to the Olympic Stadium in Berlin was to be re-named after Jesse Owens.

19
War and Peace

Whatever you do, Hägg, don't do any more sport.
—Swedish doctor in 1939 to Gunder Hägg, later world
number one at middle and long distances

In the second half of the 1930s Finland reached the top as a running nation. Keen international competition was pushing standards up and encouraging inventive approaches to improving them further, particularly over the longer distances. People in other countries recognized both the advantages and the drawbacks of the Nurmi school, of which a particular trait was the exaggerated movement of the hips, shoulders and arms. The New Zealander Jack Lovelock, winner of the 1,500 metres at the 1936 Olympics, thought that training should share the character of play and he adopted a more relaxed running technique. He experimented in all kinds of ways and realized it was possible to beat the Finns if he could train better than them.

The Swedes focused on the conservation of strength in terms of their running style at the same time as they exploited their country's gentle terrain and paths. The long-distance runner Henry Jonsson Kälarne led the way, assisted by the coach Gösta 'Gosse' Holmér, whose philosophy was christened 'fartlek' or 'speed play', that is, running out in the country, not on a track, and varying the intensity of the run. They would run for up to an hour at a time, then sprint, then lower the pace, then make a longer burst – either following a pre-decided plan or simply making the changes instinctively. Fartlek developed speed and strengthened the internal organs without overloading them, and it also provided mental variety in beautiful surroundings. It made a break from the monotonous surroundings of a track or of the roads and it produced runners with more all-round competence. In 1934 Henry Jonsson Kälarne also began wading and running in snow to strengthen his legs: it built up his fitness, will and strength.

Sweden remained neutral during the Second World War and produced the world's best runners at 800 metres and upwards during that period: the impetus provided by fartlek and training out in the country proved very significant.[1]

Many runners in Germany in the 1930s had begun to follow more systematic interval training. The principle of running fast, then taking a short pause before running again as a way of building up speed and endurance was known even among the ancient Greeks. The method was used more or less consciously throughout the centuries and then, after 1900, more consciously by the British, the Finns and the Pole Janis Kuszoczinsky. The latter was a pioneer of interval training in the early 1930s though his approach was less scientific than that of the Germans.

The cardiologist Dr Herbert Reindel and the coach Waldemar Gerschler were carrying out research on the pulse and heart rate in Germany during the 1930s. Reindel was using interval training to rehabilitate heart patients. He scientifically measured the pulse of over 3,000 people after running and came up with a training norm. If the pulse rate reached 180 a minute it should take one and a half minute's rest for it to drop to 120; if it took longer than that either the speed had been too great or the distance too long.

Gerschler mainly recommended repeated distances of 100 to 200 metres, occasionally up to 2,000 metres for those who were well trained. He believed that the heart grew stronger during the breaks and consequently the rest periods were important. By stopping the runner before he stopped himself, the risk of overtraining was avoided. He also preferred shorter breaks rather than a faster pace – which would ideally come anyway as the heart grew stronger and made more repetitions possible. In addition to that Gerschler also recommended strength training, test runs and a weekly run of between one and a half and three hours to be done at a varying pace – a sort of natural interval training and a respite from the monotony of the track.

The German runner Rudolf 'Rudi' Harbig followed the stopwatch and pulse-taking regime, with numerous variations of intervals on the track – anywhere between 80 and 1,500 metres. He warmed up properly and always warmed down, was strict about his diet, never drank alcohol and was renowned for his iron will. Harbig was one of the world's finest middle-distance types ever, long-legged, fast even at 100 metres (10.6 seconds) and with a unique stride.

He set a world record of 1 minute 46.6 seconds for the 800 metres in 1939, almost two seconds better than the old record. In the same year he brought the 400 metres record down to 46 seconds flat and he continued to compete until he was sent to serve on the Eastern Front in the Second World War, dying in the Ukraine in 1944.[2]

Rudolf Harbig was the first truly international star to cultivate scientific interval training. Over the decades that followed Gerschler and Reindel's principles were adopted and developed by many people and adapted to individual needs and new combinations. 'Intervals' became a magic word and the direct road to success, but were also a hard training method in which it was easy to train until you dropped. With the introduction of intervals and every session being timed against the clock, running became more regulated and measurable than ever – in this respect it contrasted with Swedish fartlek, although the two methods had variations of pace in common.

From the 1930s on coaches, doctors and scientists became more important to top international runners. They had, of course, worked behind the scenes earlier but with the runaway development of medical research and the increasing prestige of sport they became more visible. But even though ambitious runners grew more dependent on assistance and advanced science there was still much to be gained by drawing strength from nature.

Gunder

Gunder Hägg was born on 31 December 1918 in the small and isolated community of Albacken in the Kälarne district of the Swedish province of Jämtland. The world-class runner Henry Jonsson, who later added 'Kälarne' to his surname, also came from there and he was Hägg's model.

Hägg's earliest ambition was to be a cross-country skier. He began his working life young and from the age of twelve he was swinging the axe and using the barking iron as the youngest and slightest member of a logging squad. Though less was expected from him than from any other member he gave his all to show he was up to the job. He stuck at this for five winters and became stronger than anyone expected.

He ran several kilometres to and from school, never regarding it as training, and he ran home in heavy clothes from the logging work in the forest – with hunger as the spur. His ability became apparent when he first began competing in athletic events at the age of fifteen or sixteen. His first proper meeting was at Bräcke, twenty miles from home, and he got there by hitching a lift on the back of a lorry. Even though his time of 5 minutes 2 seconds for the 1,500 metres was hardly an omen of an international star of the future, his proud father bought him a pair of running spikes. They took them with them to the logging camp and one day in June 1936 his father paced out 750 metres across country and marked the turning point.

'Run the 1,500 metres there and back against the clock,' his father said, shouting the starting signal and checking the alarm clock.

'4.45!' his father called excitedly when Gunder returned breathless and exhausted.

The time seemed a fantastically good one.

'Wasn't it out by one minute?'

'No,' his father answered. He had cut a notch in the chair with his sheath knife for each minute and it was just a matter of counting them. They lay awake for a long time that night talking about Gunder's possibilities as a runner, and the father dreamt about it more than the son. There were no limits. Gunder accepted everything his father said and decided there and then in the logging cabin to put all his energies into running. Only many years later did his father reveal that he had knocked 30 seconds off the time to encourage the boy.[3]

Two months later Gunder wanted to take part in the district junior championships to be held at Kälarne sports field but Albacken, his home club, thought there was no point in him going and offered him no support. Gunder borrowed a bicycle and pedalled the twenty hilly miles to Kälarne where, to everyone's surprise, he won the 1,500 metres. He wanted to run in the 5,000 metres the following day but had no money for a night's lodging so he ran an errand – going to the shop for beer for a thirsty farmer – and was allowed to keep enough change to pay for the night. The following day he won convincingly again. Among the spectators present was a farmer, Fridolf Westman, who needed a farmworker and offered him a job.

'I'll have to ask my father', Gunder answered, embarrassed, having no idea that Henry Jonsson Kälarne had also worked on Westman's farm.[4]

Gunder Hägg was soon working hard in the steep fields, carting and spreading manure, spending long days walking behind the horse, doing joinery work, repairing things and carrying heavy loads. The farmer was amazed by the weight he could lift because the boy did not look that strong: one day when they were bringing the implements in from the fields Gunder lifted the plough with ease and put it in the cart. Occupying the same tiny room as Kälarne had lived in, Hägg rested on his bed after hard training sessions and looked out over the lake and dreamed. There was little else to do but work, train, eat well and sleep at least ten hours a night.

Westman recommended less skiing and more running. In 1937 Hägg ran a number of good races that caught people's attention and after his twentieth birthday in 1938 it was time for serious training. His coaches warned against overtraining and the gentle build-up during the winter of 1938–9 did not appeal to Hägg, who was impatient. Six miles road walking every day and a long tour of up to 35 miles every Sunday did not suit him. Why trudge through the whole winter and half the spring like that until May when you wanted to run fast?

After a failure of a season in 1939 and double pneumonia in the autumn Hägg ended up in hospital, where a doctor advised him against any more running:

'Whatever you do, Hägg, don't do any more sport.'

In December 1939 he was sent to Norrbotten, near the Finnish border, as a conscript and he was feeling well enough to start training. Deep snow and bitter cold did not put him off, rather the reverse. Hägg ran six days a week, setting off at full speed while his companions relaxed.

He mapped out a varied circuit of five kilometres: into the forest, across bogs, down into hollows, across a meadow and up a hill and down towards a river. In this section the snow was so hard that he only sank to the ankles whereas on the rest of the circuit he had to struggle through snow up to his knees, sometimes even waist deep, and every metre had to be really worked for.

It was more difficult to keep the pace up in the snow in the forest and he moved at walking pace, even that taking a great deal of effort, until the downhill section. On the flat it was all work again with snow up to the waist and having to lift his legs high – it could hardly be called running, but it was a struggle that punished the thighs and tested the will. The sweat ran off him and his breath rasped as he clawed his way across the flat section and then uphill, sometimes having to shovel away the snow with his arms. It was a

relief to reach the top and set off downhill and across a road, shaking himself free and gaining new strength before increasing speed at the river and
uphill back to the army camp. In spite of having less snow than other sections, the river was the most demanding part – the combination of a fast
pace and bursts of sprinting meant that he sometimes fell flat on his face,
losing both breath and rhythm. There was nothing for it but to get up as
quickly as possible and carry on stubbornly to the end. Hägg recognized
that these sessions were training his will and he went to sleep a slightly
tougher sportsman every night, one step closer to his aim of being the best
in the world.

The circuit consisted of 2.5 kilometres of walking in snow and 2.5 kilometres of running in snow. Snow walking meant walking as fast as possible
on trails where new snow made running impossible. If new snow had not
built up there between his training sessions he could also run those sections,
using a special technique of lifting his legs abnormally high, putting an extra load on his legs, and making vigorous arm movements. His body was
functioning well and his lungs were tolerating the cold. On bare ground
during the spring his usual daily ration was five kilometres flat out; from May
on he sometimes went twice a day with an easy five kilometres in the morning followed by a slightly shorter session in the evening with sprint bursts.

The progress was remarkable. In the middle of June 1940 Hägg brought
his personal best in the 1,500 metres down to 3 minutes 59 seconds and he
had his first season as a well-trained sportsman: his best times for the 1,500
and 3,000 metres were, respectively, four and nine seconds outside the
world records. He was convinced that hard training and physical work out
in the country would give him the best chance of succeeding. When Gösta
Olander invited him to work and train in Valådalen the following winter
it suited him perfectly.

There was no frozen river to run along at Valådalen so sections of his
five-kilometre circuit lay on the road. Tramping through nothing but deep
snow makes you slow, so work on cadence and pace-length are also essential. Hägg stamped out his training circuit on 7 December 1940 and made
a note in his diary that evening: 'I intend to do as much training as last year.
I do believe that hard training is the right way.'5 It snowed so much that the
open sections soon became impassable and the whole circuit had to be
moved into the shelter of the trees. Hägg always wore his spikes. It might
seem crazy to use such thin and cold shoes in snowdrifts but they gripped
well, both off-road and on the slippery road. And some cold and wet had
to be put up with anyway.

From the middle of March compressed snow made it possible to run
the whole circuit. It only took him twenty minutes and five weeks of that
routine improved his speed. Hägg finished working for Olander and continued his hard training during a short period back in the army: six kilometres at a pleasant steady pace in the country in the morning and then a
quarter of an hour at a fast pace on the road in the afternoon.

After a number of encouraging races, new personal bests and victories over good quality runners, Gunder Hägg broke his first world record at the 1941 Swedish championships when he did the 1,500 metres in 3 minutes 47.6 seconds.

He was, however, punished severely that summer for breaking amateur rules by accepting 350 *kronor* for taking part in a meeting: he was barred from competing from 1 September 1941 to 30 June 1942. Hägg took it badly and said to a journalist: 'If it comes to a ban I'll push off to Finland for the war against Russia.'[6]

According to rumour the man behind the anonymous allegation was a well-known football manager who, like a number of other people, feared that the crowds now flocking to athletics meetings would undermine the support for football. There was also the fact that footballers themselves were beginning to harp on about money. The decision to ban Hägg was the subject of much discussion since he was an enormously popular figure; he planned a terrific comeback in order to secure his position as the best in Sweden. The Hägg phenomenon also needs to be seen against the background of keen competition in Sweden at the time.

Sweden produced a rich crop of runners during the 1940s and they set 25 world records in athletics during that decade. Hägg's most outstanding Swedish challenger was Arne Andersson, and what a challenger he was!

Arne

Long strides and long legs, strong lungs and his chest pushed forward – that was Arne Andersson. On his first birthday he lost his mother to the Spanish Influenza that devastated the world in 1918 and his father's sister and her husband became his foster-parents. He came from a strong family: his grandfather on his father's side was called 'Long Johan' and was reputed to be the strongest man in the province of Bohuslän.[7]

Arne grew up in Vänersborg and did a great deal of canoeing and swimming – in fact, he produced the best times in the country as a junior swimmer. He developed strong lungs but had to give up canoeing because it leads to stiff thighs. He took up long-distance skiing and only began to run when he was sixteen. He was living in Uddevalla that summer and trained together with a local elite runner. He showed talent but was no infant prodigy in spite of taking part in the 1,500 metres at the national school championships against Finland in 1936 and 1937.

His breakthrough came in the 1939 Finnkamp, the prestigious annual athletics competition between Sweden and Finland. After a hard final lap and a spurt between two Swedes and a Finn, Andersson won the 1,500 metres in 3 minutes 48.8 seconds. It was a new Swedish record, just one short second away from the world record, and it was a ten-second improvement for Andersson on the year before.

Several experts thought this would prove to be a short-lived success for a strong but primitive talent who wasted his energy and needed to refine his technique. Andersson obediently followed the advice of his coaches. They forbade sessions of longer than six or seven kilometres, which were no trouble at all for him, often on forest paths and in short bursts. 'You mustn't run up hills, it will ruin your style', his coach told him. Style was important in the 1930s: it was important to look good and Andersson, who looks the perfect runner in later photographs, took strides that were too long and leaned too far forward; 'the buffalo gallop', as one journalist characterized it, a style that was rarely seen at the front of the field in middle-distance running. It was not until he was under the supervision of Pekka Edfeldt in 1943–4 that Andersson shortened his stride. At that stage he became much better at producing spurts and achieved the best performances of his career.

Doctors who examined Andersson's thorax suggested he had suffered from rickets in childhood but he had no memory of it and did not feel any discomfort apart from one occasion when he fainted in the steam bath and a doctor heard a heart murmur. This particular doctor had been in the USA and had heard of dangerous heart murmurs so Andersson was taken in for three days of tests, during which his pulse was taken, he blew into tubes and was surrounded by advanced measuring equipment. The young man was, of course, worried since both his health and his athletics career were at stake but the doctors and their machines concluded that his heart was unusually strong and there were no grounds for concern: the hospital had never had such a strong pair of lungs.

A Summer of Records

Gunder Hägg was working at the fire-station in Gävle and no longer living out in the wilds when, in December 1941, he began another pre-season following the same programme as the year before: hard in the winter, easy in the summer, fitness during the winter and speed once the snow was off the ground – four kilometres in snow and two on the road then all of it on snow-free ground from April on.

On 1 July 1942, the day after his ban was lifted, Hägg set a world record for the mile. Races and records now followed in incredibly quick succession. Two days later he beat the best time for two miles in front of a crowd of over 20,000 while thousands stood outside because there was no room in the arena. The police put up road-blocks in a vain attempt to prevent chaos.

In 1942 Hägg smashed ten world records in the course of 80 days. The distances ranged from 1,500 to 5,000 metres and the formula was short, hard training, rarely more than six miles running a day. He was competing anything up to five times a week and he won all his 33 appearances that season. Over 316,000 people attended these meetings and the whole nation was tuned in to the radio broadcasts. The radio was becoming more and more popular and the transmissions of Hägg's 1943 tour of the USA, in particular, had a magnetic attraction. The streets of Swedish towns were empty when broadcast races took place in the evening and many people stayed up to listen to broadcasts at night. One of his neighbours in Albacken went down on his knees and prayed when Hägg was running his first race against the American parson Gilbert Dodds: 'Please God, let Gunder beat that bloody parson!'[8]

There was something special about Hägg. He had charisma but it was not of the swaggering kind. He was five foot eleven and a half and in top form weighed about ten and a half stone – and he came over as a down-to-earth, likeable man of the people. With his thin face shining with the will to win and his hair combed back, he could have been the boy next door.

He ran so elegantly. Leaning forwards slightly, his arms relaxed, his thin legs perfect for distance running – it all seemed in perfect harmony when 'the Albacken Elk' won after having been out in front for some time. Hägg never learnt to spurt properly and he used to wear out the opposition long before the final sprint. He had long legs but did not take long strides, which differed from the Finnish technique of Paavo Nurmi, for instance, who held his arms high and took long strides – a slightly stiff, machine-like style. Hägg's stride in the 1,500 metres measured 180 centimetres whereas Nurmi's was almost two metres even though he was much shorter.

Hägg emerged from the forests and captured the interest of a whole nation. The newspapers played a big part in creating and shaping him as the 'divine' or 'invincible' national idol and he was idolized in the press in a quite unparalleled way. He became the symbol of all that was best in the Swedish way of life, showed what moderation and hard work out in the country could lead to. Hundreds of thousands of migrants from the countryside were living in the cities and more and more were following them, but in the great forests in the north of the country people still lived such a simple life close to nature that they had access to the primitive Swedish virtues of strength and endurance. Hägg was a Swedish Jack the Giant-killer, a figure straight out of a folk-tale. The story behind his success is as impressive and fascinating as his achievements: his witty, throwaway answers to journalists fed the myth, which was then commercialized to sell watches, shoes, bread, razorblades and clothes. Then came the books and the films and his own newspaper column.

Hard Duelling

In the forest of Swedish talent at distances of 800 metres and above Gunder Hägg and Arne Andersson towered like two mighty trees. They were different types, from different parts of Sweden, and with very different professions. Andersson was a trained teacher and athletic in every way; not so light of foot as Hägg but more energetic and capable of draining his body of its last drops of strength. The press presented them as opposite poles and printed pictures of close duels between the two, shoulder to shoulder,

Gunder with his fluid style, short stride and eyes down, Arne with stub-born determination stamped on his face, his arms working like a warrior's. The population of Sweden was split into two camps, depending on which man they supported.

News of the world war came ticking in over the wires, news of battles, invasions, sabotage and torpedoed ships. The world might be at war but in Sweden the duels between Hägg and Andersson gave the nation a respite from everyday concerns. There is something reminiscent of a boxing match when two men in their best years try to run faster than one another – it is both playful and serious since there is nothing more serious than play. Surrounded by gunfire and total war the Swedes held their contests to choose the world's best runner. Old men sat listening to the broadcasts bewitched and small boys went out afterwards to copy Gunder and Arne.

Arne Andersson was often called 'Hägg's shadow' or 'the eternal number two', but that was only true in the 1942 season. He beat Hägg once in 1940 and again in a cross-country race the following year. When Hägg was touring the USA in the summer of 1943 Andersson set world records for both the 1,500 metres and the mile. In 1944 Arne won six to one in their private reckon-ings and from then on he was the better of the two. Gunder's only victory over his rival in 1945 was when he set a new best time of 4 minutes 1.4 seconds for the mile. Across their careers as a whole the statistics are fourteen to nine in Hägg's favour.

At one moment Andersson would be breaking or equalling world records only to be beaten at the next moment by someone who was even better. His view was that success comes from defeat because it forces you to hone your skills.

These great Swedish feats during the Second World War were achieved with pacemakers, runners who ran one or two laps to keep the pace up until the record-breaker overtook them. Friends and club-mates played the role of the hare in exchange for payment. Records were expected even if the condi-tion of the cinder tracks of the time varied enormously, and records could be broken even when the weather was bad, as was demonstrated in a 1,500 metre race on the 17 July 1942 when Andersson was determined to beat Hägg.

The track was like a swimming pool after torrential rain and a world record was out of the question in the opinion of those who had taken a look at the inside lane, which resembled a muddy, churned-up forest road. The organizers of the meeting decided to move the race out to the third lane, two lanes out from the shortest way round, because it was much drier. International rules stipulated that the edge markings of the track be at least five centimetres high and so the stadium fire-hoses were laid out as mark-ing, but since they did not reach the whole way round the gap was filled with rope.

After a tough start Hägg grabbed a lead and in the last lap he found hid-den strength and set a new world record of 3 minutes 45.8 seconds. The hero of the day had run his victory lap and was waving to the cheering onlookers when there came the dreadful message that the track had not been formally measured. It turned out that he had actually run 1,500.9 metres.

Two years later, on the 18 July 1944, the two combatants met in Malmö, Hägg's new home track, to race in the mile. Up to that point in the season Andersson, who really was on form, was two to one up but Hägg was keen to show his best to his home-crowd. He flippantly laughed off his second position because he never let the smile slip even though he hated seeing anyone else cross the finishing line first: mentally he was a winner and did not count defeats on his personal balance-sheet. Records were of no importance on that day in Malmö, what mattered was beating his rival. Over 14,000 people were squashed together in the stands and another 5,000 without tickets were standing outside, where they could follow the events on the other side of the fence by the voice in the loudspeaker and the roars of the crowd.

Lennart Strand, acting as the hare, took the lead at the fastest ever pace in a mile race – 1 minute 55.9 seconds at the halfway point. Were they going to break the four minute barrier of the dream mile? The time of 2 minutes 59.8 seconds for three-quarters of a mile was a new world record. Hägg raced on and was in the lead at the finishing spurt but Andersson came up alongside him, his arms swinging desperately, took the advantage and breasted the tape in a new world record of 4 minutes 1.6 seconds.

This result showed it would be possible to achieve times in the 3.50s – the dream mile, as it was known – and that was on the mind of both Hägg and Andersson when they heard the lap times: 56.0, 59.9, 63.8 and 61.8. All they needed was a faster third lap.

Since 1943 Andersson had been working just outside Stockholm as a teacher at the Skrubba boarding school and home for boys in need of care. Some of them lived there and worked in the town, but they were all be found sitting in the front row of the stand when Arne was running in the big Stockholm meetings. All of them respected 'Sir', who was strict but also absolutely straight and fair. Andersson's everyday life was not a leisurely one in which the needs of a sporting star could be given top priority: his was not a selfish existence with plenty of rest and free time.

He woke 24 boys before 7 a.m., made sure they got dressed, ate their porridge and were ready for the school day. After school was finished he was in charge of the pupils' leisure activities: swimming, diving, football and games on the school's tiny playing field, as well as other time-consuming tasks that took him until 10–10.30 p.m. Unless he got his daily training session out of the way in the morning, he could only train when the working day was over. He would run out into the forest, find his rhythm and then sprint and ease up, sprint and ease up, all in a perfect training environment. This rural idyll of forest paths and moss-covered rocks had a positive impact on the boys from problem homes in the city and Andersson, too, found it a training paradise; he could head for the bath-house afterwards, satisfied with school life even though his working days were longer and his holidays shorter than at a normal school. Being a teacher at Skrubba was both a

lifestyle and a vocation: there was no summer vacation for the pupils there
and they had to stay until they had served their time.

Money, Money, Money

There were rumours that both Hägg and Andersson were well paid for running, earning anything up to several thousand *kronor* for an event. 'Everyone' knew about it but no one did anything until a well-known auditor was
tasked with the onerous duty of going through the accounts of suspected
clubs. The auditor found 'creative' accounting and club officials admitted
to collective cheating: payments to the stars were hidden as travel loans, sub-
sistence allowances and so on. Unlike the runners, the officials were not
making a profit for themselves, they were serving their clubs and had been
caught on the horns of a dilemma: should they ignore the stars and thus get
few spectators, or should they pay the big attractions and fill the stands?

On 7 November 1945 the stars who had been accused admitted receiving
payments in breach of the rules. The judgement was not pronounced until
17 March of the following year: Gunder Hägg, Arne Andersson and Henry
Jonsson Kälarne were disqualified for life – the latter even though he had hung
up his spikes several years earlier. Six other runners were banned for periods
of one or two years. The athletics officials were given lenient sentences,
usually disqualification for three months. As with the runners, only the
biggest fish were taken.[9]

The population of Sweden was enraged that the three most popular
sportsmen in the country had been stamped as cheap cheats. Expressions such
as 'Swedish suicide' could be heard and the leadership of the Sports Association, which had initiated the whole affair, was hounded by the press. The effect on athletics meetings was noticeable: interest fell.

Even though the Sports Association was following the rules many people felt that punishment was unnecessary. It would have been better to do what
the Finns did in 1932 when Paavo Nurmi was given an international ban as a
professional and the Finns announced he was a 'national amateur'. What is
more, both Finns and runners from other countries were competing for
money and, in the view of Swedish critics of the bans, it was only the Swedes
who were voluntarily sacrificing their biggest stars. Most people believed
that the runners earned every *krona* since they worked hard and brought
pleasure to many people.

Hägg and Andersson could, of course, have said no to the under-the-table
payments but they had joined a system in which exaggerated travel costs and
illegal money had already been current for decades. The runners assumed that
this was accepted since they had been hearing about earnings of this kind since
they were boys. Andersson earned enough to be able to study and pay his own
way, but without the payments for running study would have been impossible. The sums involved ranged from 500 *kronor* a meeting up to five or six
times that amount at the end of the war when price inflation was high.

In making its disqualifications, the Sports Association targeted those who made a living from sport. The success the Swedes had achieved was all the more noticeable and impressive because sport was on hold in other countries – in peace-time men from other nations would also have been running fast. It seems rather as if the Swedish sporting authorities were smitten by a bad conscience when they saw large parts of the world suffering from the war at the same time as Swedes were setting new records *and* breaking the rules of amateurism. With the war over and the world returning to normal this growing cancer in sport must be removed, not least because of the rules of the Olympic movement. Swedish honesty and propriety, qualities they prided themselves on and liked to show off to the world, must be preserved at all costs.

The runners themselves reacted to the bans in different ways. Hägg, as always, made a joke of it and stated that he did not really care about sport anyway. Henry Jonsson Kälarne became bitter because he thought the disqualification dishonoured his career even though that career had been over for some time: he swore he would never attend another sporting event.

Andersson was still hungry to improve and the ban was almost like a death sentence. Unable to give up, he continued to train in hope of a reprieve in time for the 1948 London Olympics, where he had been aiming at the 5,000 metres. It was agony for him to sit in the stand and watch his friends compete. He wrote newspaper articles about athletics and worked as a coach in Czechoslovakia in 1946 when the young Emil Zátopek was showing promise – the two became lifelong friends. The Czechs came to compete in Stockholm in 1946 and when Andersson walked onto the track alongside the Czechs a Swedish official said 'You are disqualified and we don't want you here'.[10] He had to stand outside like a spectator who has been thrown out.

Andersson asked for a pardon in time for the 1948 Olympics but was rejected by one vote. He got some release for his dammed-up frustrations when he ran a demonstration race against the whole relay team and showed he still had his old class. He took up cycling and turned out in the Tour of Sweden in 1953. After some good riding he had to drop out but was licensed as an amateur cyclist the following year and became an elite rider. He took part in orienteering and he played bandy – anything to compete, anything to get the frisson and pleasure of sport. He bought horses, trained them and took part in trotting events with all the enthusiasm of a top sportsman. He could not imagine a life without active sport.

Swedish running remained at a high level even after the disqualification of its greatest stars in 1945. But some of the sparkle of the war years disappeared and public interest waned, perhaps because football was attracting ever bigger crowds. The story of Swedish middle- and long-distance running during the Second World War is not only unique in the history of that country; even from an international perspective it stands out as a magical epoch, with two young Swedes dominating the world of middle-distance running while other comparable nations could think of little but the great war.

20

In the Service of the State

Young sportspeople! Remember that it is from you our new champions
will come and they will beat the bourgeois records and raise the banner
of the physical culture of the Soviet Union to new heights.

—In *Krasnyi Sport*, the Soviet Union, 1935

Zlin, Czechoslovakia, 15 May 1942. Young lads from the Bata factory are
about to compete in the annual race through the town. The management
likes to show that their employees are in good shape and everyone has to
take part. Few of them are keen and one of them, Emil, refuses until the
principal instructor comes to the boarding house.

'You're running on Sunday! Understand?'

'I'm such a bad runner.'

'That doesn't matter. Whether you come in first or last is up to you –
but you're going to run.'[1]

The lad knows that it is pointless to refuse if he wants to keep his job and
his place in the technical college, but he does not give up hope of getting
out of it. During the medical examination he limps and pretends his knee
is injured. The doctor is not taken in and tells him to turn up at the start,
but even then Emil is reluctant. Early on Sunday morning he sneaks down
to the classroom with a book, hoping to be overlooked. While he is learning chemical formulae by heart his mind goes back to his childhood and the
time his father bawled him out for running so much, wasting his energy and
wearing out his shoes. Education and work were the priorities, not sport,
his father had told him, inculcating an important lesson in the child's mind.
Emil is remembering this when the silence is broken by a friend.

'Get a move on.' They hurry to the starting point.

The distance is 1,400 metres. Many of the hundred boys try hard to
win but Emil is less concerned – until his competitive instincts are stirred.
Soon there is only his friend Krupicka in front of him.

Emil does not get a great thrill from his second place, nor from the
prize of a fountain pen. 'It's the last time I'm running anyway.'[2]

No one could have been more wrong.

Running is soon the most important thing in life for Emil Zátopek;
soon he is being congratulated and the papers are writing about him. It is
much more fun to be out of doors and feel free than to stand bent over an
assembly line in the factory where the workers are shouted at and fined
irrespective of how fast they work.

Emil Zátopek, 1951.

The Germans have not yet taken control of the sports ground and they can talk Czech there, enjoy themselves and forget the horrors of war. The dusty, sooty sports field in Zlin, to which the wind brings the pollution from every factory chimney in the town, is nevertheless a fine place for someone who spends his working day breathing in poisonous dust. Emil tries to get transferred to a different section but the response is 'Do you want to be sent to a labour camp?'

But his ambitions have been awakened. In 1942 he takes part in the Czech championships for the first time and comes in fifth in the 1,500 metres. He experiments with training whenever he has any time.

The road to the factory passed through an avenue of poplar trees. To make best use of his time he had hit upon a special sort of self-control, which he practised on the way to and from work. He practised controlling his breathing. He started by holding his breath to the fourth poplar tree but after a few days he did not breathe out until the fifth poplar. He carried on pushing himself until one day he decided to hold his breath until he was past all the poplars and level with a little clump of trees way down the road.

He walked and walked, all his will-power focused on not breathing. He could hear a roaring in his head and feel pressure in his chest and thought he was going to suffocate – but he did not breathe out. When he reached the group of trees he was aiming for he fell down in a faint.[3]

His training was so demanding that competitions seemed easy by comparison. Interval training was the recipe for success – 20 to 30 metres, but sometimes the whole 200 metres of the long side of the track – with an easy pace in between. He picked up the idea for this training method at a course supervised by the long-distance runner Hronem in 1944.

Zátopek's interval principle became well-known and initially it was much criticized. The critics were silenced by the results he achieved, as were those who criticized his style, arguing he would burn out since he put himself through such an ordeal before every competition. 'If my style had mattered, I'd have done something about it', was Zátopek's response. Anyone who studied the way he used his legs could see short, efficient strides suitable for long distances.

Emil Zátopek was born in Koprivnice in 1922, a small place in northern Moravia in the old Czechoslovakia. He was one of a family of six. His father was a carpenter at the Tatra factory, a solid, hard-working man who often sighed at his son's ideas: 'Are you going out running again? You'd be better using your energy for something useful'.[4]

On one occasion his sister sneaked to their father that Emil was running through the streets like a mad thing, red in the face and out of breath after the teacher had asked him to buy sausages. Their father disliked his brood wearing out their shoes by running and playing football. He considered sending Emil to the teachers' training college but there were many applicants and the family had little money. But when Zátopek got a job at the Bata factory in Zlin and a place at the company technical school he was assured of a living and good prospects – if he could stick the hours from 6 a.m. through to the end of evening classes at 9.30 p.m.

The monotony of the work threatened to drive the young Zátopek mad. At one point his department was producing 2,200 pairs of tennis shoes a day and his job was to cut the grooves in the stick-on soles with a toothed wheel – the same movements all day long. The workers' lives were like those in Charlie Chaplin's 1936 film *Modern Times*, a ceaseless round of work in an enormous factory, all about speed of production, assembly lines and simple monotonous tasks. Zátopek was moved to the chemical section, where he learned more but where the pollution was noticeable.

It is important to know about his youth in order to understand Zátopek's later joy in life. Running offered a refuge from everyday monotony and a way out of the factory. Like other future champions he recognized the value of having mentors such as Dr Haluza and the engineer Hronem, good Czech long-distance runners. Zátopek's salvation came with his conscription into the army and his entry into the Czechoslovak military academy in the autumn of 1945.

At this stage Emil Zátopek was one of the best long-distance runners in the country, holding national records at 3,000 metres (8 minutes 33.4 seconds) and 5,000 metres (14 minutes 50.2 seconds). Several people advised him against the military academy since it did not offer the opportunity to concentrate on athletics. But Zátopek trained when others were resting; in the winter he trained in the academy riding school, where he ran circuit after circuit while his fellow soldiers were spreading sawdust.

During the autumn of 1946 he and his fellow cadets were at a military camp with demanding duties and little free time. Around 7 p.m., immediately after supper, Zátopek would put on his army boots and run out across the parade ground to a 400-metre clearing in the woods:

> The forest tracks became silent witnesses of something they had never seen before – a soldier running back and forth, back and forth, until far into the night. No one forced him to do it, no one had ordered him to do it and he was not running nice and gently, just for fun. It was easy to see that he was pushing himself, driving himself to run faster, using all the energy he had left after a tiring day. He was merciless, running circuit after circuit, tormenting his muscles and demanding more and more of them. It was late at night before he stopped and he had to find his way back in the pitch dark with the help of a pocket torch.[5]

After spending the autumn and winter like that, competing in spikes and shorts on a track came as a liberation.

During 1947 and 1948 Zátopek secured his position as one of the top long-distance runners in the world. He raced in Paris, London, Germany, Oslo, Finland, Algeria and many other places, always eager to experiment and learn. He tried racing without a warm-up and he ran up to 25 miles a day including 60 laps of 400 metres. Zátopek became the figurehead of Czechoslovakia, with a worldwide reputation after his gold in the 10,000 metres at the 1948 London Olympics. But it was in his 5,000-metre duel with the Belgian Gaston Reiff that the public and press really became aware of his charismatic qualities.

Reiff was leading by 60 metres and was heading for victory until the Czech, arms flailing, head rolling and pain written all over his face, began unexpectedly to catch up with him. The spectators in London and the radio audience all over the world held their breath as Zátopek closed up and finished just two metres behind Reiff, who took the gold for Belgium.

'The Human Locomotive' was what one headline called Zátopek and the name stuck with him for the rest of his career.[6] He was the product of a great deal of training, rather more than most of his competitors, but it was the effort of will that was most visible. He looked as if he would die on the track. Could he really take one more lap at the same killing speed? Can he really *still* manage to up the pace?

Sporting heroes are frequently elevated to the status of divine beings in their own countries but Zátopek's popularity was world-wide – Asia, South America, wherever he went he charmed people. He was chosen as the world's top sportsman in 1949, 1950 and 1951 without losing his childlike joy in being fit, in meeting new people and in taking on challengers. Between October 1948 and June 1952 Zátopek was undefeated in 72 races at 5,000 and 10,000 metres.

In May 1952 Zátopek was wondering whether he would compete in that year's Helsinki Olympics. He was pessimistic because he was setting himself the target of two golds and that spring he had been training with a cold that developed into bronchitis. Confined to bed, he speculated about the climax of the summer, the games in Helsinki. Against the advice of his doctors, who feared he would burst his heart, he tried to train himself back to health; he left his sickbed and walked and ran to chase away his illness.

Emil Zátopek's three gold medals at the 1952 Helsinki Olympics are among the most commented on achievements in sporting history. No one before him had won the 5,000, the 10,000 and the marathon at the same

Emil Zátopek enters the stadium on his way to victory in the marathon and his third gold medal of the 1952 Helsinki Olympics.

Olympic Games. And no one was more cut out for it than Zátopek, who achieved the legendary status of Paavo Nurmi even though they were opposite poles as personalities.

Zátopek possessed a spark that is granted to few men and he was the sort of man it is impossible to dislike. The Australian Ron Clarke, the greatest long-distance runner of the 1960s and Zátopek's successor, met him behind the communist Iron Curtain in Czechoslovakia during those years. 'Accept this gift', Zátopek said to Clarke, 'but you mustn't open it until you are out of the country.' Zátopek had given Clarke, who never won a gold himself, one of his Olympic gold medals.

In 1968 Colonel Zátopek protested against the Soviet invasion of Czechoslovakia and was punished by being sent to work in the unhealthy environment of a uranium mine. He was later rehabilitated by the authorities and travelled as an ambassador for running until his death in 2000.

A Giant Awakes

Immediately after the Second World War the Soviet Union entered the international sporting world without reservations. Up until then the country had boycotted 'bourgeois sport' and had not participated in an Olympic Games since 1912. Sporting developments had nevertheless been going on under the banner of communism ever since 1917.

Working men from a number of European countries formed associations in the 1920s and organized Workers' Olympics. The breadth of Soviet sport was demonstrated by the interwar Spartiakads, in which the collective rather than the individual was the focus. A call in *Krasnyi Sport* in 1935, however, signalled a change in thinking and called for a challenge to the records of the West: 'Young sportspeople! Remember that it is from you our new champions will come and they will beat the bourgeois records and raise the banner of the physical culture of the Soviet Union to new heights'.[7]

This exhortation was a product of the Five Year Plans and Stalin's strategy for using sport in the service of socialism. Nothing could be better suited to this gigantic project than running. It was important that success should be measurable and that could be done much more clearly in races than, for instance, in football since running required accuracy both in terms of distance and time. In a marathon in the Soviet Union in 1937 several men beat the national record but it later emerged that the course was two kilometres too short. The organizer was arrested and punished severely. A number of the greatest Soviet sporting heroes of the 1930s were runners, such as the brothers Serafim and Georgij Znamensky, who between them held every Soviet record between 800 metres and 10,000 metres. The country invested a great deal in training up good runners but it took time before the level was high enough to compete against the West.[8]

In 1948 the Central Committee of the Communist Party launched an ambitious plan: in addition to raising the physical fitness of the masses the aim was for Soviet sportsmen to be world leaders in a number of important sporting disciplines within a few years. An editorial in *Pravda* two years later declared: 'The duty of our young sportspeople is to beat old records'.[9] What mattered was competing against and beating the West, particularly the USA. The Soviet Union should be superior in industry, agriculture, science and sport, and the superiority in sport would be proof of the ideal state and the classless society in contrast to decadent Western nations.

The Soviet Union participated in the Olympics from 1952 on with growing success and by the end of the decade was the leading sporting nation in the world. From the viewpoint of the West the Soviets, who regarded the running track as a war zone, were reminiscent of the Spartans. They were focused and serious and had little interest in mixing and communicating with other competitors.

The consequence was that Westerners distrusted the communist regime and Soviet involvement in general. There were all kinds of rumours, such as the story of the Hungarian runner in 1951 who was all set to win but who was pushed and kicked by Soviet competitors and consequently lost the race. They could not tolerate defeat in the home arena and would do anything to win. The ingrained suspicion of the West, coupled with keen competition at home and the enormous rewards for success, bred a new kind of athlete with a voracious hunger for victory. Sport was both a sweaty way to personal profit of various kinds and propaganda for the Soviet state.

Blazing Willpower

No one fulfilled the task better than the long-distance runner Vladimir Kuts (1927–1975) who, like other Soviet sportsmen, emerged from a population that had suffered and been hardened over decades.

Kuts was born in a village in the Ukraine and saw the havoc and death caused by famine in his childhood. He was fourteen when the Germans occupied the area and in spite of his youth he was one of the 'men' the Germans forced into heavy, slave labour. The young Kuts was not naturally servile: there was a strong streak of the rebel in him, particularly when it came to helmeted Germans roaring orders. The normal method of punishment was a beating with a club and on one occasion Kuts took 25 blows without a whimper. The experience as a forced labourer burned itself into Kuts' body and soul and he wanted to get away and fight for his country rather than build roads for the German war-machine. Before his sixteenth birthday he escaped from the village and joined up with the Russian armoured forces that were pushing the Germans back. He lived with a gun in his hand and death at his shoulder in the battle for the Soviet Union.

After the war Kuts returned to his village in the Ukraine only to find it had been burnt down. He was nineteen years old, with nowhere to go, no job and no prospects at home. He had never had anything to do with running, hardly thought about sport and in those years it took cunning and a good deal of luck simply to survive. He joined the navy.

He was used to a tougher, more physically demanding life than the navy called for so he began to take part in sports. He lacked the speed to be a sprinter and given his thickset body – five foot seven and a half and eleven stone four pounds – he looked best suited to weight-lifting or wrestling. It was Zátopek who inspired Kuts. He began to train in the same spirit as Zátopek, but even harder than his model.

Kuts really ought not to have been able to hold his own internationally when he was discovered at the age of 25 and sent to train with Nikiforov in Leningrad. He was on the slow side but what he lacked in pure running talent he made up for in toughness. Kuts had needed to do a lot of walking as he grew up, he had carried heavy loads, dug, hacked and hoed the earth and, though small, he had become a muscle man. He focused on the 5,000 and 10,000 metres and improved his speed through simple and brutal interval techniques: 400 metres absolutely flat out and the shortest possible rest before the next run. Another variation was 6 × 800 metres with minimal rests or 3 × 1,200 metres, always breathless and on the verge of cramp but never giving up.

He inured himself to being in a state of near exhaustion, with the taste of blood in his mouth and lead in his legs. He had to be so tough because his opponents were faster and superior to him in the final spurt. He would take a rest day after the hardest sessions, with a long hot bath and a massage to restore his body. Under his strictest training regimes he would rest two days a week to ensure he did not suffer burnout, and life in the navy provided him with the perfect conditions.

Kuts emerged like a little Soviet bear at the 1954 European athletics championships, where he beat both Zátopek and the Englishman Chris Chataway in the 5,000 metres, setting a world record in the process.

Kuts was the personification of the Western stereotype of Soviet man. His clear blue eyes and square face radiated will-power and strength, his blond mop of hair made him look like a Finn but he looked angrier than the Finns. His body language said: 'Here comes the Soviet Union. We suffered most in the world war and refused to back down. We are communists, standing together against the capitalists. We are workers and the agents of a socialist world revolution, we are not the lapdogs and yes-men of the Americans.' Such were the thoughts Kuts evoked among spectators in the West the propaganda had achieved the desired effect.

He would open at a killing pace and often run the first half much faster than the second, clearly exhausted towards the end but always man enough to retain the lead. The tactic was to frighten off the opposition, to get clear of them and demoralize them while tormenting himself out in the lead. What was a race compared with German forced labour and torture?

Before the 1956 Olympics Kuts was ranked as the world's number one 10,000 metre runner and at 5,000 he was ranked number two, just behind the British runner Gordon Pirie. He had only lost twice at international meetings and on both occasions his opponent had to break the world record to win. In Kuts' view, both defeats had been close and a matter of luck. His defeat by Gordon Pirie in Bergen in 1956, when Pirie had stuck with him and then sprinted away on the last lap, encouraged him to adopt suicidal tactics at the Olympics: not the usual changes of pace but all-out sprints two or three times each lap in order to crush the opposition totally.

In the autumn of 1956 Kuts acclimatized himself to Australia, trained hard and then took a rest day, during which a newspaper asked for a photograph of him in a fast car. Kuts loved fast cars, pushed his foot to the floor, lost control and hit a telegraph pole, banging both his knee and his chest. It was a shock but fortunately he had three days to recover before the 10,000 metres.

The race was a duel between Gordon Pirie and Vladimir Kuts. The two of them were soon alone out in front, Pirie like a shadow just behind Kuts and refusing to be dropped. Even when the Russian sprinted for 200 metres the Englishman stuck with him, to Kuts' annoyance. But about four laps before the end Kuts pulled away and went on to the gold whereas Pirie succumbed and finished eighth. In the 5,000 metres Kuts again beat Pirie.

Gordon Pirie wrote about these races in his book *Running Wild* (1961). On the victor's podium Kuts' eyes had a glazed and abnormal appearance and Pirie believes that it might have been due to drugs, possibly amphetamines or some other stimulant. Amphetamines were commonly used, particularly by European professional cyclists, and their eyes frequently seemed glazed, possibly as a result of drugs or perhaps by the effort. If Kuts was not on drugs but simply both exhausted and moved by the occasion, his eyes could easily have been filled with tears of joy.

For a man of Kuts' background victory over the arch-enemies in the West was a sweet triumph. Kuts, of course, felt personal elation at his victories but he was also bringing home success to a nation that would reward him for life for his records and triumphs. For the Soviet authorities Vladimir Kuts was the outstanding example of his country's resilience and physical condition.

Kuts retired in 1959. Age was taking its toll and his body would no longer take the hard treatment. People who met him later remember a chubby, good-natured man who had given up running – there was no point now the gold medals and state pension were in the bag.[10]

Intervals Rule!

Zátopek also inspired the Hungarians in a major way. Zátopek himself passed on ideas about interval training, even though the Czechs and the Hungarians were arch-enemies who were not keen on exchanging ideas about training. The Hungarian coach Mihaly Igloi also picked up tips about intervals from the Pole Janis Kuszoczinsky and from coaches in Sweden and

Finland. Igloi's disciples made Hungary a major power in the middle- and long-distance world for some years in the mid-1950s with the emergence of a range of runners, such as Sandor Iharos, István Rózsavölgyi and Laszlo Tabori, who between them set many national and international records. Igloi later emigrated to the United States and was very successful there – with interval training as his recurring theme and brutal method of improvement.

All elite running in Hungary in the 1950s took place on tracks in Budapest. The capital, the twin cities of Buda and Pest, was the showcase to the outside world and ambitious runners from the rest of the country had to move there. Although industry and colleges existed all over the country the clubs outside the capital received little support and worked in difficult conditions. In Budapest, however, there were coaches, masseurs and good tracks – an organized, well-supported and vibrant environment.

It was only for periods during the winter that crowds of runners went out into the city parks. Once the ground was dry and clear of snow in March they returned to their normal track environment; for the Hungarians the tracks fulfilled the same role as the forests did for the Scandinavians – a breathing space away from the bustle of the city. Running on the streets of a city with two million inhabitants was no use, there were few areas of woodland close-by, and the grass in the parks was not supposed to be trodden on. Of all the good running nations the Hungarians were the most urban. They were firmly attached to their club tracks and facilities and they had no need to travel outside the city for national competitions since 90 per cent of all meetings took place in the capital.

The idea of running for exercise did not exist in Hungary in the 1950s: you either belonged to the world of interval training and lived with intervals week after week, year after year on the same track, sometimes doing as many as 75 laps at varying speeds, or you gave up running. The purpose of intervals was solely to improve the skills necessary for a better track performance. There was a brotherhood of runners, with a few woman members over the shorter distances, whose daily existence revolved around interval training. Warming up and warming down, also an effective part of the training, provided the breathing spaces without which the Hungarians would not have survived the hard training.

Gergely Szentiványi (1940–) wanted to run even when he was just a boy of six. His grandfather was the founder of the Hungarian Centre Party and was declared an enemy of the state after the communist takeover in 1948. In the mid-1950s his grandson had to watch his step when he joined the university club in Budapest since even the relations of enemies of the state could be banned.[11]

Gergely took advantage of the benefits enjoyed by sportspeople and ate bread rolls and luxuries like yoghurt after training, since it was the coach who distributed rations. Many people joined sports clubs simply for the food. In the Second World War Hungary had been on the losing side against the Soviet Union and had to pay reparations in goods as well as money. Trainloads of grain, meat and butter left Hungary for the Soviet Union every day: meat was a rarity in Hungary before 1955 and grain and butter were in short supply. The situation was similar to that in various other European countries where ration cards were part of everyday life well into the 1950s.

People who took part in sports received what was called 'calorie money', monthly payments of 300 *forints* or more to cover their increased food requirements. They were a welcome addition to tight budgets and they varied according to the level of sporting achievement: the best got most and the payments were adjusted in line with results.

In 1958 Gergely produced the best international 1,500 metre time for an eighteen-year-old (3 minutes 49 seconds). His club wrote to the director of a cable factory inquiring whether there was a job for Gergely and the director was keen to have a top performer on the books since it brought status. Gergely trained in the mornings and then arrived at work when it suited his schedule, usually an hour and a half after his workmates; he also finished a little early in the afternoon in order to have another training session. He still received the full wage for an eight-hour day, however, and earned more than his workmates. Gergely and other Hungarian sportsmen lived well and, in contrast to their Western competitors, they did not have to worry about having their wages cut because of absences from the workplace.

The process of reaching this level was, however, extremely demanding and an individual had to carry on achieving in order to stay in the system. Rewards in the form of wages and material and social benefits made the sportsmen keen to improve. A member of a national team risked being downgraded if his performance level fell drastically and he could no longer be sure of a permanent place. On the other hand, sportsmen who were in the armed forces in communist countries were promoted whenever they broke a world record.

For many years East European sportsmen and their managers smuggled goods home when they travelled abroad: the opportunity to profit from small-scale smuggling was another of the motivations to be involved in sport. Hungarian sportsmen passed through the strictly policed borders of their homeland with smuggled goods concealed in their tracksuits, trouser pockets and bags. As well-known personalities they passed easily through the customs checks. Ballpoint pens from the West were popular in the 1950s and 500 of them sold discreetly provided an extra income as well as some excitement. The black market was also hungry for nylon stockings. The demand for Western consumer goods seemed bottomless, partly because many things were in short supply but also because Western goods had status value. Anything that is rare makes easy money even though it may be of no use.

Gergely used to cross the borders between East and West with something sellable in his baggage. When he was competing in Romania in 1958 he sold his tracksuit for 200 *forints*. There was a shortage of black pepper in Hungary at that point and he invested his profit from the tracksuit in pepper, which he sold for four times as much in Hungary. The following year the team was competing in East Germany where there was a shortage of cigarettes. The Hungarians bought cartons of cigarettes before leaving home and sold them singly on the street in the German Democratic Republic at a steep price. In Poland Gergely sold hard liquor on the street and bought himself a record player with the profits.

They were always under surveillance, particularly abroad where there was the danger they might defect. Gergely had two watchers on his trips abroad – in Switzerland, for instance, two hefty hammer throwers from the Hungarian police club did not let him out of their sight.

'I'm going for a walk', Gergely would say. 'I'll come with you, then', one of the hammer throwers would reply and collect his colleague. They had been tasked by the Hungarian authorities with ensuring that Gergely did not defect. Thousands of people were being watched and thousands more were doing the watching. No one trusted anyone else and everyday life was characterized by suspicion.

In the 1960s when Hungarian runners began to move out into the woods and parks for more distance training and fartlek work they might suddenly hear the word 'Halt!' shouted and find themselves face to face with an armed Russian or Hungarian soldier guarding a restricted area. There were military bases all over the country, one Russian and one Hungarian in each place, and the Soviet Union had its supporters at all levels.

Gergely often thought of defecting but he mentioned it to no one but his girl-friend Irma. Once, close to the border, he was tempted to defect but common sense stopped him. He was, however, well prepared for defection in that he had a sports passport and, as a sportsman, had taken a German course during his working time; he also had contacts and was familiar with conditions in German-speaking countries. Irma had worked on a market stall in Vienna the summer before and also wanted the chance of making a future for herself away from the iron grip of communism.

The couple were under suspicion of being potential defectors. When Irma had been working in Vienna and wanted to extend her visa her application was rejected because Gergely was competing in Hanover at the time. Their plan was to defect if Gergely did not qualify for the Olympic Games of 1968: if he was selected they would stay in Hungary. He was not selected for the Olympics but they could not risk fleeing that year since someone had informed on them.

They took the chance a little later. The train was not a realistic option for the small family – their daughter Nora was a small baby and the customs would immediately recognize them as defectors and send them back. The sports passport, with its distinctive colour, offered possibilities since he and his partner had different surnames. Gergely did not reveal their plans to anyone. He and Irma, who was carrying the eleven-month-old baby, boarded a boat on the Danube, headed in the direction of Vienna. There were American journalists on board but there were no ordinary Hungarian passengers. The group of ten or twelve, apparently a party of Americans both fascinated by Eastern Europe and thoroughly glad not to live there, watched the passing countryside as they sailed up the river. Gergely talked English to the journalists and lived through five tense hours. Neither customs men nor policemen came aboard and Vienna welcomed them, as it had thousands of other Hungarian refugees.

After the Second World War the differences between the Eastern Bloc and Western Europe in terms of government, lifestyle and living conditions remained enormous for two generations. The day-to-day existence of sportsmen was defined by political circumstances and national rivalries had the effect of pushing standards upwards. There were, however, still some people in the middle of the twentieth century who wanted to become top runners for pure and noble amateur motives. While state professionalism was still in its infancy in the East, there were young men – particularly from the declining world power Great Britain – who were out to prove the continuing vitality of their countries.

21

The Dream Mile

I collapsed almost unconscious, with an arm on either side of me. It
was only then that real pain overtook me. I felt like an exploded flash-
light with no will to live; I just went on existing in the most passive
physical state without being quite unconscious.
—Roger Bannister, on being the first to run the mile in under
four minutes, 1954

'No one can run a mile in less than 4.01.66' was the conclusion reached by
Brutus Hamilton, a coach at the University of California, in 1935.[1] Ambitious
runners saw fewer limitations but no one knows for sure who was the first
to fantasize about breaking the four-minute barrier. Nor is it absolutely clear
who achieved it first although the English runner Roger Bannister is officially acknowledged to be the first with his time of 3 minutes 59.4 seconds
on 6 May 1954.

At the beginning of the twentieth century no one knew that the Pawnee
Indian Koo-tah-we-Coots-oo-lel-hoo, Chief Great Hawk, was reputed to
have done a mile in 3 minutes 58 seconds in the United States in 1876.
American army officers timed him with a stopwatch over two runs and the
hands stopped in the 3.50s both times. But there is no proof that the distance
was accurately measured or that the gradient of the track would have satisfied twentieth-century regulations for the ratification of records.[2]

Various rumours in the interwar years tell of sub-four-minute miles
being run in the course of training, with empty stands, no press presence
and only coaches and colleagues as witnesses. The American world record
holder Glenn Cunningham is supposed to have done it in the 1930s, and the
New Zealander Jack Lovelock is said to have achieved it twice in absolute
secrecy during the same decade.

That last story came to public knowledge rather like a spy's revelations.
The English doctor John Etheridge wrote a letter to the *British Medical
Journal* after reading a reference to a biographical novel about Lovelock.
Etheridge claimed that he was the timekeeper when Lovelock, who was also
a medical student, ran in Paddington in London and at Motspur Park in
Surrey in the 1930s. He had described everything in detail in a diary: conditions, the reliability of the distance and of the stopwatches. Half a century
later he could not remember the exact times without looking at the diary
but he thought he remembered 3.56 at Paddington and 3.52 at Motspur Park
– without a pacemaker. Etheridge died before the diary entries were located.[3]

After the hiatus caused by the Second World War people had a healthy
appetite to watch international sport again. In 1945 Roger Bannister, then

a sixteen-year-old, sat with his father and 57,000 other spectators in the White City Stadium, watching the world's best milers. Bannister found the experience overwhelming and it planted a seed in his mind. He was physically rather awkward and ungainly but still wanted to take part in dramatic races at great sporting arenas.

Roger Gilbert Bannister was born on 23 March 1929 in the north London suburb of Harrow. His father was a civil servant and his mother a trained teacher, though not practising. The two children in the family grew up in a bookish environment and were taught to fill every available hour with something productive. Bannister was by nature diligent and systematic: his dream was to become a doctor and in 1946 he won a scholarship to study at Oxford. He spent five important years there before moving on to St Mary's Hospital in London to complete his medical education. Bannister was not, then, still a student at Oxford when he broke the record though he still had good contacts there.

The environment he was part of there was rich in tradition and had produced a number of middle-distance Olympic champions, Jack Lovelock among them. Student sportsmen in Oxford lived a good life – there were track facilities within walking distance, a considerable emphasis on sport and a system in place to foster good sportsmen. And the majority of students at Oxford came from fairly affluent families and were part of a social elite. A working-class boy who wanted to go in for athletics in 1950s Britain would have been in a much less advantageous position. He would have started work at the age of fifteen, probably not have had either tracks or coaches available locally and would have little free time compared with a student.

Professor John Bale has studied Roger Bannister's athletics career and challenged the myth of him as an amateur.[4] Bale stresses that he was, of course, a thoroughbred amateur in that he did not earn money from athletics. But as a scholarship holder at Oxford he had important advantages and his years as a student there provided him with social and cultural capital which later benefited his professional career and his personal economy.

From the day Bannister made his debut in the mile with 4 minutes 53 seconds in 1946 he gradually refined his training and toughened up his body. He was tall – six feet two inches – and slim and few middle-distance runners have trained so systematically and scientifically. He was not keen to admit it in public because a true British amateur should not take sport that seriously. Every race was an experiment, the ultimate goal being to produce a mile in under four minutes. And while on tour in Germany he had the benefit of meeting the famous German coach Waldemar Gerschler.

As a student and future doctor Bannister spent much time in the laboratory. He would adjust the speed and gradient of a motor-driven treadmill and in this way he studied the body's reactions at maximum performance: 'In time I learnt to repeat my performance on the treadmill so that I could study the effect on my performances of changes in body temperature, in the acidity of the blood, and in the composition of the air breathed in'.[5] He experimented on himself, breathing air that contained 66 per cent or 100 per cent oxygen. It was so easy to run when the oxygen percentage was 66 per cent that he stopped because of boredom rather than exhaustion. Signs of exhaustion came after seven or eight minutes with ordinary air compared with 22 or 23 minutes after taking oxygen.

All of this was quite considerably more than the 'common sense' training of an amateur. It was extremely advanced for its day: a very rare example of a researcher and a sportsman aiming at a world record – a combination unique in running history.

In the magazine *Athletics Weekly* in 1951 Bannister claimed that he trained three times a week for 45 minutes. In his book *The First Four Minutes* (1955) he admits to four training sessions a week, although the truth was that there were even more.[6] Bannister did not want to reveal his preparation methods and he was following a good Oxford tradition of not wanting to appear to be trying too hard. One should not take things too seriously, whether studies or sport, because it might lead to one being thought of as pushy, over-ambitious, a swot – all of which were unpopular.

Bannister set a British record for the distance in 1953 and was focusing everything on the following season. A number of others were doing the same, including Wes Santee in the USA and John Landy in Australia, as well as Scandinavians, British, Hungarians and others, all sensing that the barrier was ready to fall. Landy appeared to be the strongest contender and his 4 minutes 2 seconds in December 1953 without a pacemaker equalled Bannister's personal best. By that stage Bannister had been planning his campaign for a month.

Together with the McWhirter twins, both Oxford graduates and the originators of the *Guinness Book of Records*, and several other friends, Bannister set the date for 6 May 1954 and the place: Iffley Road in Oxford. The Austrian coach Franz Stampfl, a recent arrival in the city, and two of Bannister's friends from his student days, Chris Brasher and Chris Chataway, were also involved in the preparations. The first of these two was to be the pacemaker and a test run showed him to be up to the job.

It was no accident that these preparations were taking place in the spring of 1954 since news was coming in from the USA and Australia that Santee and Landy were coming into top form. Bannister's shoes were hand-made and all superfluous weight was removed. He sharpened the spikes himself on a grindstone in the laboratory and covered the soles in graphite so that dirt would not stick to them and increase the weight.

Roger Bannister and Franz Stampfl took the train from London to Oxford on 6 May 1954, finally ready after six months of preparation. Bannister seemed nervous: was it really possible to break the four minutes? Stampfl calmed him down: he knew that Bannister was properly prepared and capable of achieving 3 minutes 56 seconds on a perfect day assuming his form, the game-plan, the wind and the weather all clicked.

Things look bad when they arrive in Oxford and find the wind whipping across the Iffley Road track. Bannister tests his spikes, eats a light meal and relaxes. An hour before the start he, Chris Chataway and the journalist Joe Binks go to the track, where somewhere between 1,000 and 2,000 spectators are waiting. Norris McWhirter has tipped the BBC that a record time is a possibility and a cameraman is rigging the equipment to film it for that evening's sports news. The McWhirter twins are there as writers for their own athletics magazine and Norris is also the announcer at the meeting as well as running in the sprint relay. Ross is in position as unofficial timekeeper at the 1,500 metre mark of the mile race in case a world record time is also produced at that distance.[7]

Because of the unstable weather Stampfl has advised Bannister to consider the conditions before deciding whether to give his all and go for it – he might need to spare his strength for a later occasion. A quarter of an hour before the start Bannister is saying no to the attempt – the wind is too strong and an attempt at the record is not on the cards: he refuses to try for it in the conditions.

Suddenly the wind drops and six men line up: Bannister, Chris Chataway, Chris Brasher, the American George Dole, Alan Gordon and Tom Hulatt. The latter is a working-class lad and the only one of them unconnected with university life. Only Bannister is a world-class miler even though Chataway later sets a world record for the 5,000 metres and Brasher wins the Olympic gold in the 3,000 metre steeplechase two years later.

It is a scientific experiment in which Bannister has two assistants, Chataway and Brasher, whereas Hulatt is told to run his own race. Brasher is to lead for two laps and then hand over to Chataway before Bannister takes over for the decisive spurt. Everyone in the field knows his place and they know that it is all about the record.

After a false start they fall into their agreed positions and the front of the field passes the half-way mark in 1.58 – ahead of their schedule. Once into the last lap Bannister takes the lead, running with long, elegant strides and passing the 1,500 metre mark in 3.43. He is giving it everything and reaches the line with a gladiatorial effort and his face contorted with pain. He gasps for air and puts his head in his hands as if asking 'Is it a new record? Is it under four minutes?' The stopwatches of the three timekeepers show 3 minutes 59.4 seconds.

He has done it! So many spectators push forward that the last two runners are unable to finish the race. The result is recorded and given to Norris McWhirter, who makes a melodramatic announcement:

> Ladies and gentlemen, here is the result of event number nine, the one mile: first, number 41, R. G. Bannister, of the Amateur Athletics Association and formerly of Exeter and Merton Colleges, with a time which is a new meeting and track record and which subject to ratification will be a new English Native, British (National),

British (All-comers), European, British Empire and World Record.
The time is three minutes, fifty nine point four seconds.

Jubilation erupts and the crowd senses the tidal surge of history.[8]
Bannister is totally exhausted. It takes three hours for his pulse to drop
to its normal 40–50 beats per minute and his colour vision is blurred. He
appears modest in front of the television camera and says he is happy to
have succeeded. It is great to break time barriers but even greater to win
international titles. He assures the world that running is his hobby and that
he races as a true amateur. Only those in the know are aware that there are
few runners in 1954 who train in such an advanced way as he does, even
though he works hard as a doctor and does not receive payment for his
sporting achievements.

Bannister's name flies round the world and newspapers everywhere
splash the news on their front pages. The photograph of him immediately
before he breasts the tape, in his final effort to break the record, symbolizes
a superhuman feat in the same category as the ascent of Everest the year
before. The British Empire may be wobbling, the inhabitants of many
colonies demanding independence, but here is a young man who can show
that Englishmen are still the best in the world in the sport they claim to
have invented. The mile is a true British measure, a symbol of the breadth
of the Empire, a distance superior to the metric distances that are pushing
their way in. The mile is the measure that brings order to the world and it
is right that it is an Englishman who breaks the dream barrier.

There is, however, also some criticism of the use of pacemakers, a practice far from being fully accepted. Commentators in the USA and Australia
say that this is *one* way of doing it but not the most authentic way. The
record is a result of pace-setting, not of a proper competition.

Paavo Nurmi and many other experts forecast rapid improvements –
the limit has certainly not been reached.

The summer of 1954 was the summer of two middle-distance records.
A month after Bannister's race Wes Santee in the USA set a new world 1,500
metres record of 3 minutes 42.8 seconds, thereby beating Gunder Hägg's
ageing record. Not long after, however, Santee was found guilty of professionalism and banned for having received excessive expenses for appearing.

The third of the world's best milers, John Landy, came over from
Australia to tour Scandinavia in the spring of 1954. After a number of meetings he arrived at the stadium in Turku in Finland on 21 June. Landy took the
lead from the 700 metre mark and led from there on, setting a new world 1,500
metres record of 3 minutes 42.8 seconds and a new mile record of 3 minutes
57.9 seconds – with a smile on his face. This achievement was more clearly a
solo effort rather than a careful experiment with chosen assistants.

Roger Bannister's record had survived for 46 days.

A meeting between him and Landy was obviously high on the agenda.
It came at the Commonwealth Games in Vancouver in August 1954 and

was billed as the 'Miracle Mile'. Bannister won in 3 minutes 58.8 seconds, with Landy coming in at 3.59.6 even though he had a clear lead at the halfway stage. Bannister undoubtedly held the crown for the mile during the 1954 season.

In 1957 Dr Herbert Berger from the USA claimed that the use of amphetamines explained the avalanche of sub-four-minute times for the mile. By then twelve runners had broken the magic barrier on eighteen occasions and this, according to Berger, was suspicious. His claims led to international debate among doctors and other experts while the runners, feeling stigmatized, stated that middle-distance running was free of any use of stimulants such as amphetamines. These drugs were easily available in many countries in the form of pills or sprays and in 1957, in the USA alone, six billion amphetamine pills were produced. The debate soon faded away without having led to anything apart from claims being made and then followed by denials from the milers.

But Berger's claims revealed that scepticism about the way records were going started early. The West was characterized by a strong faith in progress and in the ability of science to solve all imaginable and unimaginable problems. Simply to ask the question whether advances in sport might be due to cheating conflicted with the then current optimism about the future – the belief that everything could and should go faster. To suggest anything else was contrary to the natural way of things.[9]

22

Africa Arrives

Cattle rustling is the traditional sport for many young men
from various tribes.
—On the Kalenjin tribe in Kenya, where the young men run
for up to 100 miles in groups to steal cattle

By the 1960s the population in large parts of the West had access to television and the summer Olympics of that year were the first to be broadcast
on TV. People flocked to wherever there were TV sets or stood in crowds outside shops with screens in the windows and were fascinated by the new
medium. At last the people of the world could receive the most important
sporting events direct into their living rooms. TV increased the interest in
sport and added a new dimension. It was a magical medium that changed
its viewers' world and their perception of it.

Two runners made a particularly strong impact at the Rome Olympics
of 1960. Wilma Rudolph from the USA took three golds with her long legs
– the 100 metres, the 200 metres and the sprint relay. She became the first
black queen of sprint in history. Quite sensationally, moreover, she was a
former polio sufferer, only twenty years old and the mother of a little girl.
Rudolph was also an early female sex symbol for running – she was graceful and feminine and a revelation for photographers and cameramen.
Men, typically enough, characterized her as a sex object rather than judging
her by her speed – earlier the lack of femininity among female runners had
often been used as an argument against them. Wilma Rudolph may not have
been the first black woman runner to have made an impression at the international level but she opened the way for successors in a world that was
calling for change, particularly in the areas of race and racial prejudice.

Another new phenomenon also emerged in the 1960 Olympic marathon:
Abebe Bikila from Ethiopia, hitherto unknown as a sporting nation.

This was the first time that the Olympic marathon neither started nor
finished at a stadium, and the race also set off at 5.30 p.m. rather than the
usual early morning start. The course ran past many of the great sights of
Rome and was a journey through history, from its start in Michelangelo's
creation, the Piazza di Campidoglio, to its finish in the dark of night.
Soldiers lit the way with torches, their flames evoking associations with the
ancient Olympics.

The favourite was Sergei Popov, the world record holder from the
Soviet Union.

At the halfway stage Abebe Bikila and the Moroccan Rhadi ben Abdesselem were in the lead. Few people knew anything about the Ethiopian, who was running barefoot not because he had no shoes, as rumour suggested, but because the running shoes he had brought from home were worn out and a new pair he had bought in Rome did not fit properly and gave him blisters. Bikila kept trying them in the days before the race and then discarded them just before the start on the advice of his coach Onni Niskanen, a Finnish-born Swede.

The two Africans stuck together like each other's shadows until the Piazza di Porta Capena, where Bikila saw the Obelisco de Azum, a famous Ethiopian statue which the Italians had plundered from Ethiopia during the invasion of 1936. The gold went to Bikila, 25 seconds up on the Moroccan and with a new world record of 2 hours, 15 minutes and 16.2 seconds.

When Bikila arrived home in Ethiopia in 1960 he rode through the streets of Addis Ababa on the back of a lorry together with one of the emperor's lions and received the acclaim of his people. He was promoted to corporal and became a favourite of the emperor.

Bikila heralded a new age. To European eyes he was the first black African to win an Olympic gold. Two white South Africans had won the Olympic marathon in the early 1900s and Boughera El Quafi from Algeria won the gold in 1928 while representing France. The Frenchman Alain Mimoun who won in 1956 was also really from Algeria. Bikila disproved Western theories that blacks could not run long distances.

The games in Rome were something very special for Ethiopia since Italy had attempted to colonize Ethiopia as long ago as 1896. They had then invaded the country in 1936 and occupied it for five years, earning the hatred of the population and of the emperor, Haile Selassie I, who returned home in 1941. So it was a very special triumph when Bikila won and his victory echoed across the whole of Africa, exciting a continent that was in the process of throwing off the shackles of European colonialism. In the West Bikila was seen as a symbol of raw African talent in long-distance running; in Africa he signalled hope and demonstrated that they could also challenge and beat white supremacy in the sporting arena.

Ethiopia was a poor and underdeveloped country with only 280,000 school places for its 18,000,000 inhabitants. At least 90 per cent of its people were illiterate and the country's only public hospital was in Addis Ababa. Hyenas and jackals scavenged the rubbish in the towns and leprosy, smallpox and tapeworms were widespread. Nevertheless, more people than ever before could read in this highland country in which the emperor was absolute ruler and people often prostrated themselves on the street when he was driven past in his smart Cadillac. Ethiopia was a feudal society with a long and independent history and, since the country had been Christianized as early as the fourth century, the Coptic church was strong.

People in the West knew little about Ethiopia, which was secretive about internal conditions and received aid from the Soviet Union. Many people assumed that Bikila was untrained and succeeded because of his raw talent but, as is often the case with outsiders, there was a long and planned development behind him. As early as 1947 the Ethiopian authorities had appointed Onni Niskanen to organize sport in the country.

Niskanen (1910–1984) was born in Pihtipudas in Finland and some time between 1929 and 1936 he moved to Sweden and became a Swedish citizen. He was involved in the working-class sporting movement and was selected for the Barcelona Workers' Olympics of 1936 but, because of the outbreak of the Spanish Civil War, the games were cancelled the day before they were due to open. During the Second World War Niskanen fought on the Finnish side against the Soviet Union, was wounded and was later promoted to lieutenant. Niskanen was an excellent choice for the job of building up Ethiopian sport: he had experience of sport at home, he had a military training and, moreover, he came from a society that valued running.[1]

Abebe Bikila was born on 7 August 1932 in the village of Jato, six miles from the town of Mendida in the Debre Birhan mountain region. His father was a herdsman and the family, which consisted of four boys and a girl, was split up when the Italians invaded the country in the 1930s. When the family returned home in 1941 after the Italians had withdrawn, young Abebe Bikila also became a herdsman. During a visit to Addis Abbeba sometime around 1950 he saw the royal bodyguard training and was so impressed that his brother, who was already a member, helped him to enlist. The bodyguard was an exclusive group to work in and its members were on duty for two two-hour periods a day, which allowed them plentiful opportunity to take part in sports.

Sometime early in 1957 Bikila saw some soldiers with particularly smart uniforms – they hade taken part in the Melbourne Olympics and been given the clothes as a reward. Bikila wanted similar clothes and his Olympic dream was born. He intensified his training and began running even outside work – to his mother's distress since she thought he would destroy his health. She tried to get him to stop by serving him less food in order to diminish his energy. Bikila put up with it, only to be nagged at for wasting money by eating out. Bikila was invited to take part in a cycle race, a sport Ethiopia was also focusing on, and he did some serious training. His mother's worries continued and she wanted to arrange a marriage for him so that he would have no time to train. Bikila was victorious in the cycle race and won the first trophy of his life.

There were rumours that the Ethiopians were considering dropping their plans for the 1960 Olympics since they had won no medals in 1956. Onni Niskanen, who was working for the Red Cross at that stage, reacted to the rumours and spoke directly to Emperor Haile Selassie I, explaining the importance of having good sportsmen. He referred to Finland, his own native country, and suggested that Ethiopia could gain recognition and respect in the world in the same way. The emperor gave his permission for continued preparations and the Finn had a sauna installed, to the amazement of the Ethiopians, who wondered why they should need even more heat than they already had.

Hundreds of Ethiopians on the military bases around the country ran in the selection process. Bikila, too, was involved and came sixth in the 5,000 metres and ninth in the 10,000. The intention was that the national military championships of 1959 would sort out the candidates for the 1960 Rome Olympics. On the day of a military parade in Addis Ababa that year Bikila won his first marathon.[2]

The traditions of Western sport were absent among the Ethiopians, who lived according to their own ideas and perceptions. If things went badly, for instance, they would blame 'evil spirits' and invisible forces. They saw no point in pushing themselves to the limit, since the spirits were all-powerful in any case. Niskanen tried to eradicate attitudes of this kind, which led runners to give up or slow down for no apparent reason even when they had plenty of energy left. Eventually Niskanen's rational message got through.

During the summer of 1960 they trained ferociously. Niskanen drove a jeep, with the runners in a group either behind or in front. Every one of them was a soldier with permission for unlimited training and they steadily became stronger, both in body and mind. Niskanen gave his commands with a whistle while his Ethiopian assistant took care of the stopwatch, noted times and interpreted the results with him. They usually had two training sessions a day in hilly terrain and then they sweated even more in the sauna after their training.

Before a five-mile run back to the army camp Bikila was having trouble getting his shoes on when all the rest set off, so he put his shoes in his pocket and set off barefoot. Niskanen studied Bikila's training times both with and without shoes: on the 28 June he ran twenty miles barefoot on roads in 1 hour 45 minutes and two days later ran the same distance in shoes in 1 hour, 46 minutes and 30 seconds.[3]

Just a month before the Rome Olympics Bikila achieved 2 hours 21 minutes in a marathon in Addis Ababa, which lies 8,000 feet above sea-level. In contrast to the assumptions of many in the West, when Bikila arrived at the Olympics he was no hobby runner captured in the mountains and coaxed to run.

In December 1960 the Ethiopian emperor's bodyguard mutinied while the emperor was on a state visit to Brazil. The rebels arrested all the members of the royal family and held the ministers as hostages. The American ambassador attempted to mediate between the rebels and the army but the army were not prepared to compromise. The rebels then massacred all the hostages with machine guns before fleeing. Meanwhile, the emperor had been informed and flew in from abroad.

The mutiny was put down and the emperor was profoundly disappointed by the disloyalty of some of his officers, a number of whom were hanged. Bikila was connected to the mutiny simply through his job, but he had no desire to overthrow a friend. He was imprisoned for a short while and could have ended up on the gallows, but there was no proof of any active involvement on his part and the emperor's goodwill was decisive. The emperor could not have the country's great hero executed.

Bikila's marathon career continued. Over his career he won twelve of his fifteen races at that distance, including the 1964 Tokyo Olympics when, after finishing, he impressed TV viewers the world over by performing stretching exercises and gymnastics on the grass without any signs of exhaustion. He was as tired as the rest of them but grimly determined to complete the exercises while millions of viewers followed his every movement. The exercises were well stage-managed to secure his status as an African phenomenon. The emperor promoted Bikila to lieutenant, gave him a house and a Volkswagen – about the poshest thing an Ethiopian could possess.

One rainy day in March 1969 Bikila was driving his Volkswagen to his farm after a training session. The roads were slippery and visibility bad. A bus going in the opposite direction came over a bridge at full speed and the two vehicles collided. The passengers recognized the injured man in the car and behaved as if they had crashed into a god.

When he regained consciousness, surrounded by his wife, his mother and the medical staff, Bikila was unable to move. They assumed at first that his paralysis was a result of having been unconscious for so long – the world's greatest marathon runner wanted to start running again as soon as he came round. But his condition did not improve: he was paralysed from the chest down. The best doctors in the country did what they could and then the patient was sent to England for further treatment, but there was no miraculous cure available. Any ordinary Ethiopian with similar injuries would have been left in his hut in the care of his family but Bikila was transported all over the world by car or by plane, always surrounded by the curious, who found it particularly tragic that legs that had once been so nimble could no longer move. He gave training advice from his wheelchair, took part in sledging competitions in Norway and tried his hand at archery.

In the autumn of 1973 he suffered severe stomach pains. His condition deteriorated in hospital and the emperor asked his doctors to transfer him to England for specialist treatment. Bikila died before they were able to do so. He was 41 years old and Ethiopia went into national mourning at the news of his death on 22 October 1973. People wept openly in the streets and tens of thousands attended his funeral.

In Addis Ababa the General-Secretary of the Organization for African Unity expressed his condolences:

> The honour that Abebe brought to Ethiopia will be enduring, not just for Ethiopia but for the whole of Africa. With Abebe's death Ethiopia and the rest of Africa have lost a man who has made Africa renowned in the arena of international athletics. As the double

winner of the Olympic gold in the marathon he proved that Africans can compete successfully against their international colleagues. Even more important was the fact that he made history and gave racists a reminder of their prejudices.[4]

From a Western standpoint it is difficult to comprehend Bikila's position in Africa. People in the West thought of him as a phenomenal runner who emerged from nowhere, won, won again, was crippled and died a tragic death. He was far more than that to Ethiopians and to Africans: he was a fairytale figure who became a demi-god and, after his death, even a martyr. He proved what the ancient Greeks knew – that sport and the worship of sporting heroes has a unifying effect on a country, and that one shining example can act as a spur to others. It was Bikila's good fortune that he was competing in the age of television and photography, at a time when African countries were achieving independence from colonial rule, and when blacks in the United States were freeing themselves from the lingering fetters of past slavery.

The Kenyan Avalanche

Seen from the West it often looks as if African runners are natural talents who come straight from their highland countries and compete with virtually no training. The Kenyans in particular are seen in that light. But when did the Kenyans actually begin running?

The standard of track racing in Kenya before the Second World War was poor compared with the best in the West. Nyandika Maiyoro, the first Kenyan runner of international standard, was born in 1931, the son of a well-known hunter. The foundations of his good physique were laid as a herdsman in the hilly Kisii district. Maiyoro did not have to go to school but he saw a sports meeting at a Catholic missionary school and, without asking his father, he attended a meeting there and won. From then on his father allowed him to represent the school in races.

The colonial power saw that Maiyoro had great potential and in 1949 removed him from school so that he could train full time. He was moved to a fenced and guarded concrete house. The British wanted to create a world class runner and a model for other Kenyans. His fellow tribesmen, however, did not look up to a man who had to run 28 miles a day and live a prison-like existence without a wife or girlfriend, but his status began to rise when he performed well in the East African championships.

The British also wanted to put an end to the cattle-rustling that was common among the Kalinjen tribe. One approach was to divert their energies elsewhere by organizing running competitions and promoting running, particularly among the Nandi. In 1959 the district commissioner in the Rift Valley stated that, 'Cattle rustling is the traditional sport for many young men from various tribes', and the slogan 'Show your bravery in

Wanjiru leads Kebede in the London Marathon 2009. This is at mile 24 and a half, along Mid Temple right by Temple Place. Samuel Wanjiru is here a few seconds short of 1:56:00, and went on to finish in a personal best and new course record of 2:05:09. Kebede finished second.

sports and games and not in war' tells us a good deal about the intentions of the colonial power.[5]

In 1949 an Englishman, Archie Evans, became the Colony Sports Officer and manager of the Kenyan athletics team. Under his leadership the system became more organized with, for instance, national championships without racial barriers. He also aimed at participation in international events, including the 1954 Commonwealth Games in Vancouver, Canada. The team stopped over in London on the way and Lazara Chepkwony ran in the six-mile race at a meeting at White City, the first time a Kenyan runner had competed in Europe.

The barefoot African caused a stir in a field that also contained the charismatic Englishman Gordon Pirie. Chepkwony stayed with the leaders, suddenly spurting for a couple of hundred yards and running very unevenly – a tactic the crowd applauded. But he pulled a muscle in the fifteenth lap and had to drop out. Press reaction showed that the Africans were not taken seriously and Chepkwony's performance was considered odd and untamed. There was a myth in the West that blacks could not run far: they had neither the musculature, the strength of will nor the talent to deal with long distances. Chepkwony's sprinting, his injury and his dropping out of the race in London in 1954 was held to be proof of this.

The following day Chepkwony's countryman Nyandika Maiyoro appeared in a three-mile race in front of 30,000 spectators. When the starting pistol went he set off at a furious pace and, to the amazement of the crowd and the surprise of the keen competition, took a clear lead of something like 45 yards before getting a touch of cramp and being caught. He nevertheless sprinted home in 13 minutes 54.8 seconds as number three, beaten by Fred Green and Chris Chataway, both of whom beat the world record.[6]

Even though 1954 was something of a breakthrough for Kenya as a running nation it was only those with a particular interest in athletics who noticed it and picked up the rumours of other great talents in waiting – such as two fifteen-year-olds who had run three miles in under 15 minutes 30 seconds. At this stage the Kenyans did not stand out as people with particularly good, natural pre-conditions for running.

Kenyan demands for independence grew during the 1950s. There was anger that white settlers were taking land from African farmers and an elite of Africans educated in Europe was working hard to bring about independence. Jomo Kenyatta and 183 other nationalists were arrested and Kenyatta was sentenced to seven years gaol for planning the Mau Mau rebellion that lasted from 1952 to 1959. Of the 13,000 people who died during the struggle for independence fewer than 100 were British and the British had to all intents and purposes won by the time they arrested and executed the guerilla leader Dedan Kimathi in 1956. There were also elements of civil war about the emergency in that there were Africans on the European side and not all the African chiefs renounced their loyalty to the colonial power.

Part of the effort to suppress the rebellion consisted of compulsorily resettling Africans in 'protected villages' surrounded by barbed wire and ditches filled with sharpened bamboo stakes – anyone in breach of the ban on leaving such a village might be shot on sight. During the whole period of the uprising the colonial authorities encouraged sport as a way of diverting Kenyan thinking away from politics and rebellion.

Largely unnoticed by the world around, however, developments took place during the 1950s that laid the foundations for the future of Kenya as a running nation. A number of big international names from the USA and Britain visited the country and advised on training. In 1963 Kenya achieved independence and the following year Jomo Kenyatta became president.

For the first time the Kenyans could now compete for their own independent country and they had the support of President Kenyatta who recognized the value of sport as a political tool: it unified the nation, had a positive impact abroad and testified to the character and strength of the people. The Berlin Conference of 1884–5 had divided Africa up into colonies which cut across linguistic and cultural boundaries with the result that differing ethnic groups were forced to become part of the same nation. Sport, running in the case of Kenya, bonded the nation together. A Kenyan minister greeted the successful Olympic team in 1964 with the following words: 'You have shown the rest of the world that there is a country with the name of Kenya, in which there live people of such talent, energy and potential that they have to be reckoned with.'[7]

This is reminiscent of Finland in the 1920s – a newly independent nation affirming its place in the world. And just as with Finland, the runners from Kenya became much better known abroad than the politicians and artists. Another element in common with Finland was good organization and good assistance with coaching. In the case of Kenya, the coaches were mainly British, one of whom was John Velzian.

It was John Velzian who 'discovered' Kipchoge Keino in 1962, when the latter ran a mile in 4 minutes 21.8 seconds. Velzian became his coach. Keino, who won Olympic gold in both 1968 and 1972, won the same status in Kenya and Africa as Abebe Bikila, and he came from the same background – a herd-boy from a poor family, who started school late. In the 1960s Keino became the black phenomenon of the track at 1,500 metres and he abolished the usual pattern of running evenly. No one could put in a merciless spurt for a lap or for two hundred metres like Keino, splitting open a field of top international runners and demolishing major stars. Keino developed further the spurt technique that African runners had tried much earlier but failed with because of poor coaching. But he could do it.

Stories were told that underlined his legendary position in Africa. As a ten-year-old he was supposed to have met a leopard and run away from it – which is what inspired him to become a runner. Keino himself gave the lie to the tale. No human being could outrun a leopard, certainly not a small boy, but he had been tending the family goats when a leopard killed one of them and tried to drag it away. Frightened that the leopard would disappear with the goat Keino had grabbed hold of it and tugged against the leopard until it let go and moved off.

But is is true that Keino was suffering so badly from gallstones both before and during the 1968 Mexico City Olympics that he was unable to take solid food for the eight days the games lasted. And this is how he got to the start of the 1,500 metres in time: 'It was five miles from the Olympic Village to the Stadium and I knew that if I took the bus I would never get there in time because of the heavy traffic. So I decided to run there. I overtook most of the busses carrying the competitors to the stadium and got there in time.'[8]

Keino took the gold in the thin air 7,400 feet above sea-level – and it also happened to be Kenya's national day *and* the day his wife gave birth to their first child. Kenya's total of three golds, four silvers and a bronze in 1968 announced to the world that Kenya had arrived as a running nation.

In 1972 Keino took in five orphans who had been roaming around eating dirt while looking for food. Three years later he and his wife moved to Eldoret in Kenya and started a children's home, which was home to 82 children by the year 2000. Kip Keino's feats on the track pale by comparison with his later humanitarian contributions and he provided a model for several generations of Kenyans who saw running as a way out of poverty.

Success made the Kenyans internationally desirable. At the end of the 1960s the first runners started going to American universities on scholarships

Mohamed Gamoudi of Tunisia beating Kenyans Kipchoge Keino and Naftali Temu into second and third place respectively at the 1968 Mexico City Olympics.

and by 1974 Jim Wambua, coach of the national team, was complaining that the Americans were draining Kenya of running talent to raise the standard of their universities with imported runners. Paradoxically the Kenyan invasion also caused controversy in the USA, where it was argued that the imports were blocking out American talent. In the years between 1971 and 1978 no fewer than 168 Kenyans took part in American student championships, virtually all of them in races of 400 metres and over. At least 200 male Kenyan runners were living on scholarships in the USA in the years around 1980. The country was systematically exporting runners who wanted to get an education and to support large families.[9]

23
Loving the Landscape of Pain

God is not there, I am not with you, your mother and father are not
there with you, and you have to prove everything on your own.
—Percy Wells Cerutty's advice to middle-distance runners

Personal crises often lead to valuable new insights. People tell of despair,
chaos and tragedy in their lives before they got back on their feet, renewed
and stronger than before.

The Australian running coach Percy Wells Cerutty (1895–1975) began
his life's work after that kind of phase in his life. In 1939 he weighed 99 lb
(45 kg), his digestive system was not working properly and he had severe
migraines and rheumatism. Powerful drugs had destroyed his inner organs
and a doctor gave him a couple of years to live.

Cerutty had an ecstatic experience in a Melbourne library that year,
came to a new, religious insight, underwent an awakening in which he
recognized his true nature as a spiritual being. It was as if he was transformed and he remained in a state of ecstasy for five days.[1]

Cerutty was given six months leave from his job in order to regain his
health. As a result of his illness he had lost the right to drive and had to walk
everywhere. One sleepless morning he visited the Caulfield Racecourse in
Melbourne where the horses were out training at dawn. Ajax, an elegant and
highly rated horse, swept past Cerutty who was watching him with childlike curiosity, and Cerutty felt the horse was sending him a message. On
the way home he had a sudden urge to run, at first slowly, then faster, and
then flat out, inspired by the horse, until his heart was pumping hard. He
had not run for decades and it felt as if he was being reborn, as if life was
beginning anew.

He stopped smoking and changed his diet to fruit, vegetables and muesli
– all vegetarian. He ate nothing but raw food for three years apart from
lightly steamed vegetables. He walked, ran, swam and went hiking in the
outback. The more effort he put in, the better he felt in mind and body
afterwards. He read philosophy, immersed himself in religious literature
and revisited the wisdom of the Bible and the Ancients with manic fervour. He devoured knowledge, studied books by yogis and by winners of
the Nobel Prize in medicine. Cerutty had always felt that he would achieve
something great, would earn a place in world history, and now he had
found his path.

Arthur F. H. Newton, who wrote the book *Running* in 1935, was a major influence in the running world: he recommended slow and gradual training at a gentle speed before moving to a faster pace and more intense training sessions. Running did Cerutty good and his migraines disappeared. He joined the Malvern Harriers in Melbourne, the same club he had belonged to in his youth. He was 47 years old and he rose at dawn to watch the horses, which he studied to learn their running technique. There were several tracks alongside each other and the thin, white-haired man ran along with the horses, imitating them, trotting and galloping for hours in the morning mist, sticking his face over the fence to see. The jockeys and trainers shook their heads despairingly at the energetic old fellow. Cerutty noted that all the horses moved in the same way, unlike human beings. The horses had rhythm and flow, moved gracefully using little energy, but still reached high speeds. There were no unnecessary movements even though they were using their whole bodies.

Cerutty began to lift weights, which was contrary to the running theories of the 1940s. He also lifted rocks over his head. He was thin and sinewy but nevertheless capable of impressive lifts, and he was always barefoot in shorts, wearing as few clothes as the law allowed.

Cerutty experimented with every imaginable and unimaginable way of moving: raising his knees high or a shuffling run or varying the length of stride or the use of his arms. He visited Melbourne Zoo to watch gazelles, panthers, leopards and apes and he came up with new theories about running technique. In terms of technique the best runners of the future would be a cross between horses, gazelles, leopards and panthers. And even Frederick Mathias Alexander, the man behind the Alexander Method used by dancers and actors, agreed with Cerutty.

The originally perfect human being has been destroyed by what Cerutty most despised – the softness of civilization. Nothing has done more to spoil man physically and spiritually. In reality, the so-called advances of civilization have been huge reverses for humanity. He himself had used nature to become healthy after his doctors had pronounced a sentence of death.

Cerutty saw the Aborigine as a living relic of the way primitive man had moved: 'It seems to me that, until they are ruined by civilization, they are the only ones in the world who move in a perfect way – in terms of posture, walking and running. They move differently to all other people, put their feet down differently, have a different posture and carry their arms in a different way. That is what I am trying to teach'.[2]

Cerutty wanted to be teacher, coach and mentor. The new type of men he desired to coach into existence were called 'stotans' – a name derived from the word 'stoic', meaning 'unmoved by sorrow or joy', linked with the word 'spartan', meaning 'simple', 'unassuming'. A fifteen-square-metre cabin at Portsea, on the coast 60 miles from Melbourne, became the first hatchery for stotans.

A manifesto of six typewritten pages provided a comprehensive plan, not just about diet, regular sleep and training but also about man as a whole, the laws of the universe and the purpose of life. Sacrifice was demanded and the life was not for weaklings. The central theme was the need for hard physical activity in order to come as close as possible to one's true nature. Only by going outside his comfort zone could a human being truly achieve growth. Man becomes stronger and more harmonious through performance and pain, a kind of stress which exists in natural circumstances where everything is struggling for survival. Runners should push themselves as if they risked death if they were to lose; only then would they perform to their maximum ability. In addition to growing as people they would also be purified mentally and achieve a higher spiritual level. For Cerutty running was a primitive act, a return to man's primeval state and, essentially, acute violence against the self.

A man could find his inner stotan by communicating with nature, sleeping out under the stars, listening to the song of birds, running barefoot in the sand, smelling flowers and listening to the lapping of the waves. These were old thoughts in new packaging but original in that Cerutty was different from his contemporaries.

In particular he saw the need to train lethargic businessmen, to restore lost manhood and to act as personal trainer at a time when there were few such people in Australia. Such ideas had been experimented with for some decades among Hollywood film stars and American health reformers such as Bernarr McFadden (1868–1955), who in some ways was a predecessor of Cerutty. Whereas McFadden recommended walking, a simple diet and all-round strength training, Cerutty extended the principles to include running and weight-training. Men of eccentric tendencies in many countries were voicing the same themes as Cerutty, writing books recommending a more active, 'natural' life as a counter to the advance of civilization. But Cerutty stood out among them because his particular focus was on running.

After the circulation of his stotan manifesto in 1946 Cerutty tried to qualify for the Olympic marathon in London in 1948. He was then 52 years old, ran it in 3 hours 2 minutes and was hopelessly far back in the field, with no chance of being chosen for the squad. He recognized that he was too old to make his mark internationally and that it was only through others that he could win the attention and recognition he so desperately sought – his father had been an alcoholic whom he had only seen three times after his parents separated when he was three years old.

Cerutty was prepared to try anything.

Warming up is unnecessary, particularly in the hot climate of Australia, was his thinking in 1948 after Les Perry ran out of steam after three miles because of the heat in Melbourne. Perry was one of Cerutty's first successes.

John Pottage was also a pupil of Cerutty and had been sitting in the shade while the runners warmed up on the day Perry had problems. Pottage took a cold shower before the start and poured a bottle of cold water over himself as they were called to the starting line. Cerutty had 'proved' the effect of this by pouring iced water over a sleeping cat, which leapt up and shot up a tree. Neither cats nor other animals warm up, Cerutty argued with stotan logic. The tactic was successful. Pottage did not notice the heat for the first two miles and came in third.

Cerutty advertised his services in the newspapers and attracted runners who, having heard the rumours, came banging on his door. The lives of many of them were changed by listening to this untamed and uninhibited coach with an unusual ability to inspire, and not just in sport. Even in later life Cerutty's disciples benefited from his advice.

Cerutty trimmed and tested training philosophy. Stotans underwent six months of basic training, with runs starting off short and becoming longer, and then moving up to eight or nine miles, combined with weight-training. This was followed by three months leading up to the season, but still with little track work. The stopwatch and the track were not good, it was better for the runners to be breathing sea air and doing hill intervals in the sand-dunes, where the ageing Cerutty demonstrated an impressive ability over short distances. Cerutty would lie in ambush in the bushes, jump in among the young men during the final spurt and win, in order to humiliate them and boost his own ego. Winning was what mattered.

Running on the track was a lonely business and brutally measurable, a metaphor for a life stripped bare. 'God is not there', Cerutty said, 'I am not with you, your mother and father are not there with you, and you have to prove everything on your own.'[3]

Cerutty believed that demanding sports were not suitable for women. Too much training made them hard and unfeminine and, when they lost their bosoms and rounded form, they became like men. His ideas annoyed many people in Australia in the 1950s and he had a very particular ability and urge to feed the press, which liked outspoken people. Cerutty loved to be in the limelight and he lacked a self-censor. When he was invited into people's homes he might suddenly undress, jump up on the table surrounded by the dinner guests and sit there in a lotus position in his underpants, talking philosophy, showing off his muscles and telling of the primeval needs of mankind. People laughed and stared in amazement – he got up many people's noses, but few forgot this man with his desperate desire to find the perfect running candidate to turn his theories into reality.

The Australian athletics championships were held in Adelaide in February 1955 and included a mile and a half-mile race for juniors as additional events. Both distances were unexpectedly won by a sixteen-year-old from Perth, Herb Elliot. Later that year Elliot heard Cerutty lecture in Perth, ran a trial mile in 4 minutes 22 seconds and was warmly praised by Cerutty, who promised he would be running it in under four minutes within two years.[4]

Elliot's parents invited the coach to their home and it was the beginning of a unique partnership. Elliot was really inspired, though he was still a schoolboy who smoked, liked to party and had a girlfriend, which was something stotans should not have since girls destroyed their concentration and sapped their strength. When he finished school in 1955 Elliot worked for his father's company, smoked 30–40 cigarettes a day, drank beer with his friends and thought less about sports. His parents hoped that a trip to the Melbourne Olympics in November 1956 would reawaken his desire to run. Would it be possible to live with Cerutty afterwards?

'Absolutely', came the answer in one of Cerutty's many inspiring letters.

So Herb Elliot sat in the stand in Melbourne and was impressed by the aggressive running of Vladimir Kuts: Elliot, too, now wanted to compete at the highest international level.

Elliot stayed on in Melbourne after the Olympics, took a badly paid job as a TV-fitter and, along with several others, accompanied Percy and his wife Nancy out to Portsea. Eight or nine of them from the city went out there every Friday to train and live the simple life for the weekend and Cerutty moved out there more permanently later with athletes from Australia and overseas. Cerutty and his wife took them in and the lads worked for their keep, taking casual jobs in the area and gathering around Cerutty's dining table like an extended family of ever-varying size.

Bill Stacey hitchhiked there on Saturday afternoon in August 1959 and knocked on the door.

'I want to learn to run.'

'What's your name? I've never heard of you', Cerutty said and then shouted to Nancy: 'Another mouth to feed!'[5]

Elliot became a part of this environment and quickly showed that he had more than ordinary potential. He was only eighteen but he came from a secure and harmonious background and was mature both physically and mentally. He absorbed the wisdom and listened to Cerutty's monologues about the 'Jesus consciousness', a consciousness of pain in training and of competition as a purification, which led to a better understanding of the suffering of Jesus on the cross. If one could endure the pain then miracles would happen on the running track, and the whole of humanity would be elevated through the self-sacrifice of individuals. Anyone who aspired to achieve insight and be the best had to visit the landscape of pain: he had to love pain as a valuable and dear friend because it gives so much in return.

There were plenty of fast legs and strong wills at Portsea but no one came close to Elliot. In May 1957 he ran a mile in 4.00.2 and, although only eighteen, was all-time number eleven in the world at that distance. Cerutty prophesied that the young man would do the mile in 3.43 given optimal physical training.

At Portsea Elliot found the perfect training environment: the views of the shore, the cliffs and the trees gave him the urge to run and Cerutty knew that people run better and more easily in beautiful surroundings. Training on the track meant nothing to him, nor to Elliot who saw the beauty in running but not on a track and not with a stopwatch. Nor did they do trial runs of a mile or so. Cerutty did not stand there with a whip; instead he provided inspiration and let the runners decide much for themselves. They had to help themselves, torment themselves in isolation in order to become familiar with their inner landscape. On the other hand, he would become enraged if they did not put enough into it, if they did not run hard enough – in which case he would turn off the hot water in their only shower in the winter.

Elliot and Cerutty went to the USA in 1957 and both of them reacted against the lifestyle there. America was full of overweight people chasing material goods. Their statements made headlines in the newspapers and the young senator John F. Kennedy noted Elliot's remarks: 'Money seems to mean so much in their way of life. It seemed to me that people have forgotten the simple joys of life, family life and an awareness of nature, in their chase for material things. A nation that spoils itself so thoroughly is bound to become weaker both physically and spiritually.'

Elliot and Cerutty worked well together, though the pupil got embarrassed when his coach put on his most blustering performances in front of the press and other competitors, as if it was open warfare: 'We slaughtered them, we made mincemeat of them', and so on. Cerutty revelled in the role of successful coach and would rather die than be beaten in a race. He hated the opposition and disliked shaking hands and patting people on the back just to be friendly.[6]

Cerutty was hardly the ordinary husband. He was divorced from his first wife in 1954 and married Nancy two years later. She was 21 years younger than him and his perfect female stotan. They would argue violently and on one occasion she smashed a milk-bottle on his head while they were drinking tea at Portsea. Percy was cut and did not wash the blood away for a week, proudly strolling around Portsea with blood in his hair like a boy unwilling to clean up the wound. Yet he would also listen devoutly to the music of Beethoven and Verdi and admire the works of Leonardo da Vinci and Michelangelo.

Fixed routines were important when it came to races. The day before Elliot's important races he and Cerutty would go to a track where the old man would run four laps, driving himself to the absolute limit. 'You can maybe run faster than me but you don't push yourself so hard', he would say, to egg Elliot on to push himself to the limit and then beyond.

Before the Olympic 1,500 metres in Rome in 1960 they had agreed as usual that Cerutty would give signals from the stand. If Elliot was looking close to a world record or if there was someone just behind him Cerutty would wave a handkerchief. Elliot was nervous and did not listen properly and when his coach was waving like a madman during the last lap he had no idea what it meant other than that he should increase his pace.

Elliot won, setting a world record of 3 minutes 35.6 seconds. Cerutty leapt over the barriers to celebrate the moment with Elliot but the police grabbed him and put him under arrest.

The chemistry between Elliot and Cerutty was good, which was not the case with Cerutty and Ron Clarke. At the 1964 Olympics Clarke was in the changing room getting ready for the 5,000 metres after only taking the bronze in the 10,000 race, in which he had been clear favourite. In the last tense minutes before the start a well-known voice was heard in the changing room: 'You haven't got a chance, Clarke, you've always been a weakling' – this to the world's best long-distance runner, a man who had broken the world records in the two longest track events. Giving that kind of dressing down at tricky moments was a brutal tactic typical of Cerutty; and sometimes it worked, angering runners into showing this loudmouth what they could do and performing above their level. But Clarke needed encouragement, not abuse. He raced one of his worst races and came in ninth.

Percy Wells Cerutty's name will always be linked with that of Herb Elliot but the hundreds of other runners he coached during his twenty years of activity at Portsea should not be forgotten. He never received the acknowledgement he longed for and was frequently thought of as a cantankerous man with crazy ideas. He suffered ill-health towards the end of his life and could scarcely speak or swallow, but there was no question of going to the doctor until his wife forced him to. He was diagnosed with motor neurone disease, which makes it difficult to swallow and to eat.

Percy Wells Cerutty died on 15 August 1975, one week after going to the doctor.

Arthur Lydiard

Another Australasian coach also made a valuable and lasting contribution to coaching. Arthur Leslie Lydiard was born in Auckland, New Zealand, on 6 July 1917. He was a small, thickset boy who won races at school without any coaching, but he was more interested in rugby even after he had joined the Lynndale running club in Auckland. Running was a diversion between matches and training and it was painful for the untrained body.

In the mid-1940s Jack Dolan, president of the Lynndale club, took Lydiard with him on a five mile run. Dolan was older but well-trained and Lydiard struggled to stay with him. If he was getting that exhausted at 27, what was going to happen to his body later? Arthur Lydiard had needed to recognize his own poor level of fitness before he was motivated to train seriously.[7]

He began by experimenting with running seven days a week and reading running literature, determined to train to the level where running became a pleasure rather than the suffering that followed a weekly 800-metre race. Most authorities recommended walking but he cut that out and increased his daily distance to twelve miles. At the extreme, he would do up to 250 miles a week. When he was getting up at 2 a.m. to drive a milk lorry before going on to work in a shoe factory (there were a wife and four children to be supported), he had to limit his training to the weekends.

Lydiard was still not particularly successful in races. But a hard training run of say 20 miles could always be followed by an easy session the following day. Eight or ten days later the body would feel stronger. It had
been broken down and then built itself up to a higher level, and it was all
about finding a balance in the training.

Lydiard experimented alone for the most part. Lawrie King, one of his
workmates at the shoe factory, began to accompany him and showed
impressive progress, winning the junior two miles at the Auckland championships in 1945. He was Lydiard's first success on the track. Two others,
Brian White and Tom Hutchinson, won the national cross-country championships the same year.

Initially Lydiard had no plans to become a coach but when young runners achieved success after listening to his advice to train more than usual
it encouraged him to do so. After disagreements and administrative difficulties with Lynndale he left the club and formed a group of runners in
Owairaka, drawing on runners from virtually the same district. 'In four
years,' Lydiard said. 'Owairaka will be beating Lynndale.' Lynndale was the
best running club in the country – but Lydiard was right, almost to the day.[8]

It took Lydiard nine years to perfect his ideas. When he was coaching
for the marathon his group would cover up to a hundred miles a week, including a long run of 22 miles every Sunday during the preparatory phase.
They built up a phenomenal fitness base without exhausting themselves
because the training was done at talking pace but without being slow. In the
run-up to the season they dropped the amount and concentrated on hill
running and speed in order to bring them to peak form, which would then
last for a long time since their fitness base was so good.

This was going on from the early 1950s, a time when middle and long-
distance running was totally dominated by interval training. Lydiard,
however, was recommending running long distances at an even pace. What
was new in his system was the greater amount of running, his periodization,
and long runs of 20 miles even for middle-distance runners. Lydiard's
runners trained as if for the marathon but competed at every distance from
800 metres up. The example *par excellence* was Peter Snell, who dominated
international middle-distance running at the beginning of the 1960s.

They were not slow, these runners, and the most persevering of them
had most of their energy left to give in the final spurt if their training had
peaked properly. 'Train, not strain', Lydiard said and coached strength *into*
the body, not out of it. His starting point, after all, was a belief that running was fun, was enjoyable – as long as the runner was well-trained.

Many thought it was risky for young people to double or treble their
training distances to up to as much as a hundred miles a week. There was
a feeling among doctors and people at large that too much running could
damage the internal organs, and the fear of pushing themselves too far
and overstraining themselves was widespread even among active runners:
the heart would get too enlarged and the body exhausted. But by lowering

the pace and training for long periods the body became stronger and gradually capable of tolerating more.

No other twentieth-century coach had anything like the same significance as Lydiard. During a long and active life he travelled a great deal, talked to hundreds of journalists, gave lectures and worked as a coach in several countries, and as a result his method was copied and developed with endless variations. His greatest contribution was the idea of building up an aerobic fitness base by steady, long-term and enjoyable training. The same principle is followed in many other branches of sport, indeed, in life itself, where the formative years of childhood and youth are the foundation of adult physical health.

Lydiard had a good deal in common with his Australian colleague Percy Wells Cerutty. Both of them noticed the lack of fitness and physical degeneration in themselves before running and later coaching became their life's work. They were small, energetic men with strong opinions and a desire to put themselves on public view, internationally oriented and ambitious that their athletes should be the best in the world. Both made and left a deep impression on the history of running but Lydiard was the one with the widest appeal. Cerutty's message was more spiritual and difficult to take in and, unlike Lydiard, he did not serve up a training programme, he relied more on instinct. What they had in common was a devotion to life and to running that lasted into old age. It was all about performing at one's best and living as passionately as possible through running – which was a metaphor for life.

24
The Jogging Revolution

Suddenly tears were running down my face and I felt an unimaginable
strength from the universe and optimism about my life. I was a child
of the universe.
—Craig D. Wandke, a newly converted jogger in California
in the 1970s, out running

In the United States in the 1970s there was a story going round about
an office worker who arrived home from work one evening nervous and
depressed, no longer able to deal with the pressures of society. He decided
to commit suicide, but since suicide would bring misfortune to his family
and stigmatize them he decided to run himself to death. Since he was an
overweight, middle-aged chain-smoker he thought running would give him
a heart attack.

The man ran as fast as he could, that is to say, slowly and panting dread-
fully. He waited in vain for his heart attack. Thinking that his preparations
had been insufficient he went to bed earlier and ate a little less that evening.
The next morning he set off at an easier pace so that he would be able to
run farther and suffer his fatal heart attack. He got twice as far along the
street before becoming breathless – and still no heart attack. He turned for
home and noticed that he was not feeling depressed for the first time in
months, indeed, he felt elated. 'If running isn't going to kill me then maybe
it will cure me', he thought.

The following day he bought expensive jogging shoes and first-class gear.
That same evening, having run even farther than before, a lorry hit him as
he crossed the street – and killed him.[1]

Lydiard's Infectious Initiative

After the 1960 Olympic Games, at which the New Zealanders Peter Snell
and Murray Halberg sensationally won gold medals in the 800 and 5,000
metres respectively, their coach Arthur Lydiard was asked about his recipe
for success. The Tamaki Lions club in Auckland wanted to know why New
Zealand was suddenly producing such good runners. Lydiard's answer was
that even when they had run a long distance his men could still finish their
races faster than other runners. He was thinking of Peter Snell in particular, whose final spurt was already legendary. The secret was systematic and
rational heart and fitness training by a lot of steady running, followed by
a period of bringing them to peak condition.

After the talk at the Lions club three retired businessmen came up to Lydiard and told him about their heart problems. One of them had the idea that heart patients could perhaps run themselves back to health. But the problem in New Zealand in 1960, as in other countries, was that doctors usually forbade heart patients from taking exercise. Patients who had suffered heart attacks were ordered to stay quietly in bed for many weeks. Even if they did not die – possibly as a result of the lack of activity – the heart muscle was certainly not strengthened.

Lydiard was not a medical expert but he did know that parts of the body would inevitably degenerate if not used. With the permission of a doctor these men ran to the harbour in Auckland by walking from one telegraph pole to the next, trotting to the next, and so on until they had done a mile. It started in this small way but gradually they could run the whole distance and increase their speed up to eight miles an hour. This was quite sensational given their physical condition just a few months earlier.

Some of the Auckland pioneers visited business contacts in Christchurch on the South Island of New Zealand, where their hosts thought they were looking slim. They attributed it to running: they were no longer ill and they felt better than ever before. Lydiard was sent for so he could preach the message and the South Islanders began running.

A couple of years later Lydiard met Colin Kay on a flight. Kay was a former sportsman, sport administrator and later mayor of Auckland and he had a wide circle of contacts and was a good organizer. He was also unfit and a little overweight. Lydiard was always ready to talk about his ideas and he suggested that Kay should get fit.

Kay knew a number of businessmen with heart problems and he gathered them and the cardiologist Dr Noel Roydhouse at his house one Sunday morning. There Lydiard explained the effects of gentle running and of gradually increasing the pace, and the cardiologist filled in the medical aspects. That same morning they all went out for a run, with Lydiard warning them against being competitive and, since they were unfit, not pushing themselves so hard that they could do serious damage.

This group of plump, good-natured businessmen trotted and walked to Auckland harbour, where some of them had a swim before plodding back the same way. The distance was no more than a mile or so but none of them had run that far as adults. Another cardiologist, Jack Sinclair, a former New Zealand national champion in the mile, added medical weight to the project and the group, which began to meet every Sunday, became the Auckland Joggers Club and attracted many members.

They called this pleasant form of running 'jogging'. The word was not new: it was used in seventeenth-century England to describe a kind of gentle running, either by people or by animals, and in England the word had often been used about trotting horses. In his 1884 novel *My Run Home* the Australian novelist Rolf Boldrewood had referred to his 'morning jog', but the word was hardly known outside English-speaking countries.[2]

Auckland's Cornwall Park became the meeting place for the growing numbers of joggers. The park had a central location and offered a variety of paths and tolerably hilly bits. They built a clubhouse there and met to practise this individual activity which, however, also had a social side in that Lydiard recommended a 'talking pace' as a way of controlling their speed during basic training. It was not all trouble-free, however. As they ran along these pioneers were sometimes the recipients of abuse, mockery and ridicule from drivers and other road users, while passengers threw the odd beer-can out of the window and drivers honked and cut across their paths. Even in New Zealand it was unusual to see runners on the roads. One friend of Lydiard trained in the dark from a naval base north of Auckland: a police car slowed down and asked him what he thought he was doing.

'I'm running for the good of my health.'

'Oh yes, we know all about that!' They arrested him and kept him overnight on the grounds that no one runs in the dark for the sake of his health.[3]

The author and journalist Garth Gilmour, another of Lydiard's friends, worked all day and trained at night for his first marathon. After one nocturnal session a police car drew up alongside him, a torch shone in his face and a policeman addressed him brusquely.

He explained he had deadlines in the morning, which was why he was out running now, but the policeman was suspicious and answered sarcastically: 'So you're just running, are you?'

Gilmour was wearing running shoes and shorts without pockets, hardly the standard dress for a criminal – and he was not carrying any swag. After repeating what he was doing he said he was writing a book about running and did not have time to train in daylight: the policeman accepted the explanation but only after following him for half a mile.[4]

In New Zealand in 1960, as in most other countries in the world, a solitary runner at night risked being treated with considerable suspicion. Why would mentally healthy and law-abiding citizens bother to go running along the streets, and in the dark?

The jogging movement spread around New Zealand. In Hamilton it was a cardiologist who had had a heart attack himself who took the initiative; in Dunedin Dr Norie Jefferson was the central figure. He put 80 runners on a three-month programme and tested them. With Lydiard getting the support of doctors, the jogging movement attracted more and more people, though many medical men remained sceptical: most of these smoked cigarettes even though both research and common sense said they were a danger to health.

In December 1962 Bill Bowerman, a coach at the University of Oregon, visited New Zealand with his runners. He and Arthur Lydiard knew each other and swopped experiences. The day after they arrived was a Sunday and Lydiard took him to Cornwall Park, where members of the Auckland Joggers Club of all ages were on the move. The American was over 50 but considered himself fairly fit for his own kind of exercise – walking and running for 400 or 500 metres. Obviously he joined in with Lydiard's joggers.

Bowerman handled the speed and the terrain for about half a mile until they came to a steep hill where he became breathless and panicky while Lydiard shot off out of sight like a squirrel. An old fellow there understood the American's situation and formed a rearguard with him, led him on a short cut and chattered away, although Bowerman could not manage to respond and had to mobilize all his will-power to complete the shortened run. His kind helper, Andrew Steedman, had to wait for him: in spite of being 73 years old and the survivor of three heart attacks, Steedman was in better shape than he was.

That run changed Bowerman's life.

Bowerman trained almost every day of the six weeks he was in New Zealand and he interrogated Lydiard about jogging. Who did it and why? How did they get started and what were the advantages? Bowerman lost nine to ten pounds in weight and returned home to Oregon bearing a message he believed the United States needed. A journalist asked Bowerman to summarize his impressions of the tour and he held up jogging as the most important thing he had learned.[4] The resulting article by Jerry Uhrhammer in *The Register General* in Eugene also contained an invitation to people to come to the local track at Hayward Field and hear about the miracle of jogging.

What is This?

On 3 February 1963 about 25 people turned up to learn. They walked and trotted and went home with new knowledge. The following Sunday the numbers had doubled and on the third Sunday there were over two hundred people, a quarter of them women. Uhrhammer wrote a follow-up article and *Life Magazine* made plans to document this rare phenomenon occurring in Eugene. On the fourth Sunday somewhere between two and five thousand people came to the track – so many that it scared Bowerman, who was worried that with so many unfit people someone would have a heart attack and die. He suggested that people go home and run in their own neighbourhoods until he could get things better organized. He telephoned Dr Ralph Christensen, who put him in contact with Waldo Harris, a Eugene cardiologist.

Bowerman and Harris put together a training programme, each drawing on his specialist knowledge: the starting pace would be a mile in twelve minutes, a little faster than a walk. Four members of the university in Eugene took part in a pilot study, which consisted of three months of gradually increasing training sessions.[5]

Charles Esslinger, dean of the university's Physical Education Department, gave his support to a larger study. They recruited a hundred middle-aged individuals, mostly men, who, split up into ten groups, were to train three times a week. The results were positive and the majority improved their fitness, lost weight and felt revitalized both physically and mentally.

Spurred on by this success and eager to spread the New Zealand message (he remained in regular correspondence with Lydiard), Bowerman and Harris wrote a pamphlet in 1966. This was followed a year later by *Jogging: A Physical Fitness Program for All Ages*, a slim volume that sold in millions. Bowerman was not the only one in the USA to be promoting jogging but he was by far the best known.

'Do you want to earn a bit of money – two or three dollars a time?' Bowerman asked the members of the university running team. A Norwegian, Arne Kvalheim, happened to be studying at Eugene on a running scholarship in the second half of the 1960s and he agreed to act as instructor to joggers before the start of work.

The joggers would arrive by car at 6.30 a.m., some fat, some thin, some unfit, some in slightly better shape, and they enjoyed being supervised by acknowledged star runners. They followed Bowerman's plan by beginning very carefully, walking a hundred yards and then trotting the same distance: it is hard and often tedious for unfit people to run continuously for a mile or so. Kvalheim had not come across an initiative of this kind in Norway and the set-up was also unknown to Americans. There were people in many places who did run even if they did not do it competitively, but in the middle of the 1960s it was rare to find the ordinary citizens of an industrial country running in groups. This new breed of runner was of a completely different cut to the skinny racing men – and their speed was a good deal slower. They were running for different reasons: not to win or to set personal records but to get some exercise and lose weight.

The Eugene group began by alternately running and walking for two miles – eight circuits of the track. The load gradually increased over the three months of the course. They met three times a week and were aware of rapid progress – the fitness curve for an unfit person rises rapidly. A sturdily built dentist weighing 265 pounds jogged for two miles without a break after six weeks, an impressive achievement in view of his weight.[6]

The upsurge in jogging had spread from New Zealand to the USA and from there to Europe. Once the Americans had begun running in substantial numbers, people from other industrialized countries followed suit.

An Obese, Unfit Doctor

The best-known doctor to promote running on a national scale was Kenneth Cooper and he also produced marketable books. His 1968 book *Aerobics* seems rather banal 40 years later because it treats training and fitness on an almost childish level. But Cooper had to pick his words carefully in a country in which the car was king and the population, only one generation away from the hardships of the 1930s, had virtually forgotten how to take exercise. Unhealthy food and a lack of exercise had led to a rise in heart disease and those other diseases of civilization – diabetes and obesity – had become more common.

The messages Bill Bowerman and Kenneth Cooper were sending out were aimed at counteracting the sedentary lifestyle. President John F. Kennedy had encouraged physical education. He himself suffered from Addison's Disease and was periodically reliant on crutches even if the public did not see this. Specialists in physical education such as gym teachers, physiotherapists and the personnel responsible for basic training in the military were all recording declining physical standards in the population of the USA.

Kenneth Cooper had run both at school and at university. As with most of his contemporaries, his physical decline after that was noticeable and he put on a lot of weight. In 1960, after completing his studies and his first year in the military, he tried what had been his favourite hobby, water-skiing, and found that he could only hang on to the tow-rope for a few seconds before becoming breathless. This experience, along with higher blood-pressure and various small ailments, were symptoms of Cooper's loss of vitality. He was 29 years old and should have been at his physical peak in terms of age.

Other doctors in the West had noted the same things and attempted to solve their own problems with pills. Cooper, however, was a doctor in the air force and he went for fitness training and noted that his blood-pressure returned to normal and his other aches and pains disappeared. He also began recommending running to his patients.

A number of cases of heart attacks among young fliers gave him food for thought. They had to pass strict entrance tests before flight training and their vision and other senses had to be of the highest standard. But that did not help if their hearts gave out in the air or when the pilot was in stressful situations. Once again, running was proving to be important in the military, even in a high technology arm, precisely because advanced technology tended to undermine endurance. Cooper recognized something that many others often forgot – that the heart is a muscle which becomes stronger and more efficient with sensible exercise. Without it, it will grow weaker.[7]

Millions of Americans took part in sport at school and rather smaller numbers continued to do so as students. But after their student days, which usually finished at 22 or 23, they normally ceased to do so altogether when working life, family responsibilities and adult life took over. Running was something for children and young people and the minority that carried on running after that was almost invisible. Sport and the education system are closely linked in the United States and there is not the same club system as exists in Europe and elsewhere. So joggers started up their own clubs.

'How can we best test endurance?' Cooper asked. He tested himself and servicemen, sending them out on running tests that ranged from a few seconds to twenty minutes, measuring pulse rates and distances and logging the results, whether achieved on the track or on the treadmill. After much experimentation he reached the conclusion that twelve minutes running and the distance covered in that time provided a perfect test of fitness. It gave an approximate measure of the oxygen intake. Thousands of airmen, soldiers and sailors completed the test during the 1960s and the test – known as the Cooper Test – spread beyond the USA, leading to the most exhausting sessions in physical education classes as fitness was tested! Very few Europeans during the 1970s and later knew anything about Cooper and how his name became attached to an enduring fitness test, but they knew the 'Cooper Test', and the name alone brought the taste of blood into their mouths.[8]

Cooper was inspired to apply for two years' leave to study public health at Harvard. His subjects were preventive medicine, training physiology and space medicine. John F. Kennedy had declared that America would land a man on the moon before 1970 and the requirements and training of astronauts was given a great deal of attention. Simultaneously there was a significant increase in the American health budget. Physical fitness had become a national concern.

After Harvard, Cooper took over responsibility in 1964 for NASA's physical conditioning programme for astronauts. Little was known about the body's reactions in space but it was, of course, necessary for the astronauts to be extremely well-prepared. The stated aim of the programme was to build up astronauts' physical condition and endurance but there was also a need to develop a training programme to prevent astronauts losing physical condition while in flight.

In 1965 the journalist Kevin Brown visited the research centre to write about the simulation of weightlessness. Cooper told him that what was really new and quite sensational about the training programme was that it was suitable for people of differing standards and from different age-groups. Brown was very keen on the idea and an article, 'Exercise the Astronauts' Way', was published in the Family Weekly of January 1966 and read by millions.

The article caused great excitement. Was it really possible to train like an astronaut? Was there some kind of magic formula that worked for ordinary people as well as for these hand-picked supermen who were training for one of the greatest and most advanced journeys into the heavens? The word 'astronaut' stimulated the imaginations of a nation hungry to know about the mysteries of space: the space race between America and the Soviet Union fascinated Americans and many of them dreamt of becoming astronauts.

The publishers of the Family Weekly asked Cooper to write a book about his discoveries and exactly two years later Aerobics was on the shelves, published at the perfect point in time, one year after Bowerman's book. The two books taken together were enough to ensure that the tide of jogging rolled on and Cooper and Bowerman were united in their recipe for improving the endurance of beginners: a slow and gradual build-up of distance and speed.

Cooper did not simply recommend running: swimming, cycling, cross-country skiing and any other activities that improved the heart and endurance were good, including walking. Unfit and very overweight Americans should start off by walking and gradually increase their pace until they were running. The word 'jogging' was not used in the 1968 book but was then taken over from Bill Bowerman and made its first appearance in the following book.

For a long time Kenneth Cooper ran 25 miles a week, a distance which in his own view was rather more than was necessary to maintain a good and lasting level of fitness. In an interview with the American magazine *Runners' World* in September 1970 he admitted that he did not like running and six years later he confirmed that: 'I don't run for pleasure. I run because of the great benefits it brings. If I stop for a couple of days I can feel myself getting physically and mentally weaker.'[9]

He ran to get fresh air, to counteract the stress of concentrated mental work, and as a form of all-round relaxation. And when a close friend died of a heart attack it motivated him further. As far as he was concerned, running was a form of preventive medicine with many beneficial side effects. Many of the people involved in the early phases of jogging came up with virtually the same answer when asked why they ran: 'Because I feel so much better.'[10]

Cooper and Bowerman tested out their principles on themselves and that perhaps explains much of their success. They lived what they preached and set a good example rather than simply being salesmen with a healthy message. And both of them made a very healthy financial profit out of running.

Religion or Sport?

Runners belonged traditionally to a slightly exclusive circle who took their sport seriously but did not try to influence others to join their company. Many other people, however, had been put off running completely by school PE classes – they saw running as a form of punishment. As joggers increased in number in New Zealand and the USA during the 1960s they talked of their new and joyful discovery: running for fun! This is what lay behind the jogging movement.

Joggers discovered what Scandinavian cross-country skiers had known for years: that training can have religious overtones and spiritual insights are achieved along the way. Going for a run out in the country might take the runner into unspoilt surroundings and, particularly in the United States, the land of the automobile, these experiences of nature were exotic, were a path to spiritual growth. Runners borrowed the vocabulary of religion and talked of being 'saved', being 'born again', as if it was all about salvation. The daily run became daily meditation.

Some of the runners' rituals are reminiscent of religious practices. They would meet for long runs on Sunday morning rather than going to church. Instead of listening to ministers of the church they would talk among themselves about their mental and physical purification, after which they would shower and eat. Runners believed in specific diets and specific training programmes, they followed the advice of their gurus and they worshipped their idols. In running they found friends, understanding and comfort, and the day before important competitions was devoted to rest as sacred as any Sabbath. The great god was 'form', and the process of finding form left no room for sin: deviations from established routines could only be justified if they improved form – but they might also impair it.

Some people become Christians as adults. They are born anew, catch a glimpse of spiritual things, gain new insights that 'save' them and mark out a new course in life. Something similar happened among runners, often middle-aged runners, who suddenly began doing a lot of running, losing weight drastically and changing their appearance and personality.

American running magazines received reports from readers who had experienced ecstasy when out jogging. Craig D. Wandke in California in the 1970s wrote:

> Suddenly tears were running down my face and I felt an unimaginable strength from the universe and optimism about my life. I was a child of the universe. I looked down at my feet as they hit the ground and felt fresh summer air filling my lungs. The feeling of ecstasy lasted perhaps for 30 seconds and then my tears dried and I continued to run, my soul immensely enriched by this short experience.[11]

It is possible that the effect of endorphins is one part of the explanation, along with the fact that the runner was exhausted. But reactions of this kind might also have to do with the environment, with the force of nature, the magic of sun, air and summer. It is worth asking whether people in a different age and different culture might also have experienced this kind of thing when running. Was it a spiritual release brought on by running, something Wandke would also have experienced had he been a Native American in eighteenth-century California? Perhaps Wandke and Americans like him, living in civilized society and distant from natural things, lacked insights that were automatic to people living close to nature and could only achieve them by running and becoming part of nature? Perhaps running provided some sort of compensation for the lack of contact with the primeval self, and the run became a space free from the regulation and confinement of everyday life, a glimpse into eternity?

Not everyone can have the kind of experience Wandke reported; some people have their senses and perceptions more fine-tuned than others. Wandke was living in a time and in a culture when young people were on the look-out for a 'high', whether it came from music or drugs. The younger inhabitants of California in the 1960s and '70s were known for their drug culture and meditation was widespread, along with an interest in Eastern philosophies. The spirit of the age was all about expanding horizons and distancing oneself from the lifestyle of the older generation. Wandke might well have had the same intense experience while sitting in the lotus position, standing on a surfboard or tripping on LSD.

Ed Muzika was a disciple of Zen in Los Angeles in the 1970s. He was also a jogger and believed that running and meditation had similar effects. At the start running and meditation feel different from everything else but gradually the practitioner becomes so used to the condition that he feels a permanent 'high' without thinking about it. Runners and Zen priests and monks rarely talk about this until the condition has disappeared.[12]

People listened earnestly to the spokesmen of the jogging movement. On one occasion Kenneth Cooper spoke to an audience of 240,000 at a stadium in Brazil about the connection between physical fitness and psychological well-being. Cooper was a deeply religious man and sometimes shared the stage with Billy Graham, the internationally known American evangelist. For religious reasons Cooper would not talk about running on Sundays and as a speaker he resembled a minister of the church, having an ability to rouse his listeners and to spread his message.

New converts to running were the most likely to try to influence others to follow their lead. The veterans had lived with their eccentricity too long and were less likely to be evangelists. 'If it is good for me it is good for everyone' was the slogan of the converted, and their colleagues and families noticed both physical and personality changes in joggers – their way of life became more energetic, there was more bounce in their step and they suddenly became engrossed in the mysteries of running. They cut out cigarettes, made new circles of friends and some of them even divorced because they found it impossible to live with an obese, cigarette-smoking partner.

The puritanical slogan 'time is money' developed a new variant during the jogging craze – 'time is health'. Time can be used to achieve better health and a slimmer body and so it became permissible to take some leisure-time since it benefitted your health: jogging was an investment that paid both a short-term and a long-term dividend.

A healthy run in the middle of the day beat a heavy lunch and a drink. Running boosted body and mind instead of weighing them down and enlarging the waistline. Running was also a way of creating order and regulating your own physical condition – unless injury struck, of course. Jogging offered new possibilities to control your weight, your fitness and your mental state.

Seen from the standpoint of non-runners, joggers might appear to be egotists, living narrow lives that focused only on training. The high point of their day was the training run and mealtimes and rest had to be adjusted to suit it. Weekend activities were dominated by competitions. To non-runners new converts to jogging were fanatics whose lifestyle was as extreme as the one they detested. Runners had always been considered to be ascetic oddballs but only young and active sports people used to be involved: now, however, jogging had spread running upwards in age and outwards in standards – it had become a source of youth and a way of filling leisure time.

Towards the end of the 1970s a woman runner expressed what had become a common view: 'The satisfaction I get, the high points, the time to think and solve problems, the energy – all these prove that running works. Which is why my devotion to running makes me happier and makes my life better. It's the same thing that religion does for many people. It gives meaning to their lives. I don't really understand why but running has given my life a new meaning that it did not have before'.[13]

The woman stresses that running has nothing to do with a belief in God, rather with a belief in oneself, in one's own strength and the possibility of controlling one's own life through discipline. Many people felt they had lost control over and contact with their own bodies and running enabled them to win them back. Along with the revitalization of body and mind it was this spiritual dimension that was particularly powerful.

Bob Anderson, publisher of *Runners' World*, the most important magazine for joggers in America and, indeed, the world, was asked in the 1970s what his religion was. Without being at all flippant he answered 'I am a runner.'[14] Jogging in moderation was a healthy and sensible solution and counter-balance to physical degeneration and to the epidemic of obesity in the United States. Jogging as an American phenomenon was also a short-lived fashion which many people started and soon gave up.

Away from the Psychiatrist's Couch

The psychiatrist Thaddeus Kostrubala (1930–) in San Diego, California, was a practitioner of Freudian principles who used analysis to untie the knots of the mind. Early in the 1970s he began jogging and noticed the positive impact it also had on his mental state. In 1972 he started a rehabilitation programme for heart patients and the following year gave a talk on the joys and mysteries of running from a psychiatric perspective. The audience listened but none of them asked questions afterwards and he thought he had made a fool of himself. But many of them then came up to him and stated that they had had similar experiences: they too had noticed that running stimulated the mind, releasing what amounted to a flow of elation. Medical circles were already beginning to accept that running improved fitness and had other beneficial physical effects but medical science traditionally made a distinction between the body and the mind.

Thaddeus Kostrubala's 1976 book *The Joy of Running* was one of several that appeared in the same genre. It argued that running had a therapeutic effect, that it was a cure for depression and melancholia and perhaps even for more serious mental illnesses. Kostrubala went out running with his patients rather than just talking to them and he knew of other psychiatrists who were doing the same thing. Instead of handing out prescriptions for pills Kostrubala prescribed running. Naturally enough he was at the receiving end of criticism from his colleagues – highly regarded professionals with twenty years of education behind them could hardly recommend something *that* simple. The answer to complicated mental problems must surely demand more advanced methods, preferably methods that resulted from sophisticated technology and scientific research – new types of pills, for instance. Kostrubala was therefore up against a very powerful economic lobby even though he conceded that running was not the answer to all psychiatric problems.

Running had been used in the United States in the medical treatment of psychologically damaged war veterans in the 1940s, when psychiatrists had observed that their patients became calmer and better able to escape their problems. But psychiatrists had moved away from solutions of that kind in favour of treating patients with a torrent of sedatives and other chemical substances. Kostrubala was challenging the psychiatric paradigm of the time which, as far as the USA was concerned, was identical with the advertising slogan of DuPonts, the country's richest family: 'Better things for better living . . . through chemistry.'[15]

Physiologists and doctors studied whether there was any link between depression and running but found themselves on uncertain ground since depression was such a vague diagnosis. The things a well-fed American in the 1970s might call depression were frequently trivial or problems of luxury in the eyes of poor Asians or Africans. Countries like the USA, with an abundance of material wealth, witnessed the rise of new problems, neuroses and diagnoses that emerged as the population sank into a state of physical passivity – a sort of negative bonus of affluence. American psychiatrists were awash with patients suffering from various levels of depression, many of whom would have reacted positively to running or, indeed, to any kind of physical activity.

Thaddeus Kostrubala was critical of his colleagues' diagnostic methods:

There is a strange system of values in our society that says that worries and anxiety are not good. Some worries are absolutely essential to survive in our society, as is some level of depression. If we go round saying that all fears and paranoia are dangerous or pathological then we have misunderstood the situation. There are many other more serious mental illnesses in present-day society and in many cases long-distance running can provide a surprising cure – much more so than psychiatrists are willing to accept.[16]

Major American magazines like *Newsweek*, *Time* and *People* put jogging on their front pages. American readers and television viewers in the 1970s could not fail to be aware of it and well-known rock musicians like

Alice Cooper, Brian Wilson of the Beach Boys and the singer Linda Ronstadt all said that jogging had helped them to get off drugs.

Rune Larsson, who later became a world-class Swedish ultrarunner, was an exception in that he fell into depression in the middle of a run. One Sunday morning, after the nineteen-year-old had been studying hard and had achieved a marathon in 2 hours 36 minutes, his mind just went bang and depression troubled him for the next five years. When Larsson felt low at the start of a run his mental state deteriorated during the course of it. Training did not function as therapy, quite the reverse, and he would find himself sitting down and freezing in the forest in the middle of a training session, hardly capable of going on – but never weeping, though he should perhaps have allowed himself to do so. Later, when his depressive state eased, he became one of the most positive and sparkling characters in ultrarunning, using his excess of energy and humour both to win major ultra races and to encourage others. The difficult years tempered his character and he grew as a human being.[17]

Endorphins

'Runner's high' describes the elevated mental state a runner feels during or after a run. It was a 1970s concept but well-known long before that, though there was no scientifically tenable explanation of it.

A biochemical explanation of the sense of well-being felt by runners was discovered in 1975 by two teams of researchers working independently of each other. In Scotland John Hughes and Hans Kosterlitz isolated what they called *enkephalines* from a pig's brain. Around the same time the Americans Rabi Simantov and Solomone H. Snyder found the same substances in calf's brain. Independently again of them, Eric Simon had discovered endorphin, 'morphine produced naturally by the body'.

Endorphins are biochemical substances that ease pain and affect the will to eat, drink and sleep. The substance is released into the body during running or training, when falling in love or sustaining an injury. After they are produced, endorphins can remain in the blood for hours and in large doses can induce ecstasy.

It is possible that stimulated runners are feeling the effect of endorphins. There is no doubt that the body begins to produce endorphins after fifteen to twenty minutes of running but later research has questioned whether it is endorphins or some other chemicals that produce the elevation felt by runners. Could it be fresh air or using the muscles (running uses about 60 per cent of the 660 muscles in the body), or just the fact that the runner is performing a little personal physical feat? Could the surroundings, the beauties of nature, soft paths, good companions and sunshine be the cause?

Studies during the 1980s evaluated the link between endorphins and runner's high and found that even when the runner being tested had been

Jogging, Upper
East Side, Central
Park, June 2008.

dosed with an agent that blocked the production of endorphins he or she still experienced runner's high. The fact that scientists were unable to produce the effect with absolute certainty in the laboratory is an awkward one since it makes it more difficult to study endorphins and to prove whether they are or are not the cause. Scientists attempting to study stimulated runners are faced with a concrete but nevertheless indefinable phenomenon that varies from individual to individual. Very fit individuals have higher levels of endorphins.

If the experiments were carried out with individuals running on an indoor treadmill, the treadmill should be moved outside, since the combination of fresh air and endorphins has a powerful effect.[18]

Women runners, in particular, have compared runner's high to orgasm. The bodybuilder Arnold Schwarzenegger compared his hard training sessions in the weights room to sex. The resemblances between sex and running are an intense awareness of presence, great effort and a powerful flow of blood to certain parts of the body. After hard running the runner feels an enhanced sense of well-being and some believe that the enhancement is in proportion to the effort expended. Stress and pain trigger the production of endorphins during a run and they dull the pain – which is perhaps an ancient survival mechanism from hunting runs. It is possible that primeval man was able to exert himself more because chemical substances in the body eased the pain produced by exertion. If that is the case then it is a sensible evolutionary characteristic.

Running Gurus

The bible for joggers was *The Complete Book of Running* (1977) by James F. Fixx – known as Jim Fixx.

He began running in 1967 at the age of 35, at which stage he was smoking two packs of cigarettes a day and weighed 240 lb (109 kg). By the time his muscular legs graced the cover of the book that unexpectedly went to the top of the 1977 bestseller list he was 60 lb (27 kg) lighter and an ardent jogger. The book made him a celebrity and he appeared on national and international television shows and at major running events.

Fixx gave the jogging movement a public face in the United States but the movement was already well under way there. His book was more important for jogging in Europe, where there was a tendency to snap up American trends eagerly even in areas beyond films and music. The jogging movement reached Europe at the end of the 1970s and rolled on for the whole of the following decade. At last America was exporting something useful, something healthy, rather than just cigarettes and chewing gum.[19]

The other great American running guru to emerge in the 1970s, George A. Sheehan, was a cardiologist himself and also the son of a cardiologist of Irish extraction. Sheehan, who grew up in Brooklyn in New York as the eldest of a family of fourteen, ran while he was a student but stopped when he started his own family – which ended up with twelve children. Not until 1963 when he was already 45 years old did he start running short circuits of his garden in New Jersey, embarrassed to be doing such a thing as a middle-aged man. Soon he was routinely going for a lunchtime run and Sheehan became a typical 'born again' runner.

He came alive again, became his old self – that slim athlete who had lived for his daily training and for competitions. Perhaps this was the result of a mid-life crisis – whatever it was, it gave his life a boost. 'Running liberated me. I stopped worrying about what other people thought. It freed me from rules and restrictions that had been imposed. Running allowed me to start afresh.'[20]

Running was both a source of youth and a source of wisdom. It provided him, the cardiologist who had studied and worked with the human body, with a new familiarity with his own body, with wider horizons and with enhanced professional knowledge. The runner's body had its own brain and intelligence and they set defined demands. It could not tolerate all types of food the same day as it raced and it demanded that its stomach contain very little if it was to perform at its best. Its intestines called for water on hot days and its thighs complained in the winter wind since Sheehan preferred to run in shorts.

Running enriched George A. Sheehan's existence in an amazing way. Few writers took such a metaphysical view of running and few put such a banal activity into the bigger perspective. Like some Messiah of running Sheehan could hold a large audience spellbound but he was no soft, sentimental son of nature romanticizing about running. He grew up in the city and preferred running on asphalt. He raced a great deal and lived by the stopwatch, keen to set new personal records and have his times prove that running kept the ravages of age at bay. He ran to stay in form but recorded mercilessly how his pace was becoming slower.

He ran because he had to. Physical fitness cannot be put in the bank and withdrawn as and when necessary so he ran every day. Without training he would go into decline and since his personality and his self-image were constructed around being fit he had to carry on. The image he had of himself – that of the runner – needed to be continually topped up with training and competition. Without running there would be a reduction in his mental and emotional well-being and all his past investment would go to waste. Sheehan ran in order to be today what he had been yesterday and to be tomorrow what he was today.

His column in the *Runners' World* started in the 1970s and later reached millions of readers. He expressed what joggers felt and experienced and he described their inner lives and mental universe.

Sheehan's greatest achievement was his ability to view running in both micro and macro perspectives and he used it as a metaphor of life in America in the second half of the twentieth century. His thoughts provided the opponents of running with good ammunition: they thought of Sheehan as a fool, a quasi-philosopher, a sweaty clown, endlessly trying to turn back the tide of old age and physical decline. Sheehan accepted that, for non-runners, that was his role and he knew he was easy to find arguments against. But Sheehan was most at home in his running shoes and could not care less what the outside world thought as long as he could run. There was a lot of vigour and ambition in what he wrote, a boyish urge to show who can run fastest, but he stated bluntly that there were only two kinds of people – those who ran and those who did not. Mutual understanding between them was impossible: he knew because he had belonged to both camps.

Sheehan and those like him recognized something that runners had always known – that running, particularly on a hard surface, can often lead to injuries such as runner's knee, plantar fasciitis, Achilles tendonitis and other afflictions, especially after marathon runs on a hard surface. What had previously been one of the topics of conversation among a small sect of runners – the risk of injury and the frustration at being unable to run – now became the talking point among millions. Many people simply gave up when they suffered injury, unaware that the cause may have been the wrong shoes, too hard a surface or a faulty running style.

Right from the start George Sheehan experimented with remedies other than rest, medicines, injections and surgery when he or his patients were injured. He had a number of injuries himself which not even the most skilled of his colleagues could help with but there was never any question of him giving up. It was up to the individual jogger to find a solution, preferably with the help of an expert, but there were few of those in the early 1970s and even they had little experience.

Sheehan told the story of David Merrick, a good runner at school who later suffered from severe knee pain. The medical advice was fourteen months' rest, exercises to ameliorate the damage, medicines, cortisone injections and finally an operation. The surgical procedure was the last resort but that did not help either. The same process was gone through again for another eighteen months until the doctors recommended another operation. By this stage the young man was sick of it and consulted Sheehan.

He recognized that Merrick's feet needed to be properly adjusted. After a week with special insoles he started training again, six weeks later he won an indoor championship and after a further three months Merrick won the university cross-country championship. A cheap supporting insole in his shoe succeeded where several years of advanced – and unsuccessful – medical treatment had failed.

Sheehan and his colleagues learned to look for what was causing the damage, such as, for instance, a biomechanical peculiarity. And they thought more holistically. Apparently inexplicable injuries could often be corrected by simple means as long as they had not gone too far. Occasionally an operation would be necessary, though the South African Professor Timothy Noakes, author of the definitive *Lore of Running*, advised against operating unless it was absolutely necessary.[21]

Doctors and foot specialists gained a better insight into running injuries from the 1970s on. Self-help, however, was the ideal and a flood of information circulated among runners. Injuries were often discussed in the way patients talk of their diseases: as a possession you will never get rid of, that you have a close relationship with, that you have to take account of – and accept.

George A. Sheehan was diagnosed as having prostate cancer in 1986 but carried on writing and training as long as he could. He died in 1993, leaving us with eight books and hundreds of articles with running as their central theme.

Positive Addiction?

Seen from the outside, this does seem to be an odd message. Does running become a compulsion in spite of the runner's praise for his hobby?

The American psychiatrist William Glasser presented theories about the addiction to running in his book *Positive Addiction* (1976), which was based on an investigation announced in *Runners' World* two years earlier.

At home in California Glasser had been struck by the thought that running was a new, spreading but rarely discussed addiction.[22]

According to Glasser there are negative addictions, such as eating until you are obese or being a chain-smoker, but there are also bright spots in the human tendency to addiction. There are some addictions that can invigorate and enrich life, unlike alcoholism or drug addiction, which destroy the mind and the body. Glasser thought that positive addictions can increase people's mental strength. Someone with a positive addiction enjoys the habit without it dominating his life – unlike the heroin addict who is constantly seeking the rush and is content to live *for* his addiction.

As might be expected, 75 per cent of those who responded to his enquiry and who had run at least six times a week for a year were, according to the psychiatric definition, addicts. The answers to questions such as 'Do you suffer if you have to refrain from going for a run?' and 'Do you always enjoy your runs?' were particularly revealing. The addicts laughed and were perfectly happy with their vice. They had started with the intention of getting fit but become ensnared and now they neither could nor wanted to give up.

The symptoms the runners showed during periods of involuntary abstinence were similar to the symptoms of negative addicts: apathy, lack of mental clarity, loss of appetite, sleeplessness, headaches and stomach-aches. Some of them suffered from twitching legs at night and felt depressed. People who were normally happy and bright were overcome by a sense of gloom that only going out jogging would dissipate.[23]

There are a number of examples of people who have run every day of the year for the last three or four decades irrespective of illness or injury because they loved it but also in order to keep up their personal statistics. The best known of these is Ron Hill, European marathon champion in 1969 and only the second man in the world to break 2 hours 10 minutes – his time was 2 hours, 9 minutes and 28 seconds. From December 1964 through to 2008 he ran every single day, frequently twice, even though interruptions for injuries, operations and long flights sometimes limited his runs or forced him to run indoors in corridors and airport waiting rooms. But he has done at least a mile a day, including the occasion when it took him 27 minutes to cover a mile on crutches straight after an operation. There can be few people in history who have clocked up a higher mileage than Hill, who often ran to and from work and who certainly did not have an easy life even outside his training sessions.

An addiction to running does not emerge quickly. The potential addict had to be able to manage an hour of continuous running and have achieved a certain level of fitness, and it would take six months or more before he or she became addicted. Older people became addicted quicker and remained addicts into old age, as long as they were able to run – even if they were in prison. In the USA there were prisoners with a life-sentence who clung on to their daily run in the exercise yard: they would run on a hard-packed track close to the prison wall in order to have the longest circuit possible and they ran the same monotonous circuit day after day, year in and year out. Jogging became an important therapy and a welcome addiction for many prisoners.

Some runners resorted to cycling when they were injured but this did not provide the same satisfaction for true runners. It had something to do with the movement and Glasser believed that running was a primeval human activity, a deep need to move in the ways human beings had originally had to move in order to survive. He pointed to the way small children instinctively run.

In Glasser's view running fulfilled all the criteria for a positive addiction. It is a voluntary exercise, easy to perform and demanding little mental energy. It can be done alone and has value for the individual. Positive addiction provides a sense of success that encourages the individual to continue. Runners, moreover, have to accept themselves while doing it: it is impossible to be self-critical when running and still become an addict – that is likely to lead to the particular individual giving up the activity.

Glasser's enquiry revealed much of interest, everything from elevated experiences to instances of bad conscience. The 24-year-old Timothy Charles Masters, for instance, said: 'When I miss a training run I feel as if I've let myself down'. He had a sense of guilt until his next run. Other people felt fat, lazy and apathetic if they did not get out, a sense that their sin was being punished by a feeling of moodiness and a heavier body. They were sinning against themselves, against their own ideal image, not against a god or a doctrine. In spite of an often relaxed attitude to times and personal records, the unstated driving force for many joggers was to achieve a particular weight or particular shape. Any interruptions in their training meant that they were delaying their achievement of this dream or self-delusion: and over-eating and drinking might reverse the process. Even a positive addiction can cause spiritual and physical dilemmas: there were examples of pathological thinness caused by eating disorders, either eating too little or eating too much and then vomiting.

Most joggers, however, were satisfied with simply feeling better and, unlike psychologists and psychiatrists, felt no need to seek more closely for potential imbalances and abnormalities. 'It makes me so happy', 'I feel so well', or 'It's so much fun' were the standard responses among those who carried on running. Perhaps the tendency of psychiatrists to want to diagnose all such so-called abnormalities was at least as much a symptom of imbalance as running was?

Timothy Charles Masters liked having his pangs of conscience because they forced him out for a run, which made him fit, kept him slim and boosted his self-confidence – in his view this last point was one of the great benefits of training. Running was both an inner journey and physical activity of a kind he did not get in his job. It had, moreover, altered his outlook on life, making him more philosophical and less materialistic.[24]

Many runners felt a bit superior because they believed they had a better life than other people. It was not so much an egocentric emotion as a belief that running had raised the quality of their lives. They were able to think more clearly and quickly, they had more energy, and some of them had lost the desire to drink excessively. To the jogger's mind humanity fell into two categories: those who ran and the rest. How could anyone voluntarily miss out on something so life-enhancing?

One important consequence of the jogging craze was that millions of people began running without ever giving a thought to competition. Jogging at a pleasant, steady pace, LSD – long slow distance, as it was called – brought a new dimension to running. The point was the exercise itself, not setting the fastest possible pace or keeping an eye on the clock. The main aims were improved health, well-being and fun rather than personal records. This was in the spirit of Arthur Lydiard, this was what lay behind his experiments to find the secrets of long-distance running. The masses only began running once training routines had become more enjoyable.

The great family of runners now had more freedom, more diversity and fewer inhibitions and there was room for all age groups, all shapes and sizes, not just the lean and skinny. Running in the streets and marathon running also implied an escape from enclosed tracks and flat, strictly regulated surroundings out into the tarmac territory of the car. They all knew the roads but now they were trying them without wheels and engines and discovering that everything felt completely different when travelling on foot. It was all up to you, up to your own strength and performance and nothing to do with the accelerator pedal. Rather than buy a posh car and fill up with petrol you had to get out there and train in order to achieve and retain a good standard.

Writing in Runners' World Joe Henderson argued for seeing gentle running in the perspective of a whole lifetime, as part of the good life. He was perceptive enough to see that running was not for everyone: some people hate it irrespective of whether they have tried it or how much others rabbit on about its potential benefits. They prefer team sports or golf or tennis or walking the dog. Henderson recognized that there are many who run for months and years and then give up, or run off and on depending on injuries. But non-joggers can still draw some advantage from their bitter experiences of running: if the thought of running sticks in their craw they might, for instance, find some other way of keeping fit.

Negative Addiction?

In 1978 the sports psychologist William P. Morgan responded professionally to William Glasser's hypotheses about running and positive addiction. Morgan was of the opinion that long-distance running, like alcohol and drug abuse, had negative side-effects in that runners ignored injuries and pain in order to continue training and competing. He was also critical of the social sacrifices made by runners, such as their limited lifestyle and neurotic asceticism.

According to Morgan, jogging resembled cigarette smoking in its early phases. It initially felt damaging and unpleasant and the jogger became breathless, sore and possibly exhausted. If he continued, however, he would feel a sense of elevated mood and of increased physical wellbeing that could only be retained by increasing dosages of training. Even though Morgan accepted that a runner might find inner peace as long as he was permitted to train he did not consider that to be something positive if the runner became indifferent to the world around. Jogging, said Morgan, could become the most important thing in life and everything that stole time or attention from it would be considered negative.

It is certainly true that hundreds of thousands of joggers in the 1970s became so self-absorbed as to be both comical and bizarre. The jogging craze was part of an ego-trip that washed over the Western world. Running fulfilled the desire for self-realization and eternal youth achieved by one's own efforts. The following decades witnessed innumerable new fashions in the name of health and Mammon and jogging was often the first physical trend these new 'seekers' in life experimented with – running is, after all, the mother of all sports. Technological advances together with the huge rise in living standards in the years after the Second World War gave the American baby-boom generation the freedom and opportunity to search for a meaning in life over and above family and work. Morgan took the view that this energy and abundance ought to be used for some meaningful purpose rather than being dissipated out on breathless running trips.

What Morgan did not recognize was that a society such as the USA, with its enormous health problems, widespread obesity and lack of exercise in everyday life, was bound to react against these things. There had never been a time in the history of mankind when people had so little necessity to move around as part of their everyday existence, and many other countries were following in the wake of the United States. The jogging movement and other training trends, healthy or not, were necessary reactions if the population was not to be reduced to utter helplessness.[25]

Running, for the most part, gave people more energy for the rest of the day and training enabled them to cope with stress and office life. Even President Jimmy Carter ran in the second half of the 1970s. When he collapsed, completely exhausted, in a 10-kilometre race in 1979 the incident was used as a metaphor for his lack of presidential qualities, his physical weakness being juxtaposed with his poor leadership skills. The unfinished run came to symbolize a lack of energy and will and it was exploited by his successor Ronald Reagan, even though the latter preferred to restrict himself to posing on horseback on his ranch.

As the tide of joggers rose higher so did the average age since many people of a mature age took it up and continued as pensioners. Slowing down the aging process became a time-consuming process for serious joggers and they measured it against the clock. Even though recent recruits could still set personal best times in, say, the marathon even in their sixties, the aging process always wins, partly because pushing oneself hard can easily lead to injuries as one gets older.

Veteran sport and running was a revolt against existing conventions. Why should we stop doing something we love doing? It was part of the Western trend that put more emphasis on youth and vitality. People did not want to age as fast as earlier generations had done, they did not want to stagnate physically and mentally or be restricted to the behaviour and attitudes considered appropriate to a particular stage in life.

The world of Hollywood led the chase for eternal youth. The rejuvenation industry had already been attracting film stars and the rich for many years and in the decades following the 1960s it began to stretch its tentacles out to catch the population at large. The film stars' techniques for keeping themselves young and vigorous – running, for instance – were now marketed as part of a package to increase both the quality and the length of life.

25
Big City Marathons

I would never have believed that the New York City Marathon could
make one weep. It's a vision of Doomsday.
—Jean Baudrillard, on watching the marathon in the mid-1980s

On 13 September 1970 126 runners took part in the first New York City
Marathon. The 55 runners who finished had completed four circuits in
Central Park without attracting the attention of the press or the television
and they were clapped home by family, friends and enthusiasts. Few of the
other people who happened to be in the park that day – skaters, dog walkers and courting couples – knew anything about the marathon apart from
the fact it was a strange Olympic event and one that attracted cranks.

A man with a beard, Fred Lebow, came in at number 45. He was one
of the initiators of the race and had come up with much of the meagre
$1,000 that the event cost, mainly for the purchase of drinks and cheap
watches as prizes. He had started running alone the year before but soon
sought the company of the New York Road Runners Club, of which he
became president in 1972.

Lebow wanted the whole world to run – adults, young people, children, women and the elderly – and he wanted them to run long distances.
This Romanian immigrant, who spoke English with a strong accent, was
bubbling with ideas and he became one of the world's most persistent
advocates of mass running in the years that followed.

New York offered opportunities Lebow could not have dreamt of when
he was growing up in Arad in Romania, where he was born in 1932 as the
sixth of a family of seven. The Lebowitz family were orthodox Jews and
Lebow's father was a merchant from whom he inherited the outgoing social
attitudes that stood him in good stead in later life. The family escaped being
sent to a concentration camp during the war and emigrated to Israel at the
end of the 1940s. Fred stayed behind in Europe, leading a rootless life as, among
other things, a diamond and sugar smuggler, until he went to America in
1951 on a student scholarship. He worked his way up and by the start of the
1970s was involved in the ready-to-wear clothing business.

Fred Lebow loved running above all else. He was not one of those
worthy traditional organizers in a suit and tie, a pillar of society with a wife
and family, he was both an active entrepreneur and an enthusiast, who
found in New York the right mental climate for his drive and his life's

La Salle Bank Chicago Marathon, 2005.

passion. As often happens with successful entrepreneurs his work and his hobby became one. Lebow *was* the New York City Marathon, to the outside world anyway, even though he was assisted by a large team which worked rather more anonymously.

The great boost came in 1976 when the New York City Marathon ran through all five boroughs for the first time. The idea of changing the route came from Ted Corbitt, one of the city's marathon and ultramarathon legends, who thought the change would increase public awareness of the race. Lebow was initially against it since, given the growing numbers of entrants, it was already difficult enough to organize the race in Central Park. How could it possibly work out on the ordinary streets of the busiest city in the world? Getting police permission did not prove easy and even the city authorities were against the idea. On top of all that, the 1975 race, which had 500 finishers, lost money.

In 1976, however, helped by the United States bicentennial celebrations and new-found enthusiasm on the part of the city authorities, the police gave their permission and the family of Samuel Rudin came up with $25,000 in sponsorship support. (Rudin was a rich businessman who had died that year but had been a runner 50 years earlier.[1]) Lebow, with five good assistants and Ted Corbitt as the man with the local knowledge, set off through the maze of New York streets in December 1975 to work out a route. Lebow wanted the fewest possible traffic problems, the fewest possible street crossings and traffic lights and preferably not too many bridges. The men measured out the distances on foot and by car, checked and rejected alternatives until they came up with a route that crossed four bridges and included 220 street crossings.

'Out of the question!' was the first reaction from the police: it would lead to total chaos and accidents as well as gridlock in the wheezing, hooting anthill of New York traffic. But since the highest authorities in the city were insistent and since it was the 200th birthday of the USA, opposition and scepticism turned to enthusiasm and a 'can-do' determination to show the rest of the country and the world that New Yorkers can handle anything.

In the early summer of 1976 Lebow called a press conference to announce the fantastic event. Not a single journalist came and Lebow recognized that he would need the stars of national and international running in order to whip up interest. Frank Shorter and Bill Rodgers were the top names in American marathon running and they promised to take part, as did Ron Hill and Ian Thompson from Britain and Franco Fava from Italy. Lebow was now making contacts at the highest level in the world of running.

Even in 1976 the organizers were already relying on computer registration of the participants. The problem that year was that the man doing the inputting had been doing it in his girlfriend's flat until she threw him out. Unfortunately there were 200 entry forms still waiting to be input and the angry girl was refusing to let her ex-boyfriend or anyone else into the flat to collect the forms. Lebow negotiated with her over the telephone, using all his histrionic skills: 'It's obvious your boyfriend has treated you badly but that's no reason to punish the whole of the New York City Marathon. There are forms there from some of the best marathon runners in the world – surely you don't want to punish them?'[2]

It made no impression on her even though Lebow begged and pretended to cry on the telephone. It meant that the organizers had to get 200 unfortunate runners to fill in new registration forms immediately before the start of the race. In later years the organizers put a lot of resources into making sure they had copies of all the applications that came in.

Lebow had nightmares in the run-up to the race, waking up as sweaty as if he had been out for a run, his mind full of horrific images of what might happen in an event that had never been tried in a city before. He drove the course in a delivery truck on the morning of the race, following the blue line on the tarmac that marked out the route. Most things were in order but, as tense as a theatre director before the first night, he saw potential traps everywhere. Halfway round, the police had erected the barriers incorrectly so that the runners would be led out onto the roadway between Brooklyn and Queens instead of staying on the footpath. Lebow leapt out of the truck and set about moving the barriers like a maniac – he cursed and pushed a policeman so hard that he was threatened with arrest but fortunately his driver came to the rescue and dragged him back into the truck.

The race was a huge success. *The New York Times* estimated that half a million people were lining the sidewalk to watch runners, 1,549 of whom finished the race, including 63 women. There were runners from 35 of the states of the USA and from twelve other countries. Five hundred applications had arrived too late and had to be rejected.

Lebow and his gang of organizers were overwhelmed but ready to continue their efforts. A tradition had been established. There was something both magical and contradictory about the New York City Marathon. The great city was an exotic destination, the driving force behind modern finance as well as the criminal capital of the USA, but here were runners of all standards chancing their luck out in the middle of the main streets between towering skyscrapers. It was an amazing situation – on one day a year the city was allowing people on foot to be given precedence in the realm of the car. Little people were given control of the metropolitan jungle and, what is more, they were being cheered on by a wall of spectators.

Fred Lebow was permanently on the move to other countries to spread the word about street running and city marathons. He gloated over the increasing numbers in the New York City Marathon: 11,400 in 1978, 17,000 in 1983 – and 44,000 had been turned down. The numbers continued to rise to double that and in 1983 Lebow handed out over 2,000 press accreditations for the day of the marathon. It is estimated that there were 100,000 joggers in the United States in 1968; eleven years later that figure had become 27 million.

The marathon had become less of a competition to achieve a good placing or good time and more of a ritual to be gone through, a symbol of vigour and will. Before the marathon trend of the 1970s courses were usually closed after four hours. In 1981, however, over a third of those taking part, more that 4,000 runners, took longer than four hours in the New York City Marathon and the number of slow runners increased year on year. The timekeepers stayed at their posts and the spectators cheered to the last.

Running at this level during these years did not involve all the social classes. In New York it was upper-middle-class people who flooded in to the marathon and in 1983 almost 90 per cent of the members the New York Road Runners Club had a higher education.[3] Well-educated, white people ran to and from work or laced up their jogging shoes during their lunchbreaks. The marathon, which had earlier had low status and been seen as an event for eccentrics (unless money was involved), now gained high status and offered big prize-money. In 1976 Bill Rodgers received $2,000 under the table for taking part in the New York City Marathon and Frank Shorter also received a tidy sum. Payments for the marathon and other athletic events were unofficial at that date although everyone involved knew that they happened: not until 1982 was payment officially allowed.

Television broadcast the race live and the television rights paid much of the cost. Street running and the marathon now became popular televised sports. The budget for the race grew to $1.3 million in 1983 and continued to grow, partly because some 30 million Americans called themselves joggers by this time. The membership of the New York Road Runners Club had reached 24,000 by 1984, making it the biggest club of its kind in the world. Some 35 paid employees worked at the club headquarters and more than 4,000 others worked for the club voluntarily, organizing hundreds of events throughout the year. And over them all, like an enthusiastic, smiling little king in training bottoms and a cycling cap, sat Fred Lebow, the personification of the jogging craze.

The club also led the world in terms of technology. Allan Steinfeldt, a runner and computer expert, was in charge of the computer section and set the standard for other race organizers who used computers. Around 1978 they developed coded slips that were attached to runners' starting numbers: the slips were torn off at the finishing line and read by electronic scanners.

Every year the staff wanted to improve on the previous year's marathon. Progress was the name of the game – just as in the business world it was no good to rest on the laurels of past success. Success should be a springboard for something even better and more spectacular, which included outdoing other big city marathons. From the end of the 1970s there was rivalry between the biggest races in the USA and, indeed, the rest of the world: they competed to attract the stars and come up with the best appearance fees, entry lists and bonuses for the victors. Like other growth industries, big city marathons passed through several phases. At first they ran at a deficit, relying on volunteers and idealism, but then bigger sponsors entered the picture, along with television rights, advertising opportunities and the need for their own financial experts. This happened in New York within just a few years of the first race: long-distance running for the masses became a business, not just a sweaty hobby.

A Sceptical Philosopher

I would never have believed that the New York City Marathon could make one weep. It's a vision of Doomsday. Is it possible to talk of voluntary suffering in the same way we talk of voluntary servitude? They are all seeking death, the death from exhaustion that was the fate of Philippides more than two thousand years ago when, let us not forget, he brought to Athens the news of the victory at Marathon.

Doubtless these marathon runners also dream of bearing a message of victory but there are too many of them and their message no longer has any meaning: it is no more than the message of their arrival at the goal of their effort – an obscure message about a superhuman and futile effort.[4]

The French philosopher Jean Baudrillard watched the New York City Marathon in the middle of the 1980s.

He recognized the beauty of sport and of top-level sport, but he was dismayed that anyone could take part and thus pollute the aesthetic aspects of what had been an exclusive arena. It had become a show with thousands of legs. Elegance had been replaced by grey figures who lacked the talent to inspire the spectators, their only motivation being self-satisfaction based on the marketable illusion that drudgery was somehow of value. The New York City Marathon was the symbol of this madness – the marathon had become a heroic feat that lacked all meaning. It was like climbing a mountain or landing on the moon, a programmed attempt to achieve something that led nowhere at all and thus extinguished dreams. It was a kind of public suicide, simply to demonstrate that one could finish it, but to what purpose and at what price?[5]

Baudrillard was looking behind the happy tide of joggers, behind the contented, reasonably fit hordes that sought companionable physical challenges in a society that virtually lacked them, at least in working life. The New York City Marathon was the joggers' Olympia and they made pilgrimages from afar simply to take part in its tough rituals.

To Fred Lebow these mediocre participants represented a victory over inactivity and that victory was at least as great a triumph as the achievements of the elite. They were living the sporting ideal that taking part is in itself the accomplishment.

Baudrillard argued contentiously against the marathon. It is unhealthy, the participants suffer during it and their pain stays with them for days and weeks afterwards in the form of stiffness and torn muscles. He was critical because he was fascinated by it – even if his fascination was despairing.

A Lasting Trend?

As the jogging craze spread its tentacles ever wider, big city marathons became a trend from the 1980s on, at first in the West and then in other parts of the world. City authorities saw the value of this kind of modern carnival since it offered profits and publicity and a complete contrast to the vehicle-dominated everyday life of the city. Television pictures and photographs of tens of thousands of legs at the start of a marathon were broadcast to the world, showing a snaking, slow-moving queue of people at the back of the field. But they were all moving and they all had a noble goal in mind.

In the decades after the 1970s the population growth of the world's great cities continued as people moved in from country areas. The metropolis thus became ever more important to identity, even for those who lived far from it: if you imitate metropolitan trends you can be sure of not being left behind by new developments. Look to the metropolis – that is where modern man can learn the lessons of efficiency and consumption. City tourism was a growth area and the link between running and tarmac became a desirable demonstration of the attractions of the city – all of which was brought to life by television pictures and plugged by city authorities and financial forces. The big city marathon was a wonderful mixture of commercial interest and festival for enthusiasts, a win-win

Verrano Bridge, New York Marathon, 2005.

situation for the organizers, the sponsors and the participants which made them worry less about the financial outlay and the wear and tear on the human body.

The big city marathon in New York had entertainment calculated down to the second. It was a timed, modern sphere for lasting exertion, the preparation and training for which were reminiscent of both religious devotion and the work ethic of industrial society. It took stubborn and methodical people to take on so many monotonous miles on a surface designed for the car, with three times the runner's body weight crashing through his muscles and skeleton every yard of the way.

In the hierarchy of joggers it felt natural to aim to complete a city marathon. It was not only a test of manhood it was also a proud, if breathless, symbol of mankind's need to take on physical challenges in the company of others. The lives of most joggers did not involve hard physical teamwork in agriculture or industry and by running in a crowd they experienced companionship and a sense of belonging at the same time as satisfying their competitive instincts. They felt inner joy and intense pain on a number of levels, at the same time as feeling pride and exclusiveness in that they were sharing a starting line with the international elite. The city marathon was a journey into a fascinating urban jungle, a voyage into the unexplored areas of the soul and an expansion of one's own physical horizons. Races like this, even those over shorter distances, among tourist attractions and skyscrapers, would become a memory for life. Fred Lebow and those like him recognized this and spread the message with all the fervour of apostles.

When the idea of the New York City Marathon was conceived the aim was to get more people to run. The way the event developed may be seen as an extension of those original ideals along with a successful business enterprise. It is that combination that has made the race so successful.

26
Marathon Women

One of them was weeping in despair, their faces were distorted and ugly, and they were trembling as if suffering from severe typhoid.
—A Norwegian journalist after the 1928 Olympic 800 metres for women

Well into the twentieth century, in civilized Western societies anyway, it was thought that women should not run long distances. Women among the Tarahumara in Mexico ran for hours without coming to any harm, but they were children of nature like the Native Americans in the USA, whose women also covered long distances until the apathy of reservation life changed things.

The Chinese knew that women were designed for endurance and the women in the revolutionary Red Army in the 1930s lived a hard life. Poor Chinese women in the countryside only knew a life of toil and, when they donned uniforms, running became obligatory. The woman soldier Zhao Lan recounted that they rose early, trained, did weapons training and all sorts of physical exercises: 'We also did a long-distance run every day. We liked all kinds of sport, particularly long-distance running, since it helped us when we were fighting.'[1]

Wei Xiuying, another soldier, was sold by her parents as a child bride when she was only five. While growing up she toiled in the fields from dawn to late at night with little to eat and beatings as punishment. When the Red Army arrived in her village she cut her hair short as a protest and enlisted. Wei and the other hardy girls could run and march long distances and carry heavy loads.

The communists in the Soviet Union, too, recognized women's strength and endurance. In Soviet sport between the wars women were put on an equal footing with men since equality was enshrined in the socialist programme of the 1917 revolution. Soviet women were considered strong, tough and capable of virtually the same performances as men. Similar ideals existed in working-class and small-farm communities in the West, where heavy work and frequent pregnancies were the norm. Olympic sport, however, was dominated by a bourgeois ideology that defined women as weaker, more sensitive and without the drive or the ability to train for and compete in long races. These were actually considered to be harmful and, in the view of specialists, could endanger fertility.

The women's 800 metres at the 1928 Olympics left a deep scar. The race took place on a hot day and several of the runners collapsed at the finish.

One of the Norwegian journalists present wrote:

> The two words women and athletics should never be uttered in the same breath since there is such a glaring disharmony between them. We saw it last and most clearly at the Olympic Games in Amsterdam. Women's participation in the 800 metres was an absolute horror. They set off groaning, arms flailing away; one dropped out halfway with a tired gesture whereas the others finished the race utterly shattered. One of them was weeping in despair, their faces were distorted and ugly, and they were trembling as if suffering from severe typhoid.[2]

The journalist in the German magazine *Der Leichtathlet* took a different and more positive view. He commended the winner's fitness and physique and her long strides, and he judged it as an athletic performance, not as an odd sideshow. After a good deal of criticism resistance to women's races had been partly overcome in Germany – though press and public opinion had needed time to get used to the idea. Athletics were strong in Germany and women students at the College of Physical Education had to run 3,000 metres within a set time.

The sight of the exhausted women collapsing after the 800 metres led to the event being excluded from the Olympics and not re-introduced until 1960. Women's athletics were nevertheless advancing in Europe, Oceania and the United States during the 1930s, with the sprint as the running event. The first official mile race in Britain in the modern period was held in 1936.

The women pioneers of long-distance running have left few traces in the history books. Great events like the 12-kilometre race in Paris in October 1903, when 2,500 shop-girls ran and the winner came in in 1 hour 10 minutes, did not lead to a mass movement. At least 20,000 spectators – mostly men – watched and whistled and cheered at the girls running in their working or best clothes. The winner was given a singing spot at the famous Olympia review theatre and was a celebrity for a while. In France women's races were something that many people took seriously.

A number of women's races in Germany in 1904 show that there was a growing interest. The spectators, once again mostly men, noted that the women's arms and legs were covered – otherwise it really would have caused a sensation. The distance run by women was increased in Germany and soon, racing in rather more practical clothing, women were running 1,000 metres and more.[3]

Whether women lost their femininity and became masculine through taking part in sports was a topic of debate in the USA, Britain, France, Germany and elsewhere. The French writer Emile Zola approved of all forms of physical exercise as long as it was not pushed to excess. But what was excess? And what were women's motives for taking part in sports? The critics' view was that they did so out of a desire to provoke, to show off, to flirt with something new, but women – like men – took up sport, including running, for a variety of reasons.[4]

Long races for women were rare in the Western world and even more rarely did they get into the papers. Well into the twentieth century we have only snippets of historical information about the longest distances. Marie-Louise Ledru was alone among a crowd of men when she completed a marathon in France in 1918. Violet Piercy, an Englishwoman, was equally non-traditional and the cause of open-mouthed amazement among the spectators when she ran in the Polytechnic Marathon in Chiswick in 1926. After the start she modestly took up position back in the field and stayed there, achieving a time of 3 hours 40 minutes 22 seconds, which became the first unofficial record for women over that distance.[5]

The Second World War was to come and go before an important new pioneer for distance running emerged. The German Ernst van Aaken was the father of the women's marathon in Europe and an early advocate of distance running for men, women and children. He was a pioneer of jogging in line with Arthur Lydiard and, like Lydiard, Van Aaken uncovered the secrets of distance running in the 1940s. According to Van Aaken women were built for endurance. When he recommended the 800 metres for women in 1953 and 1954 it led to a debate in the German press. The press expressed doubts about Van Aaken's competence, when he, as an all-powerful doctor, urged women to run non-stop for more than two minutes, torturing themselves publicly and stripped of all femininity and womanliness, in order to create 'Zatopecs' with plaits. At the German 800-metre championship in 1954 one journalist was of the opinion that they would need doctors, ambulances and camp-beds at the finishing line to deal with the exhausted runners.

The same commentator changed his view after the initial races: 'Marianne Weiss flowing over the finishing line was a marvellous image of elegance and beauty.' But even in West Germany, which was far ahead of the rest of the West in terms of longer races for women, it was to take another fifteen years before the 1,500 metres was officially introduced, even though the event had been suggested back in the 1950s.[6]

Women and the marathon enjoyed a minor breakthrough in the 1960s, a decade characterized in the West by rising affluence, political protest movements and an increased population of young people. Young people in many countries were challenging authority and women were beginning to enter new areas of society. The intellectual climate was conducive to experimenting with new ideas, and this also held for running, where middle distances were attracting an increasing number of adherents.

In 1964 the New Zealander Ivan Keats asked his training companion Millie Sampson whether she would like to take part in the marathon. His club needed an extra boost for a projected meeting and the world record of 3 hours 37 minutes held by the American Mary Lepper was within reach.

Millie Sampson agreed immediately and they added extra mileage to their training runs in the weeks running up to August 1964. The night before the race there was a social evening and the dancing and entertainment went on until late with the result that Sampson's alarm clock failed to wake her the following morning. When she woke up she saw that time was too tight for her to take part so she dozed off again. Keats, however, convinced her to get up and she set off without any breakfast as the only woman in the race. Even with a break at eighteen miles to eat ice-cream and chocolate, she did it in 3 hours 19 minutes 33 seconds and set a new world record.

The *New Zealand Herald* had a front-page article about 'The housewife who ran the marathon in record time' but few paid any attention, either in the press or in the athletics world. Only one daily newspaper referred to it and Millie Sampson did not achieve celebrity as a pioneer of the women's marathon.

The American Kathrine Switzer did, however, achieve celebrity. In 1967 she told Arnie Briggs, a veteran of the Boston Marathon, that she wanted to run in the event. Even though she ran nine or ten miles every evening he told her that women cannot run marathons.[7]

Several women had already tried the Boston Marathon, the first of them in 1951, although neither her name nor her time is known. In 1964 Roberta Gibb applied but was rejected, so she concealed herself at the start, joined in with the field and finished in 3.21.40 without it causing any fuss.

Kathrine Switzer tried out the distance in training and performed well. Without knowing that women were not admitted to the Boston Marathon and convinced of her ability, her training partner entered her for the race in 1967 as K. V. Switzer. Kathrine's boyfriend Thomas Miller, a hammer-thrower, also joined the group.

The press car informed Jock Semple, co-director of the race, that there was a woman out in the field. He leapt out of his car, ran after her and grabbed her in an effort to stop her but Kathrine's boyfriend put up strong resistance. The photographers had a grandstand view and the following day many newspapers printed photographs of Semple attacking Switzer and three men defending her. Her finishing time was 4 hours 20 minutes and the Amateur Athletic Union banned Switzer from further competition on the grounds that she had illegally entered a race longer than two kilometres and restricted to men only.

The photographs could scarcely have been posed to achieve a better effect. They show a pretty Switzer being attacked by evil Jock Semple and protected by good Thomas Miller – virtually all the sympathy went to her. Switzer was protesting that certain areas of athletics were restricted to men and women were excluded: in the case of the marathon they were excluded because doctors and opinion at large held that women could neither manage nor tolerate the distance.

Roberta Gibb also completed the race in 1967 but less attention was paid to that since there were no dramatic photographs. Both represented

Paula Radcliffe, New York Marathon, 2008.

long-haired feminine beauty in a men's race that had been in existence for seventy years and was richer in tradition than any other race of its kind in the world. In a remarkable and unplanned way this incident sparked off the 1970s wave of women's marathon running.

Shortly after the 1967 Boston Marathon a world record time for women of 3 hours 15 minutes and 22 seconds was set by fifteen-year-old Maureen Wilton in Toronto. Both public and press were doubtful about the accuracy of the time. When Ernst van Aaken was asked about it he was ridiculed for his response, 'Yes, and the times will get much better.' To support his statement van Aaken asked two German runners, Annie Pede, a 27-year-old mother of two, and nineteen-year-old Monika Boers, to take part in a marathon at Waldniel in West Germany. They started 30 metres behind the men and Pede set an unofficial new world record of 3 hours 7 minutes and 26 seconds.

The following year the first Schwarzwald Marathon was held at Donaueschingen in West Germany; it was open to both sexes and attracted 51 women from five countries. The race grew to be one of the biggest of its kind with 1,151 entrants in 1970, a hundred of whom were women.[8]

While others were still focusing on the idea that women were the weaker sex, Van Aaken continued to argue that they were better suited to marathon running than men. They carry more body fat, which can be converted into energy, more protein, and they store liquids in a different way. Ernst van Aaken was a supporter of women's distance-running and the first German marathon championship for women was organized in his home-town of Waldniel in 1973.

The magazine *Spiridon*, founded by Noel Tamini from Switzerland, supported long-distance running for women and published Van Aaken's articles, which were also translated into English. By now there were people in Germany and the USA arguing that running made women more feminine and beautiful rather than masculine as critics had claimed – running was supposed to lead to the blossoming of a new femininity.

In the first years of the 1970s there was pressure in favour of women's distance-running, both in Europe and in the USA. Events organized in the USA pulled in the biggest crowds since that was where jogging was most popular: it is no accident that women's distance-running took off at the same time as the jogging trend was sweeping across the Western world. The feminists and their sisters were calling for women's rights, access to education and equality while the female pioneers in the fields of jogging and the marathon were opening people's eyes to physical education too. A number of good runners became important symbols even for women outside the sporting sphere.

The American Joan Benoit, winner of the first Olympic marathon for women at the 1984 Los Angeles games, was one of them. At last women could legally enter races over the same distances as men and no longer had to sneak in. Another woman with an unexpectedly wide appeal ended up in long-distance running by accident.

Grete

The Norwegian Knut Kvalheim took part in the New York City Marathon in 1977. He and Jack Waitz, who was married to Grete – one of the international elite at middle and long distances on the track – were talking together and thought that she should try the marathon too.

Grete was not against the idea, though she wanted to retire after the 1978 European Championships when she would be 25 years old. Grete had never competed in the USA and could not afford to pay for the journey herself so they telephoned the race office in the autumn of 1978 to enquire whether her air fare could be covered. The telephone was answered by a female secretary.

'What's your personal best for the marathon?'

'I've never run a marathon', Grete answered.

'I'm sorry, we only have a small budget and won't be able to pay for you', the secretary answered, not knowing that Grete had a World Championship gold in the cross-country, world records in the 3,000 metres and many other international triumphs. She nevertheless took a note of Grete's name so that Fred Lebow, who was in overall charge of the race, could see it when he came to the office the following day.

'Why's this name here?' he asked.

'She wants to run in the marathon but I said we couldn't invite her and her husband since she's never run the distance before.'

Fred Lebow was better informed than the secretary and reckoned that a competitor of this kind of quality would at the very least add some extra colour to the race.

'She almost certainly won't finish but she may be a good pacemaker and up the pace of the field.' Christa Valensick from Germany and Micki Gorman from the USA were aiming for world records. And Lebow, knowing that Americans loved unknown challengers, also saw the value of overseas participation. Three weeks before the race he decided to invite the Norwegian couple.[9]

Grete and Jack Waitz arrived in New York on a Thursday, three days before the race. They wandered wide-eyed around Broadway without any thoughts of pre-race nerves or a build-up. On a run in Central Park Grete thought, 'Oh, is this where the finish is?' They had not even thought it worthwhile to find out the route or to familiarize themselves with the conditions.

Grete was at the end of a long athletics career and was in New York for the first and last time and wanted to enjoy the trip. The evening before the race they ate shrimp salad, beef and ice-cream, along with a glass of red wine, and she gave no thought to loading her body with carbohydrates as the best preparation for the exhausting demands of the race.

On Sunday 22 October 1978 she rose, relaxed and ready to run the only marathon of her life. The absence of the press was a relief after so many years of arriving at the start labelled as the favourite in virtually every race. She was unbeaten in Norway since 1972 and the Norwegian press demanded both victory and new records of her at almost every meeting. She had nothing to fear in the streets of New York, having never run farther than about twelve miles in training and normally racing at 5,000 metres or less.

When Grete Waitz arrived at the start and saw 13,000 runners of all shapes and sizes warming up her first thought was, 'If all of *them* can do 26 miles, so can I.' As an elite runner she was used to competing against pencil-slim, fit runners whereas what she was looking at in the starting zone here – the whole spectrum from overweight joggers to world-class athletes in one nervously trotting throng – was her first acquaintance with the jogging craze. Now it was her turn to line up with the joggers.

The starting shot was fired and Grete immediately noticed what her husband had told her in advance: by her standards the pace was low – slow, in fact, in comparison to track races but also slower than her training pace. Her husband had advised her to stay behind the leaders in the women's class and save her strength.

That worked. After nineteen miles, on First Avenue, she passed Marty Cocksey, who had set off at a cracking pace, and took the lead. Everything went swimmingly until the 22-mile stage, which is where many people have problems because the body's store of glycogen – carbohydrates – runs out. From there on she was hard pressed to keep up steam. The distances were given in miles, which was confusing for a Norwegian. Her temper was rising because of a stitch and painful thighs and she was angry with her husband for getting her into this in the first place. He himself was standing relaxing near the finish, fit enough to have entered, although he had not even considered it.

Grete Waitz heard all the non-stop clapping and cheering, heard talk of a world record and all kinds of compliments, but no one, not even the excited commentator at the finish, had any idea who Number 1173 was. She was a late entry, her name was not in the programme and her number had been hand-painted for lack of anything else. She won, however, setting a new world record of 2 hours 32 minutes and 30 seconds, two minutes better than the old time.

A microphone was stuck in her face but she did not want to talk to television reporters; she strode over to her husband to bawl him out in Norwegian for getting her into something that had hurt so much towards the end. She tore off her shoes and hurled them at Jack: 'Come on, we're going! I don't want to stay here any longer.' Grete's legs were stiff, she had blisters on her feet and she was angry.

Her mood soon calmed down. But they could not hang around after the finish since they were flying home straightaway. There was no time even for the prize-giving. Back at the hotel they received an important telephone call.

'At 6.30 tomorrow morning a limousine will be there to pick you up so that Grete can appear on the TV show *Good Morning, America*.'

'We're flying home this afternoon – Grete has to be back at work tomorrow.' She was a secondary school teacher and she had not asked to take the following day off.

This was not understood in America where no one said no to an appearance on live national television. Grete, however, did not like to ring her headmaster in Norway and ask for an extra day off so Arve Moen, the Norwegian who had arranged the air tickets, rang the Bjølsen School claiming to be telephoning on behalf of the organizers. Everything was sorted out, the limousine collected them at the hotel and they drove to the television studio where the winners of the 1978 New York City Marathon, Bill Rodgers and Grete Waitz, were the guests of honour.

Rodgers was a jovial superstar and used to the media. Waitz came over as modest and taciturn. All she had done was win a race and now she had to get home and back to work as soon as possible. Was a marathon victory really something to make a great fuss about?

The Americans took her attitude to be typically Scandinavian. It was a personality trait they found charming in its simplicity and naivety, and they understood the values behind it even if it did not represent something they idealized in their own culture. Her down-to-earth manner immediately made her popular and the Americans loved the story of this tall, fair-haired Scandinavian emerging from deep forests to outclass everyone in the city. There was a Cinderella element to Grete Waitz's debut in the New York City Marathon – she had won it all on her own and in addition had unexpectedly set a world record. A fresh, European face was quickly emerging among the host of women's marathon stars in America.

Grete and Jack Waitz received $20 in taxi fares in 1978, that was all, and then they went home, richer in memories and fairly certain that Grete would retire.

For the Christmas holidays that year Grete and Jack had booked a cabin at Sjusjøen along with Grete's brother and his family. They received an unexpected telephone call from Bob Anderson of the *Runners' World* in California inviting them to Palo Alto outside San Francisco, where there were to be races, running seminars and selections during the Christmas holidays: events of this kind, where newcomers would eagerly garner all the information they could about their sport, were typical of the early phase of the jogging craze. Waitz said no – they had paid a deposit on the cabin and being with the family was the priority anyway.

'Can't you bring your family with you?' Anderson asked, dangling the offer of free travel for all of them.

So Grete and Jack, along with Jan Andersen and his wife and two children, all had a ten-day Christmas holiday in Palo Alto. The Norwegians were beginning to understand the burgeoning power of the financial forces at work within the jogging movement. Grete had always bought her own running equipment and was not used to getting anything for nothing.

Grete was also in the process of cutting down on her athletic involvement and was playing handball for the Romsås Housewives team in the winter of 1979. Jack was terrified, fearing injury every time sturdy housewives tackled his slender wife, but she could sprint away from all of them. She was also doing cross-country skiing and had been in the lead in the major Vidarløpet ski race until the last two kilometres, when bad waymarking had led her off route and she lost the race.

Grete Waitz was still training but not going all out. When they rang from New York to enquire whether she would be back in the autumn of 1979 her attitude to the marathon was still relaxed though she had done several long runs of close to 20 miles on Jack's recommendation. There was a new world record this time, too – 2 hours 27 minutes and 33 seconds, an improvement of five minutes – and even more of a fuss than before, but she was still not fully concentrating on the marathon.

Not until the autumn of 1980, *after* the Moscow Olympics that many Western nations boycotted in the hostile political climate of the Cold War, did Waitz decide to continue. She dropped track running and concentrated fully on road races and marathons. Her decade on the track and heavy training sessions had fortuitously prepared Grete for longer distances; they had forced her to cultivate all the speed she was capable of. She was a typical front-runner on the track, a runner with the will and ability to take the lead and to keep it. This suited her for road races and for the marathon, where she had more space to work hard without crowding and jostling and without a final spurt just a few minutes after the start. Long races were calmer.

This new direction in her career came at the perfect moment. Marathons and road races were taking off in many countries and Grete became the great female star. She got on well in the United States, liked the atmosphere and the people and their direct manner as well as all the opportunities the country offered. And she shed her shyness and diffidence.

Waitz took leave from her teaching job in 1980 and started running full-time, since women as well as men were now beginning to earn money from the sport. Her first contract with Adidas was the equivalent of her teacher's pay in Norway and she did not dare to ask for more. She had neither thought nor dreamt of earning money from athletics – the joy of running and a desire to produce her best had always been the driving force.

Grete Waitz was a charismatic runner without recognizing it herself. There was no tormented facial expression, no heavily rolling torso in the style of Zatopec from her. It was rarely the final sprint that decided the result and there was no wild rejoicing afterwards. She often outdistanced the competition and did much of her running alone. Waitz was a very visible marathon runner because she challenged ingrained gender stereotypes. There was something touching about seeing two pigtails or a swinging ponytail among the cropped hair and beards of the men: tough, feminine charm in an arena where it was not expected.

It was inspiring for everyone to see a woman lying well up in a marathon field and beating most of the men. Women recognized that they too could take part in endurance events in fine style and men were deeply impressed. Because of the rules, men and women rarely competed at the same time in the same sport and the spectators loved seeing Waitz in a crowd of men, sometimes in front, sometimes behind or in the middle, apparently steering a steady course towards yet another marathon victory. Even though her husband might hear her talk and moan about all sorts of problems along the way there was something Nurmi-like and unbeatable about Grete Waitz at her best: it was as if no other competitor stood a chance – and if they did, Waitz would just up the pace.

That is not how she felt herself. She went through all the torments of the race and never took victory for granted.

There are photographs of the field at the start of races, for instance, at L'Eggs Mini Marathon in New York in 1980, a 10-kilometre race that Grete won for the third time. Waitz is standing a little to the left of the many other starters: her concentration seems absolute, she is staring down at the ground, taut and ready to perform at maximum level. None of the other thirty runners in the front row are as focused as she is. They are relaxed, looking to the side, chatting with the woman alongside and smiling. It is as if they are taking part in a different and less serious competition.

Everyone in the race considered Grete Waitz to be the favourite but she was still taking the job more seriously than anyone else there, and so she won. Year after year Waitz stood at the starting line as clear favourite, knowing that everyone expected her to win. It was just a race, a trivial thing seen in the larger context and nothing to moan about, but such thoughts are meaningless to performers with an all-consuming interest in their discipline. They are like creative artists and, caught up in the excitement of events, they live their lives through competition.

The public that watched her win in sovereign style time after time might well believe that it came easy to her. They knew nothing of the steely training sessions when she was down on her knees on the track between 400-metre interval sprints, panting and on the point of tears, physically and mentally exhausted. 'Fifteen seconds again', Jack would say calmly and receive a breathless grunt in reply. 'We can stop now' – while his wife was still panting like a racehorse. She would get up from her knees and run another lap, sink down and feel ill again. 'Fifteen seconds again, we can finish now', Jack repeated, knowing that you can wear yourself down too much in training. Grete would mobilize all her reserves and stick to the schedule to the bitter end. It was this stubborn attitude in training that led her to keep the same pace of one kilometre every 3.45 minutes irrespective of the terrain, and she would push harder on uphill stretches.

Grete and Jack Waitz would often arrive in strange towns late at night. The following morning the two Norwegians would step out of their hotel at 5.00 a.m. into the darkness and run 25 minutes in one direction and then return, having completed their stipulated 50 minutes. That is how they always lived when travelling – they got up early and did the required training. On one occasion when it was snowing in Seattle Grete ran the length of the bus terminal 60 times in order to put in her 15 kilometres. If they finished a planned run in 52 minutes and the programme required 55 minutes she would run an extra lap. If the training plan said 15 x 300 metres at 46–8 seconds, Grete would do them at 46 seconds, always choosing the harder option.

The Waitz couple became world citizens of running during the 1980s. They spent time at month-long training camps at the home of the wealthy Norwegian businessman Erling Dekke Naess in Bermuda – he was fond of Grete and often pressed them to visit him. There was training in Switzerland and winter tours of New Zealand and Australia – the latter with a large group – and everywhere she went Grete was welcomed as an ambassador for women's running. It was not until 1988 that the couple bought an apartment in Florida.

Grete Waitz' career was a family project. Few women runners have received so much assistance from brothers, boyfriend and husband and she rarely trained alone. Her husband Jack loyally turned out for the morning session. They were renowned as early birds in their district of Oslo, always punctual and speedy while the paper-boys and working people were sleepily leaving home and wondering how anyone could train *so* early irrespective of the time of year. Grete kept up a fast pace in the morning and even Rob de Castella, the world marathon champion, thought she was too fast. Her brother Arild was her afternoon partner for a time and her eldest brother Jan Andersen became important for her marathon career, always making himself available as a willing and fearless sparring partner: 'Use me for anything you want. I'll be there as long as I'm able.'[10]

Jan Andersen was the perfect training partner for Grete. Eight years older than her, he was a cross-country skier but had also raced on the track when he was younger and had played handball for the national junior team. Even though he just called himself a keep-fit man and never took part in the national cross-country ski championships, in 1978 he still took second place overall in the major Birkebeiner ski-marathon.

Jan and Grete began training together every afternoon from 1978–9. It was good to have a variety of training partners but only Jan could compete with her.

In the New York City Marathon, where men and women start separately and only join up after eight miles, the two of them always found one another. Jan had a tendency to open too hard and his little sister usually caught up from behind. Jan was ready to sacrifice everything for his sister and would ask: 'How's it going? Do you need water?' He knew she would beat him but never saw it as a defeat. They would run together until she began to draw away since she often ran the second half faster than the first.

Jan cut the length of his stride so as to have the same tempo as his sister. During the 1980s the two of them did a lot of running in and around Oslo, in the Nordmarka forest area or along the Frognerkilen bay, where long intervals were done during the winter. 'How *do* they manage it?' ordinary people asked on seeing these two slim runners with notably similar features, always shoulder to shoulder and often chatting away eagerly in spite of their fast pace. At other times they were silent and serious, as if it was a matter of life or death. Jack was never far away – this was a three-man team. He drove the car or cycled, took the times and said 'Easy now, easy' when Grete set off at an explosive pace, but he knew his warnings were of little use once his wife had found her rhythm. For long runs from Maridalen to their home at Nordstrand they would put bottles of water in the waste-bins at bus-stops along the route. It was the winter holidays in Norway and people waiting at the bus-stops were taken aback to see two frost-covered runners grabbing the bottles and swallowing their contents before running on.

From December 1982 to February 1983 Jan took unpaid leave from his job at a printing works and he did the same the following winter so that he could train overseas with his sister. During these periods Grete paid her brother the equivalent of his normal net wage so he could support his wife and two children.

Her brother took on the job and performed it conscientiously. It was no great burden, rather the opposite: it was an adventure with the chance to travel, to live an active life and meet world-class athletes and all kinds of interesting people. As a big brother he was proud of and impressed by Grete's achievements but she was still just his little sister, a girl he had seen growing up.

Jan and Jack had a good influence on Grete. Her big brother joked and Jack calmed her down. They were solid anchors to hold on to in the whirl of journalists, microphones and intrusive people at the major foreign meetings.

To have a family to lean on in stressful situations is special, it gives strength and security, particularly abroad.

During their morning runs in Central Park in New York passing police-cars would turn on their loudspeakers and say 'Good morning, Mrs Waitz'. On the day after L'Eggs Mini-Marathon passers-by clapped Jan and Grete as they trained in Central Park. The openness and spontaneity with which she was treated in the USA made her particularly happy in that country, per-haps because it was so different from the more reserved Norwegian atti-tudes. But even though she was prepared to sit writing autographs or give interviews after her victories she could also be uncompromising when it came to filtering out approaches. It was Jack who did the negotiating while his wife rested in her hotel room.

'There's someone who wants to talk to you . . .'

The answer was often no – not because of any moodiness but because there are limits to how many approaches an athlete can tolerate when she needs time to recover. Jack would slip downstairs and explain the situation, give a diplomatic refusal, and perhaps even give it another try on behalf of the individual.

The Norwegians even said no when there was a telephone call from President Ronald Reagan's White House staff after Grete's triumph in the 1982 New York City Marathon. They had been away for three weeks and wanted to get home, and they did not have any smart clothes. But it is impossible to turn down an invitation from the American president and Jan and Jack bought their finery at the White House's expense.

First of all there was a photo shoot and press conference on the White House lawn. Then they went into the Oval Office, the president's official of-fice, were introduced to the president and shook his hand before he gave them an account of a 400-metre race he ran as a student.

'Time's up', an aide said after the allotted time and the company was ush-ered out into the corridor where others were waiting for the same purpose.

The three Norwegians received the same invitation the following year. Once again they stood in the Oval Office and once again Ronald Reagan told them word for word the same story of his student race.

Grete had her dark days, too. Brother and sister entered the Boston Marathon in April 1982. They did the first six and a quarter miles in 32 minutes, better than Jan's personal ten-kilometre best and inside a world record time.

Jan soon dropped out, however, and Grete continued alone at a mur-derous pace that looked set to beat the world record by five minutes. But she was teetering on her personal pain threshold and felt the cramps seeping into her until they suddenly became crippling. Even the most phenomenal effort of will could not drive her legs on and she had to be virtually carried into the shower. At the hospital they measured higher levels of pollutant residues in her muscles than had been recorded before. When they visited the Adidas headquarters in Germany a few days later and were going to take their first run Grete could only walk and was so stiff that she could only descend a hill backwards.

Grete Waitz retired in 1990 at the age of 37 but she continued to move in running circles as an ambassador of the sport. She never won an Olympic gold and other women soon passed her in the statistics of the marathon but not even the most grudging competitor could deny her position as a queen of running. She was a symbol of the millions of women who laced on their running shoes during the 1980s and began to lead more active lives. Articles about Waitz and interviews with her have often featured in the culture pages of the newspapers because her life's work as a runner has ranged beyond the narrow confines of sport. There is a statue of her at the Bislett Stadium in Oslo.

Ingrid

There should actually have been two Norwegian women at the start of the New York City Marathon in 1978. Ingrid Kristiansen (née Christensen) was also invited but had to take an exam in Trondheim the following day. She had run a student marathon in 2 hours 45 minutes in Trondheim the year before and had many long-distance races under her belt as a ski-racer. Running long distances had been Ingrid's great passion from the time she moved into the elite level in 1971 at the age of fifteen. Ingrid and Grete Andersen (later Waitz) met for the first time that year when they shared a room at the Helsinki European Championships. As two newcomers they shared the experience of international athletics at close quarters and had no idea of the changes the future would bring to their athletic careers.

Ingrid was the world best of her particular year when it came to the 1,500 metres, the longest championship distance for women at the time, but she was just as much a cross-country skier with a phenomenal basis of fitness as a result of the many forest and cross-country ski-tours of her youth. She was a prodigy without equal in Europe at a time when children's and youth athletics were permitted in Norway. The girl with legs like a daddy-long-legs and a will of iron was built for long-distance running.

'You must turn up at Lerkendal to do some distance running', her coach told her when she was fifteen and she dutifully appeared at the stadium in Trondheim.

'Why should I run round here?'

'It's important you maintain your stride and to time the kilometres,' her coach said.

'But I'd rather train out in the country.'

'That's not the right way for you', her coach said.

Before a national championships meeting in Oslo the fifteen-year-old met up with Grete Andersen for a long run around Sognsvann lake. The fine, gentle paths and flat terrain around this picturesque lake was where the great stars trained before the big meetings at Bislett Stadium. The two girls ran around the lake once, barely five kilometres, and Ingrid wanted to carry on. No, that was the whole training session and, according to the male coach, girls should not run farther than that. Ingrid felt cheated: it was only after a few kilometres that the real pleasure kicked in – once you were properly warmed up, had found your rhythm and were gliding through the forest sensing the delights of hard exercise in the open air. That is not what a Norwegian girl was supposed to think in 1971. Ingrid, however, was rare enough as a 1,500-metre runner and she was a new type of girl – one who could take on boys of the same age.

Norway, small as it is, produced two absolutely top-class long-distance women in the 1980s and both of them found their true athletics métier by changing direction relatively late in their careers.

Ingrid was also a cross-country skier of international standard. She was the best of the women skiers on snow-free ground but she lost against the best on snow, particularly over easier parts of the course where poling technique became increasingly important as the 1970s progressed. On the athletics track she seemed a little heavy on her feet in comparison with the specialists even though she was fast. Every spring cross-country skiing would persist in her physical memory and deceive her into believing that the thighs rather than the lower leg should do the hard work in running as well. It took her some time to adjust her stride to running on the track.

Around about 1980 Ingrid Kristiansen cut out cross-country skiing and focused completely on running. She shed muscle mass in her upper body, lost a little weight and refined her stride. She also noted how different the milieux of the two sports were: at the cross-country ski training camp she had shared a double bed with her fiercest rival for half the year, whereas in athletics the competitors tended to keep themselves to themselves. She felt that the athletics world was more secretive, less open and above-board, particularly at international level.

After taking the bronze in the marathon at the 1982 European Championships – the first international marathon championship for women – Kristiansen concentrated fully on the new athletics world championships of the following year and on the 1984 Olympics.

At the turn of 1983 she was working full-time as a bio-engineer and training twice a day, hungry for success as never before. In the middle of January she won the Houston Marathon, returned to Norway to catch up on lost working time and then went off to two big road races in the USA in order to compete against international elite runners. She was rather tired and feeling the cold, but that was normal for anyone who had been crossing timezones along with heavy training routines and full-time work. Things got worse during the world cross-country championships in England later in the spring: she made very heavy weather of it there and came in 35th place.

That evening her coach Johan Kaggestad was talking to his wife, who had watched the championships on television. 'I think Ingrid looks as if she's pregnant', she said – her bust looked bigger.

Ingrid Kristiansen of Norway; a dominant force in 1970s and '80s distance running.

On the flight home Johan did not dare ask Ingrid whether she was pregnant but she went to the doctor and it turned out that she was expecting a baby in August. As with many top-level sportswomen her menstruation was irregular and its absence was not a sure sign of pregnancy.

Ingrid's son Gaute was born on 13 August 1983 in the middle of the world athletics championships. Ingrid watched the men's marathon on television in the maternity ward, not in the least resigned to giving up, even though childbirth frequently spelled the end of a top-level athletics career for women. 'It's time to stop running now,' Ingrid's mother said. 'You've kept going for a long time, now it's time to settle down and have a family.'

But Ingrid had no desire to give up. If male colleagues in the national team could have children and continue so could she. The interest in women's long-distance running was growing rapidly, the number of competitions was increasing and one championship was following another. With hindsight it turned out that her pregnancy had come at just the right moment.

In 1983 Ingrid was living in Stavanger since her husband was working in the oil industry and spent much of his time on the North Sea oil-rigs. Ingrid sought out suitable places for training. She would leave the pram and run backwards and forwards, short stretches, uphill stretches – just a few moments away from the pram but enough to be effective as training. It may have looked strange and rather desperate and it was certainly an unusual sight in Norway or anywhere else in the world – but there was no other way.

There were few Norwegian women in 1983 who were both breastfeeding and focusing on elite-level sport. The world cross-country ski champion, Ingrid's friend Berit Aunli, had had a baby six months early without retiring so Ingrid knew at least one person in a similar situation to her own while she was trying to combine child-care and a running career. Moreover her body felt stronger and she had a higher pain threshold than before the birth; and babies enrich an otherwise egocentric existence. For Ingrid a baby was the greatest gift of all, proof that in the greater context sport is unimportant: she suddenly found herself with a new and very vocal boss who gave her a new and much wider perspective on life. Even though those around her thought she should settle down as the mother of a small baby, Ingrid herself saw child-care as something fine and positive, and what could have marked the end of an only partially fulfilled running career became instead an advantage that served to lift her to a new level.

But Grete Waitz was lurking in the background. Ingrid had never beaten her in a race they both finished in the thirteen seasons since they first competed against each other in 1971. After her pregnancy she confided in her coach Johan Kaggestad, who said: 'You train just as much and just as hard as Grete and you can be just as good.' As always, he was enthusiastic and his pleasure in sport and performance was infectious.

Willy Railo had been a sprinter and was a specialist in sport psychology. After ten minutes conversation with Ingrid he said:

'You have a problem. You have a Grete Waitz complex.'

'I know that. That's why I'm here.'

Railo had methods of erasing complexes of this kind. Known as mental training it was not a new discovery but it was Railo who introduced the system to Norway. It was carried out for five or ten minutes daily during or immediately after training and Ingrid was to visualize that she was always out in front, that she could not see any backs in front of her in the imagined races.

'How long will it be before this has any effect?'

'A month', Railo said his soothing voice.

The Norwegian cross-country championships were held in Hønefoss less than three weeks later. Ingrid won the short race and was also entered for the long-distance race – and beat Grete Waitz for the first time. Just sport, of course, but nevertheless a fantastic experience for Ingrid.

Immediately afterwards she beat both Grete Waitz and Zola Budd from South Africa in the Sentrumsløpet race in Oslo. But her respect for Grete remained so great that in the 1984 Olympic marathon she stayed behind Grete, positioning herself in relation to her, and it was Joan Benoit from the USA who put on a spurt and won. In her later career Ingrid did not listen to the advice of others about race tactics and followed her own intuition instead.

After the 1984 Olympics Grete and Ingrid rarely competed against each other. They did not train together and each of them took her own road through life.[11]

In 1981 Ingrid discovered that she could draw energy from the crowd, enabling her to run faster. Grete Waitz was trying to set a new world record for the 5,000 metres at the Bislett Stadium in Oslo that year. The crowd was shouting encouragement clapping and hammering on the advertising bill-boards until Grete dropped out. For ten to fifteen seconds there was absolute silence until the crowd noticed that Ingrid was lying in second place and transferred its support to her.

Year by year, helped by Johan Kaggestad and his wife, she learnt to be a more independent competitor: their influence stimulated her and made her believe that anything was possible. Kaggestad took his wife's advice on the thought processes of top-class sportswomen since they differed to some extent from those of men – as did the practical aspects of their lives. To a great extent, however, they followed the same recipe as male runners. Ingrid could both tolerate and enjoy a lot of training and there were few competitors who took so much pleasure in training.

In 1984 the Kristiansens moved to Oslo and installed a specially made treadmill in their house since they could not afford an American model. Financial support for women distance runners in Norway was meagre and Ingrid's initial budget was only 5,000 Nkr a year, and that included paying Kaggestad as her coach.

She began to run full-time and set aside an hour in the morning and another in the afternoon for training, often on the treadmill, which was a welcome relief from slushy winter surfaces. No other Norwegian runner had covered so many miles on a treadmill and it made her stride lighter and quicker. It was a full life in other respects, too, and she had a wide social circle and many interests. Running was both a cherished hobby and a job that was bringing in a growing income – and Ingrid Kristiansen still wanted to break records.

She certainly did break records: in 1986 she held the world records in the 5,000 metres (14 minutes 37.33 seconds), the 10,000 metres (30 minutes 13.74) seconds and the marathon (2 hours 21 minutes 6 seconds). In 1987 she turned out in the London Marathon with a painful scrape on her calf which she managed to 'put out of her mind' for 21 miles, at which point she seemed on course for 2 hours 18 minutes, but the last few miles were considerably slower. The 1987 Sandnes Half Marathon was another very fast race: she won in 1 hour 6 minutes 40 seconds, immediately behind the men and with a personal record of thirteen minutes at the 5,000-metre mark. No other woman long-distance runner before or since has been number one in the world at so many distances at the same time.

No one, however, is immune to injury. There is nothing worse for runners at the peak of their training than to have to put off their planned preparation for days or weeks before major events.

Ingrid was among the top runners in the 1980s who began using the new, alternative training method of running in the water while wearing a life-jacket. The jacket gives the body some support so that the feet do not touch the bottom and the legs then run at a high cadence. It is gentle on the legs but, in Ingrid's view, rather boring and it made training an effort. To make the hours in the pool pass more quickly she trained even harder and became overtrained in the build up to the 1987 World Championships when, because of injury, cycling and water-running were the only forms of training open to her. For the only time in her life Kristiansen was overtrained.

On her return to Norway from the training meeting in St Moritz in Switzerland in preparation for the World Championships just one month later, Ingrid was unable to run normally. She went to her doctor Hans-Gerhard Hovind and his response was, 'I'll take charge of you for 48 hours.'

He gave her electro-acupuncture twice on the first day and after 24 hours she was able to trot. Continued specialist treatment improved things further and was crowned by her victory in the 10,000 metres at that season's World Championships.

She found it useful to train with men and joined the training sessions of the BUL Club in Oslo. It was advantageous to both sides. It was unusual for men of a good level to have a woman training with them and Ingrid was always visible in the middle of the crowd of men both when training and in competition. In international marathons she came across a strange brand of male. In televised races certain men focused on running among the leading group of women in order to give TV-exposure to a sponsor. It was easy enough for a well-trained man to stay with the lead women for a while, where he might disrupt the tempo and cause an uneven pace since he did not need to complete the race. If the women stuck with him it could have a negative impact later on when the man either eased off and cruised to the finish or simply dropped out. International road races were a shop-window for all kinds of clowns.

During Ingrid's third pregnancy in 1993 she suffered even more sickness than during her second, when she had been in poor health for seven months. In 1993 she spent large parts of the day in her bedroom, unwell, feeling and being sick. She was unable to hold down even liquid food and drink. The days dragged out while her eldest boy was at school and the second at nursery. It was wearing, both physically and psychologically. The vomiting fits meant that she was taken to hospital on a number of occasions to have her nutritional and liquid balance restored: she was informed that some 3 per cent of Norwegian pregnancies are afflicted by this level of nausea and sickness.

Half an hour after the birth her nausea disappeared and she felt good – strong and motivated enough to start thinking of the 1996 Olympics. She started off carefully with something like a run five days after giving birth, her body feeling light after having put on something like sixteen or seventeen pounds and then losing it. It ought to be possible to return to the international elite for the third time.

But physically something was not right. Sensations she had occasionally had in races such as the 10,000 metres at the 1991 World Championships, when she had felt she was running outside her own body and came in seventh, pointed to some kind of imbalance. At the Osaka marathon she had felt fine at the eighteen-mile drink station but had to drop out a few minutes later, unable to continue. She was checked for diabetes but no one came up with anything until she was examined by the kinesiologist Terje Skriver. His diagnosis was hypoglycemia: the pancreas produces too much insulin, which can lead to a rapid drop in the levels of blood sugar. Drastic dietary changes were necessary. Coffee, tea and all fast carbohydrates such as bread were forbidden whereas protein and fat were good. She adapted to the new diet very quickly but was unable to build up the motivation to fulfil her plans for 1996. She retired the year before without any sense of defeat, having set her mark on international long-distance running and having simultaneously held the world records at all distances from the 5,000 metres to the marathon – the only person in history to do so.

Her hypoglycemia was possibly a result of the frequent sickness during her pregnancies. It is difficult enough to carry and bear a child but if we add to that the effort to get back into the international elite of distance runners then the strain on body and mind is multiplied.

Ingrid Kristiansen put herself through a lot in order to achieve her goals, tried much that was unusual for the mother of small children. The most important motivation behind an international career that spanned two decades was the vibrant joy in movement that was with her from her forest tours in Trondheim's Bymarka as a small girl to when she was collecting world championships and grand titles in the international arena. She was one of the few who came into elite running as a teenager in the years when distance running for women was in its starting phase. She kept at it through her years as a student, at work and as mother of a growing family, and she went from being a lone wolf to being part of a mass movement for the women of many countries. Ernst van Aaken was right: long-distance running suits women. The critics were silenced when women of all ages and shapes laced up their jogging shoes.

27
Mr Comeback

He ran faster and faster, almost forgetting where he was, even though
his fellow prisoners lined up cheering and clapping something they
had never seen in a prison before.
—Henry Rono running 20 kilometres in a 70-metre-long
common room in a US prison in 1986

Some people are dancers in everything they do. Irrespective of how they
move the dancer in them is visible even though it is not always easy to
point to what it is – but there is a certain something, an elegance and grace-
fulness.

Some people are runners through and through. Henry Rono from Kenya
is one of them, hand-crafted by nature to run far and fast, an antelope on
two legs.

Rono stuck out from the crowd at Pullman, Washington State University in the USA, not just because he was an African in a town with few black
people but because there was something about his flowing gait, long legs and
swaying back that seemed adapted to moving across the savannah. Everything about his posture pointed to a man not brought up with tarmacadam
and motor traffic. People used to worry because he crossed the road without
a sideways glance, as if cars did not exist.

The environment in an American university town in 1976 was very different from that of the Kenyan Highlands. Rono's native language was Nandi
and he hardly spoke English when he arrived in the USA. Language problems
made everyday life hard, not least because his coach John 'Motormouth'
Chaplin spoke very quickly and was difficult to understand.

Rono won virtually all of his races. He had no choice but to adapt to the
lifestyle in the richest country in the world, where he was living on a scholarship and getting a free education. No one was very particular about his
studies and if the grades were poor Chaplin's contacts would make sure
that everything was straightened out. Rono was grateful to have been
given free entry into the American university system and simultaneously
into the world's biggest athletics arena. But few people understood how
little he liked it and how homesick he was. It was not just that he needed to
quickly become Americanized, to recognize the cultural codes and behave
properly. Would an American sportsman resident in Kenya have managed
to adapt quickly to the Kenyan life-style and Kenyan attitudes? Would he
have managed the so-called primitive life in the Rift Valley without being
homesick or being seen as odd?

Henry Rono was born in Kiptaragon, a village in the Nandi Hills in the Rift Valley in 1952. As a two-year-old he fell off the back of his uncle's bicycle, caught his leg in the spokes and broke his ankle. To his mother's distress, the boy could only crawl for the next four years and he was six before he could walk normally.

Like many local men his father was working for a white farmer at this stage while Henry's mother and the children looked after the family plot and milked their cows. As his father was ploughing the fields one day a huge snake appeared over the front wheel of the tractor: Henry's father was so frightened he leapt off the tractor and landed on the plough. He was killed instantly.

It was a hard blow for the family, particularly for a small boy since among the Nandi it was mothers who brought up sons until they were six and fathers took over thereafter. At the age of ten boys took on the duties of a man – hunting, working the fields and tending the animals. Henry was raised by two strong women, his mother and his grandmother, but felt the lack of a father. Once he had learnt to walk again he worked as a herd-boy for a neighbour until the authorities complained that he was not attending school. He started school at the age of ten and completed elementary school.

These two childhood events had an effect on Henry's personality. Few if any of those who later watched him perform in the great athletics arenas knew about the poverty of his background, his struggle to survive and all the dreams those things had engendered. Rono was tempered by harsh conditions but he also had deep scars in his soul.

Henry's family adhered firmly to the traditions of the tribe. When he was ten his family became more exposed to Western culture through the medium of school and church. He also had two front teeth extracted from his lower jaw. This tribal ritual, in which the child sat still throughout the extraction, without anaesthetic and without showing pain, was gradually becoming less common. The man who performed the procedure was surprised when Henry came to his hut and opened his mouth: 'I thought you'd just started school. You won't be able to speak English properly because the air will escape through the gap.'[1]

His mother had wanted her son to undergo the symbolic but painful ritual, though there was also a practical aspect to it: if people became ill and their mouths swelled up it was possible to feed them through the gap.

Rono played football at school but finding the money for school was a burden. His mother had to marry off Henry's sister to a soldier for a dowry of five cows, five sheep, two goats and 500 Kenyan shillings – almost enough to pay the school fees – and Henry worked the land for a tea-planter to cover the rest. It was not until 1968 that he had any dreams of becoming a runner.

That was the year that Rono heard on the radio that that Kip Keino had won the 1,500 metres gold in the Mexico City Olympics. The news spread like wildfire through Kenya and changed the country forever – from then on it was called a land of runners. Keino, himself one of the Nandi tribe, was the new national hero, an inspiration to thousands of youngsters, including Rono who decided there and then to drop football and become a runner. Three years later Keino came to the sports arena eight miles from Rono's home to talk to the people and an expectant Henry was there among the crowd gathered to see the hero, who had to raise his arms to show where he was. Keino's words and presence captivated Rono and he ran home, excited as a child, without stopping or slowing down and with a profound desire to become the best runner in the world. It is reminiscent of a religious experience or vocation: Rono's call in life was to become the world's best runner.

Many people dream of becoming the best in the world at their particular sport or occupation and only one in a million pull it off. Natural selection takes place along the way. Most people's talent and willpower are not up to the task, they cannot make the necessary sacrifices and feel that striving for the top is actually unimportant – at least when it means sacrificing personal happiness.

That, however, is not the way Henry Rono and others destined for the top think. Apart from education running was the most important thing to Henry and in order to gain access to the optimal training conditions he had to join the Kenyan army. When he enlisted in 1973 at the age of 21 he was given his first pair of shoes – army boots, which he proceeded to run in. He soon changed them for a lighter variety. Up until then Rono had been working on his own, running barefoot through the hilly countryside at home, talking to other runners and gathering their experiences. He was self-willed, with an independent streak that was to characterize the rest of his career. It was not that he was difficult – quite the reverse, he was modest and quiet – but he had an untamed quality and this independent streak would sometimes come to the surface. This unpredictability and his ability to surprise or disconcert people contributed strongly to the legendary status he achieved later. No one could predict what might come. He functioned on his feelings, had a sanguine outlook, but was unusually tough too.

The conditions for runners in the Kenyan army at the start of the 1970s were pretty well perfect. They had two or three training sessions a day and, along with the runners in the police and prison service, belonged to a small and privileged class of sportsmen. Kip Keino, for instance, was in the police force and the group of state-employed athletes got together for meetings and annual championships. In terms of practical benefits the Kenyan runners were not disadvantaged in comparison to their European and American competitors: their position was rather like the state professionals of Eastern Europe, where the authorities provided for their sporting elites by means of military ranks and wages.

Henry suffered depression for the first time in 1975. Eager for success, he threw out all his jogging shoes and spikes and began wearing heavy army boots with the idea that a hard training regime in them would strengthen his legs. After a couple of months the ankle that had been damaged when he was a child began to cause problems. Treatment was of no help, neither modern nor traditional medicine, and Rono resorted to a witch-doctor in desperation. He himself believed the problem was a psychological one which could perhaps be traced back to his childhood traumas. But the Nandi also believed that sudden success could lead to jealous people putting bad spells on the successful individual, which is why a witch-doctor was needed to drive away the evil. The injury healed itself and was later shown to have been caused by the boots.

Then Henry moved to the United States. The coach John Chaplin treated his white runners differently from the way he handled Rono and the other Kenyans. The Africans felt the whites received fewer tongue-lashings and more humane treatment.

Henry Rono used alcohol to dull his anxiety and misery. After the second training session of the day he would go straight to the bar and stay there until closing time at 2 a.m., talking to the other customers – who frequently stood him drinks – or sitting on his own mulling things over. He would go to sleep at 2 or 3 a.m., bloated with beer and unhealthy bar-food. Training with a hangover was the next task and morning after morning he forced himself out of bed in the apartment he shared with other Kenyans, tired, with bloodshot eyes and in no real state to train. But willpower can move mountains and Rono would go out and sweat out the impurities, the alcohol and the bad food. Henry brooded over things. 'Loosen up a bit. Don't take everything so seriously', Chaplin told him.

His coach recommended having some fun, a party now and again, a jollier attitude to life – but he disapproved strongly when Henry got a girlfriend. Alcohol was acceptable, women were not; and Henry's performance was noticeably worse when he had a girlfriend.

In 1977 Henry Rono regularly noticed that there was blood in his stools and the doctor diagnosed chronic stomach ulcers brought on by alcohol, stress and anxiety. Henry was only 25 and his organs were already showing dangerous signs of wear and tear.

Many people asked why John Chaplin did not see to it that his best runner was dried out. 'What harm does Henry do when he drinks?' he said, 'He doesn't hurt anyone, does he?' That was true – but he was, of course, hurting himself. The coach said nothing as long as Henry was winning. The exception to that was on 6 May 1978 when Henry was storming around the University of Oregon track in Eugene in the 3,000 metres steeplechase. His time was clearly up on the world record of 8 minutes 8.0 seconds held by Anders Gårderud from Sweden and the crowd was cheering hard in anticipation of a historic moment.

Suddenly John Chaplin began to wave a white handkerchief, telling Rono to slow down. 'This state doesn't deserve the world record', he said, referring to the rivalry between the states of Washington and Oregon when it came to running. Rono was not supposed to bring glory to Oregon but to keep his records for more appropriate occasions.

Rono was broken-hearted. It was like being physically tortured. The crowd understood what was happening and began booing, some of them even climbing over the fence and jumping down on the track to berate Chaplin. Newspapermen clustered around Rono and the atmosphere was chaotic. It was a nasty experience and a salutary lesson: like most sportsmen, Rono listened to his coach and looked up to him but the incident in Eugene showed Chaplin's worst side.[2]

In 1978 Henry Rono was named the world's top sportsman, irrespective of which branch of sport. That year he broke four world records over distances from the 3,000 metres (7 minutes 32.1 seconds) and 3,000 metre steeplechase (8 minutes 5.4 seconds) to the 5,000 (13 minutes 8.4) and the 10,000 metres (27 minutes 22.5). He appeared in 60 races that season, winning 56 of them. His defeats were over shorter distances or when he was acting as pacemaker before dropping back. There was still much for him to do on the athletics track but he was basking in success and picking up hefty prize-money.

But Rono also experienced the down-sides of success, learnt what it was like to be hurled from anonymity into the limelight of international fame. It was not all roses for a man of independent mind to be on Nike's wage bill from 1978 to 1983, with the huge sum of $60,000 as a guaranteed honorarium in that last year. The relationship ended when Rono did not take part in the 1984 Los Angeles Olympics and the parting was not without friction. Rono felt that Nike was controlling him too much but Nike, naturally enough, had demands of its own and had no wish to be paying an alcoholic whose athletics performances had become extremely unpredictable and who was forever trying to get back into the top ranks.

Henry was Mr Comeback. There are few world record holders who have trained themselves back in – or tried to do so – so often and then fallen so low again. It became a pattern, a comfort almost, something to attach his identity to. Even if he drank himself senseless, became physically bloated and hit bottom again, there was still the chance to train hard and return to record-breaking form. He had done it in 1981 after all, when people who knew him saw him in Boulder, Colorado, in the spring and he could hardly run for half an hour. People who met him trotting breathlessly along the paths around Boulder laughed at his plans for further records. Leave him alone, he is living in hope, they thought, feeling sorry for him, particularly when he arrived in Europe in June after desperately telephoning European contacts asking to be invited to events. The rumour mill said he was in the grip of the demon drink while Rono pleaded to be given a chance. He went to Finland where, given his overweight condition, he was outclassed by club runners and took over fifteen minutes to finish the 5,000 metres. His fitness was on an upward curve, however, while his weight was going down and in September 1981 he broke his fifth world record at Knarvik outside Bergen, doing the 5,000 metres in 13 minutes 6 seconds.

Then Rono went back to Kenya to celebrate his record with long binges and loose living with friends old and new. He failed to appear at a pre-arranged meeting in Australia so the Australian Maurie Plant jumped on a flight to Nairobi to find him, having no idea where to start. They bumped into each other in the premises of the Kenyan Athletics Federation in Nairobi where Rono happened to be, knowing nothing about the Australian and his errand.

'I'll have to go home first', Rono said, meaning the Nandi Hills 160 miles or so away.

Plant rented a car and they set off late in the evening but the car broke down in the middle of the night in the middle of nowhere. Plant, who had never been to Africa before and was unprepared to spend the night on a dark and deserted African country road, feared they would be attacked by hungry lions.

They found a car to tow them but the rope was so short that Plant almost crashed into the back as they lurched at suicidal speeds along bendy and bumpy roads. Australian newspapers published sensational stories about the man who had gone to Kenya on the off-chance of finding Rono but who was now feared dead since no one had heard anything from him.

On the way back to Nairobi an increasingly inebriated Rono wanted them to pull in at various drinking dens. By the time they arrived back there at two in the morning Plant was sweat-soaked and exhausted but happy to be alive and still have Rono with him. They flew to Australia at the end of five days of confusion. No organizer has ever risked so much to get his star attraction to an event.

Rono trained seriously in Melbourne for a few days and put in some good performances.

Alcohol was Rono's comfort in turbulent times. When he was winning everyone wanted to talk to Rono but few people were interested in him as a man. Few people really took him seriously and understood that he too thought about things other than running: he was not just a running machine on whom they could simply pin a starting number and expect him, in some mysterious way, to outrun everyone else.

Some of Rono's performances in these years were incredible. In Australia in the winter of 1980 he disappeared on a two-day binge immediately before a meeting, was found and delivered back at his hotel in a virtually unconscious state. The English promoter Andy Norman commanded Rono down onto the track at four o'clock the same afternoon saying if he did not appear he would be sent back to Africa.

Norman flogged him round the track for ten laps. Rono did each of them in 60 seconds flat followed by a 20-second break, throwing up four times. Four days later there was a 10,000 metre race on the programme and Rono seemed to be right out of the game. At the halfway stage the leaders came close to lapping him but he suddenly pulled himself together and set off at a ferocious pace, passing runner after runner and winning in 27 minutes 31 seconds, the world's best time of the season. That fight-back simply served to bolster the legend around the man.

Many of the people who saw Rono at close quarters in the 1980s were shocked. The combination of that much alcohol and training was unprecedented. For years he used his morning session to take the edge off his hangover before training properly during his afternoon session.

The next step was to drink away the rest of the day after the first training session. As he sank even further he could not even manage the morning session and would break off and shamble away in frustration. There were periods when everything revolved around drink. 'The drinking became the race', he said and he went at it as hard or harder than he had running, drinking up to 40 beers a day. His friends and the athletics public would come across Rono as a spectator at events, reeling around since the organizers did not have the heart to throw out a legend.

Much of his prize money was sent home to Kenya, as was the prize for a marathon in the autumn of 1986. Rono went into a New Jersey bank:

'Hello, I want to open an account.'

'That will cost $25.'

'I'm very hungry after running this morning. I'll have breakfast first and come back.'

Rono went out, meeting two aggressive policemen on the way.

'Can I see your identification?'

Rono showed them and had no idea why they were asking so brusquely.

'Are you certain you're Henry Rono?' He had not noticed that his name had been misspelt as Rond and the police believed his identity card was false.

'Do you recognize this man?' They showed him a picture of a black man suspected of having robbed several banks in the area.

'No.'

'We think this is you.'

'No, he's nothing like me.'

'Where do you live?'

'Two blocks away.'

'Let's go there.'

'Have you got a key?'

Rono handed over the key and they handcuffed him.

They let themselves in and ransacked the apartment without finding anything suspicious apart from a cassette player on the dining-table. Switching it on, they listened to a lesson on motivation for sportsmen given to Rono by his coach John DeHart. The policemen listened to the end, by which time they were even more certain they were dealing with a hardened criminal. They went out and got into two cars: five policemen altogether, two of them in uniform and three plain clothes, plus the bank clerk who had pointed out the criminal.[3]

At the police station Rono swore he was a runner, not a criminal, and gave his coach's name as a reference. But DeHart did not want to provide a reference since they had only known each other two months and, given Rono's risky reputation, DeHart did not rely on him.

Rono was put in a cell. He was given an opportunity to talk to his coach on the telephone and DeHart explained that Rono was suspected of several bank robberies in New Jersey. The police believed he had run to the banks, robbed them and run away – all under the guise of a training programme. He had a motive and was fit enough to make his escape by running through the streets in broad daylight. It was a brilliantly simple way – or so the police thought – for a faded and bankrupt running star to get hold of money. And both in the USA and elsewhere they were familiar with jogger robbers – criminals in training gear.

Rono ended up in gaol, in a section for black prisoners, separate from whites and Latinos. A doctor at the check-in recognized him and suspected something was amiss but could do nothing to help.

An inmate came up to him after breakfast the following morning: 'You were a famous runner, weren't you?'[4]

It was not long before all the prisoners in the dormitory knew and came crowding round him, eager to know how he had ended up there and honoured to have someone so famous sharing their fate.

Rono was in despair. He had two comfort blankets in life, running and alcohol, and drink was certainly not available here. He looked at the 70-metre-long room. Could he do some training here? He moved the beds, made a passage between the bunks and the inmates and began to run slowly, stiff and tired after so little sleep. He ran faster and faster, almost forgot where he was even though the prisoners lined up cheering and clapping at something they had never seen in prison before. 'I've seen him on TV', said one; 'Look at those easy strides', said another. Rono was excited, he had an audience, admirers, it was almost like being out on the track. He was in prison but running was freedom and they could not take that from him even if a warder did shout, 'You try and escape and I'll shoot you.'

Did the warder really believe he was going to escape because he was a good runner? If so, it was as stupid as the police believing he was a running bank-robber. The police and the warders thought that someone so quick on his feet was out of their control. He might shoot off and disappear down a back street. In a society full of waddling, fat people anyone like Rono was a reject. And he was also so obviously an East African. Black Americans are rarely long-distance types. They can produce top speeds for a minute or two, or sprint with an American football or basketball in their fists. But this black man, with his two missing bottom teeth and an unusually good physique, did not fit in. Rono was the man in the fairytale who ran to the end of the world to fetch the tea-water. The prisoners and the warders saw him in that light – a fantasy figure and not just a sportsman. He was the same colour as them and he was in prison, but he was also something quite different and unknown, someone who lived by and for running – and he clung on to that in every situation.

These training sessions in prison were very special. Henry Rono really discovered how much running meant to him, how wonderful it was to stride out in an enclosed situation. He ran for almost an hour and a half that first morning and felt transformed by it, full of endorphins and the juices of joy. In the evening he added some more circuits so that the day's total reached 30 kilometres.

Henry was soon asked to accompany a warder. He was put in a car, taken to another prison where the facilities were better and given a cell to himself – food brought to his cell, a shower in the room, television and plenty to read. The only disadvantage was that there was no room to run. He continued training on the spot instead, lifting his knees and pretending to run for over an hour.

The following Monday Rono heard how things stood. He was accused of robbing four banks in New Jersey, crimes so serious that if proven they would lead to a sentence of many years in gaol. But he had been mistaken for a criminal with a similar name and his lawyer plugged away at that. After eighteen hours of negotiation Rono was at last a free man, painfully aware that he had escaped with only six days in prison because he was a famous runner: if that had not been the case, even though he was innocent, there was every chance he would have been found guilty.

The bank, which had of course caused his arrest by misidentifying him, wanted to avoid a suit for damages and offered him $50,000 compensation. Rono's lawyer, however, said they should sue for $10 million: the case lasted two years and the bank was forced to pay $75,000. The lawyer took $35,000, leaving the rest for Henry – which was less than he would have got had he not sued.

After his release in the late autumn of 1986 Henry signed into a clinic for alcoholics in Philadelphia but two weeks later moved in with a friend in Boston and quickly fell back into his old drinking habits.

Rono lived a rootless existence, moving between the east and west coasts of the USA, living with old friends, scraping an existence from prize money. There was no one else in the same situation – a former world record holder roaming from place to place and running for a living in between drinking bouts. Homelessless and athletic effort eroded body and soul.

State support and welfare benefits were not an option in Rono's case since he did not have a Green Card or official documents. He did not have what was necessary to get them and he lacked the right contacts until an Italian-born lawyer took up his case.

'Rono', the lawyer said, 'surely you're not the famous runner?'

Henry liked reactions of that kind. A number of earlier American star runners worked for shoe companies, had started businesses or lectured about the secrets of running, but Rono was not part of that network and was in no position to take advantage of his earlier achievements. He felt ex-cluded because he was foreign and because he was black.

People said that Rono was unable to hold down a job but it was not always that easy just to take a lousy job and keep it. He had only been at a chicken factory in Eugene in Oregon for a few hours before rumours were spreading among the employees about the new man with the elegant walk.

'Who are you?' a supervisor asked and Rono was sacked because the boss of the factory did not want any mentions in the press. Journalists and photographers followed in his footsteps as he meandered from job to job, a day here, five days there, sometimes a few weeks, always afraid of being revealed as a former star in the athletics world and so losing the job. It is hardly surprising that he kept very quiet about his past: in his situation any talk of his own achievements could easily be taken for deception or delusion.

So Henry did not talk about his time as a star. The inhabitants of hostels and shelters for the homeless rarely talk voluntarily about their past and when they do it is usually to embellish or lie about it. The dialogue of the disempowered homeless is silence and trivia.

Henry, bloated as he was, tried to get back into physical shape. When the Salvation Army closed the doors every morning and told the inmates to return at the end of the afternoon Henry would sometimes take a training run through the streets. Who would believe that that overweight jogger was one of the greatest long-distance stars of the age? An observant eye might have noticed that this was no ordinary jogger trying to get rid of his pot-belly because Rono would quickly fall into a flowing rhythm and his face take on the characteristic expression that said 'I'm running and for me there is nothing better in the world, problems don't exist and everything is just fine.' He would forget the misery of homelessness, or almost anyway, since the excess weight was a burden to a man who had run slim and light as a feather. Perhaps I can manage yet another comeback?

The approach of another Olympic Games might shake him from his trance and binges and in 1988 Gordon Cooper wanted to sponsor Rono's preparation for possible participation in the Seoul Olympics of that summer.

Rono could not refuse. Anything was better than drifting homeless and broke from town to town in the USA, living on friendships that were wearing thin. A training camp would at least mean free board and lodging for a while and Rono probably did not think farther ahead than that when he and the coach James Mibey went to the selected locality, an island off the coast of Tijuana, a paradise for wealthy anglers. 'Be focused,' Cooper said, 'this is the perfect training place for you.' 'Make sure he doesn't drink', he said to Mibey.[5]

Rono was completely unbalanced. Earlier bad experiences with Mibey made him deeply unhappy when they were living together. Rono was like a bankrupt boxer who wanted to get back into top form but lacked the willpower and inner drive to do so, however much he desired to rediscover his old self. He was not a helpless drinker without any direction in life, he was a dedicated sportsman; drinking and drifting were things of the past; he just had to take himself by the scruff of the neck and everything would be fine. That is what he hoped and thought in his brighter moments, until his thoughts turned back in a negative direction again.

Rono trained on the island but drank himself stupid every evening. At the same time he was corresponding with a sports psychologist at Oregon

State University who was sending him psychology books. For the umpteenth time in his career the conditions for a comeback by Henry Rono had been put in place.

The diagnosis was depression – depression because he drank so much and so destroyed all the possibilities, but also because he did not get on with Mibey. Rono's lifestyle was destructive. Alcoholics do not only drink because their internal organs are screaming for more liquid poison, they drink because they are living miserable lives. The force of habit is strong and Rono could not discipline his habit.

'Why don't you stop drinking and train properly?' Mibey asked. 'You've got more talent than anyone in the world and you're throwing it away.'

'You don't understand', Henry said, stirring up more trouble. One day he almost flew at Mibey in fury and, after another quarrel, he lay awake drinking hard while Mibey was asleep in his room. In the early hours of the morning Rono burst in yelling, 'You want me to train! Come on then we'll train!'[6]

Mibey looked afraid and thought his companion had gone mad. In the darkness they ran for hours on the beach to the sound of the waves, both of them drunk, until Mibey could not take any more.

The coach thought that Rono had failed and stopped complaining about the drinking and lack of training. Rono, meanwhile, buried himself in psychology books in an effort to achieve an insight into his chaotic inner life.

Immediately after the incident in the hotel and the nocturnal run Cooper visited the island and berated Mibey for dereliction of duty. Once Cooper had gone, however, they fell back into the old routine and it was not until their next big quarrel and another visit from Cooper that there was any change in their everyday lives.

After his third visit Cooper recognized that the situation was hopeless. Even though the Seoul Olympics were still six months away there was no magic solution to getting Rono back into shape. He was too depressed and his alcoholism too far gone.

In February 1988, after six weeks in this parody of a training camp, Rono and Mibey were ordered to take the boat back to the mainland. The three men drove towards the United States border in silence, painfully aware that this was a repeat of the fiasco four years earlier when Rono had wasted his chances of getting fit for the Olympics. Cooper assured them he had only wanted the best for Rono and left them in a Tijuana drinking den. Mibey was on the point of tears – he did not have a passport, he said, and was frightened of the border controls.

Henry crossed the US border without problems, dressed in a smart suit Cooper had bought him. Mibey, however, so Henry heard, was arrested at the border and ended up in a Mexican gaol. And so this, one of the strangest attempts to get an Olympic runner back into form, ended in failure.

Rono became even more depressed and signed himself into a detoxification clinic in Rochester in New York State. He knew that he had to run in order to achieve and keep his mental balance. He had nothing else in the United States, no relatives there and few friends outside running circles. His whole existence was centred on athletics.

He moved to Albuqerque in 1990 after a spiritual visit to Portland, where he developed an appreciation of meditation and Bible study. Things looked more optimistic when he met his fellow-countryman Sammy Sitonik. The two of them completed half the Duke City Marathon in 1 hour 14 minutes and Sitonik invited the 38-year-old Rono to come home with him to Las Vegas in Nevada, where they trained together in the hilly desert.

The healthy, alcohol-free life-style had an immediately positive effect on Rono. After only two weeks he ran a Las Vegas half-marathon in 1 hour 4 minutes. The press got hold of the story of the runner who had been denied the chance of two Olympics because of boycotts and had wrecked his chance of two more because of alcoholism. Henry Rono was finally on the right track and on his way to his fifth planned Olympic Games. If he really trained properly a gold in Barcelona was a possibility. Rono's victory in a half-marathon in Austin in 1.04 whipped up expectations among the experts, who reckoned that he could improve on that time by several minutes.

But Rono could not handle the pressures of high expectations and rash journalists. The more attention he received the more he doubted his own ability. And whoops, he was drinking again! He fell out with Sitonik and had to move out. Carrying his few possessions in a bag he checked into a crisis centre in Las Vegas and after a week moved again to Albuquerque to train with Abrahim Hussein, a sound Kenyan marathon runner.

Rono focused seriously on the 1992 Olympic marathon. In May 1991 he earned $2,000 dollars by taking part in the Pittsburgh Marathon and lived on that for some months but soon the organizers of earlier races were demanding to be repaid for races he had missed in past years. Once again Rono resorted to drink and then again to detoxification, this time for some months in clinics run by Alcoholics Anonymous in California.

It became a pattern. He would move to a town holding a road race in order to win some money and get back on his feet. He would train a bit and perform well, and then would come another drinking bout. Once he had reached bottom he would sign into a drying-out clinic and follow its programme for however many weeks or months it lasted. It happened in California in 1992 before he moved on to race in Salt Lake City, where the clinic once again became his home. Rono became a nomad, moving from clinic to clinic, signing himself in voluntarily or with the help of friends at least seventeen times.

In spite of the healthier life and regular routine they offered, Rono, lover of freedom that he was, perceived them as prisons because they did not permit him to run. Sitting around having group discussions deepened his depression. He argued to be allowed to train and then he felt much better and ready to tackle a proper job.

In 1995, for the third time in six years, he tried to get a job with Nike. They had turned him down on the two previous occasions because they did not want to finance his drinking. In 1995 he filled out the usual forms with questions like 'Have you worked here before?' and 'How much do you earn?' He was turned down this time, too.

Rono took the rejections very badly. At the end of the 1970s he had after all been Nike's figurehead, a symbol of Nike's bold and somewhat untraditional style. Both Rono and Nike had some justice on their side when each accused the other of bad faith, but a sponsor had no obligation to support an alcoholic – and a sportsman could not expect charity even though Rono knew that other top athletes were working for Nike. He felt he was being discriminated against as an African.

He took it particularly hard in 1995 since he was getting his life into order, washing cars in Portland and paying for his own accommodation. Then the press arrived again and took pictures of the legend washing cars for a pathetic wage. The news spread from the local papers to the national and from there to agencies and the worldwide media. As usual, he was presented as a failure, a beer-sodden fool. The journalists did not write about the complex individual, they were not interested in Henry Rono the man, only in the champion and the victim. Once again it all served to fuel the rumourmill of stories about Henry Rono.

He moved on to a more regular job at the city airport in 1996 thanks to his Kenyan contacts in Albuquerque. He assisted passengers with their baggage, earning $2.17 an hour plus tips, which varied from nothing to $50 or $60 a day.

Rono still lacked the Green Card that could open the way to better paid jobs. He was right at the bottom of the pile in terms of work in America, on a par with illegal immigrants and virtually without any legal rights. There was also the fact that he and the other Kenyan runners were anything but pushy: they behaved like the modest people they were, did not boast about their earlier exploits, lived anonymous lives, socialized among themselves and did not apply for jobs that required the higher education that many of them actually had. A number of the Kenyan running stars of the past, including Peter Koech, who won an Olympic silver medal in 1988, worked as baggage-handlers in Albuquerque.

So an overweight Rono trudged around the airport, pushing cases and trolleys, muttering polite phrases and smiling to encourage tips. He sometimes met old acquaintances arriving in Albuquerque for training visits. At the end of the 1990s he met Grete Waitz.

'Hello, I'm Henry', he said and held out his hand to Waitz, who recognized him immediately. They had not met for many years and had a lot to talk about.

The contrast between them was enormous. Two decades earlier both of them had been the best runners in the world at their respective distances, they had posed together for photographs, been earning well and competing all over. Waitz was harvesting the benefits of her career, giving lectures and holding contracts that secured her a good living and a meaningful existence.

Henry Rono dried out for good in December 2002, at last free from an alcohol problem that had been the scourge of his body and mind for a quarter of a century. But now junk food became his new addiction.

What is it about America? Why did Henry and other Kenyan runners take up comfort-eating when their careers were over and gorge themselves until they were unrecognizable? Overeating led to a different kind of depression.

One evening in June 2006 Henry Rono went to bed as usual in his apartment in Albuquerque, unfit, uncomfortably overweight and unhappy, even though his alcohol problem was now a thing of the past. Something was lacking in his life, indeed, life itself was lacking – the ability to run.

At 3 a.m. he woke suddenly and heard a voice calling him.

'Get up and run, Henry. You will find yourself again, you will find the man you once were but have since lost.'

He got up, went out in the dark, turned left and then right and there it was, the Pole Star shining in the sky. He looked at it and he went towards it, slowly, but nevertheless following it, alone in the dark of the night like an Indian following a call from the gods. Never before had he thought so well and so clearly as he did on that run, even if his style was close to a waddle through streets that were empty of cars and people. He ran for two hours, a solitary journey of two hours by starlight, during which the powers of running preached their gospel to him.

He returned from that run determined to get fit again, to become his old self, to set a new world record for the mile for his 55–9 age group.

It did not happen the first year. Rono remained 20 to 30 pounds above an ideal running weight, but he continued to compete and achieve greater harmony with his true self. Running was sacred to him, the cause of both the crests and the troughs of his life. Rono's philosophy is 'I run therefore I am.' He feels a powerful bond with his own, inner, running god.

28
Stars, Business and Doping

This is all made up, bloody lies! We refuse to accept these lies and
intend to take legal action.
—Marita Koch from the German Democratic Republic, 400 metres world
recorder holder with a time of 47.60, on being accused of doping in 1991

At the beginning of the 1980s athletics and running was attracting enormous
interest in the Western world. The jogging trend meant that millions of
people easily identified with the stars of the sport. The runner as a type –
thin, legs covered with distended veins, slightly red in the face – became a
physical ideal. The models in advertisements look as if they have just been
for a run: they are slightly sweaty or just out of a shower, healthy, lungs filled
with fresh air. The cigarette-smoking, drinking models and poster pin-ups
have been replaced by athletic looking people and even rock stars ran in
order to keep their figures and be better able to tackle their hard lives.

The best runners had long been folk-heroes. The very greatest stars of
the sport, like John Walker from New Zealand, the Englishman Sebastian
Coe and Carl Lewis from the USA, had an appeal that reached beyond the
sporting public. Women liked the look of them and their shapely legs and
men wanted to be like them. Walker (1952–), in his black national strip,
became a slightly Jesus-like running icon with his long, flowing hair and
his ability to always come up fast in the final sprint. Walker was just an ambitious and talented lad who loved competing but in the eyes of the public
he had an aura that matched that of famous actors. He was a superstar with
few equals in his field – middle distance – but he became a sex symbol too.
Another 1970s sportsman who achieved an equivalent individual status was
the Swedish tennis player Björn Borg.

When John Walker set a new world mile record of 3 minutes 39.4 seconds
in Gothenburg in 1975 he spent a whole day sitting talking on the telephone
to journalists from all over the world. The best runners travelled the world
from continent to continent. They spent the winter in Oceania to get the
best summer conditions, then on to the United States and from there to
Europe where the cycle of meetings flourished at the start of the 1980s as
never before.

Every summer in the years around 1980 some 200 international athletics meetings were organized in Western Europe. The number of meetings,
road races and cross-country races rocketed and stars big and small were
invited everywhere to bring a blaze of glory to the events.

It was not until the 1980s that money was allowed into so-called amateur athletics – that is, athletics for those who wanted to participate in the Olympic Games. In 1982 the IAAF (International Association of Athletics Federations) departed from its rusty definition of amateurism. A participant's fund on a national level was allowed from 1985 and international prize money was also permitted. The decade before had been characterized by a spiralling increase in 'black' money – appearance money, free flights and inventive evasion of the amateur rules. Everyone involved knew what was going on.

At the big European meetings such as Zurich the participants used to queue up afterwards to pick up their money. Everyone had a price tag and generous organizers were popular and guaranteed a high level of participation year after year. In Eastern Europe the payment sometimes came in currencies that were difficult to exchange in the West; runners from Romania and the Soviet Union, on the other hand, were overjoyed to be paid in dollars, which gave them access to exclusive shops in their home countries. The system of illegal payments used crafty methods to avoid transfers being made through the banking system.

There were world record holders who travelled with cases of money and opened bank accounts in different European banks in order to spread their fortune. One particular Kenyan always demanded $754 for a meeting, that apparently random and meaningless sum corresponding to the price of a cow or a patch of land back at home. Thoughts of the increasing size of his herd and farm spurred him on to compete often and earn as much as possible on the European circuit in order to secure the future for himself and his family.

The sums of money grew through the 1980s and '90s. Closer links between sportsmen and sponsoring interests led to increased media attention, and an increased focus on money was characteristic of top-level sport in general.

The 1980s also saw the arrival of agents in athletics to negotiate and arrange contracts. Professionalization meant that the best athletes became dependent on intermediaries to gain access to events, to build a reputation and increase their market value. Self-reliance was not always advantageous and even some of those at the very top had been deceived by their own sponsors and needed help at the negotiating table.

The rivalry between the many big city marathons also had an effect among the runners. Organizers had their own preferences among the elite, sometimes wanting particular individuals to win because, for instance, that individual was in the pay of the main sponsor. In both road and track racing there was often a hidden game going on under the table. In order to secure their reputation as winners, runners might handpick certain races on condition that particular rivals were not taking part. If the organizer was hoping for a world record a pacemaker or two had to be part of the deal, preferably one or two from the same country or group as the potential winner. Negotiations went on to build a field that would be advantageous to competitors, organizers, sponsors and television.

The result was that certain runners hardly ever competed against one another. The two Englishmen Sebastian Coe and Steve Ovett, fantastic middle-distance runners who were at their peak around 1980, rarely appeared in the same heat. The rivalry between them was the talk of the athletics world for several years and they received so many invitations that each of them could fight the battle on his chosen front even to the extent of each of them winning his particular distance at the same meeting. Prestige and economic factors went hand in hand among sportsmen who hated to lose.

The increased financial rewards encouraged young people from Kenya, Ethiopia and other poor countries with a running tradition. Sporting ambition, the desire for education and fame had been the main motives for Africans entering the running world, along with a desire to come to, settle in and compete in the West. That in itself meant a rise in their standard of living, but not to anything like the same extent as pure cash payments did. Stories went round among African runners that just one win or top placing in the West could bring in more money than they could dream of.

An All-round Phenomenon

It happened again at the beginning of the 1980s when a young runner from an African nation made his mark. Said Aouita (1960–) from Morocco revealed a god-given talent that has rarely been equalled. He was an eighteen-year-old footballer when he was tempted into trying his skills barefoot in a school championship, with no coaching apart from football and with no idea about energy-saving tactics – he just knew it was worth doing your absolute best. In his 800-metre debut the clock showed 1 minute 49 seconds.

He was a true innocent. He knew nothing about records – his instructors stood at the side of the track shouting at this natural prodigy when to speed up or to slow down, but he was immediately master of all distances from 800 to 5,000 metres. The results were so encouraging that Aouita concentrated fully on running and that meant he had to go abroad, to France, the country of the old colonial masters.

There, strangely enough, he had difficulty keeping up with the speed of his colleagues during training but outclassed them all in races. Something had to be wrong with the training he was doing so he developed his own philosophy which, among other things, perfected a bullet-like spurt over the final 300 metres. He did not run a great mileage – 45–55 miles a week – with a lot of fartlek, speed training and uphill work.

Between 1980 and 1982, when Aouita was working his way up to the elite at his chosen distance, English runners dominated the 1,500 metres. Aouita felt that some organizers were discriminating against him and he was referred to as 'the little Arab'. He represented a new addition to the fauna of the running world. He was not just a newcomer from a Muslim

North African country receiving invitations to the biggest events, but he was also expressing himself bluntly about organizers, competitors and European arrogance.

Aouita moved to Siena in Italy, which he found a more conducive environment, and from there he mounted his campaign to conquer the world. Before events he would visualize himself as a Moroccan soldier ready to fight for his own and his country's honour. Defeats felt like being stabbed with a dagger. When he came in four hundredths of a second behind Steve Cram in the 1,500 metres in 1985 he was unable to sleep for two nights and had a stomach-ache for two weeks.

Said Aouita's Olympic gold in the 1984 5,000 metres made him a national hero and brought him the friendship of the king. Suddenly his picture hung alongside that of King Hassan II in public places and private homes all over Morocco. His injuries were treated by the royal doctor and he frequented the court. He became Morocco's first really affluent sportsman.[1]

Was Said Aouita the most complete middle- and long-distance runner the world has ever seen? He was at top international level at all distances from 800 metres to 10,000 metres. He set world records and he won 115 of his 119 races between September 1983 and September 1990. He paved the way for the later wave of great runners to emerge from Morocco and Algeria at distances over 800 metres, of whom his countryman Hicham El Guerrouj has surpassed them all.

Since Aouita began to dominate the 1,500 metres from the middle of the 1980s, runners from North and East Africa have continued to be world leaders at that prestigious distance.

Breaking Barriers

'I want to run,' said Hassiba Boulmerka (1968–) from the town of Constantine in Algeria. That meant obeying Muslim dress laws and still taking long strides, breaking norms and being prepared for the disapproval, amazement and condemnation of her society. With her head covered, in ankle-length leggings and with covered arms as the rules stipulated, she made her mark in the 1980s and won the national championships at 800 and 1,500 metres.

Algeria with its mountains and deserts, Africa's second largest country, had few women runners when Boulmerka was young. Women trained in secret and hushed up their achievements since they were considered blasphemers and exhibitionists. They had more barriers to overcome than their sisters in the West because a stern religion as well as simple seemliness and custom repressed running. Little girls and young women who announced at home that they wanted to play games and run would most often receive a firm paternal no as the answer. For those who defied the norms there was a book of rules and prohibitions to be followed. Muslim women could not run when men were watching and certainly not reveal bare flesh in a culture where even men should not uncover too much. Everyday life was full of restrictions and rules for Boulmerka, who wanted to train and sweat, go overseas and compete.

So Hassiba Boulmerka did not have a straight and easy journey to the top, which made the joy all the greater when she won the first women's athletics title for her country in the 1,500 metres in 1991 and followed that triumph up at the Olympics a year later. On her homecoming from the Olympics she was congratulated by the president of her country, who apologized for voting for a proposal to outlaw women's athletics in Algeria.

But fundamentalist Sunni Muslims accused her of blasphemy: she had raced almost naked in a stadium full of thousands of men; she had broken the laws and mocked Islam in the name of her country by running a victory lap with the flag while joyfully shouting 'Algeria! Algeria!' – as if such a dishonourable event was anything to celebrate. Boulmerka had to be given police protection and moved to France to train.

She was, however, simultaneously a popular heroine, particularly among women, and she stimulated political changes at grass-roots level. A slogan appeared in the wake of her triumph: 'Hassiba Boulmerka did not need her father's permission to win a gold medal.' Her 1991 victory and the grassroots demands that followed it was the cause of Algerian women being given the vote: fathers and husbands had spoken for them earlier and made most of the decisions.

The unrest in Algeria after the electoral victory of the Islamic Salvation Front in December 1991 and the military take-over a month later led to a long and bloody civil war that also ruined Boulmerka's everyday life. She remained a patriot and refused to emigrate permanently but had to visit Cuba and France to have the peace she needed during important periods of training. Threatening letters and telephone calls promised her death and destruction. During the 1995 world athletics championships in Gothenburg she had to move to a different hotel to the rest of her countrymen and live under strict security 24 hours a day, like a politician with the threat of assassination hanging over her.

What did she herself have to say about her brave actions and all the uproar? She considered herself a pioneer and also a good Muslim, as a woman contributing to women's liberation without losing either her patriotism or the spirit of Allah.

Within just a few years of her international victories over 8,000 girls took up running in Algeria. They cast off their long, hot and impractical garments and, like their model, ran in shorts. They felt excitement and the joy of sport, perhaps a slight twinge of conscience, but it nevertheless felt good and right when there was a crowd of them. Some of them dutifully retained certain garments and came to a compromise, as their sisters with similar interests in other countries had done. There was no need to imitate Boulmerka completely.

Hassiba Boulmerka belonged to a long tradition of women who opposed male dominance. As a runner she met many of the same attitudes as men had done in the West a hundred years earlier and women a decade or two earlier. Her Islamic burden was, however, a heavier one in that Islam was on the march and igniting radical movements in many countries. Those Muslims who accused Boulmerka of sin also viewed her career as a surrender to the main enemy, the Great Satan, the United States, because she engaged in Western sport against the words of the Prophet. Running in scanty clothing became a symbol of moral degeneracy and the infiltration of American values.[2]

Big Business

The manufacturers of running shoes became major sponsors in the financing of sport during the 1980s. The shoe industry in the USA, Europe and Asia really took off in the wake of the jogging boom, with the number of producers peaking around 1980. After that there was some shrinkage, as happens in growth industries that level off or go through some lean years.

Imternational competition also became tougher in the shoe market, reflecting a sharpening of the business climate that indicated the coming of globalization.

Nike was both the name of the goddess of victory in Ancient Greece and of an American shoe manufacturer. In the 1950s its founder, Phillip Knight from Portland in Oregon, had belonged to the running team of the legendary coach Bill Bowerman at the University of Oregon in Eugene. Knight went to Japan in the autumn of 1962 to see if it was possible to import running shoes from there to the United States – buy cheap in a low-cost market and sell to Americans at a higher price. The brand of shoes he ordered was called Tiger and the American company was registered as Blue Ribbon Sport.

It took over a year to get the first five pairs of a light type of shoe. Then, however, with Knight selling shoes from the back of a car at athletics events on the west coast of the USA and Bowerman recommending the Tiger shoes, they sold 1,300 pairs in a year.

After they achieved a turnover of $1,000,000 in 1970, increasing costs and reduced deliveries convinced Knight and Bowerman of the desirability of launching their own brand. In 1971 Blue Ribbon produced the first shoe with the Nike logo – a wing-like curve which might represent the goddess's wing and which was later known as the Nike 'Swoosh'. The shoes were made in Mexico, however, and had no tolerance for low temperatures. They tore easily and the model was dropped. Knight went to Japan and arranged for the Nike logo to appear on the popular Japanese Tiger Cortez shoes. He also ordered basketball boots, wrestling boots and ordinary trainers from his Japanese contacts.

The selection for the 1972 Olympic team was taking place in Eugene and the young runner Steve Prefontaine, who was trained by Bowerman and who tested the new shoes, was attracting a lot of attention. This charismatic long-distance runner was photographed wearing Nike shoes. In the same year Bowerman poured latex into his wife's waffle iron and recognized the possibilities of a sole with a waffle pattern.

Nike's sales grew in parallel to the increase in the number of joggers through the 1970s – and the profusion of products from Nike and other producers bolstered the jogging movement. New models with shock-absorbent properties came as a revelation to both old and new runners, whether on tarmac or cross-country, and they replaced the tennis shoes and baseball boots they were using with good, elegant and light shoes at an affordable price. Technological improvements, low production costs in Asia and the currents of capitalism all favoured and, indeed, formed the daily experience of joggers, many of whom felt that using specially designed running shoes produced miracles and increased the amount of running they did. Customers came in all ages and sizes and were increasingly willing and able to spend money on hobby items.

The Blue Ribbon company changed its name to Nike in 1978. They liked to think of themselves as the small, alternative brand that was challenging the giants Adidas and Puma and representing something new and necessary. It was a highly successful strategy. When Nike's turnover in the USA overtook that of Adidas in 1980 and it became the biggest sports shoe in the country, the company launched a collection of clothing. Sportswear and shoes was a growth industry with potentially huge profits, particularly as wages and costs in the producer countries were so much lower than in the West.

Michael Jordan, the basketball player, was very important to Nike throughout the 1980s and the company later signed up other superstars from a variety of sporting disciplines. As far as running is concerned Nike has milked most out of Steve Prefontaine (1951–1975), who was killed in a car accident but is central to Nike's self-constructed myth of itself as a company rooted in idealism.

By linking the story of Prefontaine's short career with Bill Bowerman's waffle-iron invention, Nike constructed a moving narrative that made them that little bit more than the rest, gave their products authenticity – even though they were manufactured on conveyor belts in Asia. Nike succeeded in attracting a host of loyal customers by creating the illusion that Nike represented a particular lifestyle, a style that marked Nike-users out from the rest of humanity. By buying and using Nike, by recommending the brand to others and becoming a brand patriot, users became part of a unique and cherished community. Neither the Japanese Saucony nor Asics nor, indeed, Adidas ever achieved that kind of status.

The combination of cynical commercial attitudes allied to the slave-like conditions of many workers in the Asian factories producing their goods is hardly unique to Nike among successful, multinational companies. But what is special about Nike is the linkage between Knight and Bowerman on one side and the origins of the jogging movement on the other. One precondition for the Nike founding staff in the USA and other countries was that they should be genuine running enthusiasts. Nike was, for example, one of the first companies to refuse to employ smokers. The company succeeded because it brought together the drive and enthusiasm of runners for their beloved hobby, Bowerman's team spirit and Phil Knight's overwhelming urge to grow and dominate the field. Knight never won a race under Bowerman's tutelage but he became an international star in the world of running shoes.[3]

Doping in All Its Forms

The issue of blood doping, as it is known, has given rise to much heated discussion ever since the 1970s. Strictly speaking, it was not illegal in the Olympic context because what the regulations banned was 'the use of foreign substances'. The International Olympic Committee did not ban blood doping until 1985, even though it was impossible to test for this kind of doping at that date.

Experiments in Sweden in the early 1980s demonstrated the enormous effect of blood doping. The subjects of the experiment had eight decilitres of blood (approximately 15 per cent of the total blood) withdrawn and the blood was then frozen. This normally leads to a 10 per cent drop in the maximum oxygen uptake. The subjects then continued training and after three or four weeks their blood had returned to its normal level. After four weeks the frozen blood was thawed and re-injected into the subjects with the result that their red blood cell count rose by about 10 per cent, with an equivalent increase in the oxygen uptake.

In Sweden Dr Björn Ekholm carried out many experiments in this field, not to encourage anyone to cheat but to study what it is that affects performance. One of Ekholm's research subjects was Artur Forsberg, a hobby runner whose personal best for a nine kilometre cross-country was 33.35. In the week before his blood was re-injected he ran three trial runs in 34.25, 34.32 and 34.12. Two days after his blood was re-injected he produced a time of 32.29 – one minute better than his previous personal best. Forsberg also took his morning pulse for three days before the re-injection and it was 44, 43 and 44 beats a minute; on the three days following the re-injection it measured 39, 38 and 40 beats a minute.

A 10,000 metre runner improved his time by about one minute – a result confirmed by studies in a number of other countries – and an improvement of half a minute was recorded over 5,000 metres.

There is much speculation as to whether the Finn Lasse Virén, who won the 5,000 and 10,000 metres at both the 1972 and the 1976 Olympics, used blood doping. He has denied it and his long period at peak form in both Olympic years does not suggest blood doping. His fellow-countryman Kaarlo Maaninka, on the other hand, who took the silver at 10,000 metres and the bronze at 5,000 metres in the 1980 Olympics, has admitted using blood doping.[4]

EPO (Erythropoietin) was used as a doping substance for long races from the end of the 1980s. It increases the body's production of red blood cells and can improve 10,000 metre times by around one minute. A number of Italian doctors, in particular, were willing to provide athletes with EPO.

It was in East Germany – the German Democratic Republic – that the most sophisticated state-run doping system operated. The state was founded in 1949 as a communist buffer-zone against the West and from the 1960s on it became a sporting colossus in spite of its relatively small population of seventeen million. East German success was achieved by a system that picked out children and young people early and sent them to sports schools. At a later stage the elite were selected and entered into the state-run advanced sports programmes. A huge amount of research was done into training methods and anything that could improve performance, including doping. East Germans may often have been competing against doped rivals from the rest of the world but no other country has been shown to have used system-atic state doping on such a scale.

The use of anabolic steroids became common in East Germany towards the end of the 1960s. This was also true of a number of other countries, including the USA, which has frequently taken a high moral stance *vis-á-vis* East Germany since the American authorities were not involved in organized doping. The communist and capitalist systems handled doping differ-ently and sportsmen in East Germany and the West were obviously subject to their own systems: if they wanted to reach the top they had to follow the rules of the game in their respective countries.

East German women sprinters achieved particular international promi-nence. Renate Stecher took the gold at 100 metres and 200 metres in the 1972 Munich Olympics: 'Never before have I seen a woman like her. She seems to be bigger and more muscular than Valerie Borzov' (winner of the men's 100 metres).[5] This comment was made by Charlie Francis, who later coached the sprinter Ben Johnson in Canada. Muscle mass previously unseen in women was typical of East German women sprinters. The combination of more and better training with weight-training and doping produced a body type among women sprinters, especially in East Germany, that resembles that of extremely well-trained men. Marita Koch, the 400 metres runner who ran the distance in 47.60 in 1985 and thereby set an almost unbeatable record, had the kind of athletic shape portrayed in comic strips.

Male runners in East Germany rarely took dosages greater than nine milligrams of testosterone a day; women, on the other hand, took large and almost unlimited dosages. There were examples of married couples among the elite sprinters where the woman took almost three times as much as the man. Marita Koch took about twice as much as Thomas Schönlebe, her male counterpart at 400 metres. And the East Germans were taking high dosages by comparison to their Western competitors.

Doping of this kind had an extra strong effect on women, particularly in explosive sprint events – which accounts for the amounts taken. The sprinter

Bärbel Wöckel-Eckert was taking up to 1,745 milligrams of steroids a year at the start of the 1980s. Her more famous teammate, Marlies Göhr, had an annual consumption of 1,405 milligrams of steroids.[6]

Systematic doping also occurred in middle- and long-distance running from early in the 1970s. The experts recognized that it could also be useful for slimmer competitors. Both sexes took drugs during the training and build-up phases and women also used doping at the preparation stage for competition. Runners were able to train more and recover more rapidly from both training and injuries. There was very precise research behind the East German doping programme and the research was led by some of the country's leading medical men.

Even though muscle mass was not increased in the way it was among sprinters – nor should it have been – a number of doping exposés from the end of the 1970s among, for instance, Romanian women middle-distance runners indicate that doping was widespread. In East Germany competitors were tested before being sent abroad and those who did not pass the test were kept at home.

Sportsmen involved in doping have had a tendency to deny it, perhaps because 'everyone' at the top level was doing it and they feel it would be unfair for them to be condemned when others are getting away with it. Marita Koch was interviewed on television in 1991 when the collapse of the East German regime led to revelations about the doping programme there:

'So you're sticking to the story that you've never taken anabolic steroids?'

'Yes.'

She and her husband and coach, Wolfgang Meier, said:

'This is all made up, all bloody lies! We refuse to accept these lies and intend to take legal action. These smears show that people will stop at nothing when it comes to denigrating athletes.'

Koch also threatened to sue the German magazine *Der Spiegel* for stating that she had used dope. The case never came to court.[7]

In any account of the doping system in East Germany it is easy to present those involved as factory-farmed cheats, but doping was just as pervasive at the top level in the United States – East Germany's main rival – particularly among sprinters. It was pure (and typical) American bluff when the top stars in the running circus of the 1980s and '90s claimed to be dope-free, unlike the Eastern Europeans. And the American athletics authorities also hushed up positive doping results among its athletes as, for example, before the 1984 Olympics. they protected their athletes, fearful perhaps of losing face and income. Communist countries and those of the West accused each other of cheating and, of course, such accusations were a way of explaining away your rival's successes. In surprisingly many countries 'we' equalled 'innocent' and 'they' equalled 'guilty'. In some countries doping was not even on the agenda for discussion.

The biggest farce of the 1988 Olympics was when the 100-metres winner Ben Johnson was caught by a doping test and was made a scapegoat: it showed that far from all the guilty parties get caught. Everyone with any knowledge of international athletics knew that Johnson was not the only one in the field who had built himself up on anabolic steroids. Hundreds of runners were caught later when dope tests became more frequent and the will to catch dope users increased.

One of the biggest doping scandals in the United States involved BALCO – the Bay Area Laboratory Cooperative – in San Francisco, which was led by its founder and owner Victor Conte. The company's official business handled blood and urine analysis and nutritional supplements. At the end of the 1990s Conte started up an athletics club, ZMA, to market a nutritional supplement of the same name. One of the club members was the sprinter Marion Jones who, after the demise of East Germany, was the queen of the sprinting world, with the charisma of a film star. The world had never witnessed such a combination of speed and elegance as revealed by this girl with her good-natured, open face.

BALCO was raided in 2003 on suspicion of illegal activities. The narcotics agents found growth hormones, large sums of money and lists of customers that included international stars in a number of sports. They also found reports on individuals' dosages and suggestions on how to achieve the optimal effect using the banned substances.

The most famous runner in the BALCO archive was the sprinter Marion Jones but she denied having done anything illegal – and she had never tested positive in dope tests. She could not, however, escape the suspicions that had been growing over the years, since she had tended to 'forget' important doping tests and had trained with runners and coaches who were rumoured to be involved in doping.

The case against BALCO rolled on and on and revealed the darker sides of elite sports. Jones's trustworthiness was further undermined when Conte admitted on national television in 2004 that he had personally given Jones banned substances before the Sydney Olympics four years earlier. She later admitted to having lied and was consequently stripped of the five medals she had won in Sydney and, additionally, all her results and achievements since September 2000 were annulled. She was a ruined former sprinter when she admitted her guilt in 2007 and in March 2008 she began a six-month prison sentence for having lied in court about her use of dope.

Both Marita Koch and Marion Jones were competing at a time when sprinters had to take dope to reach the top international level. International running at elite level needed a staff of good, well-educated assistants and smart agents: the runner was just one piece in a multilayered game of national rivalries, money, prestige and ambition. Elite sport had gone the way sceptics had been warning for years, but it was merely reflecting the contemporary world, just as it always had done.

29
Running with Zen

We follow the master's words, because we know it is good for us.
—Toshihiko Seko, a runner from Japan

Obedience and discipline – these are the characteristics an outsider sees in the Japanese runner Toshihiko Seko – blind obedience to his coach Kiyoshi Nakamura and inconceivable discipline when training. 'Run 90 miles a day!' his coach told him at a training camp in New Zealand and Seko covered 750 miles in eight days. 'My body was a little confused after it, but I managed it', he said afterwards.[1]

His coach Nakamura (1913–1984) had earlier been the Japanese 1,500 metres record holder and was a man who worshipped willpower. When he began his career as a coach in 1965 the good old Japanese master–pupil relationship of total subjection – the principle of *sunao* – still operated. Practitioners lived as a tightly bonded family and were not permitted to criticize the words of their master. They all had to have the same haircut and avoid any kind of loose living – girlfriends and nights out on the town were inconceivable. In the early days pupils might be given a thrashing by their coach, whom they called Satan because of the harsh regime he ran. But Nakamura, who coached over 1,000 runners in the course of two decades, knew that constructive talk was more effective than physical punishment.

Seko entered Nakamura's stable at the behest of his parents. He was born in 1956 on the island of Kyushu and from an early age showed an unusually strong will to win – his nickname 'Kaibutsi', meaning 'monster', points in that direction. Where others might weep and moan Seko would become more determined and ready for greater efforts as, for instance, when he set the 1,500 metres Japanese school record of 3 minutes 53.3 seconds in 1972. As a result of a life filled with demanding training, long training camps, races and chasing victory, Seko did not perform well at school and, to the disappointment of his family, failed to get a place at Waseda University in Tokyo.

His parents sent him to the United States but he failed to settle and longed to return home. He found solace in the company of two other Japanese sportsmen, who also wanted to go home and were not doing any serious training. Home was best for Seko; in California he was just one of the crowd.

The three Japanese boys did not handle life well in the USA and soon fell into the same pattern as other frustrated immigrants: they ate junk food and drank fizzy drinks instead of studying and training, and they lazed away their days in their rooms while painting a bleak picture of life. Seko failed to survive his first year at university and at the same time he became unfit and put on weight.

When he returned to Japan in the summer of 1976, chubby and twenty pounds heavier, there was little to remind anyone that this young man had been Japan's most promising middle-distance runner. For a while he did not run at all, simply lounged around. His parents were very concerned and realized that he needed guidance so in 1976 they took him to Kiyoshi Nakamura, who was the coach at Waseda University.

He immediately recognized Seko's talent, his flowing movement and easy stride: 'He'll be a world-class marathon runner within five years.'[2]

Seko's father doubted that: 'My son doesn't have the character or the mental attitude to be a marathon runner.' He did not think Seko was up to making the sacrifices necessary to reach the top levels. Nor did the young man believe it. He had been brought up as a middle-distance runner and was used to competing on the track for between two and five minutes, not for two hours or more on a tarmac surface. The coach, however, assured the family that Seko would succeed at the marathon if he trained suffi-ciently and properly: 'Talent has its limits but effort is unlimited.' Seko felt he either had to accept Nakamura's offer or drop the idea of a running career altogether.

Seko did not enjoy himself at the start. It was strange and difficult to submit completely to the coach. He was irritated by the dictatorial style, the strict rules and anything that set limits on how he lived his life. Every detail of everyday life was changed and adapted to the will of the master. For a period the coach would only let him eat salad leaves and one slice of bread a day in order to bring his weight down. Seko ran away in despera-tion and returned home to his parents but they telephoned Nakamura and gave him a free hand with their son.

Seko became the master's most obedient disciple, accepting the role partly out of the respect the Japanese have for their elders. It was, there-fore, perhaps not *that* extraordinary that Seko came to believe firmly that Nakamura could teach him everything he needed to reach the top: 'We follow the master because we know it is good for us. We know that he is changing us but we are aware of what is happening and we want him to do it. It is love that binds us together, not compulsion.'[3]

The runners prayed silently to Nakamura as they ran round the track. The master was a guiding force who strengthened their discipline both in the sphere of sport and that of life. They looked up to him as a holy man and submitted to him accordingly.

Nakamura had a close relationship with his runners but none of them was as close as Seko, and Seko did not know of any other sportsman in the world who had the same kind of relationship with his coach: 'We run every race together; we are the same person.' Even though Seko followed his coach's advice, however, he was not merely his machine. In 1984 he pondered how long the relationship would last: 'For ever. I see no end to our relationship. Even if I get married it will continue. I shall perhaps move to a larger house but I will still live in the neighbourhood so that I can come here and be with *sensei* every day.'[4]

Nakamura took his duties as coach very seriously and it was a considerable expense for him to feed all the runners who lived at or frequented his home. He was father, pastor, coach and dietary adviser and he asked for nothing in return but total obedience and maximum effort. He worked to create a positive, attacking attitude and he read to them every evening from the works of the great philosophers so as to give them an edge in training and in competition. One of his favourite quotations was from the Buddhist monk Daruma-Taishi: 'Welcome difficulties when they come. Be patient and work your way through your burdens. Only then will you overcome them and become stronger.'[5]

The coach told Seko and the others to study nature, the sun, the moon, the forces of the universe, and also the great runners, in order to wrest their secrets from them. There was something to be learnt from everything, even from losers because then one could learn how things should not be done.

To an outsider, particularly a foreign outsider, the set-up looked militaristic, with Nakumura commanding his troops and clicking off their times on a stopwatch at the 1,325 metre asphalt circuit outside the Tokyo Olympic Stadium. Seko ran lap after lap, up to 50 consecutive laps in a recognizable and concentrated style with his eyes fixed ahead. All the force was channelled into the running and Seko flowed onwards in a manner reminiscent of a Zen master. Zen is a form of Buddhism that originates in China: it stresses an awakening of its disciples' senses. Nakamura called his coaching philosophy *Zensoho*, 'running with Zen'. The basic aim is to liberate undreamed-of powers by clearing the mind of all detritus and allowing the body to function naturally, unhindered by thought.

Nakamura was called everything from a tyrant to a genius. People who got close to this complex man noted that he was well-read and reflective, as much of a philosopher as a coach, and certainly not a narrow sports fiend. People permitted to enter his house had to listen to disquisitions on philosophy and the miracles of nature. Nakamura was just as happy reading the well-known passages of Zen Buddhism and nuggets from other spiritual writings as he was reading training diaries and sports results. He had studied the great wise men and constructed his own coaching philosophy and he would not retreat when critics accused him of dominating and brainwashing the young. There was always a reaction from Western journalists when the coach answered questions put to Seko; Seko, however, believed that the master's words were also his words – the two of them had identical thoughts.

Nakamura believed that the Japanese had to train extra hard because they were small and had short legs – a body shape that did not lend itself to long-distance running. That implied long training sessions for Seko and the rest. Seko trained first for the 5,000 and 10,000 metres in order to ease his transition to the longer distances. His 1977 marathon debut in Kyoto with a time of 2 hours 26 minutes flat showed great progress, as did his time of 2 hours 15 minutes 1 second in Fukuoka the same year. After Seko had produced a time of 27 minutes 51 seconds in the 10,000 metres the following season, his coach ordered him to focus exclusively on the marathon. His victory over the American Bill Rodgers, the East German Olympic champion Waldemar Cierpinski and other big names at Fukuoka in the late autumn of 1978 was his international breakthrough.

Unlike many Japanese runners, who tend to do everything as a group, Seko often trained alone, with special instructions to encourage and guide him. His coach would call him to him before competitions and read quotations from the Bible while Seko listened intently. It happened in Fukuoka in 1979 when Seko won for the third time, though his coach was still displeased: he could have run *even* better and Nakamura scolded his pupil for two weeks. That was the way their collaboration worked – even great performances were followed by criticism and still harder efforts.

Seko ran with a poker face. Many runners show weakness or strength and their competitors can read what they are thinking or how much strength they have left from their facial expressions or their stride or their posture. There was no point in studying Seko in that way: whatever the situation he just kept running, apparently unmoved and unaffected. Behaviour of that kind breeds rumours and creates a mystique, particularly when those involved have no common language and cannot communicate directly.

Seko did not allow illness to stop him. After a training camp in New Zealand in 1983 he suffered from inflammation of the liver, probably as a result of too much beer-drinking in combination with an enormous amount of training. It is rare for a dedicated sportsman to drink so much alcohol but Seko had a tendency towards extremes and beer provided the relaxation his over-ambitious nature needed. Seko also had an intellectual streak and a broad perspective on life: books on Japanese history and the deeds of the *samurai*, for instance, fascinated him.

When he was suffering from injuries Seko would walk the distance he normally ran. He would remain as focused as ever and it might take him twice as many hours as usual. Once able to run again the amount of training would be pushed to new heights – anything up to six hours a day. He also wanted to respond to the challenge coming from his main Japanese rivals, the twins Takeshi and Shigeru Soh, and on one of these training runs Seko broke the world 50-kilometre record. The Japanese ran excessive distances in order to build up physical and mental strength and some of them would run for eight hours.

In his autobiography Seko provides an example of one of his training days:

6.30: Wake up and go running.
8.00: Breakfast and a nap.
11.00: Second running session; time trial if feeling good.
12.00: Lunch – noodles and sushi, followed by a sleep.
Evening: Hardest training of the day, 20–30 kilometres. Seko sometimes trained so hard that he could not eat dinner. If his stomach was all right, he would eat dinner and drink one or two beers. If he could not eat anything he would drink up to ten beers.[6]

Zen philosophy was all-pervasive in Seko's life and training. He could tolerate his exhausting training routine more because of his amazing mental strength than because his physique was in any way exceptional, though he was very robust. Zen and running were the same thing. Through practice he developed patience and a meditative state. Zen monks would sit still and meditate for hours and Seko could achieve the same trance-like state by running. He would relax and meditate along the way. Whether he had six miles or eighteen left to do was irrelevant, his legs would continue in the same rhythm. Seko transferred the mental attitudes of samurai warriors and Zen monks to the marathon. In contrast to the monks sitting motionless in a monastery, however, Seko achieved his silent ecstasy through running. Compared to Western competitors the Japanese had an almost deadly attitude to competition and they were aware that this gave them an extra weapon: they were competing more for their coach, for Zen and for Japanese tradition than against their Western rivals. Elite runners from Europe, the USA and Australia also possessed phenomenal mental strength but they lacked the philosophical foundations the Japanese had. Competition was a sacred act for Seko, something worth dying for.

In the 1984 Olympics Seko was under inhuman pressure to take the gold for Japan. He stuck with the leading group on the wide motorways of Los Angeles and seemed to be going strong until the twenty-mile mark but from there on everything went wrong. Dehydration brought on by the intense heat broke him and several other runners. The race was won by Carlos Lopes from Portugal who was experienced in these conditions and Seko came in seventeenth place, dehydrated, unusually exhausted and filled with shame.

Fellow athletes and experts understood the situation but all those Japanese viewers sitting at home in front of their television screens did not: they believed that an advanced disciple of Zen ought to have been capable of ignoring the heat and the need for liquids.

A defeated runner and an even more depressed coach had to face the press. Nakamura was used to accepting the glory and honour when his runners performed well, but he would also take much of the blame in times of defeat. The two of them stood in front of a dismayed group of journalists and, while the cameras clicked, they tried to explain the causes of the fiasco. Eric Olsen of the American magazine *The Runner* described the scene:

> Japanese newsmen surrounded them (Seko and Nakamura) pro-
> tectively, all stunned by his impossible defeat, all as silent and still
> as if they'd just learned someone dear to them had died and perhaps
> in a sense, someone had, such is the intensity with which Seko strives
> for victory and the intensity with which the Japanese demanded he
> succeed . . . The Japanese operate in an entirely different milieu
> than we do, an intense, ascetic, modern samurai tradition in which
> death is always preferred over failure . . . [7]

It was the whole nation that had shown weakness and lost, not just Seko.

Shortly afterwards Nakamura was found dead in a river after a fishing trip. Officially it was stated to be an accident but rumour said it was *jissatsu* – suicide as a result of loss of face. It is not easy to know which is true in a country in which the loss of honour has led tens of thousands to choose death.[8]

It had been a long-standing joke in Japan that running was Seko's only sweetheart; he had no time for anything else since he was also working and concentrating all out on university exams. Seko did, however, get married in the middle of the 1980s and begin to live more like an ordinary citizen. He remained an amateur and worked for the s&b company after his exams. He withdrew from elite level competition in the autumn of 1988 and marked it with a celebrated retirement run in Japan. The country's foremost marathon samurai could finally rest.

Seko now became more open and outward-looking and coached s&b employees. Since he had been through all the ordeals of running himself there were few people better qualified to guide ambitious younger runners. He took over Nakamura's place at the asphalt loop close to the Olympic Stadium in Tokyo, checking times but behaving much more gently than his master: he tried to bring his runners the pleasure that had been absent in his own career. He passed on much of what he had inherited from his master but adapted it to the modern age. No one expected the younger runners to push themselves to the extremes Seko had done in order to win.

He was right to change the regime. Nakamura's strategy was effective and built up phenomenal mental and physical strength but a more humane regime would also have been beneficial to Seko. There is, in spite of everything, a difference between running and war. Those who do not feel they are running for their lives or the honour of their coach and country may perhaps be holding the best cards. Japanese earnestness could lead things off in the wrong direction: Seko's ideal is a combination of the best in the Western tradition and the best in the East. Nakamura and Seko are not alone in having tried to bring about a fruitful union of these two traditions.

30
Running like Ostriches

Every day I'm yelled at, punished and beaten.
I really can't take any more.
—Chinese woman runner in the stable of the coach
Ma Junren

Is there a connection between chopping wood and running? The Chinese coach Ma Junren thinks there is. When chopping wood you have to pay attention to two things – the wood and the axe, and they have to come into perfect contact. A running coach also has to study the surface and what others have done earlier. The axe-blade is the method he should use on his runners.

Ma Junren said: 'If there are questions, you will get answers.'

He disliked making things complicated, but he wanted to combine Eastern and Western knowledge, to use Chinese medicine and philosophy in harmony with modern science in order to surpass everything else.[1]

Ma Junren was born in 1944, the fourth of a family of nine, and he grew up in the mountainous district of Gu Zi Gou in the province of Liaoning. The family was poor and Ma ran six miles (9.7 km) every day to and from school. He was the oldest of the family still at home when his father was taken into hospital and he had to work as well as attend school: he loaded coal into a horse and cart and delivered it to his customers. He began working full-time at the age of fourteen, when his job was to feed pigs in the prison system.

Growing up in a harsh mountain region taught him moderation and how to make use of everything in order to survive – it also implanted in him a deep desire to be rich. Ma Junren began by cultivating an expensive ornamental plant for sale. The knack was to let a dead chicken ferment and rot in water and then pour the water on the plants. They would grow enormous and provide him with a good income, as did many of his other business ideas. While on a coaching course Junren saw an untrained monkey and bought it for twenty yen. He took the monkey with him on the long train journey to Beijing and went to the busiest street in the city, where he sold the animal. Everything can be sold in China, even a wild monkey in the city, and Ma Junren multiplied his original investment.

But Ma Junren had no desire 'to rot away in the mountains', as he put it, and he went on a course that qualified him as a gym teacher in his home province. Quite soon he was showing his skills as a running coach. His pupils, running without shoes, won many school competitions. He recommended running barefoot, thought outside the traditional mould and experimented.

Ma Junren knew that Emil Zátopek had visited China for a month in 1958 and people had been inspired by his visit. He also knew that a small jogging movement had started in China in 1956 when 478 people had taken part in a run in Beijing, one kilometre for women and three kilometres for men. By 1965 it had grown to 7,000 runners and was perhaps the biggest race of its kind in the world. Similar 'round the town' runs had become common in a number of cities and were a part of the midwinter celebrations. And on 8 March, International Women's Day, the Chinese ran in crowds, though this phenomenon only happened in the towns.

Approximately 700,000 people in Beijing in the 1970s took part in a two-month running programme in memory of the 'Long March', the 10,000 kilometre march the communists made during the Chinese civil war in the 1930s. Each training group aimed to cover this distance collectively. When the jogging boom swept across the Western world, then, China was not unfamiliar with jogging. In Beijing great crowds of runners of both sexes could be seen, often running in military-style formations – runs like this were organized by their factories and workplaces.

In the course of the 1970s Ma Junren moved to larger schools and towns, determined to achieve something great and firm in his belief in his own talent. He moved to Ansha, a town with a good athletics community, and there he spent time at the stadium studying both the coaches and the runners before cycling home at eleven or twelve o'clock at night. Do, watch and study was his method – learn from the best and then construct your own, better version. He would sit among the crowds in the sporting arenas of Mao's China and stand at the roadside for road races. He read and mulled over the training literature, bursting with ambition but angrily aware that China lay far behind the West as far as running was concerned. He nevertheless saw that there *was* a road to the top, tortuous though it may be, given the right strategy for the right people.

By 1982 Junren's runners were achieving results at the top provincial level. Only four years later, as the only winners to come from Anshan that year, they took two gold medals in the provincial championships. In 1986 he visited Portugal with four of his runners and both there and in Luxembourg two years later the results caused a stir. He was appointed as the running coach for Liaoning province in 1988 and moved up the hierarchy of Chinese coaches. There are over twenty provinces in China and each of them has many tens of millions of inhabitants.

Ma Junren was not, as many in the West believed, a newcomer to coaching. Nor was he some kind of Asian charlatan, as the Western press portrayed him when it became known that he gave his runners turtle soup. Turtle soup was neither exotic nor mystical, simply one of many Chinese delicacies. Ma Junren used a large, wok-like pan in which the turtle crawled around drinking specially spiced water to acquire a particular taste before it slowly died of thirst. The white flesh of domestically raised turtles tastes rather like fish. It is not everyday food but something eaten in small quantities.

There were at least three other kinds of fortifying foods on Ma Junren's menu: donkey-skin soup – a gelatinous dish – reindeer horn and dates. The Chinese believe that foods of this kind provide extra heat. Donkey skin can be bought in a fried block, ready cooked, and kept in the freezer or refrigerator until needed, when it is boiled up with added water. Massage, acupuncture, physiotherapy and Chinese medicine all played their part in his very eclectic approach.

Ma Junren handpicked his runners on the basis of their physique and resilience. He would travel great distances to look at potential talent that had been reported to him by gym teachers and local coaches all over China. Women should resemble reindeer or ostriches, have ostrich-like legs and arms like ostrich wings. Ma Junren studied the running technique of the ostrich and considered the combination of running and hopping to be extremely effective. The women should have a short stride with minimal lifting of the knees. They would often form a line one behind the other in international fields, all with the same style and all looking as if everything had been drilled into them.

Ma Junren was just as nervous as his runners before major races: he would lose sleep and seek comfort in cigarettes and unhealthy living. This man, who would hit his runners and subject them to the strongest abuse, was also a crafty psychologist who could put on a fatherly act, organize the practical things and look after them. His bouts of temper were sparked off when things did not go according to his rigid planning and he blamed them on the pressure of work, lack of sleep and enormous ambition. It was certainly true that he worked virtually all day and all night, but other people have been able to handle similar stresses without becoming despots or resorting to physical violence. Respect, according to Ma Junren, was necessary in order to achieve good results and if the women did not respect their coach they would neither want nor be able to give of their best.

Ma Junren planned every single detail. He would position himself at races so that runners did not have to lift their heads to see him. No unnecessary energy was to be wasted and everything, including thought, should go according to the drill. In order to calm their pre-race nerves and boost their morale the women were told to think of the nation or of a group: the Chinese like to think of themselves as part of a group, so they were not running for themselves, they were running for the people. In a 1,500-metre race they were systematically to change what they were thinking about every 100 metres in accordance with Ma Junren's pre-determined plan.

Once the starter's pistol goes, the slim women set off for a 1,500 metre race, taking small steps, jostling and in a group. Ma Junren's runners remember their coach's words about the first 100 metres: calm your mind and try to relax the tension out of your body; run straight ahead and take your opponents seriously but without being afraid of them.

Mental phase two begins after 100 metres: 'I am better than all the others; I must run in the right lane and go straight ahead.' An important stage and new thoughts come after just one lap: 'Now I'm running for my country and my people; the whole country is watching me.' The people must not be let down so it is now just a matter of keeping the pace going for 600 metres, at which point new and comforting thoughts take over.

'I'm just running, it's nothing compared with what the martyr Jiang Jie went through in the 1930s when she was tortured and had splinters of bamboo driven under her nails.' Jiang Jie survived the torture without revealing anything and was then shot after appalling sufferings.

From the 1,000-metre mark on is decisive. The women are now to think of another Chinese hero, the film hero Wang Cheng, and to recognize that the torments of running are trivial by comparison. In the last 200 metres they should simply run as fast as possible and try to win.

Ma Junren was a slavedriver and easily angered. For relaxation during their free time his runners would listen to small radios – precious things in China at the time. On one occasion the coach exploded in a fit of rage, gathered all the radios and smashed them while the women watched. He forbade the reading of novels and other light reading and would burn confiscated books. The same held for women's magazines, which he would tear up in front of them to demonstrate his power and crush all opposition. They ought not to be filling their heads with silly ideas, dreams and nonsense about an unreal world.

The women were not permitted to wear make-up to make themselves attractive and they were to wear ragged clothes – they looked like a gang of well-trained tramps. People who saw them at airports and railway stations all over China were taken aback by this group of small, thin, poorly dressed and short-haired young women led by their swaggering, chain-smoking coach.

Any contact with men was banned. When they were training in Qinghai province in July 1992 Ma Junren heard that one of his runners had been talking to a man. He struck her in the face and shaved her head – she was so ashamed she ran in a cap afterwards in spite of the summer heat. She poured out her despair in a letter to her parents:

Dear Mother and Father,
When I was in Anshan I thought of coming home but you pressed me to train and sent me here to suffer. Every day I'm yelled at, punished and beaten. I really can't take any more. If I get my things together and leave he will undoubtedly punish you. He can do whatever he wants. You are not allowed to come and visit me. I'll hold out until the next time we have a holiday. On no account should you come to Qinghai and don't let anyone else see this letter or know about it.[2]

Ma Junren's sweetest triumph in the West came at the 1993 World Championships in Stuttgart. His runners took the gold in the 1,500 metres, the first three places in the 3,000 metres and the first two in the 10,000 metres.

'Doping' was the first thought that came to his critics' minds after these successes and the sensational world records over the same distances. EPO was suggested since it was being used in several endurance sports at that time. Many competitors in cycling, running, cross-country skiing and other sports were using EPO, which could not be traced in tests at that date.

From the standpoint of the West it was understandable that they suspected the Chinese of cheating since they had apparently come from nowhere. China, with all its millions, was regarded as a weak sporting nation, partly because so little information leaked out and partly because it appeared to lack any tradition of elite sport. But that was not actually the case. Journalists focused on Ma Junren's conscious disinformation about training, diet and a running style based on the ostrich but what was really important was his talent-spotting of the right physical and mental types in the rich undergrowth of talent available to him. Let us assume that the Chinese were not using dope and that none of those they were competing against in 1993 were using artificial stimulants. It is rather unlikely, but let us be naive.

In 1993 the African women had still not moved into the international elite in any numbers so the Chinese were effectively competing against Europeans, Americans and runners from Oceania. China has a population of 1.3 billion inhabitants, which is more than all its rival nations in running put together. The country was still economically and technically backward by Western standards but it was catching up fast and had a population hungry for increased welfare and material progress. Hundreds of millions of people in the countryside lived in primitive conditions and were physically very active from a young age simply to survive. Very few of them owned cars and most people walked and cycled a great deal.

In a society like that, where communism had inculcated strict ideals and had a firm grip on social life, there was a selection system in existence for sports colleges, local championships, elite sports and, at the very top level in women's running, for promotion into Ma Junren's Army. All over the world the press referred to it as an 'army' since there was something militaristic about them and about their leader.

Ambitious girls and their parents in the Chinese provinces knew of Ma Junren's success and were prepared to submit to almost anything. Those unable to tolerate the training and the strict regime disappeared and were replaced by energetic and talented newcomers. Ma Junren was sifting out potential stars from an enormous population in which toil, industriousness and obedience – particularly among poor women in the country districts – had been the norm for thousands of years. Growing up in the Chinese countryside in the 1970s and '80s was very different from growing up in the affluent West, where an abundance of food and high technology made everyday life comfortable. Many of those who passed through the Chinese sports schools possibly ended up physically and mentally warped by an upbringing that consisted of training, training and then more training. By the time the top stars in this system went out into the international scene they were well and truly hardened. Only the very best and the very toughest were allowed to represent Ma's Army abroad. After the Chinese revolution women had equal status with men and Ma was working in less complicated conditions than in the West: the system resembles the old Soviet system but the Chinese had four times the population to choose from.

The Chinese, moreover, belonged to a culture in which extreme industriousness was a virtue. An anecdote about an old Chinese man and running illustrates this. An old man was passing a stadium and could hear the sound of celebration. As the excited spectators came out he asked what it was all about,

'A new world record at the 100 metres! The old record was beaten by a tenth of a second.'

The old man thought about this and then said: 'I understand. And what's the runner going to do with the time he saved?'

This tells us a lot about Chinese humour, mentality and perception of time. Time must never be wasted, even if the anecdote itself is poking fun at the Chinese addiction to efficiency.

After the success of his women runners at the world championships in 1993 the Baishi company asked Ma Junren what kind of tonics he had given them. 'A secret nutritional drink, among other things', Ma replied. It was necessary, Ma Junren claimed (falsely), because Chinese men only have a tenth as much haemoglobin in their blood as Europeans and Chinese women only have a fifth as much. His nutritional drink remedied this difference. Baishi bought the rights to the drink for 10 million yen – almost a million pounds – and Ma Junren became a rich man.

The label lists eight ingredients: donkey skin, dates, Chinese angelica, Goji berries, the rhizomes of *Gastrodia elata*, red ginseng, deer tail and the root of Chinese milk-vetch. Once this is all mixed into a drink it is miraculously refreshing, according to Ma Junren, and only contains things that anyone in China can buy without a prescription. He founded his own health products company, which had another miracle drink among its offerings, and he went on television to advertise a company that produced turtle soup. He became a celebrity, a face familiar to all, finally realizing the colossal ambitions he had for himself. But his good fortune was not to last.

In December 1993 Ma Junren resigned from his post as coach. Early in the new year he called his runners and their parents to a crisis meeting. The women, their mothers and fathers, most of them from poor country areas, sat there and defended Ma and the case he put. They wanted the success to continue so that more money and more prestige could trickle down to them, however controversial their coach may be. The meeting demanded that others resign and leave Ma Junren in place, and they were supported by the politicians of the sports world. They only had *one* Ma Junren whereas new leaders for the sports committee could easily be found.

Ma was reinstated. The decision demonstrated his power and position in China in 1994 – and he *had* raised the status of women athletes.

Crisis after Crisis

In the summer of 1994 Ma Junren fulfilled an old dream by opening his own coaching centre. He had travelled around China and in the city of Dalian in Liaoning province he found sea views that he, a boy from the mountains, was not accustomed to. A three-storey house in Dalian now became his headquarters, though the team also moved round between several bases at varying altitudes in the mountains. The house became home to twenty young women, some of whose parents were also there to keep house. In the beginning the coaching centre also included a group of ten men.

Liu Dong spoke out about the abuses and dropped out in 1994 after several shocking episodes. Ma Junren's outburst of rage before a training camp in the mountains of Western China made her decision easier.

The women had been waiting in the bus to go to the airport that morning. Liu Dong did not arrive at the agreed time of 6.10 and the bus waited half an hour for her – she was out on a training run. The flight also delayed its departure since this was a group of the best known people in China and eventually took off twenty minutes late without Liu Dong aboard. Before leaving Ma Junren went up to Liu Dong's room on the fifth floor and hurled all of her baggage, trophies, clothes and everything else out of the window so that when she returned from her training run she found them scattered all over the street. She was, however, a world champion and was not about to tolerate that kind of treatment. She left his stable. The incident upset the rest of the women, who began to wonder who would be the next victim of the coach's volcanic temperament.

On 11 December 1994 ten women arrived in Ma's office and handed in a joint resignation. Ma Junren was dumbfounded and recognized that the situation could have been avoided. He could not sleep, he smoked incessantly, he brooded and had not been so depressed since his mother's death three decades before.

Then, on top of everything else, his father died in late December 1994 and two days later Ma Junren overturned his car on the motorway. He had reached the low point of his life. For several days he lay unconscious in hospital. On the fifth day all of his runners stood around his sickbed and looked at their suffering, rather diminished coach, who had softened a little and was full of regret: the women did at least receive some of the earnings that had been held back in their coach's care.

'Come back!' Ma Junren asked them.

The state of his health was bad and an operation for an inflamed appendix immediately after his accident made it worse.

Ma Junren has to be seen in the context of the poverty of his youth and his lack of schooling. He learnt from life, became tough and had the obstinacy typical of the self-taught. He used his late mother as a medium and she spoke to him in his dreams and prophesied the future. He passed her messages on to his runners, and these warnings tended to make them anxious and afraid for long periods: any deviation from the demands made by the medium risked punishment by the celestial powers.

Wang Junxia came from a poor home on the outskirts of Dalian. Her family effectively existed without money, relying on food they cultivated on their small plots. They rose early and spent most of the day digging in the fields, carrying water and toiling as Chinese peasants have done for thousands of years. Junxia liked running when she was a child, ran to school and soon revealed unusual physical abilities along with the willpower of an Emil Zátopek. Like thousands of others she was picked out by the system of sports schools.

After their daughter's success her parents became well known throughout the country. Her father, who had initially known very little about running,

Wang Junxia on
her way to victory
in the 10,000 metres
at the 1993 World
Championships.

became an expert commentator. As a gesture Ma Junren gave them work in his Dalian coaching centre at a good wage, since they earned virtually nothing from their land. But the chemistry between Ma Junren and Wang Junxia's parents simply did not work and their time at the coaching centre was short.

Ma Junren passed on an eerie message to Wang Junxia and it made her so anxious that she consulted a woman with second sight. The woman immediately 'foresaw' danger in the imminent New Year celebrations, particularly on the seventh and eighth days of the New Year: on these days Wang Junxia was told to shut herself in a dark room, with not even the light of a candle; she could eat but must not prepare any food.

Wang Junxia was at home on holiday at this point but on the fifth day of the New Year she travelled back to the training camp, alarmed by various bad omens. No one else had returned yet and she was uncomfortable being alone in the large house. Another one of the women returned the following day and on the seventh day of the new year the two of them went to a hotel together and took a room there. The girls got help to black out the windows and exclude the light and, with enough food for two days, Junxia and her companion stayed in the room, passive and terrified. Nothing at all happened, but the women believed in such omens and inhabited a mental world in which there were spirits and celestial beings that had to be cared for and heeded.

Ma Junren motivated his runners to give their all, threatened them with witchcraft and boosted their patriotism. He was foul-mouthed, using words like 'tart' and 'whore' in the women's presence and he would say things like 'Now we're going to beat those little Japanese' or 'We'll beat those whites with their big noses and bellies'.

In January 1995 Wang Junxia wrote a serious letter of resignation:

> I have trained hard and won prizes for my country all these years. I have done nothing that harms my country and my people. But now I am inexplicably anxious. I am afraid and I feel that despair is causing my personality to disintegrate. It might come to the point where I can't face living any more. I beg the leadership to let me go.
>
> I don't want to be spoken to because I can't bear such serious torture. I don't want to come back. I want to have an ordinary life for the rest of my life.[3]

Even Wang Junxia, the jewel in the crown of his troop, had suffered illtreatment. On one occasion when they were in Yunnan doing altitude training Wang Junxia was running in front of the group. Ma Junren leapt up in rage and accused her of showing off in front of journalists. He grabbed hold of her and hit her hard, saying: 'I'm hitting you so that the journalists can see'.[4]

Experiences of this kind in front of friends and, in this case, in front of journalists led to her dropping out of Ma's Army. Ma's military style, public rebukes and punishment of his runners were designed to make his runners respect and fear him.

A Marathon a Day?

A heavily built, authoritarian man might succeed in bossing young women around – he thinks of them as girls rather than as grown women and he knows that men would reject that kind of discipline. Which was why Ma Junren preferred to work with women, and for a long time they were afraid to oppose his regime.

Newspapers worldwide reported the inhuman training sessions. 'They run a marathon a day', Ma boasted, though he modified the claim to the journalist Zhao Yu, who stayed at his training camp in 1995. He was given to bluffing foreign journalists: his runners did not actually run over 26 miles every day, week after week, and to have done so would not have served them well, anyway. Exaggerating the amount of training was a game, he said, or was it just another lie?

Ma's Army lived just as most top runners live. They got up early, went for a morning run and then ate breakfast. Ma bought and cooked the food himself, or it was prepared by cooks indoctrinated with his culinary philosophy. On the breakfast table there would be rice porridge, good-quality sausage, boiled eggs, vegetables and bread – a good, solid, filling Chinese breakfast, after which they went to sleep.

Soup was the main dish for lunch – either fish soup, chicken or turtle. They then went back to bed, two women to a room, before a cup of donkey-skin soup that preceded afternoon training. After running they would return to a rich and varied dinner and then there would be a some of Ma Junren's specially concocted fortifying drink before bedtime at 9 p.m. Two training sessions a day were sufficient and Ma Junren was usually present for the afternoon one.

Zhao Yu wrote an account of Ma Junren and his women runners, based on a stay at their training headquarters from February to June 1995. He also interviewed the runners and their parents. The critical and negative tone of the account annoyed Ma: 'It's shortened my life by five years', he said, bitter at the thought of having given the journalist hospitality and revealed his secrets to him.

A 2004 biography of Ma Junren presented a different and, for him, rather more favourable version. It was based on many long interviews rather than on a stay at the training camp and it seems to present a balanced picture.[5]

Ma Junren was unmatched in terms of competence and knowledge. He is reminiscent of the Japanese coach Nakamura and his ambitions were at least on the scale of those of Arthur Lydiard and Percy Wells Cerutty. Ma Junren's life dream became a reality when his runners beat the rest of the world on the track. That was his way of conquering the world and showing he was best. Like some other coaches he was even more ambitious than his runners, even though he had never won anything of importance as a runner himself.

When he lost his job as coach Ma Junren began breeding an endangered Tibetan breed of dog.

31
Striding Out of Poverty

> But the real problems can't be overcome just by
> Ethiopians running fast.
> —Haile Gebreselassie from Ethiopia, one of the all-time best
> long-distance runners, commenting on poverty and famine
> in his homeland

It is the end of the 1990s and an experienced American coach is once again in Kenya to recruit new runners. Since he got in contact with Kip Keino in the 1960s and took him over to the USA many runners from the Nandi district have received student scholarships in America thanks to Fred Hardy. Keino has been the middle man, the one with the local knowledge, the one the Kenyans rely on. On this particular day they are visiting the Kurgat family, whose son Josiah has finished high school and is looking carefully at offers from educational institutions in America.

Kip Keino and Hardy are driving out to the Kurgat's farm. They turn off on to a gravel road and pass cows and goats grazing on the small farm. The house has mud walls and a corrugated iron roof. As the car roars into the farmyard three younger brothers and sisters run out. Mother and father come out too.

Hardy greets them in Swahili and they all shake hands. He then switches to English and Keino translates. 'How are things going with Ben?' Kurgat Senior asks, referring to the son who has already been recruited by Hardy and is living in the USA.[1]

'He's running well and is among the best in the university in his field', Hardy says, handing over a present from Ben – an elegant leather jacket, beyond the pocket of a poor farmer. The family is excited by the jacket and by the presence of Kip Keino, who is only one down from God in these parts. Hardy lets the family admire the gift and then says to the father:

'I'd like to talk to you and his mother about Josiah. I'm hoping he can get into the University of North Carolina.'

It is an irresistible combination, a representative from a university in the richest country in the world, offering a running career and a free education, together with the man who is the Nandi's greatest living folk-hero.

'Well, you've given me one son. I want to be sure I have your permission to take your second son. I think he'll be a success and happy at the University of North Carolina. Do I have your and his mother's permission?'

Keino translates and the Kurgats discuss it in their local dialect. 'The family will rely on you. We Kalenjin respect our elders', they say to Hardy, who is in his eighties. They all smile and the family begins to plan a *haram-bee*, a get-together to raise money, in this case for Josiah's air ticket.

They all chat peaceably together and discuss the conditions and practical details until they reach agreement. Hardy is clearly pleased when he takes them all by the hand and joins in a Kalenjin prayer.

'Many, many thanks for your son.'[2]

Hardy has recruited yet another runner for the University of North Carolina. No one knows for sure what happens to Kenyan runners in the USA or what happens after their studies are finished. Not all of them return home even though they perhaps want to. Going abroad and getting an education does not always have positive results. There is no guarantee of success even for a Nandi, but Kip Keino knows that ambitious boys still long to go. For forty years and more the Nandi have told stories of the Promised Land, which may not always be filled with milk and honey but neverthe-less offers many possibilities. In his own eyes Hardy is a benefactor who brings poor young men to a rich country with a good offer to study. Both Josiah and his family will benefit from his stay in the USA. It will bring in capital and lead to material progress.

Is there any great difference between Hardy's motives and those of the buyers of West African slaves in the USA in the eighteenth century? The slave trade was a brutal one-way ticket to a lifetime of subjection, a cynically ex-ploitative trade in human beings. Modern-day runners can become wealthy and get a sound education; they can quite literally take a step in the direc-tion of material luxury. It is an economic migration that often works to the advantage of both parties, but it also based on the fact that wealth is dis-tributed extremely unevenly and that Americans are taking advantage of the physical accomplishments of Africans. Though some of their countrymen are envious, most Kenyans consider it an honour to get a scholarship and they are prepared to put up with any difficulties.

A Tribe of Runners

The Kenyans train hard but talent can also lie latent. Rapid progress is typical of the Nandi even when they do not become world-class. Take Paul Rotich for example, who was sent to the United States in 1988 to get a de-cent education and who had no thought of sport. His wealthy father gave him $10,000 to go and he led a riotous life at South Plains Junior College in Texas. By his first spring the sum had already shrunk to $2,000 and Paul was afraid he would have to return home in shame without completing his education. So the 175 pound, 5 foot 8 inch young man began to train, at first at night since he was embarrassed by his lack of fitness. By the autumn he was a good deal thinner and had got into his school's cross-country team.

He got a running scholarship at a nearby university and made a success of it. When he went home to Kenya and told his cousin about his new, un-planned career, his cousin answered: 'If you can run, any Kalenjin can run.'[3]

The Nandi, a sub-group of the Kalenjin people, make up less than two percent of the population of Kenya, which consists of 40 African tribes plus Asians and Europeans.[4] Why has the Nandi tribe, with about 500,000 members, produced so many top runners?

Tradition is important and Kip Keino's shining example has inspired several generations. Long, slim legs and lightly built bodies are also important, along with a naturally efficient running economy. Growing up in the thin air at 5,000 or 6,000 feet (1,500–1,800 m) above sea level has a lasting effect that is advantageous in endurance sports. And the physically demanding and painful customs of the tribe must also be reckoned with – the emphasis on being tough, rather like the Spartans.

Boys are circumcised at fifteen. The operation is supervised by tribal elders who watch to see whether the boy shows signs of pain: this is a society in which it is cowardly to complain about pain. Those who do not pass the test are called *kibitet*, 'cowards', and are excluded from the most important spheres of male activity. They are not invited to join cattle-raids, not allowed to speak in the tribal council and not usually allowed to marry.

Women are also circumcised. The operation is done without anaesthetic. If they complain or cry they are called *chebitet* and risk bearing cowardly sons.[5]

The Nandi are feared as cattle-raiders and as good warriors. Cattle-raiding is an old custom, in which 40 or 50 men or more may run anything up to 100 miles (160 km) in a night to take the herd they have chosen. Endurance and the ability to run well are all-important on these raids, during which they eat and drink as little as possible and return home quickly. These raids still occur and the Kenyans do not consider them to be theft since cattle are thought of as divine property.[6]

The Nandi have lived as nomads and cultivated the soil. Their way of life in the Kenyan Highlands has made them a tribe that possesses all the qualifications necessary for fast running at middle and long distances.

Historically speaking the basic food of the Kalenjin people has been milk, blood and meat – the first two being consumed raw – but they have also grown and eaten cereals. In more recent times the Kalenjin have eaten a more varied diet than, for instance, the Masai, who have continued to stick to the older tradition.

Traditionally the Kalenjin cultivated millet and sorghum; the main crops of today, maize and sugar peas, are relatively new introductions, as are vegetables. Their carbohydrate intake is high – 465–600 grams a day, about 70 per cent of their diet. Fat makes up about 15 per cent. The main items of their diet – maize, beans, cabbage, kale, wheat and beef – are produced locally. They drink milk, coffee and tea.

A 2002 Danish study showed that 6 per cent of their total calorie intake came from milk. That was less than expected, but the consumption of milk rose before important competitions. At a pre-competition training camp two years later milk made up 13 per cent of the calorific intake, which is still far below the levels consumed by traditional nomads like the Masai. Runners from the Kalenjin tribe eat more vegetables and carbohydrates than pure nomads.

It makes sense to top up on carbohydrates quickly after hard training. In the Danish study the runners were given breakfast and dinner after the morning and afternoon training sessions respectively, which is the ideal way of replacing the glycogens quickly. Maize, which made up 64 per cent of the calorie intake, has a high glycemic index and thus provides virtually optimum replacement of glycogen.

The average Kalenjin intake of fat is 46 grams a day, which is average for the population of Kenya as a whole. The Kenyans eat little fat in comparison to the top runners from other nations.

It is often stated in the West that the great Kenyan runners have a metabolic advantage. Bengt Saltin from Sweden has measured the Hydroxyacl-CoA-dehydrogenase (HAD)-enzyme activity in thigh and calf muscles: it is an indicator of the body's ability to convert fat to energy. HAD-enzyme activity in thigh and calf muscles was respectively 20 per cent and 50 per cent higher in Kenyans than in Scandinavian elite runners. They are thus utilizing the fat efficiently. Experiments carried out by Timothy Noakes in South Africa show that this is true of black runners in general, not just the Kenyans.

Their average daily intake of protein is 75–88 grams. The increased amount of milk taken in periods of intense training adds important amino acids.

There has been little investigation of vitamins and minerals and it is uncertain how much wild plant material supplements the diet. The most comprehensive study so far looks at the pupils who are runners at a boarding school in Marakwet.

These pupils showed low intake levels of minerals and vitamins, as is usually the case in Africa. The important antioxidants – vitamins A, E and C – were consumed at levels of 17 per cent, 65 per cent and 95 per cent of WHO recommended levels respectively. The level of iron intake, on the other hand, was extremely high at 152 milligrams a day, which may perhaps be put down to the length of the cooking time or to iron-rich soil. The high iron intake did not, however, provide the Kenyans with extra haemoglobin: the type of iron they consumed is not easily absorbed by the body and, moreover, they consume only small amounts of two vitamins necessary to the absorption of iron, namely folic acid and B12. An additional factor is that many Kenyans are infected with malaria parasites and tapeworms, both of which have a negative impact on the level of haemoglobin. Their daily intake of calcium was 600 milligrams, approximately half of the amount recommended by the WHO.

Kenyan runners, then, do not have an adequate diet, especially in terms of the recommended norms for the daily intake of vitamins and minerals. But a simple diet also has advantages and Kenyan runners living overseas often try to keep to their traditional foods.[7]

Many of the Kenyan runners from the 1990s and beyond were migrant workers. They went out into the world to get rich and, like other migrant workers, they listened to rumours or followed relations and acquaintances when deciding where to base themselves in order to earn the best money. So they lived in Scandinavia, Britain, Italy, the USA, Japan, Germany and elsewhere. They often lived in overcrowded conditions, three or four to a small room, had limited social contact outside their own circle, and concentrated on running fast. Some of them changed their citizenship or, if they represented a Muslim state, their names. Those who succeeded became rich, but there was an underclass of runners who did not reach the elite level however much they tried. As migrant workers they could easily despair and end up living and working in inadequate conditions and being exploited.

Japheth Kimutai (1978–) had some success at 800 metres. What was on his mind when he joined the circus of European meetings in the mid-1990s?

He was thinking of land and of buying land, first of all for his parents and then for himself. He was thinking of grazing for cows and beef cattle, the largest possible unbroken acreage of land. That was the dream that inspired his running career. He loved running and was a great enthusiast for sport but, like other ambitious Nandi, he had asked himself what skills he had and how he could best use them to get out of poverty and achieve a better life.

Running was the best and quickest way but he had no desire to go via a long education in America. He took the shortest route into the European circus as a teenager and set an 800 metres world junior record of 1 minute 43.64 seconds.

Japheth's family farm was ten acres but he wanted three times as much land. That was the dream he had in his head when he came to Europe every summer to race in the big events. An Australian manager arranged the practical side of things and put all his appearance and prize money into a European account, from which it was transferred to an African bank.

The price of land increased during Kimutai's time and you had to be careful who you were dealing with to avoid being swindled. Much of the land was owned by politicians and it was not unheard-of for the same plot to be sold to two people so that the seller made a double profit at the same time as creating a horrendously tangled legal situation. Japheth sought the advice of earlier top runners and did as they had done.

Kimutai knew that politicians and chiefs, even from his own Nandi tribe, disliked poor boys becoming wealthy by running and then going out and buying large farms. So he was careful who he bought from: better to wait for a later deal than to buy plots of land owned by unreliable people in Kenya, one of the most corrupt countries in Africa.

After his first payment Kimutai bought land for his parents, then he began to collect land for himself. Every running season led to improvements on Kimutai's growing farm – a new tractor, new equipment, a new employee and a new car. The aim was to make improvements year by year until he had his dream farm.

By the age of thirty Japheth Kimutai had realized his dream of owning 30 acres. He has his own farm with workers to milk the cows and look after the beef cattle. Like his successful fellow runners among the Nandi he is free to follow his own interests, to help his fellows as coach and to work to improve their situation. He advises them to buy land and to invest carefully starting with their very first pay-cheque. In Eldoret, the main Nandi town, many of the tower-blocks and business premises are owned by the running stars of the past. Many of the inhabitants of the posh residential area are former runners who have invested their money sensibly. But Kimutai also knows of some who have squandered their assets or been tricked by swindlers – the Nandi are often naive and trusting in their financial dealings.

Japheth Kimutai may have a mobile telephone and use email but he has remained loyal to his deep roots in the cattle-focused, agricultural culture of the Nandi. He is also an abstainer who consciously avoids alcohol, knowing what it has done to other men in his milieu.[8]

A Kenyan with a time of 2 hours and 7 minutes in the marathon succumbed to alcohol and died as a homeless, alcoholic vagrant in Boston in 2007: the Kenyan runners in the USA collected money to send his coffin home to Kenya. A notable number of earlier Kenyan running stars have drunk themselves to death although that has not always been admitted as the cause of death. Alcohol has ruined many of them physically. The long and toilsome journey from the Rift Valley into the international arena, years abroad and contact with a completely different culture, in which human beings are commodities, is bound to leave deep traces on the body and on the mind.

Single-minded Women

Kenyan women arrived on the scene later than the men and it was not until the 1990s that there were many of them among the international elite. The Nandi dominated among them, too.

A survey in 2003 asked 250 women between the ages of twelve and fifty why they had started running. The women in the survey had either taken part in the Olympics or other international events or were showing great potential as juniors. Half of them stated they had started in order to make money; just 20 per cent said they had been inspired by their models; 1.5 per cent ran for pleasure and 3.5 per cent ran to keep fit.

The average daily wage in Kenya is less than one euro (£0.86 or US$1.40) so it is clearly tempting to take up running as a way of earning money – an annual income as small as $10,000 might be ten times what could be earned at home. When Catherine Ndereba beat the world record in the 2001 Chicago Marathon she won $75,000 as the first prize, $100,000 for the world record and a car worth $26,000. In addition to that there were appearance fees and championship bonuses: winning major marathon races is profitable and also opens the way to other money-making possibilities.

Kenyan women runners have even stronger economic motives than the men in that money can buy independence. Kenyan women are often excluded from the acquisition of land and wealth. They cannot inherit land and they usually live on land that belongs to male relatives. With money in the bank they can buy their own land, something unheard-of earlier except for those from rich families. Kenyan women can thus provide for whole families, indeed, for whole villages. And Kenyan women are often more sensible with their assets than their male colleagues: they are more conscientious, less given to squandering money and taking to drink.[9]

Foreign Helpers

Coaches from many countries have been active in Kenya for decades. One of them, Dr Gabriel Rosa, went there from Italy and organized races at all levels and for all age-groups. Unlike a number of other Italian coaches and doctors involved in running he has no doping scandals linked to his name. He has staked out his own path and not cooperated with any of those investigated for cheating. After Rosa had guided Gianni Poli to victory in the 1986 New York City Marathon several elite runners, including Moses Kiptanui from Kenya, turned to him for advice. In 1992 Rosa started the project 'Discovery Kenya', which was soon being sponsored by the Italian company Fila: a number of major foreign sponsors had seen the value of supporting Kenyan running several decades before that.

But when Rosa entered the field there was no tradition of marathon running in Kenya: in 1990 Douglas Wakiihuri was the only Kenyan ranked in the international top twenty at that distance, and the next two Kenyans came at numbers 80 and 100 in the rankings. Fourteen years later fifty of the world's best hundred marathon runners were from Kenya, the majority of them belonging to Rosa's stable.[10]

Rosa established his first training camp in 1993 and followed it up with twelve more, capable of accommodating up to a hundred runners, close to the runners' home districts. Here they get up early, run in silent and focused groups, rest, train some more, eat and go to bed early, without any access to electricity or mobile telephones. This is their university, and the runners have to graduate from it before going on to compete in Europe, the USA and Asia. Foreigners come to visit and join the groups of Kenyans, since many people are curious and keen to learn – and what they see is simplicity and discipline. There is something timeless about these training camps where the only things on the timetable are simple tasks and everyday necessities – a profound contrast to the environment that awaits the runners if they achieve an entry ticket for the international circuit. They train in the highlands of Africa and move out into a materially richer world. In Kenya in 2008 the route out is via running, in the same way that in an earlier age a career in the army could lead to individual advancement.

Rosa wanted to bring them together in groups to teach them about training and about an ascetic lifestyle. Those in the training camps have to leave their families, friends and jobs for months in order to run full-time and to live according to Rosa's philosophy: 'training twice a day, relaxation and the right diet'. The competition is fierce and leads to rising standards and the selection of the very best.[11]

Rosa employs 40 people, including cooks and coaches, in his twelve camps for 200 runners. Only the youngest, those who are still at school and have their school fees paid by Rosa's company, live at home.

The camps often have several brothers at the same time, though they will usually have different second names since the second name refers to some particular circumstance at the time of their birth. The surname of the 800-metre world record holder Wilson Kipketer means 'born on the veranda'; Kipkeino means 'born while the goats were being milked'. There are also inherited nicknames like Tergat, which means 'stands or walks with his head slightly to one side', or Barngetuby, 'father has killed a lion'. Boys' surnames often begin with Kip or Ki whereas girls have names starting with Chep or Che.[12]

European missionaries have also played their part in the success of the Kenyan runners. St Patrick's High School in Iten, established by the Patrician Brothers from Ireland in 1960, is the best-known institution, but the Cardinal Otunga High School in Kisii, founded in 1961 by the Dutch Brothers of Tilburg, has also produced its share of international stars.

The first principal of St Patrick's, Brother Simon, was an athletics enthusiast who coached the pupils. All the boys at level one have to take part, which makes it possible to pick out the most talented. Mike Boit, one of the international elite at 800 metres in the 1970 and 1980s, was an early product of the school. Foreign coaches were appointed in the 1970s to raise the standard. Later world-star runners have testified to their rewarding years at this school, where most of the running is done cross-country since it does not have a track of its own.[13]

The Scourge of Africa

Seen from Europe Africa may appear to be a continent of runners. But the jogging movement has not taken off there and the inhabitants prefer to walk if they do not have a car. Henry Rono's children do not run, not even to stay in shape, even though they live very close to a perfect training environment in Kenya. Haile Gebrselassie ran in order to make his family sufficiently affluent for his children to have no need to run in their father's footsteps.

In 2007 Africa had 690 million inhabitants spread across its 53 countries. It is mainly Kenya, Ethiopia, Algeria and Morocco that have produced large numbers of people who have made their way in the world by running.

Maria Mutola, Mozambique's best 800-metre runner, has sent large sums of money home every year for years. In 2003 she won a million dollars in the Golden League Athletic Grand Prix and donated part of it to a foundation in her homeland. There are farms and small businesses that owe their survival to Mutola's generosity – it has brought first aid to the country and wells have been dug and tractors bought.

Haile Gebrselassie from Ethiopia, the King of Long-distance, has always run in the full knowledge of how poor his country is. He ran because he had to – six miles to and from school and working in the fields afterwards – and later he felt a responsibility to fight poverty: 'When I'm training I think a lot about this – because we cannot move forward as a country until we have eradicated poverty. But the real problems can't be overcome just by Ethiopians running fast'.[14]

Globalization is a fact in sport as in everything else. Just as goods are produced wherever in the world it costs least to do so, running stars from small African tribal societies can be brought to the greatest international arenas because there is a system for refining the raw material of talent. The grandparents and great-grandparents of present-day Kenyans and Ethiopians were just as well endowed with the talent for running long distances but two or three generations ago there was no system in place to give them access to the international stage. It also has to do with the achievement of freedom from colonial rule during the post-war period, one of the consequences of which was the opportunity and the will to take part in events such as the Olympic Games.

One of the paradoxes of the situation has been that the same elements that milked Kenya during the colonial age – smart, white middle-men – have also acted as agents in the import/export of runners. Retired and still active runners in Kenya are now in the process of organizing themselves in order to present a stronger front. Many of the international stars who live in and around Eldoret are uniting to speak on behalf of the runners and to lessen the practical problems and demands the Nandi face during a running career.

The runners have travelled in the opposite direction to the colonists who subjugated Africa in the nineteenth century. They have visited Europe and the West on the white man's terms. While the colonizing powers grew rich on the exploitation of raw materials, African runners have had to toil like fleet-footed slaves on the away-stage, often against one another, in order to harvest as much as they can of the fruits of Mammon. They have been competing for themselves and for their families and countries in a foreign arena, on conditions set by others. Few outsiders have understood what that really means.

32
How Fast Can a Human Being Run?

> If you want to win something, run the 100 metres. If you
> want to learn something about life, run the marathon.
> —Emil Zátopek

There are many anecdotes about people who have learnt to run fast by living in the animal world. There is, for example, the 'gazelle boy' observed by the French anthropologist Jean-Claude Armen in the Spanish Sahara in 1963. He sat in his car and followed a gazelle boy – a boy who had grown up among the gazelles – running at a speed of 34 miles (55 km) an hour. To the amazement of those in the car, who had never seen anything like it, he loped along with all the elegance of the animals that had fostered him. The story and the speed has never been proven, perhaps because it is untrue or exaggerated, but there are well-known cases of children having been fostered by animals and adopting the way of life of the species.

If Armen was correct in his measurement of the boy's speed, he was much faster than the fastest man in the world, who has been timed at nearly 28 miles (45 km) an hour. That, however, is slow by comparison with many animal species: the cheetah can reach 70 miles (113 km) an hour, horses at 43 miles (69 km) an hour are superior to men, and even a heavy, clumsy gorilla can keep up 30 miles (48 km) an hour for over half a mile.[1]

It is endurance that is man's strong point and he will beat the horse over the long run. Since 1980 a Man versus Horse Marathon has been organized annually in Wales, in which runners, cyclists and horses race a distance a little short of a marathon across hilly country. In 2004 Huw Lobb was the first man on foot to achieve overall victory against a field of 40 horses and 500 runners. His finishing time of 2 hours 5 minutes and 19 seconds was a good two minutes ahead of the first horse.

Who is the world's fastest human being? According to an athletics definition it must be the winner of the men's 100 metre race at the world championships or in the Olympic Games. The distance might appear to be unproblematical.

Experts divide the 100 metre race into three or five phases: acceleration for the first 30 to 40 metres; top speed for 20 to 30 metres; loss of speed towards the end. 'Did you see his finish!' was a phrase often heard, for instance, about the American Carl Lewis during the 1980s and '90s: in reality it meant that he slowed down less than the other competitors. It is also usual to reckon with an extra phase right at the beginning – the reaction phase – and another phase at the end, both of which are very significant for the result.

In theory the runner who runs fastest in the race may not win – he may reach the highest speed but lose because his acceleration and final phases are slower than those of his competitors. Studies have shown, however, that there is a close correlation between high speed and final result: the man who reaches the highest speed in the 100 metres will be fairly certain to win.[2]

The actual top speed is difficult to measure since it only lasts for two or three seconds. It is simple enough to measure the speed of a rolling wheel but harder to do so with a man whose arms and legs are thrashing throughout the 100-metre dash. One tenable measurement was that made when Donovan Bailey of Canada set a world record of 9.87 seconds at the 1997 World Championships: he was running at up to 12.1 metres a second or 27.27 miles an hour.

Fifty-five men from sixteen countries had run the 100 metres in under ten seconds in approved wind conditions up to the 2008 season. None of them was white and all but one had origins traceable to West Africa, irrespective of whether they were representing African, European, Caribbean or North American countries. They were native Africans or descendants of slaves, either of single or of mixed race. The exception was the Australian Patrick Johnson, whose father was Irish and whose mother was Aboriginal. One white runner was close, Marion Woronin from Poland, as was one Japanese, Koji Ito – both of them had 10.00 seconds.

Is it an accident that no white runner has managed to break the ten-second barrier in approved wind conditions? There is definitely a psychological barrier. The huge bias in the figures has fuelled a debate as to whether black West Africans are faster than the rest of the world's population. The statistics suggest they are. But it is also likely that there is an element of the self-fulfilling prophecy about it: in the USA, for instance, since white boys and girls are always told that black runners are superior in sprint events, they go away and choose to compete at something else. And few black runners in the United States have distinguished themselves at distances over 800 metres.

None of the West African countries have long-distance runners of a high international standard. The country with the highest density of world-class sprinters in proportion to the population is Jamaica, but Jamaica has never produced runners of the highest standard at more than 800 metres. Little Jamaica has a population of 2.6 million but almost always has competitors of both sexes in international sprint finals. In addition to which, many Jamaicans have emigrated to the USA, Canada and Britain and represent those countries in sprint events: they train in different countries and different environments but they still reach the top.

Only two Jamaicans have ever run 10,000 metres in less than 30 minutes, and Jamaican women are in a similar position. The results show that long-distance running neither enthuses nor suits Jamaicans and there may be particular cultural factors that contribute to that.

Genes are important in sprinting and really talented sprinters can run fast without training, whether they happen to be black or white. A runner who lacks a high percentage of fast muscle fibre stands no chance in a 100-metre sprint and the fields of international sprinters are all approaching perfection for the particular event. There have been studies to estimate what percentage of fast muscle fibre the best sprinters have, but it is not a simple matter. The proportion of different muscle fibres is not evenly distributed through the muscle and no active world-class runner would donate the whole muscle for research. Researchers are limited to taking and testing samples that might reveal tendencies. It is unlikely that anyone has only fast muscle fibres, but if the proportion of such fibres is particularly high then that individual can more easily improve because the fast muscle fibres will be trained irrespective of what the runner is doing, even if the training is wrong.[3]

It is an interesting fact that a 100-metre runner takes the same number of strides in every race once he or she is fully grown. Among the best runners, the number of strides is between 43 and 50, with some slight variation depending on height but irrespective of whether the wind is with them or against them. The Canadian Ben Johnson took 46.1 strides whether his time was 10.44 or 9.83 at different points in his career. It demonstrates that progress is achieved through faster rather than by longer strides.

It is dangerous to claim that any one race is better than another at any activity. In men's sprinting and long-distance running, however, West Africans and East Africans respectively are outstandingly the best in 2008, though that has not always been the case.

In 1986 about half of the twenty best times at distances between 800 metres and the marathon were held by European men and about a quarter by Africans. In 2003 the European element in the statistics was 11 per cent whereas 85 per cent of the best times were due to African runners. In the same year all of the world records from 100 metres up to the marathon were held by Africans or people of African origin.

Have the Africans become stronger because they want to run their way out of poverty? That is certainly an important motivation and one they put forward themselves. Physical differences are another reason. Insufficient research has yet been done in this area and it may be that we will never know the answer since there are so many factors at play even in something as simple as running.

The picture is a rather different one among the women. A black runner holds the records at 100 and 200 metres but, with the exception of the 5,000 metres, all the records from 400 to 10,000 metres are in the hands of white Europeans or Chinese. Is this because the African women entered the international elite later than their male counterparts?

Where Is the Limit?

The Finnish researcher Juha Heikkala believes that the development of sportsmen and women is hindered if a limit is set. It would conflict with a basic concept of modern elite sport, which is that improved performance is the driving force.[4]

The world's best 100-metre time in 1900 was 10.8 seconds; in 2009 it is 9.58, using more accurate electronic timekeeping. The world record for the 10,000 metres has dropped from 31 minutes 40 seconds to 26 minutes 17.53 seconds over the same period.

The reasons are more and better training, better tracks and an increased focus on running in many countries. At the beginning of the twentieth century the naturally talented were dominant and even Olympic champions trained as little as once or twice a week. A century later the top performers do more training in a day than many of the international elite used to do in a week.

According to researchers at IRMES, the French national institute for sport medicine, we shall soon reach the limit for world records in running and other disciplines. They have studied 3,263 world records set since 1896 in various branches of sport and noted how the curve has flattened out: records were broken less frequently as standards reached a higher level towards the end of the twentieth century. Using mathematical modelling techniques they conclude that there will be virtually no new running records after 2027. One possibility would be to measure times to three decimal places in order to make more improvements possible.[5]

The researchers have estimated that the sportsmen in Athens in 1896 only utilized 75 per cent of their physical capacity. The best modern competitors use 99 per cent or more of their capacity and science has contributed to raising the level. Innumerable methods and techniques, both legal and illegal, have been used in order to run faster. Doping has led to the standard of world records being artificially high and further improvements will be difficult without the use of doping. New methods of doping, such as gene doping, for instance, whereby a gene that causes certain muscles to grow abnormally is implanted into the competitor, could be advantageous in the 100-metre sprint. The heart and its ability to pump oxygen is an important factor in distance running and that, too, can be improved by doping. Changes in the field of equipment are unlikely to lead to improvements in running.

Some of the women's world records are considered to be virtually unbeatable. Florence Griffith-Joyner from the USA produced 10.49 seconds for the 100 metres in 1988, a time that very few women a decade later are within half a second of. Marita Koch's 47.60 seconds for the 400 metres also seems untouchable. Among men, the American Michael Johnson's 200 metres in 19.32 seconds was reckoned to be the limit for a long time – his technique and the level he achieved and retained was compared to that of Jesse Owens.

Nevertheless, in 2008 the Jamaican Usain Bolt beat Johnson's record with 19.30 seconds, and currently holds a new record of 19.19 seconds.

The IRMES researchers think that the world-record beaters of the future will be from Africa. That is where there are still many great performers waiting to be discovered, to be refined and to compete internationally before they produce their optimal performances.

From the Antarctic to the Sahara

The number of ultra- and extreme runs has grown enormously in all parts of the world since the 1980s. In the wake of the jogging craze runners and organizers have been seeking new and all-surpassing challenges. Many of them want to get out and away from asphalt and exhaust, out into exotic surroundings, preferably among steep hills – anywhere you can run.

One of the oldest adventure runs, the Everest Marathon in Nepal, was started in 1987 by two Britons who had organized an impromptu run along the main Mount Everest trail two years earlier. The race starts at 5,184 metres above sea level and finishes at 3,346 metres. To reach the start the competitors do the sixteen-day walk-in as a group. The race, which is rather reminiscent of an expedition, attracts 75 overseas runners every year, along with ten Nepalese.

The expedition element is also a characteristic of a number of other extreme races that have grown up in a world in which well-off people travel, flying about more than ever before with the time and resources to pursue their hobbies. Even though extreme running and tourism have a good deal in common, the extreme runner achieves rather more than the sedentary tourist. He is more physically involved, testing himself against nature and terrain over a set distance while drawing on his bodily resources. He is more than just a lazy consumer of a new country, and he feels that he gets more in return for his visit.

In 2003 the two Englishmen Ranulph Fiennes and Mike Stroud took on a $7 \times 7 \times 7$ challenge: seven marathons on seven continents in seven days. It involved advanced logistics and a great deal of travel stress. It is perhaps typical that it was the British that undertook this, given their proud tradition of conquest.

It is all about collecting experiences. People compete to complete the most marathons, the most in one year, the most in the USA and so on. The only limits that exist are those set by their own imaginations. Runners and other expeditioners set their own goals, such as the Antarctic marathon or the North Pole marathon, in which people are recommended to use small snowshoes in case there is drifting snow.

The Indian guru Sri Chinmoy was a modern ultrarunner motivated by religion. Starting in 1977 he offered salvation to the masses in the USA with running as one of many messages. He was a well-built guru whose mantra was sport, unlike the usual fakirs who lie or sit with crossed legs. Chinmoy lifted nuggets of wisdom from Greek and Indian philosophy and preached a worldview based on harmony, which was to be achieved through a robust physical education and a healthy inner life. When he suffered injuries from too much running in the 1990s, he took up weight-lifting. His followers have organized everything from short runs to the longest annual race in the world, the 3,100-mile Self-Transcendence Race in New York, which covers 5,649 laps of its course. In Chinmoy's view such tests lead to exceptionally valuable insights.

The classic desert run is the Marathon des Sable in Morocco, which has been going on since 1986 when 23 runners completed 240 kilometres. There are few places in the world where runners have suffered worse sores and blisters than in the sand-dunes of the Sahara, and few places, too, where the runners have sweated several litres a day. It is an almost surreal sight to see these thin, pale but vigorous figures starting out in a group from the tented camp with six stages to go, rucksacks on their backs and heads covered, heading for a goal that is many miles away. It is both absurd and beautiful, an experience of the natural world *and* a hot and sweaty way to learn about yourself. It is not, of course, something that the local population invented, although some Moroccans take part and some have won. The desert race is the invention of urban white men – Frenchmen in Paris and other cities, whose everyday lives are spent in front of computer screens or on mobile telephones, find a release for their sense of adventure and achievement in the Marathon des Sables. No one would have believed when it started that, by 2005, the Marathon des Sables would be attracting 766 starters from many countries.

The participants in these extreme runs are a travel-insured and pampered version of the explorers of the past. Runners have invaded the farthest outposts of the world and raced in them, they have colonized every geographical zone and declared them conquered. There is almost no natural environment on the globe that remains untouched by the feet of joggers. Is a marathon on the moon the next step?

The Timeless Stride

Human beings have been running for thousands of years, long before the archaeological sources can tell us why and long before civilizations arose. Hunting and the other practical aspects of the struggle for survival meant that they had to do so. This fundamental way of moving from place to place has to be seen in the context of its time and of its society. Human beings have run for many reasons – just think of the difference between someone running for his life and a well-nourished jogger.

The oldest sources tell us of sacred, royal races in Egypt and Sumeria, when the king ran out to placate the gods and retain power in his kingdom. The Greeks, too, communicated with their gods at the games, though they also considered running to be beneficial to the development of the individual as well as being necessary for the defence of the city-state. For several thousand years runners had a military role as special forces or messengers. Running had a practical and a symbolic function and runners were important links in peacetime as well as the fastest legs on the battlefield.

Among peoples like the Native Americans running was practical and mythic. One of the last tribes to do so, the Tarahumara in Mexico still carry on their proud, ancient running tradition. In India, indeed, there are still message runners to deliver the post in districts without roads and they still announce their arrival by ringing a bell.

Running provided entertainment of different sorts in the Europe of the eighteenth and nineteenth centuries, something that made people laugh and fascinated them with its speed. The British brought a new dimension to it when they introduced betting on races and timekeeping accurate to the second. They also spread their civilization, which included the British approach to sport and to the formation of character by physical pursuits. Industrial society demanded efficiency and measurable progress and these demands were transferred to the new sports fields. Running became more organized and gave meaning to the clock-bound everyday lives of people at the start of the twentieth century.

In the national rivalries that followed the reintroduction of the Olympic Games, Finland was the first nation to consciously use running for nation-building and as symbolic of the character and identity of the nation. Other nations later followed Finland in this.

Running, however, had still not actively captured the masses: it was something to watch and read about, a chase in which the self-evident watchword was 'faster'. Well into the twentieth century runners formed an eccentric clique with a penchant for tormenting themselves, strange fellows who had discovered something that few others recognized – that running can offer a profound inner satisfaction. Many doctors, however, considered it to be an activity dangerous to the heart and other vital organs. It was only with the arrival of the 1960s that jogging started to be regarded as good for the health, as something overfed people needed as a proper counterweight to their sedentary everyday lives. Running became part of a lifestyle aimed at preserving health and controlling weight, a daily leisure interval devoted to movement. It was pleasure and duty, a fashionable phenomenon with a variety of side-effects.

Jogging proved to be the salvation of many hearts and the ruination of many knees and other joints. It caused a torrent of injuries and minor pains which these previously unfit enthusiasts did not know existed. It was a great experiment for millions of people to swarm out onto the roads and paths, often badly shod and with a poor and uneconomical running style, and with no prior understanding of the unaccustomed loadings and stresses. Never before had so many people tried to improve their performance curve at an age when their ancestors would long since have given up physical competition. The jogging wave has not swept ashore everywhere, it has mostly been a feature of the Western world, but few countries have completely escaped the many, multi-legged herds of competing joggers.

The Olympic Day Run was first organized in 1987 to commemorate the foundation of the International Olympic Committee in Paris on 23 June 1894. Every year runners all over the world get together for it in their respective homelands and even in countries not traditionally associated with mass runs – Mongolia, for instance – tens of thousands have joined in. In Mongolia they recorded the highest proportion of participants in the world when 250,000 of the country's one million inhabitants took part in different runs on the same day in 1988. In the last ten years China has experienced unprecedented economic growth and a dramatic rise in the standard of living; by 2008 a quarter of the adult population was overweight and the diseases of civilization had become common. The population has to some extent imitated the lifestyle of America and has introduced many of the health problems that accompany it. Perhaps the next wave of jogging will come in China.

There is something enchantingly simple about running. It is a childish activity that adults can easily slip into, offering a sense of freedom that can be felt anywhere but is enhanced by fresh air and beautiful natural surroundings. There is something beautiful about the sight of a good runner that appeals even to those who do not run themselves – the graceful flight and coordinated harmony of the muscles as the runner glides across Mother Earth in such a self-evident way. That is how we should move, we feel, perhaps we are not so advanced after all and have lost something truly valuable.

Biologists think that we became human beings when we began to run. Perhaps we have to walk and run a great deal in order to remain human beings, so that we do not seize up physically and mentally and become sluggish creatures that have to be transported by machines. Research has shown that diagonal movements like running and walking promote contact between the right and the left sides of the brain, thus improving our creative ability – a central characteristic of human beings. The profound satisfaction people get from movement is one of the many reminders of our biological nature in a world that is becoming more and more mechanized. Look at children – and the way they run instinctively in joy and in play.

Modern runners are imitating something primeval man did in his struggle for survival. We run and walk for our lives in a way that is very different but just as human, since doing it makes us feel so much better and counterbalances sitting still. The runner rarely thinks about it, but he is moving just as our ancestors in Africa did when they ran across the savannah in order to survive – just as the Kenyans do today.

References

1 Messengers and Forerunners

1 Stephan Oettermann, *Läufer und Vorläufer. Zu einer Kulturgeschichte des Laufsports* (Frankfurt am Main, 1984), p. 19.
2 Louis Baudin, *Dagligt liv hos Inkaerne* (Copenhagen, 1967), pp. 220–21; Alberto F. Cajas, 'Physical Activities in Ancient Peru', *Olympic Review* (1980), pp. 150–52.
3 Baudin, *Dagligt liv hos Inkaerne*, p. 63.
4 Ibid., pp. 79–83.
5 Oettermann, *Läufer und Vorläufer*, p. 15.
6 Ibid., p. 18.
7 Ibid., p. 17.
8 Ibid., p. 8.
9 Ibid., p. 33.
10 Montague Shearman, *Athletics and Football* (London, 1887), p. 20.
11 Oettermann, *Läufer und Vorläufer*, p. 35.
12 Ibid., pp. 36–7.
13 Ibid., p. 40.
14 Andy Milroy, 'The Great Running Traditions of the Basques', at www.runtheplanet.com/resources/historical/basques.asp, accessed 3 July 2009.
15 Oettermann, *Läufer und Vorläufer*, pp. 57–75.
16 Matti Goksøyr, 'Idrettsliv i borgerskapets by. En historisk undersøkelse av idrettens utvikling og organisering i Bergen på 1800-tallet', doctoral dissertation, Norges idrettshøgskole (Oslo, 1991), p. 23.
17 Oettermann, *Läufer und Vorläufer*, p. 86.
18 Ibid., p. 93.

2 A Primordial Human Trait

1 Dennis M. Bramble and Daniel E. Lieberman, 'Endurance Running and the Evolution of *Homo*', *Nature*, CDXXXII (18 November 2004), pp. 345–52; Bernd Heinrich, *Why We Run* (New York, 2001).
2 Bramble and Lieberman, 'Endurance Running and the Evolution of *Homo*'.
3 Vera Olivová, *Sports and Games in the Ancient World* (London, 1984), pp. 21–4.
4 Aschehougs verdenshistorie, *I begynnelsen* (Oslo, 2007), pp. 136–42.
5 Deane Lamont Anderson, 'Running Phenomena in Ancient Sumer', *Journal of Sport History*, XXII/3 (1995), pp. 207–15.
6 At www.cesras.ru/index.php, accessed 3 July 2009.

7 Wolfgang Decker, *Sport and Games in Ancient Egypt* (London, 1992), pp. 24–34, 61–6.
8 I. Weiler, *Der Sport bei den Völkern der alten Welt. Eine Einführung* (Darmstadt, 1981), p. 51.
9 Ibid., pp. 62–3.

3 In Honour of the Gods

1 Norman E. Gardiner, *Athletics of the Ancient World* (Chicago, IL, 1978) and *Greek Athletic Sports and Festivals* (London, 1910); H. A. Harris, *Sport in Greece and Rome* (London, 1972); Leo Hjorts, *Graeske guder og helte* (Copenhagen, 1984); David Matz, *Greek and Roman Sport* (London, 1991), p. 25; Stephen Miller, *Arete: Greek Sports from Ancient Sources* (London, 2004) and *Ancient Greek Athletics* (London, 2004); Cleanthis Paleologos, 'Argeas of Argos: Dolichon Runner', *Olympic Review*, 87–88 (Jan–Feb 1975); Tony Perrottet, *The Naked Olympics* (New York, 2004); Panos Valavanis, *Games and Sanctuaries in Ancient Greece* (Los Angeles, CA, 2004).
2 Gardiner, *Greek Athletic Sports and Festivals*, p. 293.
3 Miller, *Arete*, pp. 172–3.
4 Matz, *Greek and Roman Sport*, p. 25.
5 John Mouratidis, 'The 776 BC Date and Some Problems Connected With It', *Canadian Journal of History of Sport*, XVI/2 (December 1985), p. 1–14; T. H. Nally, *The Aonac Tailteann and the Tailteann Games in their Origin, History and Ancient Associations* (Dublin, 1922).
6 Miller, *Arete*, p. 13.
7 William Blake Tyrrell, *The Smell of Sweat: Greek Athletics, Olympics and Culture* (Mundelein, IL, 2004), p. 58.
8 Miller, *Ancient Greek Athletics* (London, 2004), p. 11.
9 Perrottet, *The Naked Olympics*, pp. 159–60.
10 Thomas P. Scanlon, *The Ancient World* (Chicago, IL, 1984), pp. 77–90.
11 Harris, *Sport in Greece and Rome*, p. 41.
12 Gardiner, *Greek Athletic Sports and Festivals*, p. 154.
13 Hugh M. Lee, 'Modern Ultra-long Distance Running and Phillippides' Run from Athens to Sparta', *The Ancient World*, IX/3–4 (1984), pp. 107–13.
14 Gardiner, *Athletics of the Ancient World*, p. 102.
15 Walter Umminger, *Toppraestationer. En idraettens kulturhistorie* (Copenhagen, 1963), p. 31.
16 Ibid., p. 28.
17 Gardiner, *Greek Athletic Sports and Festivals*, p. 131.
18 Miller, *Arete*, p. 217.
19 Umminger, *Toppraestationer*, pp. 13–14.
20 Allen Guttman, *From Ritual to Record: The Nature of Modern Sports* (New York, 1978), pp. 49–51.
21 Matz, *Greek and Roman Sport*, p. 68.
22 At http://en.wikipedia.org/wiki/Zeno_of_Elea, accessed 3 July 2009.

4 Roman Games

1 H. A. Harris, *Sport in Greece and Rome* (London, 1972), pp. 68–69; *Seneca in Ten Volumes* (London, 1970), p. 261.

2 Jerome Carcopino, *Keistertidens Roma. Daglig liv i det første århundre* (Oslo, 1998), pp. 158–62.
3 Norman E. Gardiner, *Greek Athletic Sports and Festivals* (London, 1910), pp. 181–2.
4 H. M. Lee, 'Athletics and the Bikini Girls from Piazza Armerina', *Stadion*, x (1984), pp. 45–76.
5 Zarah Newby, *Greek Athletics in the Roman World* (Oxford, 2005).
6 Ernst Jokl, *A History of Physical Education and Sport* (Tokyo, 1975–6), pp. 53–8.
7 Edward S. Sears, *Running Through the Ages* (Jefferson, NC, 2001), p. 17.
8 Walter Umminger, *Toppraestationer. En idraettens kulturhistorie* (Copenhagen, 1963), p. 110
9 H. A. Harris, *Greek Athletics and the Jews* (Cardiff, 1976), p. 62.
10 Ibid.

5 Elephant Races and Chinese Tales

1 The story 'Kuafa Ran After the Sun' is described in the books *Shan Hai Jing*, *Lie Zi* and *Huan Nan Zi*. Cui Lequan, a researcher at the Chinese Museum of Sport, wrote the article 'Chinese Sport in Ancient Times'.
2 Zhou Xikuan, 'China: Sports Activities in Ancient and Modern Times', *Canadian Journal of History of Sport*, xxii/2 (1991), p. 69.
3 S. H. Deshpande, *Physical Education in Ancient India* (Delhi, 1992), pp. 200–1; Jeannine Auboyer, *Dagligt liv i gamle Indien* (Copenhagen, 1968), pp. 256–7.
4 Deshpande, *Physical Education in Ancient India*, p. 37.
5 Ibid., p. 85.
6 V. S. Saksena, 'Historical Background of Marwar Postal System', at www.mirdhadak.com/mps.htm, accessed 3 July 2009; 'History of the Indian Post Office', at http://pib.nic.in/release/rel_print_page1.asp?relid=4070, accessed 3 July 2009; 'Scinde Dawk', at http://en.wikipedia.org/wiki/Scinde_Dawk, accessed 3 July 2009.

6 The Running Monks

1 Alexandra David-Néel, *Det hemmelige Tibet* (Oslo, 1987), pp. 178–92.
2 Ibid., p. 180; Lama Anagarika Govinda, *The Way of the White Clouds* (London, 1969), pp. 80–84.
3 John Stevens, *The Marathon Monks of Mount Hiei* (Boston, MA, 1988), p. 58.
4 Ibid., p. 59.
5 Ibid., p. 71.
6 Ibid., p. 82.
7 Ibid., p. 93.

7 Racing against Horses

1 Bertil Wahlqvist, *Ville vikinger i lek og idrett* (Oslo, 1980), pp. 40–44, 191–2.
2 Ibid., p. 51.
3 T. H. Nally, *The Aonac Tailteann and the Tailteann Games in their Origin, History and Ancient Associations* (Dublin, 1922), pp. 8, 27.
4 Bjørn Bjarnason, *Nordboernes legemlige uddannelse i oldtiden* (Copenhagen, 1905), p. 1.

5 Ibid., p. 23.
6 Wahlqvist, *Ville vikinger i lek og idrett*, p. 180.
7 Ibid., p. 181.
8 Ibid., p. 183.
9 Bjarnason, *Nordboernes legemlige uddannelse i oldtiden*, p. 38.
10 Wahlqvist, *Ville vikinger i lek og idrett*, p. 182.
11 Bertil Wahlqvist, 'Idrottshistoriska källproblem i de islendska sagorna – ett par exempel', *Idrott, Historia och Samhälle. Svenska idrottshistoriska föreningens årsskrift* (1981), pp. 69–77.
12 Wahlqvist, *Ville vikinger i lek og idrett*, p. 46.
13 Bjarnason, *Nordboernes legemlige uddannelse i oldtiden*, p. 100.
14 Ibid., pp. 85–6.
15 Wahlqvist, *Ville vikinger i lek og idrett*, p. 50.
16 Ibid., pp. 53–4.
17 'Carnethy 5 Hill Race', at www.electricscotland.com/poetry/carnethy5_hillrace.htm, accessed 3 July 2009.
18 Gerard Redmond, *The Caledonian Games in Nineteenth-century America* (Madison, NJ, 1971), p. 26.
19 Dante Alighieri, *The Divine Comedy*, xv.121–4, written between 1308 and 1321; Edward S. Sears, *Running Through the Ages* (Jefferson, NC, 2001), pp. 42–3; Indro Neri, *Dante era un podista* (Florence, 1995).
20 Karl Lennartz, *Olympic Review* (May 1978) pp. 272–5. See also Lennartz, *Olympic Review* (June 1978), pp. 378–83.
21 Celia Haddon, *The First Ever English Olimpick Games* (London, 2004), p. 76; *Physical Education*, pp. 249–66.
22 Allen Guttmann, *Women's Sports* (New York, 1991), pp. 62–5.
23 At http://en.wikipedia.org/wiki/Adamites, accessed 3 July 2009.
24 Arndt Krüger and John Marshall Carter, eds, *Ritual and Record: Sports Records and Quantification in Pre-Modern Societies* (London, 1990), pp. 126–7.
25 Henning Eichberg, *Det løbende samfund* (Slagelse, 1988), pp. 226–31.

8 Wagers, Clocks and Brooms

1 Edward S. Sears, *Running Through the Ages* (Jefferson, NC, 2001), p. 48.
2 Ibid., p. 52.
3 Ibid., p. 51; Allen Guttmann, *Women's Sports* (New York, 1991), pp. 67–8.
4 Mats Hellspong, *Den folkliga idrotten* (Stockholm, 2000), p. 142.
5 Walter Umminger, *Toppraestationer. En idraettens kulturhistorie* (Copenhagen, 1963), pp. 196–201.
6 Guttmann, *Women's Sports*, p. 67.
7 Francis Burns, *Cotswold Olimpick Games (Established 1612)* (Bristol, 2000), p. 5.
8 Ibid.
9 Roger Robinson, *Running in Literature* (New York, 2003), pp. 65–7.
10 Peter Radford, 'Women and Girl Runners of Kent in the Eighteenth Century', unpublished article, lent by Peter Radford; interview with Peter Radford, Oxford, England, 2 October 2007.
11 Ibid.
12 Guttmann, *Women's Sports*, p. 73
13 Radford, 'Women and Girl Runners of Kent in the Eighteenth Century'.

14 Peter Radford, 'Women's Foot-Races in the Eighteenth and Nineteenth Centuries: A Popular and Widespread Practice', *Canadian Journal of History of Sport*, xxv/1 (May 1994), pp. 50–61.
15 Peter Radford, *The Observer*, 2 May 2004.
16 Interview with Peter Radford.
17 *The Observer*, 2 May 2004.
18 Peter Radford, *In Puris Naturalibus: Naked Runners in England in the Long 18th Century*, lent by Peter Radford.

9 French Enlightenment and German Health Education

1 Jean-Jacques Rousseau, *Emile. Eller om oppdragelsen*, i (Copenhagen, 1962), p. 159.
2 Ibid., p. 160.
3 Ibid., p. 161.
4 Ibid., p. 162.
5 Rousseau, *Emile*, iii, pp. 121–2.
6 Earle F. Zeigler, *A History of Sport and Physical Education to 1900* (Champaign, il, 1973), p. 296.
7 Ibid., pp. 279–80.
8 Ibid., p. 305.
9 Ibid., pp. 280–83.
10 Ibid., pp. 277–87.

10 Mensen Ernst and Captain Barclay

1 Bredo Berntsen, *Løperkongen. Nordmannen Mensen Ernsts eventyrlige liv* (Oslo, 1986), pp. 19–21.
2 Anders Enevig, *Cirkus og gøgl i Odense* (Odense, 1997), p. 87.
3 Berntsen, *Løperkongen*, p. 50.
4 Ibid., p. 55.
5 Ibid., p. 92.
6 Ibid., p. 97.
7 Berntsen, *Løperkongen*.
8 Peter Radford, *The Celebrated Captain Barclay* (London, 2001), pp. 2–14; interview with Peter Radford, Oxford, England, 2 October 2007.
9 Radford, *The Celebrated Captain Barclay*, p. 88.
10 Pierce Egan, *Sporting Anecdotes* (Philadelphia, pa, 1822), pp. 58–61.

11 Buffalo Heart for Breakfast

1 Morris E. Opler, 'The Jicarilla Apache Ceremonial Relay Race', *American Anthropologist*, n.s., v/46 (1944), p. 81.
2 Peter Nabokov, *Indian Running: Native American History and Tradition* (Santa Barbara, ca, 1981), p. 23.
3 Ibid., pp. 11–13.
4 Ibid., p. 132.
5 Ibid., p. 134.
6 Ibid., p. 137.
7 Opler, 'The Jicarilla Apache Ceremonial Relay Race', p. 77.
8 Ibid., p. 77.

9 Ibid., p. 76.
10 Ibid., p. 84.
11 Nabokov, *Indian Running*, p. 143.
12 Ibid., p. 27.
13 James H. Howard, 'Notes on the Ceremonial Runners of the Fox Indians', *Contributions to Fox Ethnology* (Washington: Bureau of American Ethnology), LXXXV (1927), pp. 1–50, at pp. 8–9.
14 Ibid., p. 23.
15 Ibid., pp. 23–25.
16 Nabokov, *Indian Running*, p. 17.
17 *Runner's World*, September 1978, pp. 54–5.
18 Charles Hughes, *Eskimo Boyhood* (Lexington, KY, 1974), pp. 116–17; Nabokov, *Indian Running*, pp. 84–5.
19 Ibid., p. 92.
20 Ibid., pp. 94–5
21 David Maybury-Lewis, *The Savage and the Innocent* (Boston, MA, 1988), p. 87.
22 Carl Lumholz, *Blandt Mexicos indianere. Fem års reise i Sierra Madre og andre lidet kjendte dele af det vestlige Mexico* (Kristiania, 1903), I, pp. 220–21.
23 Lumholz, *Blandt Mexicos indianere*, p. 215–30.
24 Nabokov, *Indian Running*, p. 68.
25 Stewart Culin, *Games of the North American Indians* (Lincoln, NE, 1992).

12 Bluffing and Handicapping

1 John Cumming, *Runners and Walkers: A Nineteenth-century Sports Chronicle* (Chicago, IL, 1981), pp. 65–7.
2 Ibid., pp. 65–7; Edward S. Sears, *Running Through the Ages* (Jefferson, NC, 2001), pp. 93–4.
3 Cumming, *Runners and Walkers*, pp. 14–17.
4 Ibid., p. 34.
5 Colin Tatz, *Obstacle Race: Aborigines in Sport* (Sydney, 1995), pp. 95–6.
6 Joe Bull, *The Spiked Shoe* (Melbourne, 1959), pp. 24–5.
7 Ibid., pp. 41–2; Tatz, *Obstacle Race*, p. 92.
8 Bull, *The Spiked Shoe*, pp. 46–7.
9 Ibid., pp. 47–8.
10 Peter G. Mewett, 'Discourses of Deception: Cheating in Professional Running', *The Australian Journal of Anthropology*, special issue 14 (2002), XIII/3, p. 298.
11 Ibid., p. 298.
12 Bull, *The Spiked Shoe*, p. 70.
13 Cumming, *Runners and Walkers*, p. 85.
14 Ibid., pp. 101–28.
15 Ibid., pp. 89, 90, 77–100.
16 David Blaikie, 'Running and Alcohol: A Long and Storied History', at www.ultramarathonworld.com (no longer extant).
17 Cumming, *Runners and Walkers*, pp. 101–5; Dahn Shaulis, 'Pedestriennes: Newsworthy but Controversial Women in Sporting Entertainment', *Journal of Sport History*, XXVI/1 (1999), pp. 29–50.
18 Peter Lovesey, *The Official Centenary History of the Amateur Athletic Association* (London, 1979), p. 19.
19 Ibid., p. 22; see also Harvey Taylor, 'Play Up, But Don't Play the Game: English

Amateur Athletic Elitism, 1863–1910', *The Sports Historian*, XXII/2 (November 2002), pp. 75–97.

20 Richard Mandell, 'The Invention of the Sports Record', *Stadion*, II/2 (1978), pp. 250–64; Henning Eichberg, *Det løbende samfund* (Slagelse, 1988), pp. 231–2; *Stadion*, XII–XIII (1986–7).

13 The Revival of the Olympic Games

1 Pierre de Coubertin, *Olympism*, ed. Norbert Müller (Lausanne, 2000), pp. 36–7.

2 Ibid., p. 20.

3 Ibid., p. 37–9. See also Cyril Bracegirdle, 'Olympic Dreamer', *Olympic Review* (June 1991), pp. 276–8.

4 Coubertin, *Olympism*, p. 333, 574.

5 Karl Lennartz, 'Following the Footsteps of Bréal', *Journal of Olympic History*, VI/2 (Summer 1998), pp. 8–10.

6 Hugh M. Lee, 'Modern Ultra-long Distance Running and Phillippides' Run from Athens to Sparta', *The Ancient World*, IX/3–4, p. 112.

7 Nicholas Geoffrey Lemprière Hammond, *Studies in Greek History* (Oxford 1973), pp. 225–7.

8 John A. Lucas, 'A History of the Marathon Race – 490 BC to 1975', *Journal of Sport History*, III/2 (1976), p. 122.

9 Ibid., p. 125.

10 Ibid., p. 126; see also Jal Pardivala, 'The Saga of the Marathon', *Olympic Review*, CCVI (December 1984), pp. 974–80.

11 Karl Lennartz, 'That Memorable First Marathon', *Journal of Olympic History* (Winter 1999), p. 24.

12 Anthony T. Bijkerk and David C. Young, 'That Memorable First Marathon', *Journal of Olympic History* (Winter 1999), p. 19.

13 David E. Martin and Roger W. H. Gynn, *The Olympic Marathon: The History and Drama of Sport's Most Challenging Event* (Champaign, IL, 2000), p. 21.

14 Lennartz, 'That Memorable First Marathon', p. 26.

15 Bijerk and Young, 'That Memorable First Marathon', p. 7.

16 Martin and Gynn, *The Olympic Marathon*, pp. 14–15.

17 Bijerk and Young, 'That Memorable First Marathon'; Lennartz, 'That Memorable First Marathon'.

18 Martin and Gynn, *The Olympic Marathon*, p. 18.

19 Karl Lennartz, 'Two Women Ran the Marathon in 1896', *Journal of Olympic History*, II/1 (Winter 1994); Anthanasios Tarasouleas, 'The Female Spiridon Louis', *Journal of Olympic History*, I/3.

20 Ibid.

21 Tom Derderian, *Boston Marathon: The First Century of the World's Premier Running Event* (Champaign, IL, 1996), pp. 3–7.

22 Martin and Gynn, *The Olympic Marathon*, p. 27.

23 Ibid., pp. 38–54.

24 Ibid., p. 41.

25 Ibid., p. 48.

26 Christian Lindstedt, *Mellom heroism och idioti* (Göteborg, 2005), p. 94.

27 Ibid., p. 106.

28 James C. Whorton, 'Athlete's Heart: The Medical Debate over Athleticism

(1870–1920)', *Journal of Sport History*, IX/1 (Spring 1982), pp. 30–52.

14 Running Round a Track

1 'Alexis Lapointe', at http://en.wikipedia.org/wiki/Alexis_Lapointe, accessed 8 July 2009.
2 Ibid.
3 Sigmund Loland, 'Rekorden: Grensesprengning som dilemma', *Kunnskap om idrett*, I (1997), pp. 15–18 and 'Record Sports: An Ecological Critique and a Reconstruction', *Journal of the Philosophy of Sport*, XXVIII/2 (2001), pp. 127–39; Henning Eichberg, 'Stopwatch, Horizontal Bar, Gymnasium: The Technologizing of Sports in the Eighteenth and Early Nineteenth Centuries', *Journal of the Philosophy of Sport*, IX (1982), pp. 43–59.
4 John Bale, *Running Cultures* (London, 2004), p. 48.
5 Ibid., p. 47.
6 Peter R. Cavanagh, *The Running Shoe Book* (Mountain View, CA, 1980), p. 343.
7 Ibid., p. 17.
8 'Adidas', at http://en.wikipedia.org/wiki/Adidas, accessed 8 July 2009.
9 John Bale and Joe Sang, *Kenyan Running* (London, 1996), pp. 47–50.
10 Ibid., p. 64.
11 Louise Mead Tricard, *American Women's Track and Field: A History, 1895–1980* (London, 1996), pp. 29–30.
12 Norsk Folkeminnelags arkiv, Universitetet i Oslo, Minneoppgaver for eldre, 1981. Oslo 29, p. 15.
13 Tricard, *American Women's Track and Field*, pp. 78–81.
14 Ibid., p. 138.
15 Robert Stevenson, *Backwards Running* (1981), available at www.backward-running-backward.com/PDF.Stevenson.pdf, accessed 8 July 2009.

15 Finnish *Sisu*

1 Erkki Vettenniemi, *Joutavan Jouksun Jäljillä* (Helsinki, 2006), p. 160.
2 Ibid. See also Mervi Tervo, 'A Cultural Community in the Making: Sport, National Imagery and Helsingin Sanomat, 1912–1936', *Sport in Society*, VII/2 (Summer 2004), pp. 153–73.
3 Vettenniemi, *Joutavan Jouksun Jäljillä*, pp. 462–71.
4 Ibid., p. 406.
5 Toivo Torsten Kaila, *Boken om Nurmi* (Stockholm, 1925), p. 25.
6 David Miller, *Athens to Athens* (London, 2004), p. 78.
7 *Sportsmanden*, 20 July 1921.
8 Charles Hoff, *Fra New York til Hollywood* (Oslo, 1927), p. 12.
9 Kaila, *Boken om Nurmi*, p. 135.
10 Hoff, *Fra New York til Hollywood*, p. 97. See also John Lucas, 'In the Eye of the Storm: Paavo Nurmi and the American Athletic Amateur-Professional Struggle (1925–29)', *Stadion*, VIII/2 (1992)
11 John Bale, *Running Cultures* (London, 2004), p. 69.

16 Ultrarunning as Nation-building

1 'Ekiden', at http://en.wikipedia.org/wiki/Ekiden; 'Hakode Ekiden', at http://en.wikipedia.org/wiki/Hakone_Ekiden; oral information from Midori Poppe, Oslo.
2 Morris Alexander, *The Comrades Marathon Story* (Cape Town, 1982).
3 Arthur F. H. Newton, *Running* (London, 1935), pp. 99–103; David Blaikie, 'Running and Alcohol: A Long and Storied History', at www.ultramarathonworld.com (no longer extant).
4 Mark Dyreson, 'The Foot Runners Conquer Mexico and Texas: Endurance Racing, Indigenismo, and Nationalism', *Journal of Sport History*, xxxi/1 (Spring 2004), p. 31; see also Richard V. McGehee, 'The Origins of Olympism in Mexico: The Central Games of 1926', *The Internal Journal of the History of Sport*, x/3 (December 1993), p. 313–32.
5 Ibid., p. 4.
6 Ibid., p. 22.
7 Ibid., p. 24.

17 Race across America

1 James H. Thomas, *The Bunion Derby: Andy Payne and the Great Transcontinental Foot Race* (Oklahoma City, ok, 1980); Charles B. Kastner, *Bunion Derby: The 1928 Footrace Across America* (Albuquerque, nm, 2007); Paul Sann, *Fads, Follies and Delusions of the American People* (New York, 1967), pp. 47–56; 'The Great American Footrace', at www.itvs.org/footrace/runnerbio/bio1020_1.htm#anderson, accessed 8 July 2009.
2 James E. Shapiro, *Ultramarathon* (London, 1980), p. 123.
3 Thomas, *The Bunion Derby*, pp. 86–7.

18 Dubious Race Theories

1 Matti Goksøyr, 'One Certainly Expected a Great Deal More from the Savages: The Anthropology Days in St Louis, 1904, and their Aftermath', *International Journal of the History of Sport*, vii/2 (1990), pp. 297–306.
2 Ibid.
3 John Entite, *Taboo: Why Black Athletes Dominate Sport and Why We Are Afraid to Talk About It* (New York, 2000), p. 178.
4 Ibid., p. 176.
5 Ibid., pp. 176–7.
6 Ibid., p. 177.
7 Ibid., pp. 251, 255–6.
8 Ibid., p. 178.
9 Ibid., p. 250. See also John Hoberman, *Darwin's Athletes: How Sport has Damaged Black America and Preserved the Myth of Race* (Boston, ma, 1997); David K. Wiggins, 'Great Speed but Little Stamina: The Historical Debate over Black Athletic Superiority', *Journal of Sport History*, xvi/2 (Summer 1989), pp. 158–85.
10 Entite, *Taboo*, p. 249.
11 Ibid., p. 250.
12 Ibid., p. 250.
13 Ibid., p. 251.

14 William J. Baker, *An American Life* (New York, 1988), p. 118.
15 Donald McRae, *In Black and White: The Untold Story of Joe Louis and Jesse Owens* (London and New York, 2002), p. 188.

19 War and Peace

1 Gösta Holmér, *Veien til rekorden* (Oslo, 1947), p. 11.
2 Fred Wilt, *How They Train* (Los Altos, CA, 1959), pp. 5–6.
3 Gunder Hägg, *Gunder Häggs dagbok* (1952), p. 8.
4 Henry Eidmark, *Fantomer på kolstybben* (1945), p. 8.
5 Hägg, *Gunder Häggs dagbok*, p. 26.
6 Henry Eidmark, *Sanningen om Gunder Hägg* (1953), p. 54.
7 Eidmark, *Fantomer på kolstybben*; interview with Arne Andersson,Vänersborg, June 2007.
8 Hägg, *Gunder Häggs dagbok*, p. 58.
9 Karen Wikberg, 'Idealism eller professionalism? En studie i den stora amatør-råfsten 1945–1946', *Del 1 Idrott, Historia och Samhälle* (1993), pp. 109–49 and *Del 2 i Idrott, Historia och Samhälle* (1994), pp. 85–122.
10 Interview with Arne Andersson,Vänersborg, June 2007.

20 In the Service of the State

1 Frantizek Kozik, *Emil Zatopek* (Oslo, 1955), p. 8.
2 Ibid., p. 13.
3 Ibid., p. 27.
4 Ibid., p. 9.
5 Ibid., pp. 42–3.
6 Ibid., p. 73.
7 Henry W. Morton, *Soviet Sport* (London, 1963), p. 35. See also K. A. Kulinkovich, 'The Development of Knowledge of Physical Culture History in the USSR', *History of Physical Education and Sport*, vol. III (Tokyo, 1975–6), p. 126.
8 Robert Edelman, *Serious Fun: A History of Spectator Sports in the USSR* (New York, 1993), pp. 75–7; Joseph Marchiony, 'The Rise of Soviet Athletics', *Comparative Education Review*, VII/1 (June 1963), pp. 17–27.
9 Morton, *Soviet Sport*, p. 34.
10 Ron Clarke and Norman Harris, *The Lonely Breed* (London, 1967), pp. 155–65.
11 Interview with Gergely Szentiványi, Spring 2008.

21 The Dream Mile

1 John Bale, *Roger Bannister and the Four-minute Mile* (London, 2004), p. 17.
2 Joseph B. Oxendine, *American Indian Sports Heritage* (Lincoln, NE, 1988), p. 87.
3 Bale, *Roger Bannister and the Four-minute Mile*, p. 10.
4 Ibid.; interview with John Bale at Keele University, 1 October 2007; John Bale and David Howe, eds, *The Four Minute-Mile: Historical and Cultural Interpretations of a Sporting Barrier* (New York, 2008).
5 Bale, *Roger Bannister and the Four-minute Mile*, p. 54.
6 Ibid., p. 57.
7 Ibid., p. 79.

8 Ibid., p. 84.
9 John Hoberman, 'Amphetamine and the Four-minute Mile', in *The Four-minute Mile*, ed. Bale and Howe, pp. 99–114.

22 Africa Arrives

1 Leonard Mosley, *Haile Selassie. Den seirende løve* (Oslo, 1964); Paul Rambali, *Barefoot Runner: The Life of Champion Marathon Runner Abebe Bikila* (London, 2007); www.runningbarefoot.org/?name=AbebeBikila, accessed 10 July 2009.
2 Rambali, *Barefoot Runner*, pp. 108–14.
3 Ibid., pp. 116–17.
4 At www.runningbarefoot.org/?name=AbebeBikila, accessed 10 July 2009.
5 John Bale and Joe Sang, *Kenyan Running* (London, 1996), p. 65.
6 Ibid., p. 5.
7 Ibid., p. 82.
8 Dirk Lund Christensen, *Washindi: Løberne fra Kenya* (Copenhagen, 2000), p. 92.
9 Ibid., p. 163.

23 Loving the Landscape of Pain

1 Graem Sims, *Why Die? The Extraordinary Percy Cerutty, 'Maker of Champions'* (Lothian, Melbourne, 2003), p. 33.
2 At www.livingnov.com.au/personal/slpersonalstories8.htms.
3 At www.abc.net.au/rn/talks/8.30/sportsf/stories/s226385.htm.
4 Sims, *Why Die?*, p. 173.
5 Radio interview, 11 October 2004.
6 Sims, *Why Die?*, p. 199.
7 At www.abc.net.au/rn/talks/8.30/sportsf/stories/s823522.htm.
8 Garth Gilmour, *Arthur Lydiard: Master Coach* (Cheltenham, 2004), p. 32.

24 The Jogging Revolution

1 *New Guide to Distance Running* (Mountain View, CA, 1978), p. 153.
2 'Jogging', at http://en.wikipedia.org/wiki/Jogging.
3 Garth Gilmour, *Arthur Lydiard: Master Coach* (Cheltenham, 2004), p. 201.
4 Kenny Moore, *Bowerman and the Men of Oregon: The Story of Oregon's Legendary Coach and Nike's Co-founder* (New York, 2006), pp. 146–7.
5 Ibid., p. 152–5.
6 Interview with Arne Kvalheim, February 2008.
7 Kenneth Cooper, *Aerobics* (New York, 1968), p. 70.
8 Ibid., p. 33.
9 *Runner's World*, June 1976, pp. 18–23.
10 *Runner's World*, September 1976.
11 *New Guide to Distance Running*, p. 362.
12 Ibid., p. 363.
13 *Runner's World*, May 1978, pp. 75–9.
14 *New Guide to Distance Running*, p. 365.
15 Ibid., p. 158.

16 Ibid., p. 157.
17 Interview with Rune Larsson, Trollhättan, Sweden, 10 September 2007.
18 'Endorphin', at http://en.wikipedia.org/wiki/Endorphin.
19 'Jim Fixx', at http://en.wikipedia.org/wiki/James_Fixx.
20 George Sheehan, *Running and Being: The Total Experience* (Teaneck, NJ, 1978), p. 27.
21 Tim Noakes, *Lore of Running: Discover the Science and Spirit of Running* (Champaign, IL, 2001), pp. 739–41, 756.
22 William Glasser, *Positive Addiction* (New York, 1976), p. 45.
23 Ibid., p. 103.
24 Ibid., pp. 107–9.
25 Darcy C. Plymire, 'Positive Addiction: Running and Human Potential in the 1970s', *Journal of Sport History*, pp. 297–313.

25 Big City Marathons

1 Fred Lebow and Richard Woodley, *Inside the World of Big-time Marathoning* (New York, 1984), pp. 64–5. Interview with Grete and Jack Waitz, Autumn 2007.
2 Lebow and Woodley, *Inside the World of Big-time Marathoning*, pp. 71–2.
3 Pamela Cooper, 'The "Visible Hand" on the Footrace: Fred Lebow and the Marketing of the Marathon', *Journal of Sport History*, XIX/3 (Winter 1992), p. 246.
4 Jean Baudrillard, *Amerika* (Oslo, 1986), pp. 32–3.
5 Ibid., p. 34.

26 Marathon Women

1 Fan Hong, '"Iron Bodies": Women, War, and Sport in the Early Communist Movement in Modern China', *Journal of Sport History*, XXIV/1 (1997), p. 7. See also Tony Hwang and Grant Jarvie, 'Sport, Nationalism and the Early Chinese Republic, 1912–1927', *The Sports Historian*, XXI/2 (November 2001), pp. 1–19.
2 'Chat', *Sportsmanden*, LXXXVIII (1928), p. 6; Gerd Von der Lippe, 'Endring og motstand av feminiteter og maskuliniteter i idrett og kroppskultur i Norge', doctoral dissertation, Norges idrettshøgskole, Institutt for samfunnsviten-skapelige fag (Bø i Telemark, 1997), pp. 236–8.
3 Allen Guttmann, *Women's Sports* (New York, 1991), p. 103.
4 Ibid., pp. 133–4.
5 At www.runtheplanet.com.
6 Ernst Van Aaken, *Van Aaken Method* (Mountain View, CA, 1976), pp. 81–2.
7 Annemarie Jutel, '"Thou Dost Run as in Flotation": The Emergence of the Women's Marathon', *The International Journal of the History of Sport*, XX/3 (September 2003), p. 17–36, at p. 19.
8 Karl Lennartz, 'Violence at the Women's Marathon Race', at www.cafyd.com/HistDeporte/htm/pdf/2-23.pdf, pp. 1–6.
9 Interview with Grete and Jack Waitz, Autumn 2007; Jan Hedenstad, ed., *Grete Waitz – i det lange løp* (Oslo, 1983); Gloria Averbuch and Grete Waitz, *World Class* (Oslo, 1986).
10 Interview with Jan Andersen.
11 Interview with Ingrid and Arve Kristiansen, 2007 and 2008; interview with

Johan Kaggestad, 2008; Kirsten Lien Garbo, *Med Ingrid mot toppen* (Oslo, 1985).

27 Mr Comeback

1 Henry Rono, *Olympic Dream* (Bloomington, IN, 2007), p. 7.
2 Ibid., p. 80–82. Interview with Henry Rono, 2006–8.
3 Rono, *Olympic Dream*, p. 175.
4 Ibid., p. 179.
5 Ibid., p. 188.
6 Ibid., p. 189.

28 Stars, Business and Doping

1 *Springtime*, June 1988, pp. 23–7.
2 'Hassiba Boulmerka', at http://en.wikipedia.org/wiki/Hassiba_Boulmerka, accessed 15 July 2009; 'Islamic Sports', at http://en.wikipedia.org/wiki/Islamic_sports, accessed 15 July 2009; 'Algeria', at http://en.wikipedia.org/wiki/Algeria, accessed 15 July 2009.
3 J. B. Strasser and Laurie Becklund, *Swoosh: The Unauthorized Story of Nike and the Men Who Played There* (New York, 1993); Aaron Frisch, *The Story of Nike* (Mankato, MN, 2004); Robert Goldman and Stephen Papson, *Nike Culture* (London, 1998); George H. Sage, 'Justice Did It! The Nike Transnational Advocacy Network: Organization, Collective Actions and Outcomes', *Sociology of Sport Journal*, XVI/3 (1999), pp. 206–32.
4 *Springtime*, 3, 1985.
5 Brigitte Berendonk, *Doping, gull, aere, elendighet* (Oslo, 1993), p. 50.
6 Ibid., p. 134.
7 Ibid., p. 231.

29 Running with Zen

1 Michael Sandrock, *Running with the Legends: Training and Racing Insights from 21 Great Runners* (Champaign, IL, 1996), p. 359.
2 Ibid., p. 348; see also interview in *Runner's World*, June 1981, pp. 45–7.
3 *Springtime*, October–November 1984, p. 18.
4 Ibid., p. 14; see also *Springtime*, 2 (1984), pp. 12–15.
5 Sandrock, *Running with the Legends*, p. 353.
6 Ibid., p. 361.
7 Ibid., p. 363.
8 Peter Matthews, *The Guinness Book of Athletics: Facts and Feats* (London, 1982), p. 284.

30 Running like Ostriches

1 Yu Zhao, 'Majiajun diaocha', *Zhongguo zuojia*, III (1998), pp. 1–213.
2 Ibid., p. 137.
3 Ibid., p. 194.
4 Ibid., p. 196.
5 Ke Yunlu, *Wen Quing Ma Junren* (Kina, 2004); James Riordan and Dong

Jinxia, 'Chinese Women and Sport: Sexuality and Suspicion', *The China Quarterly*, CXLV (March 1995), pp. 130–52.

31 Striding Out of Poverty

1 John Entine, *Taboo: Why Black Athletes Dominate Sports And Why We Are Afraid To Talk About It* (New York, 2001), p. 55.
2 Ibid., p. 56.
3 Ibid., p. 62.
4 John Bale and Joe Sang, *Kenyan Running* (London, 1996), pp. 39–40.
5 Yannis Pitsiladis, John Bale, Craig Sharp and Timothy Noakes, eds, *East African Running: Towards a Cross-disciplinary Perspective* (New York, 2007), p. 47.
6 Ibid., p. 53.
7 Dirk Lund Christensen, 'Diet and Endurance Performance of Kenyan Runners: A Physiological Persepective', in ibid., pp. 102–17.
8 Interview with Japheth Kimutai, Oslo, 4 June 2008.
9 Grant Jarvie, 'The Promise and Possibilities of Running in and out of East Africa', in *East African Running*, ed. Pitsiladis et al., pp. 33–4; see also Mike Boit, 'Where are the Kenyan Women Runners?', *Olympic Review*, May 1989, pp. 206–10.
10 Jürg Wirz and Paul Tergat, *Running to the Limit* (Aachen, 2005), p. 133.
11 Ibid., p. 137.
12 Dirk Lund Christensen, *Washindi: Løberne fra Kenya* (Copenhagen, 2000), pp. 35–7.
13 Lars Werge, *Wilson Kipketer* (Copenhagen, 1998), p. 23.
14 Jarvie, 'The Promise and Possibilities of Running in and out of East Africa', p. 35.

32 How Fast Can a Human Being Run?

1 Juan-José Fernández, 'Man is a Poor Runner in Comparison with the Animals', *Olympic Review*, CCXL (October 1987), pp. 522–5.
2 Interview with Leif Olav Alnes, 2008.
3 Ibid.
4 John Bale, *Running Cultures* (London, 2004), p. 22.
5 *Illustrert Vitenskap*, X (2008).

Bibliography

Adelman, Melvin L., *A Sporting Time: New York City and the Rise of Modern Athletics* (Chicago, IL, 1987)

Alexander, Morris, *The Comrades Marathon Story* (Cape Town, 1992)

Amato, Joseph A., *On Foot: A History of Walking* (New York, 2004)

Ashe Jr, Arthur R., *A Hard Road to Glory: Track and Field: The Afro-American Athlete in Track and Field* (New York, 1998)

Askwith, Richard, *Feet in the Clouds* (London, 2004)

Athletics and Outdoor Sports for Women (New York, 1903)

Auboyer, Jeannine, *Dagligt liv i det gamle Indien* (Copenhagen, 1968)

Averbuch, Gloria, and Grete Waitz, *World Class* (Oslo, 1986)

Baker, William J., *An American Life* (New York, 1988)

Bale, John, *Roger Bannister and the Four-Minute Mile* (London, 2004)

—, *Running Cultures: Racing in Time and Space* (London, 2004)

—, and Joe Sang, *Kenyan Running* (London, 1996)

—, Mette K. Christensend and Gertrud Pfister, eds, *Writing Lives in Sport* (Aarhus, 2004)

— and David Howe, eds, *The Four-Minute Mile: Historical and Cultural Interpretations of a Sporting Barrier* (New York, 2008)

Bannister, Roger, *The Four-Minute Mile* (Guilford, CT, 989)

Barney, Robert K., 'Setting the Record Straight: The Photograph Portraying the Start of the 1896 Marathon', *Olympika: The International Journal of Olympic Studies*, XII (2003), pp. 101–4

Bascomb, Neal, *The Perfect Mile* (Boston, MA, 2004)

Batten, Jack, *The Man Who Ran Faster Than Everyone: The Story of Tom Longboat* (Toronto, 2002)

Bauch, Herbert and Michael A. Birkmann, '… die sich für Geld sehen lassen …', *Über die Anfänge der Schnell- und Kunstläufe im 19: Jahrhundert* (Marburg, 1996)

Baudin, Louis, *Dagligt liv hos inkaerne* (Copenhagen, 1967)

Baudrillard, Jean, *Amerika* (Oslo, 1988)

Stasser, J. B., and Laurie Becklund, *Swoosh: The Unauthorized Story of Nike and the Men Who Played There* (New York, 1991)

Benyo, Richard, and Joe Henderson, *Running Encyclopedia: The Ultimate Source for Today's Runner* (Champaign, IL, 2002)

Berendonk, Brigitte, *Doping, gull, aere, elendighet* (Hamburg, 1992)

Bertelsen, Herman Appelsin-Herman, *Gjøgleren som ble millionaer* (Høvik, 2004)

Berntsen, Bredo Løperkongen, *Nordmannen Mensen Ernsts eventyrlige liv* (Oslo, 1986)

Bijkerk, Anthony T., and David C. Young, 'That Memorable First Marathon', *Journal of Olympic History* (Winter 1999)

Birley, Derek, *Sport and the Making of Britain* (Manchester, 1993)

Bjarnason, Bjørn, *Nordboernes legemlige uddannelse i oldtiden* (Copenhagen, 1905)

Blaikie, David, *Boston: The Canadian Story* (Ottowa, 1984)

Blue, Adrianne, *Grace under Pressure: The Emergence of Women in Sport* (London, 1987)

Boit, Mike, 'Where are the Kenyan Women Runners?', *Olympic Review* (May 1999), pp. 206–10

Booth, Dick, *The Impossible Hero: A Biography of Gordon 'Puff Puff' Pirie* (London, 1999)

Booth, Douglas, *The Field: Truth and Fiction in Sport History* (London, 2005)

Bracegirdle, Cyril, 'Olympic Dreamer', *Olympic Review* (June 1991)

Brailsford, Dennis, 'Puritanism and Sport in Seventeenth-century England', *Stadion*, I/2 (1975), pp. 316–30

Bramble, Dennis M., and Daniel E. Lieberman, 'Endurance Running and the Evolution of *Homo*', *Nature*, CDXXXII, 18 November 2004, pp. 345–52

Bruant, Gérard, *Anthropologie du geste sportif* (Paris, 1992)

Bryant, John, *3.59.4: The Quest to Break the 4-Minute Mile* (London, 2004)

Bull, Joe, *The Spiked Shoe* (Melbourne, 1959)

Burfoot, Amby, *The Runner's Guide to the Meaning of Life: What 35 Years of Running Have Taught Me About Winning, Losing, Happiness, Humility, and the Human Heart* (Richmond Hill, ON, 2000)

Burns, Francis, *Cotswold Olimpick Games (Established 1612)* (Bristol, 2000)

Butcher, Pat, *The Perfect Distance* (London, 2004)

Cajas, Alberto F., 'Physical Activities in Ancient Peru', *Olympic Review*, 150–52 (1980)

Calabria, Frank M., *Dance of the Sleepwalkers: The Dance Marathon Fad* (Madison, WI, 1993)

Cavanagh, Peter R., *The Running Shoe Book* (Mountain View, CA, 1980)

Cerutty, Percy Wells, *Sport is My Life* (London, 1966)

Chodes, John, *Corbitt* (Los Altos, CA, 1974)

Christensen, Dirk Lund, *Washindi: Løberne fra Kenya* (Copenhagen, 2000)

Christie, Linford, *To Be Honest with You* (London, 1995)

Clarke, Ron, and Norman Harris, *The Lonely Breed* (London, 1967)

Clarke, Simon, 'Olympus in the Cotswolds: The Cotswold Games and Continuity in Popular Culture', *The International Journal of the History of Sport*, XIV/2 (August 1997), pp. 40–66

Clayton, Derek, *Running to the Top* (Mountain View, CA, 1980)

Coffey, Wayne, *Kip Keino* (Woodbridge, CT, 1992)

Cockerell, William, *50 Greatest Marathon Races of All Time* (Brighton, 2006)

Cooper, Kenneth, *Aerobics* (New York, 1968)

—, *The New Aerobics* (New York, 1970)

Cooper, Pamela, 'The "Visible Hand" on the Footrace: Fred Lebow and the Marketing of the Marathon', *Journal of Sport History*, XIX/3 (Winter 1992)

Culin, Stewart, *Games of the North American Indian* (New York, 1975)

Cumming, John, *Runners and Walkers: A Nineteenth-century Sports Chronicle* (Chicago, IL, 1981)

David-Néel, Alexandra, *Det hemmelige Tibet* (Oslo, 1987)

Decker, Wolfgang, *Sport and Games of Ancient Egypt* (London, 1992)

Delany, Ronnie, *Staying the Distance* (Ireland, 2006)

Denison, Jim, *Bannister and Beyond: The Mystique of the Four-minute Mile* (New York, 2003)

—, *The Greatest: The Haile Gebrselassie Story* (New York, 2004)

Derderian, Tom, *Boston Marathon: The First Century of the World's Premier Running Event* (Champaign, IL, 1996)

Deshpande, S. H., *Physical Education in Ancient India* (Delhi, 1992)

Donohoe, Tom, and Neil Johnson, *Foul Play: Drug Abuse in Sports* (England, 1986)

Donovan, Wally, *A History of Indoor Track and Field* (El Cajon, CA, 1976)

Dreyer, Danny, *Chi-Running* (New York, 2003)

Dyreson, Mark, 'The Foot Runners Conquer Mexico and Texas: Endurance Racing, Indigenismo, and Nationalism', *Journal of Sport History*, XXXI/1 (2004), p. 31

Edelman, Robert, *Serious Fun: A History of Spectator Sports in the USSR* (New York, 1993)

Egan, Pierce, *Sporting Anecdotes* (Philadelphia, PA, 1824)

Eichberg, Henning, *Det løbende samfund* (Slagelse, 1988)

—, *Leistung, Spannung, Geschwindigkeit* (Stuttgart, 1978)

—, 'Stopwatch, Horizontal Bar, Gymnasium: The Technologizing of Sports in the Eighteenth and Early Nineteenth Centuries', *Journal of the Philosophy of Sport*, IX (1982), pp. 43–59

—, ed., *Die Veränderung des Sports ist Gesellschaftlich* (Münster, 1986)

Eidmark, Henry, *Fantomer på kolstybben* (Stockholm, 1945)

—, *Sanningen om Gunder Hägg* (Stockholm, 1953)

Enevig, Anders, *Cirkus og gøgl i Odense: 1640–1874*, vol. III (Odense, 1995–8)

Entine, John, *Taboo: Why Black Athletes Dominate Sports and Why We Are Afraid to Talk About It* (New York, 2000)

Fernández, Juan-José, 'Man is a Poor Runner in Comparison with the Animals', *Olympic Review*, 240 (October 1987), pp. 522–5

Fixx, James F., *Den store boken om løping* (Oslo, 1979)

Fontana, Bernard L., with photographs by John P. Schaefer, *Tarahumara* (Tucson, AZ, 1997)

Frisch, Aaron, *The Story of Nike* (Mankato, MN, 2004)

Futrell, Alison, *The Roman Games* (Oxford, 2006)

Gamboa, Pedro Sarmiento de, *The History of the Incas* (Austin, TX, 2007)

Garbo, Kirsten Lien, *Med Ingrid mot toppen* (Oslo, 1985)

Gardiner, E. Norman, *Athletics of the Ancient World* (Chicago, IL, 1978)

—, *Greek Athletic Sports and Festivals* (London, 1910)

Giller, Norman, *Marathon Kings* (London, 1983)

Gilmour, Garth, *A Clean Pair of Heels* (London, 1963)

—, *Arthur Lydiard: Master Coach* (Cheltenham, 2004)

—, *Run to the Top* (London, 1962)

Glasser, William, *Positive Addiction* (San Francisco, CA, 1976)

Goksøyr, Matti, 'One Certainly Expected a Great Deal More from the Savages: The Anthropology Days in St Louis, 1904, and their Aftermath', *The International Journal of the History of Sport*, XII/2 (1990), pp. 297–306

—, *Idrettsliv i borgerskapets by. En historisk unders:kelse av idrettens utvikling og organisering i Bergen på 1800-tallet*, doctoral thesis, Norges idrettshøgskole (Oslo, 1991)

Goldman, Robert, and Stephen Papson, *Nike Culture* (London, 1998)
Govinda, Lama Anagarika, *The Way of the White Clouds* (London, 1969)
Greenberg, Stan, *Running Shorts* (London, 1993)
Griffis, Molly Levite, *The Great American Bunion Derby* (Austin, TX, 2003)
Gundersen, Sverre, and Edvard Nilsen, eds, *Norsk fri-idretts historie fra 1896 til 1950* (Oslo, 1952)
Guttmann, Allen, *A Whole New Ball Game: An Interpretation of American Sports* (North Carolina 1988)
—, *From Ritual to Record: The Nature of Modern Sports* (New York, 1978)
—, *Sports Spectators* (New York, 1986)
—, *Women's Sports: A History* (New York, 1991)
Haddon, Celia, *The First Ever English Olimpick Games* (London, 2004)
Hadgraft, Rob, *The Little Wonder: The Untold Story of Alfred Shrubb, World Champion Runner* (Southend-on-Sea, 2004)
Hägg, Gunder, *Gunder Håggs dagbok* (Stockholm, 1952)
—, *Mitt livs lopp* (1987)
Hammond, Nicholas Geoffrey Lemprière, *Studies in Greek History* (Oxford, 1973)
Harris, H. A., *Greek Athletics and the Jews* (Cardiff, 1976)
—, *Sport in Britain: Its Origins and Development* (London, 1975)
—, *Sport in Greece and Rome* (New York, 1972)
Harris, Norman, *The Legend of Lovelock* (London, 1964)
Hedenstad, Jan, and Jan Greve, eds, *Det lange løpet:* (Oslo, 1983)
Heidenstrom, Peter, *Athletics of the Century: 100 years of New Zealand Track and Field* (Wellington, 1992)
Heinrich, Bernd, *Why We Run* (New York, 2002)
Hellspong, Mats, *Den folkliga idrotten* (Stockholm, 2000)
Hemingway, Ernest, *Afrikas grønne fjell* (Oslo, 1955)
Henderson, Joe, *The Runners Diet* (Mountain View, CA, 1972)
Hewson, Brian, and Peter Bird, *Flying Feet* (London, 1962)
Hoberman, John, 'Amphetamine and the Four-Minute Mile', in *The Four Minute-Mile: Historical and Cultural Interpretations of a Sporting Barrier*, ed. Bale and Howe
—, *Darwin's Athletes: How Sport Has Damaged Black America and Preserved the Myth of Race* (Boston, MA, 1997)
—, *Testosterone Dreams: Rejuvenation, Aphrodisia, Doping* (Berkeley, CA, 2005)
Hoff, Charles, *Treneren og hans oppgaver* (Oslo, 1944)
—, *Fra New York til Hollywood* (Oslo, 1927)
Hole, Christina, *English Sports and Pastimes* (London, 1949)
Holmér, Gösse, *Veien til rekorden: Del 1, løp* (Oslo, 1947)
Hong, Fan, '"Iron Bodies": Women, War, and Sport in the Early Communist Movement in Modern China', *Journal of Sport History*, XXIV/1 (1997), pp. 1–23
Hughes, Charles, *Eskimo Boyhood* (Lexington, KT, 1974)
Hwang, Tony, and Grant Jarvie, 'Sport, Nationalism and the Early Chinese Republic 1912–1927', *The Sports Historian*, XXI/2 (November 2001)
Illeris, Niels, *Traek af legemsøvelsernes historie* (Copenhagen, 1947)
Jamieson, David A., *Powderhall and Pedestrianism* (Edinburgh, 1943)
Jennison, George, *Animals for Show and Pleasure in Ancient Rome* (Philadelphia, PA, 2005)
Jendrick, Nathan, *Dunks, Doubles, Doping: How Steroids are Killing American Athletics* (Guilford, CT, 2006)

Jinxia, Dong, 'The Female Dragons Awake: Women, Sport and Society in the Early Years of the New China', *The International Journal of the History of Sport*, XVIII/2 (June 2001), pp. 1–34

Johnson, Michael, *Slaying the Dragon: How to Turn Your Small Steps to Great Feats* (New York, 1996)

Jokl, Ernst, *A History of Physical Education and Sport* (Tokyo, 1975–6), pp. 53–8

Jones, Marion, *Life in the Fast Lane: An Illustrated Autobiography* (New York, 2004)

Jordan, Tom, *Pre: The Story of America's Greatest Running Legend, Steve Prefontaine* (Emmaus, PA, 1997)

Juilland, Alphonse, *Rethinking Track and Field* (Milan, 2002)

Jukola, Martti, *Athletics in Finland* (Porvoo, 1932)

Kaila, Toivo Torsten, *Boken om Nurmi* (Helsingfors, 1925)

Kastner, Charles B., *Bunion Derby: The 1928 Footrace Across America* (Albuquerque, NM, 2007)

Ke, Yunlu, *Wen Quing Ma Junren* (Kina, 2004)

Kelley, Graeme, *Mr Controversial: The Story of Percy Wells Cerutty* (London, 1964)

Kennedy, John G., *The Tarahumara* (New York, 1989)

Kidd, Bruce, *Tom Longboat* (Markham, 2004)

Kiell, Paul J., *American Miler: The Life and Times of Glenn Cunningham* (New York, 2006)

Korsgaard, Ove. *Kampen om kroppen* (Danmark, 1982)

Kozik, Frantizek. *Emil Zatopek* (Oslo, 1955)

Kramer, Samuel Noah, *History Begins at Sumer* (Philadelphia, PA, 1981)

Krüger, Arnd, and John Marshall Carter, eds, *Ritual and Record: Sports Records and Quantification in Pre-modern Societies* (London, 1990)

Kulinkovich, K. A., 'The Development of Knowledge of Physical Culture History in the USSR', *History of Physical Education and Sport*, III (1975–6), p. 126

Kummels, Ingrid, 'Reflecting Diversity: Variants of the Legendary Footraces of the Rarámuri in Northern Mexico', *Ethnos: Journal of Anthropology, National Museum of Ethnography, Stockholm*, LXVI/1 (2001), pp. 73–98

Kyle, Donald G., *Sport and Spectacle in the Ancient World* (Oxford, 2007)

Lamont, Deanne Anderson, 'Running Phenomena in Ancient Sumer', *Journal of Sport History*, XXII/3 (1995), pp. 207–15

Lawson, Gerald, *World Record Breakers in Track and Field Athletics* (Champaign, IL, 1997)

Lebow, Fred, and Richard Wodley, *Inside the World of Big-time Marathoning* (New York, 1984)

Lee, Brian, *The Great Welsh Sprint* (Pontypridd, 1999)

Lee, Hugh M., 'Modern Ultra-long Distance Running and Phillippides' Run from Athens to Sparta', *Ancient World*, IX (1984), p. 113

Lee, H. M., 'Athletics and the Bikini Girls from Piazza Armerina', *Stadion*, X (1984) pp. 45–76

Lenk, Hans, *Social Philosophy of Athletics: A Pluralistic and Practice-oriented Philosophical Analysis of Top Level Amateur Sport* (Champaign, IL, 1979)

León, Pedro Cieza de, *The Incas* (Norman, OK, 1959)

Lewis, David Maybury, *The Savage and the Innocent* (Boston, MA, 1988)

Lewis, Frederick, *Young at Heart: The Story of Johnny Kelley Boston's Marathon Man* (Cambridge, MA, 2002)

Lindhagen, Sven, *Dan Waern: Vägen til drömmilen* (Stockholm, 1960)

Liquori, Mart, and Skip Myslenski, *On the Run* (New York, 1979)

Lindroth, Jan, *Idrottens väg til folkrörelse* (Uppsala, 1974)
Lindstedt, Christian, *Mellom heroism och idioti* (Göteborg, 2005)
Loader, W. R., *Testament of a Runner* (London, 1960)
Loland, Sigmund, Rekorden: 'Grensesprenging som dilemma', *Kunnskap om idrett*, 1 (1997)
—, 'Record Sports: An Ecological Critique and a Reconstruction', *Journal of the Philosophy of Sport*, XXVIII/2 (2001), pp. 127–39
Lovesey, Peter, *The Official Centenary History of the Amateur Athletic Association* (London, 1979)
—, *The Kings of Distance* (New York, 1968)
Lucas, John A., 'A History of the Marathon Race – 490 BC to 1975', *Journal of Sport History*, III/2, pp. 120–38
Lucas, John, 'In the Eye of the Storm: Paavo Nurmi and the American Athletic Amateur-Professional Struggle (1925–29)', *Stadion*, VIII/2 (1992)
Luckert, Karl W., ed., *Rainhouse and Ocean: Speeches for the Papago Year* (Tucson, AZ, 1979)
Lumholz, Carl, *Blandt Mexicos indianere: Fem års reise i Sierra Madre og andre lidet kjendte dele af det vestlige Mexico* (Kristiania, 1903)
Lundberg, Knud, *Olympia-håpet* (Oslo, 1955)
Lydiard, Arthur, and Garth Gilmour, *Running to the Top* (Vienna, 1998)
McCloskey, John, and Julian Bailes, *When Winning Costs too Much: Steroids, Supplements, and Scandal in Today's Sports World* (New York, 2005)
McConnell, Kym, and Dave Horsley, *Extreme Running* (London, 2007)
McIntosh, P. C., J. G. Dixon, A. D. Munrow and R. E. Willetts, *Landmarks in the History of Physical Education* (London, 1957)
McNab, Tom, Peter Lovesey and Andrew Huxtable, *An Athletics Compendium* (London, 2001)
McRae, Donald, *In Black and White: The Untold Story of Joe Louis and Jesse Owens* (London, 2002)
Mandell, Richard D., 'The Invention of the Sports Record', *Stadion*, II/2 (1978), pp. 250–64
Mangan, J. A., ed., *Europe, Sport, World: Shaping Global Societies* (London, 2001)
Manners, John, 'Kenya's Running Tribe', *The Sports Historian*, XVII/2 (November 1997), pp. 14–27
Marchiony, Joseph, 'The Rise of Soviet Athletics', *Comparative Education Review*, VII/1 (June 1963), pp. 17–27
Martin, David E., and Roger W. H. Gynn, *The Olympic Marathon: The History and Drama of Sport's Most Challenging Event* (Champaign, IL, 2000)
Matthews, Peter, *The Guinness Book of Athletics: Facts and Feats* (London, 1982)
Matz, David, *Greek and Roman Sport* (London, 1991)
Mewett, Peter G., and John Perry, 'A Sporting Chance? The 'Dark Horse Strategy' and Winning in Professional Running', *Sociology of Sport Journal*, XIV/12 (1997), pp. 121–42
Mewett, Peter G., 'Discourses of Deception: Cheating in Professional Running', *The Australian Journal of Anthropology*, special issue 14 (2002), XIII/3, pp. 292–308
Michelson, Truman, *Notes on the Ceremonial Runners of the Fox Indians: Contributions to Fox Ethnology* (Washington, DC, 1927)
Miller, David, *Athens to Athens* (Edinburgh, 2003)
—, and Sebastian Coe, *Running Free* (London, 1981)

Miller, Stephen G., *Ancient Greek Athletics* (New Haven, CT, 2004)
—, *Arete: Greek Sports from Ancient Sources* (Berkeley, CA, 2004)
Moore, Kenny, *Bowerman and the Men of Oregon: The Story of Oregon's Legendary Coach and Nike's Co-founder* (Guilford, CT, 2006)
Morris, Andrew D., *Marrow the Nation: A History of Sport and Physical Culture in Republican China* (London, 2004)
Morrow, Don, 'The Knights of the Snowshoe: A Study of the Evolution of Sport in Nineteenth-century Montreal', *Journal of Sport History*, xv/1 (Spring 1988), pp. 5–40
Mosley, Leonard, *Haile Selassie: Den seirende løve* (Oslo, 1964)
Mouratidis, John, 'The 776 BC Date and Some Problems Connected with It', *Canadian Journal of History of Sport*, xvi/2 (December 1985), pp. 1–14
Müller, Norbert, and Pierre de Coubertin, eds, *Olympism: Selected Writings* (Lausanne, 2000)
Murphy, Frank, *On a Cold Clear Day: The Athletic Biography of Buddy Edelen* (Kansas City, MO, 2000)
—, *The Last Protest: Lee Evans in Mexico City* (Kansas City, MO, 2006)
—, *The Silence of Great Distance: Women Running Long* (Kansas City, MO, 2000)
Møst, Aage, ed., *Raskest, høyest, lengst: Norsk friidrett 1896–1996* (Oslo, 1995)
Nabokov, Peter, *Indian Running* (Santa Barbara, CA, 1981)
Nally, T. H., *The Aonac Tailteann and the Tailteann Games in their Origin, History and Ancient Associations* (Dublin, 1922)
Nelson, Cordner, and Roberto Quercetani, *Runners and Races: 1500m/mile* (Los Altos, CA, 1973)
—, and —, *The Milers:* (Los Altos, CA, 1985)
Neri, Indro, *Dante era un podista* (Florence, 1995)
New Guide to Distance Running (Mountain View, CA, 1978)
Newby, Zarah, *Greek Athletics in the Roman World* (Oxford, 2005)
Newton, Arthur F. H., *Running* (London, 1935)
Nielsen, Henning, ed., *For sportens skyld* (Copenhagen, 1972)
Noakes, Tim, *Lore of Running: Discover the Science and Spirit of Running* (Champaign, IL, 2001)
Nordberg, Terje, *Løpetid – om gleden ved å løpe* (Oslo, 1984)
Oettermann, Stephan, *Läufer und Vorläufer. Zu einer Kulturgeschichte des Laufsports* (Frankfurt am Main, 1984)
Olivova, Vera, *Sports and Games in the Ancient World* (London, 1984)
Olson, Leonard T., *Masters Track and Field: A History* (Jefferson, NC, 2001)
Opler, Morris Edward, 'The Jicarilla Apache Ceremonial Relay Race', *American Anthropologist*, n.s., xlvi/1 (January–March 1944), pp. 75–97
Osler, Tom, *Ultramarathon* (Mountain View, CA, 1979)
Oxendine, Joseph B., *American Indian Sports Heritage* (London, 1995)
Palenski, Ron, *John Walker Champion* (Auckland, 1984)
Paleologos, Cleanthis, 'Argeas of Argos: Dolichon Runner', *Olympic Review*, 87–88 (Jan–Feb 1975)
Papalas, Anthony, 'Boy Athletes in Ancient Greece', *Stadion*, xvii/2 (1991), pp. 165–92
Parker, John L., *Once a Runner* (Tallahassee, FL, 1978)
Pardivala, Jal, 'The Saga of the Marathon', *Olympic Review*, ccvi (December 1984), pp. 974–80
Parmer, Vidar, *Teater, pantomime, linedans, ekvilibristikk, menasjeri, vokskabinett,*

kosmorama etc: På Fredrikshald (Halden, 1965)

Patriksson, Göran, *Idrottens historia i sociologisk belysning* (Malmö, 1982)

Perottet, Tony, *The Naked Olympics* (New York, 2004)

Pharo, Helge, *Tjalve hundre år* (Oslo, 1990)

Phillips, Bob, *The Commonwealth Games* (Manchester, 2002)

—, *Zá-to-pek! Zá-to-pek! Zá-to-pek! The Life and Times of the World's Greatest Distance Runner* (Keighley, 2002)

Pihkala, Lauri, *Gossarnas idrottsbok* (Helsingfors, 1915)

Pirie, Gordon, *Running Wild* (London, 1962)

Pitsiladis, Yannis, John Bale, Craig Sharp and Timothy Noakes, eds, *East African Running: Towards a Cross-disciplinary Perspective* (New York, 2007)

Plymire, Darcy, 'Positive Addiction: Running and Human Potential in the 1970s', *Journal of Sport History*, pp. 297–313

Radford, Peter, *The Celebrated Captain Barclay* (London, 2001)

—, *The Observer*, 2 May 2004

—, 'Women and Girl Runners of Kent in the Eighteenth Century', unpublished article lent by Peter Radford

—, 'Women's Foot-Races in the Eighteenth and Nineteenth Centuries: A Popular and Widespread Practice', *Canadian Journal of History of Sport*, xxv/1 (May 1994), pp. 50–61

Raevuori, Antero, and Nurmi Paavo, *Jouksijain Kuningas* (Helsinki, 1997)

Rambali, Paul, *Barefoot Runner: The Life of Marathon Champion Abebe Bikila* (London, 2006)

Redmond, Gerald, *The Caledonian Games in Nineteenth-century America* (Madison, NJ, 1971)

Riordan, James, and Jinxia Dong,'Chinese Women and Sport: Sexuality and Suspicion', *The China Quarterly*, CXLV (March 1995), pp. 130–52

—, *Sport in Soviet Society* (Cambridge, 1977)

Rohé, Fred, *The Zen of Running* (New York, 1974)

Romano, David Gilman, *Athletics and Mathematics in Archaic Corinth: The Orgins of the Greek Stadion* (Philadelphia, PA, 1993)

Rono, Henry, *Olympic Dream* (Bloomington, IN, 2007)

Rousseau, Jean-Jacques, *Emile: Eller om oppdragelsen*, 3 vols (Copenhagen, 1962)

Rothstein, Klaus, *Frisk fisk til inkaen* (Copenhagen, 2002)

Roys, Ralph L., 'A Maya Account of the Creation', *American Anthropologist*, n.s., xxII/4 (Oct–Dec 1920), pp. 360–66

Ryun, Jim, and Mike Phillips, *In Quest of Gold* (New York, 1984)

Quercetani, Roberto, *Athletics: A History of Modern Track and Field Athletics: 1860–2000* (Milan, 2000)

—, *A World History of Long Distance Running (1880–2002)* (Milan, 2002)

—, and Pallicca, Gustavo, *A World History of Sprint Racing: 1850–2005* (Milan, 2006)

—, *A World History of the One-Lap Race* (Milan, 2006)

—, *Wizards of the Middle Distances: A History of the 800 Metres* (Milan, 1992)

Sage, George H., 'Justice Did It! The Nike Transnational Advocacy Network: Organization, Collective Actions and Outcomes', *Sociology of Sport Journal*, XVI/3 (1999), pp. 206–32

Sandrock, Michael, *Running with the Legends: Training and Racing Insights from 21 Great Runners* (Champaign, IL, 1996)

Sandblad, Henrik, *Olympia och Valhalla* (Göteborg, 1985)

Sann, Paul, *Fads, Follies and Delusions of the American People* (New York, 1967)
Scanlon, Thomas F., 'The Footrace of the Hereia at Olympia', in his *The Ancient World* (Chicago, IL, 1984), pp. 77–90
Schraff, Anne, and Rudolph Wilma, *The Greatest Woman Sprinter in History* (Aldershot, 2004)
Schwartz, Bob, *I Run, Therefore I am Nuts!* (Champaign, IL, 2001)
Scrivener, Leslie, *Terry Fox: His Story* (Toronto, 2000)
Sears, Edward S., *Running Through the Ages* (London, 2001)
Shapiro, Jim, *On the Road: The Marathon* (New York, 1978)
Shapiro, James E., *Ultramarathon* (New York, 1980)
Shaulis, Dahn, 'Pedestriennes: Newsworthy but Controversial Women in Sporting Entertainment', *Journal of Sport History*, XXVI/1 (1999), pp. 29–50
Shearman, Montague, *Athletics and Football* (London, 1887)
Sheehan, George, *Running and Being: The Total Experience* (Teaneck, NJ, 1978)
Sims, Graem, *Why Die? The Extraordinary Percy Cerutty: 'Maker' of Champions* (Lothian, Melbourne, 2003)
Simmons, Al, *The Ballad of Cliff Young* (Cheltenham, Victoria, 1983)
Simons, William, 'Abel Kiviat Interview', *Journal of Sport History*, XIII/3 (Winter 1986), pp. 235–67
Smith, Tommie, and David Steele, *Silent Gesture* (Philadelphia, PA, 2007)
Snell, Peter, and Garth Gilmour, *No Bugles: No Drums* (Auckland, 1965)
Spathari, Elsi, *The Olympic Spirit from its Birth to its Revival* (Athens, 1997)
Spectrum Guide to Kenya (Nairobi, 1993)
Spitzer, G., ed., *Doping and Doping Control in Europe* (Tyskland, 2006)
Stevens, John, *The Marathon Monks of Mount Hiei* (Boston, MA, 1988)
Stevenson, Robert, *Backwards Running* (1981)
'Stonehenge', *British Rural Sports* (London, 1881)
Strohmeyer, Hannes, 'Die Wiener "Läufer" und ihr Fest am 1. Mai (1822–1847)', *Stadion*, XII/XIII (1986–7)
Strutt, Joseph, *The Sports and Pastimes of the People of England* (London, 1875)
Studier i idrott, historia och samhålle (Sverige, 2000)
Tangen, Jan Ove, *Samfunnets idrett. En sosiologisk analyse av idrett som sosialt system, dets evolusjon og funksjon fra arkaisk til moderne tid*, doctoral dissertation, Institutt for sosiologi og samfunnsgeografi, Universitetet i Oslo (1997)
Tatz, Colin, *Obstacle Race: Aborigines in Sport* (Sydney, 1995)
Taylor, Harvey, 'Play Up, But Don't Play the Game: English Amateur Athletic Elitism, 1863–1910', *The Sports Historian*, XXII/2 (November 2002), pp. 75–97
Tervo, Mervi, 'A Cultural Community in the Making: Sport, National Imagery and Helsingin Sanomat 1912–1936', *Sport in Society*, VII/2 (Summer 2004), pp. 153–73
The History of the International Cross-Country Union: 1903 to 1953 (England, 1953)
Thorstad, B. Marianne, 'Idrett, fritid og kvinner i det tidligere Sovjetunionen', dissertation, Universitetet i Oslo (Spring 1993)
Tibballs, Geoff, *The Olympics' Strangest Moments: Extraordinary But True Tales from the History of the Olympic Games* (London, 2004)
Thom, Walter, *Pedestrianism* (Aberdeen, 1813)
Thomas, James H., *The Bunion Derby* (Oklahoma City, OK, 1980)
Trengrove, Alan, and Elliot Herb, *The Golden Mile* (London, 1961)
Tsiotos, Nick, and Andy Dabilis, *Running with Pheidippides: Stylianos Kyriakides, the Miracle Marathoner* (Syracuse, NY, 2001)

Tyrell, Blake, *The Smell of Sweat: Greek Athletics, Olympics and Culture* (Mundelein, IL, 2004)

Ueberhorst, Horst, *Friedrich Ludwig Jahn* (Bonn-Bad Godesberg, 1978)

Ungerleider, Steven, *Faust's Gold: Inside the German Doping Machine* (New York, 2001)

Valavanis, Panos, *Games and Sanctuaries in Ancient Greece:* Los Angeles, 2004)

Van Aaken, Ernst, *Van Aaken Method* (Mountain View, CA, 1976)

Vega, Garcilaso de la, *The Incas* (New York, 1961)

Vettenniemi, Erkki, *Joutavan Jouksun Jåljilå* (Helsinki, 2006)

Wadler, Gary I., *Drugs and the Athlete* (Philadelphia, PA, 1989)

Wahlqvist, Bertil, 'Idrottshistoriska kållproblem i de islendske sagorna – ett par exempel', *Idrott, Historia och Samhålle, Svenska idrottshistoriska føreningens årsskrift* (1981), pp. 69–77

—, *Ville vikinger i lek og idrett* (Oslo, 1980)

Ward, Michael, *Ellison 'Tarzan', Brown: The Narragansett Indian Who Twice Won the Boston Marathon* (Jefferson, NC, 2006)

Webster, F.A.M., *Fri-idretten idag* (Oslo, 1930)

Weiler, I., *Der Sport bei den Völkern der alten Welt: eine Einführung* (Tyskland, 1981)

Werge, Lars, *Wilson Kipketer* (Aarhus, 1998)

Wheeler, C. A., *Sportascrapiana: Facts in Athletics, with Hitherto Unpublished Anecdotes of the Nineteenth Century, from George IV to the Sweep* (London, 1868)

Whorton, James C., 'Athletes' Heart: The Medical Debate over Athleticism (1870–1920)', *Journal of Sport History*, IX/1 (Spring 1982), pp. 30–52

Wibe, Anne-Mette, 'Norske tårer og russisk svette', Skriftserie fra Norges idrettshøgskole (1998)

Wiggins, David K., 'Great Speed but Little Stamina: The Historical Debate Over Black Athletic Superiority', *Journal of Sport History*, XVI/2 (Summer 1989), pp. 158–85

Wikberg, Karin, 'Idealism eller professionalism? En studie i den stora amatørråf-sten 1945–1946', *Del i Idrott, Historia och Samhålle* (1993), pp. 109–149; *Del 2 i Idrott, Historia och Samhålle* (1994), pp. 85–122

Willis, Joe D., and Richard G.L.E. Wettan, 'Myers, World's Greatest Runner', *Journal of Sport History*, II/2 (1977)

Will-Weber, Mark, *The Quotable Runner* (New York, 2001)

Wilson, Jean Moorcroft, *Charles Hamilton Sorley* (London, 1985)

Wilt, Fred, *How They Train: Half Mile to Six Mile:* (Los Altos, CA, 1959)

—, *How They Train*, vol. II: *Long Distances* (Los Altos, CA, 1973)

—, *How They Train*, 2nd edn, vol. I, *Middle Distances* (Los Altos, CA, 1973)

—, *How They Train*, vol. III, *Sprinting and Hurdling* (Los Altos, CA, 1973)

Wirz, Jürg, and Paul Tergat, *Running to the Limit* (Aachen, 2005)

—, *Run to Win: The Training Secrets of the Kenyan Runners* (Tyskland, 2006)

Zakariassen, Allan, *Mit løberliv* (Danmark, 1999)

Zamperini, Louis, and David Rensin, *Devil at my Heels* (New York, 2004)

Zeigler, Earle F., ed., *A History of Sport and Physical Education to 1900* (Champaign, IL, 1973)

—, *History of Physical Education and Sport* (Toronto, 1979)

Zhao, Yu, 'Majiajun diaocha', *Zhongguo zuojia*, III (1998), pp. 1–213.

Zhou, Xikuan, 'China: Sports Activities of Ancient and Modern Times', *Canadian Journal of History of Sport*, XXII (1991), pp. 68–82

Young, David, *The Olympic Myth of Greek Amateur Athletics* (Chicago, IL, 1984)

Journals

Canadian Journal of History of Sport, 1981–1995. Windsor, Ontario.
History of Physical Education of Sport, 1973–1976. Tokyo.
Friidrett, 1950–2008. Oslo.
Idraetsliv, 1914–1932. Kristiania/Oslo.
International Journal of the History of Sport, 1987–2008. London.
Journal of Olympic History, 1992–2004, Oostervolde, Nederland.
Kondis, 1970–2008. Oslo.
Norsk Idraetsblad, 1881–1915. Kristiania.
Norsk Idraetsblad og Sport, 1916–1925. Kristiania/Oslo.
Olympic Review, 1974–2006. Lausanne.
Olympika: The International Journal of Olympic Studies, 1992–2006. London, Ontario.
Runner's World, 1970–2006. Emmaus, PA.
Springtime, 1980–1996. Stockholm.
Sociology of Sport Journal, 1984–2006. Champaign, IL.
Sport, 1908–1915. Kristiania.

Sport in History

The Ancient World, 1978–1984. Chicago.
The Sports Historian (1993–2002) and *The Journal of the British Society of Sports History* (1982–1992). Leicester, England.
Sportsmanden, 1913–1965. Kristiania/Oslo.
Stadion, 1975–1991. Helsinki.

Acknowledgements

Thanks to Li Yuen Hem for translations from the Chinese and Gun Roos for translating from the Finnish. Thanks to Midori Poppe for help with the Japanese material. Thor Kristian Gotaas has also provided translations from various languages the author is unfamiliar with. Bredo Berntsen willingly shared his wealth of knowledge about Mensen Ernst. Ole Magnus Strand Jensvoll was computer literate when the author's skills in this area proved inadequate. Benedicte Strand helped and managed to live with an author who was, at times, despairing.

Thanks to Kjell Vigestad and Runar Gilberg of the editorial team at the magazine *Kondis* for lending me back copies of the magazine. Thanks to Per Lind for tipping me off about a useful book that led to considerable enhancement of the source material. Thanks to Barbara Mitchell in England. Thanks too to Professor John Hoberman in Texas for constructive encouragement, and thanks to Maurie Plant, Australia, for amusing anecdotes.

The following people have read the whole or parts of the manuscript and given me useful advice: Marius Bakken; Kjartan Fløgstad; Matti Goksøyr; Thor Kristian Gotaas; Andreas Hompland; Jakob Kjersem; Roger Kvatsvik; Knut Anders Løken; Sigmund Hov Moen; Lars Myhre.

Particular thanks are due to Professor John Bale and Professor Peter Radford, both in England, for having given up much time to be interviewed and for having responded to my many inquiries. John Bale's books and articles have led me to see the material with new eyes. Peter Radford's enthusiasm for the history of running and his willingness to let me borrow material from his private, unpublished collection of source material have been an enormous help. Matti Goksøyr, Professor of Sport History at the Norwegian School of Sport Science, made very important contributions in the final stages of my work. Thanks too to Hans Petter Bakketeig, my publisher's editor, for his great help and for his faith in the project.

Henry Rono also deserves my great gratitude. He has provided detailed answers to my very numerous questions over a long period. There are few people more interested in the history of running than Henry Rono.

Thank you to the helpful staff of the following institutions: Library of the Norwegian School of Sport Science, Oslo; British Library, London; National Library, Oslo, particularly the Inter-Library Loan section – Else, Britt, Hilde and Sidsel –Ringsaker Public Library, Brumunddal; University Library, Oslo.

Photo Acknowledgements

The author and publishers wish to express their thanks to the following sources of illustrative material and/or permission to reproduce it:

British Museum: p. 29; Library of Congress: p. 101; Martineric: p. 268; Matt Semel: p. 274; SNappa2006: p. 227; Thomas Sly: p. 263; Ed Yourdon: p. 253.

Index